Well-Remembered Friends

Well-Remembered Friends

Eulogies on Celebrated Lives

collected by

ANGELA HUTH

JOHN MURRAY

First published in Great Britain in 2004
by John Murray (Publishers)
A division of Hodder Headline

2 4 6 8 10 9 7 5 3 1

A CIP catalogue record for this title is available from the British Library.

ISBN 0 7195 6487 5

Typeset in 10.75/13 pt Monotype Bembo by
Rowland Phototypesetting Ltd, Bury St Edmunds, Suffolk.
Printed and bound in Great Britain by Clays Ltd, St Ives plc.

John Murray (Publishers)
338 Euston Road
London NW1 3BH

Contents

The eulogies are arranged in the chronological order of the memorial services.

Preface

Not long ago I became aware that I had reached the time of life when I was required to go to more funerals and memorial services than I was to weddings – four funerals to a wedding, it seemed, rather than the other way round. It was at these sad, beautiful services that I began to reflect on how searingly and brilliantly many of the eulogists evoked the person whose life we were remembering, and it occurred to me what a pity it was that so few people were able to hear these fine tributes. That may have been the subconscious spur that led to this anthology. But when it came to me very clearly one morning, for no particular reason, that a published collection of eulogies might be of interest, it felt like an out-of-the-blue idea.

The eulogy is a very different form from the obituary. The one is a professional matter, the deceased's career skilfully garnered from press cuttings and reference books, his or her achievements duly noted, quirks of character lightly inserted. They are embellished *curricula vitae,* and to make them memorable is a considerable art. But as obituaries are often written by people who have no acquaintance with the subject, they are necessarily devoid of the personal memories chosen by the eulogist as he takes his place (few women, strangely, are called upon) in Westminster Abbey or the parish church. The nature of eulogies is to be emotionally charged.

It should be remembered by the reader of this anthology that writing words to be spoken requires an especial technique that differs from the high polish of words designed for publication. It also means that liberties with punctuation and emphasis are sometimes taken which may jolt a reader's eye, but sound right when tempered by the human voice.

The eulogist can never escape by a sense of detachment: it's for this reason that writing a eulogy is so notoriously hard. I have been called upon to give only one. It took me two days to write a few hundred words, and I was still left unsure as to whether I had conveyed even a fragment of my friend's spirit. As T.S. Eliot observed, 'the longer and more intimately one has known a man, the more difficult it is to choose, in brief memorial phrases, the memories to evoke, the gifts and qualities to emphasise, and the achievements to celebrate.' Besides which, the speaker, in a state of anxiety compounded by both grief and desire to do well by the deceased, must face a congregation of relations and friends who knew and loved the subject of the eulogy. So a path of the utmost delicacy must be chosen. Hard choices of what to include and what to leave out must be made, clichés must be avoided. While foibles can be alluded to in the name of honesty, difficulty lies in listing the character's many virtues without making him or her sound too saintly. Then there is the question of tone: should there be jokes, for instance? If they are relevant, and serve to illuminate some part of the dead person, most people feel there should. When they work, jokes are often the most remembered part of a eulogy. The late Lord Longford gave an address on the journalist William Clark. He told a story of how he had once teased his friend about a certain propensity for name-dropping. 'Funny you should say that,' answered William Clark, 'the Queen Mother has just said the same thing.' This fragment of Lord Longford's address is still quoted.

My method of finding good eulogies was not by scholarly research. I simply wrote to friends and acquaintances who I thought might have one filed away, and many did: it seems people do remember outstanding addresses. It was then just a matter of tracking them down – no easy matter, as many were lost. And I missed a few apparently excellent ones because the speakers – Joanna Lumley and Sir Peter Hall, for instance – had taken the courageous line of just standing up and speaking spontaneously without notes. Others were misremembered, and I spent considerable time stumbling down what turned out to be false trails. In my desire to have disparate worlds represented I found there was a great richesse in those I know best: the arts, academia and country life. But I admit to having been almost flummoxed by the sports world – not my natural habitat.

A kind cricket commentator came to my rescue and sent me tributes paid to cricketers, some of whose names I just remembered from my childhood. As for football . . . I much enjoyed the days I spent talking to helpful people in various football clubs in an attempt to get hold of Jimmy Armfield's eulogy on Stanley Matthews. Its eventual arrival produced especial satisfaction.

In the study of so many eulogies it became clear to me where pitfalls and difficulties lie – not least, how to merge achievement with a pertinent sense of character. It's no wonder, faced with so many predicaments when they come to write an address, people are obliged to struggle hard to acquire the very particular art. Even those used to speaking in public and paying tribute on civic and other occasions admit it's a challenge, due to the special requirements of a eulogy. The late John Morgan, journalist and expert on matters of style, wrote in *Debrett's New Guide to Etiquette and Modern Manners* that 'At one time Memorial Services tended to be reserved for only the great and the good. Today, many far less illustrious people have them.' Recently, an enlightened funeral company, witness to the difficulties of prospective eulogists both famous and unknown, commissioned a pamphlet of helpful advice. They called upon Andrew Motion to contribute the foreword. 'Within the ceremony,' writes the poet laureate, 'the eulogy has pride of place. It is the moment at which the deceased is brought close, and also the time when he or she steps away. It is at once a greeting and a letting go . . . It must be specific, particular, even intimate – and thereby seal the sense of occasion. This is the secret of the eulogy's power: it might move us to tears, but it will start to heal us, too.'

'Time assuages our grief in the wrong way, by teaching us to forget. The better way is by remembering,' wrote the late John Sparrow, Warden of All Souls, in his eulogy on Harold Nicolson. 'For if we can summon up an image of the friend we have lost and keep that image undimmed before the mind's eye, then we shall not have lost him altogether. That, I take it, is the purpose, or one of the purposes, of a memorial service.'

But to stir remembrance of those who have died untimely deaths, or sudden tragic deaths, or prolonged deaths, is perhaps the hardest challenge. I have included several such eulogies (permission generously granted by relations): a young man killed in a car crash, a woman who had spent much of her life flayed by addiction, the writer who spent his life in a wheelchair and suffered a horribly slow death, among others. They are exemplary. There's also a tribute to a first girlfriend of many years past, and one to a man who never did anything much beyond exuding life-enhancing charm: both different, but not easy challenges. It would be good to think that this collection of eulogies are not only reminders of disparate lives, but might also be of some help and inspiration to succeeding generations called upon to write encomiums in the future.

And it seems that such callings are increasing. After the last war, memorial services scarcely existed, and those that did take place were for the nationally famous. Today, whether under the title of a thanksgiving for a life, or a celebration of a life, whether in a church or a concert hall or a field, there are many more memorial gatherings than there used to be. It's at the memorial service that representatives of various official parts of the deceased's life choose to swell the congregation while funerals, nowadays, for those who will have a memorial service as well, are likely to be less well attended: family and close friends and those 'who can get there'. So the demand for eulogies is likely to grow rather than diminish, and while the art of the outstanding address will remain elusive, eulogists will continue to strive, in Andrew Motion's words, 'to bring the deceased into the mind's eye of the congregation . . . and to let us enjoy their company a moment longer'.

Angela Huth
Oxford
May 2004

Acknowledgements

My grateful thanks to all the eulogists who have contributed to this anthology, many of whom had to spend time and trouble trying to find scraps of paper they had put away years ago. When it came to tracking down elusive speakers, many kind people gave me help. These include Diana Baring, John Woodcock, Robin Hanbury-Tenison, Tarquin Olivier, Ronald Blythe, Maldwin Drummond, Humphrey Wakefield, Candida Crewe and Jonathan Fuller, chief executive of Stoke City Football Club.

My particular thanks go to John Byrne who, hearing of my idea, generously offered me the pick of his own private collection of eulogies which he had gathered over many years. Some fifteen herein are from his collection, including several which I doubt I would have ever known about, or managed to acquire myself.

As for the technical side of things, at which I'm hopelessly incompetent, Sarah Jane White typed, re-typed and e-mailed copy with incredible patience and speed. My thanks and gratitude to her are boundless.

Neville Chamberlain (1869–1940)
Prime Minister, 1937–40

by Sir Winston Churchill
(Prime Minister, 1940–5 and 1951–5)

*Eulogy delivered at the Houses of Parliament, London,
on 13 November 1940*

Since we last met, the House has suffered a very grievous loss in the death of one of its most distinguished Members and of a statesman and public servant who, during the best part of three memorable years, was First Minister of the Crown.

The fierce and bitter controversies which hung around him in recent times were hushed by the news of his illness and are silenced by his death. In paying a tribute of respect and of regard to an eminent man who has been taken from us, no one is obliged to alter the opinions which he has formed or expressed upon issues which have become a part of history; but at the lychgate we may all pass our own conduct and our own judgements under a searching review. It is not given to human beings, happily for them, for otherwise life would be intolerable, to foresee or to predict to any large extent the unfolding course of events. In one phase men seem to have been right, in another they seem to have been wrong. Then again, a few years later, when the perspective of time has lengthened, all stands in a different setting. There is a new proportion. There is another scale of values. History with its flickering lamp stumbles along the trail of the past, trying to reconstruct its scenes, to revive its echoes, and kindle with pale gleams the passion of former days.

What is the worth of all this? The only guide to a man is his conscience; the only shield to his memory is the rectitude and sincerity of his actions. It is very imprudent to walk through life without this shield, because we are so often mocked by the failure of our hopes and the upsetting of our calculations; but with this shield, however the fates may play, we march always in the ranks of honour.

It fell to Neville Chamberlain in one of the supreme crises of the world to be contradicted by events, to be disappointed in his hopes, and to be deceived and cheated by a wicked man. But what were these hopes in which he was disappointed? What were these wishes in which he was frustrated? What was the faith that was abused? They were surely among the most noble and benevolent instincts of the human heart – the love of peace, the toil for peace, the strife for peace, the pursuit of peace, even at great peril and certainly to the utter disdain of popularity or clamour. Whatever else history may or may not say about these terrible, tremendous years, we can be sure that Neville Chamberlain acted with perfect sincerity according to his lights and strove to the utmost of his capacity and authority, which were powerful, to save the world from the awful, devastating struggle in which we are now engaged. This alone will stand him in good stead as far as what is called the verdict of history is concerned.

But it is also a help to our country and to our whole Empire, and to our decent faithful way of living that, however long the struggle may last, or however dark may be the clouds which over-hang our path, no future generation of English-speaking folks – for that is the tribunal to which we appeal – will doubt that, even at a great cost to ourselves in technical preparation, we were guiltless of the bloodshed, terror and misery which have engulfed so many lands and peoples, and yet seek new victims still. Herr Hitler protests with frantic words and gestures that he has only desired peace. What do these ravings and outpourings count before the silence of Neville Chamberlain's tomb? Long and hard, hazardous years lie before us, but at least we entered upon them united and with clean hearts.

I do not propose to give an appreciation of Neville Chamberlain's life and character, but there were certain qualities, always admired in these islands, which he possessed in an altogether exceptional degree. He had a physical and moral toughness of fibre which enabled him all through his varied career to endure misfortune and disappointment without being unduly discouraged or wearied. He had a precision of mind and an aptitude for business which raised him far above the ordinary levels of our generation. He had a firmness of spirit which was not often elated by success, seldom downcast by failure and never swayed by panic. When, contrary to all his hopes, beliefs and exertions, the war came upon him, and when, as he himself said, all that he had worked for was shattered, there was no man more resolved to pursue the unsought quarrel to the death. The same qualities which made him one of the last to enter the war, made him one of the last who would quit it until the full victory of a righteous cause was won.

I had the singular experience of passing in a day from being one of his most prominent opponents and critics to being one of his principal lieutenants, and on another day of passing from serving under him to become the head of a government of which, with perfect loyalty, he was content to be a member. Such relationships are unusual in our public life. I have before told the House on the morrow of the debate which in the early days of May challenged his position, he declared to me and a few other friends that only a National Government could face the storm about to break upon us, and if he were an obstacle to the formation of such a government, he would instantly retire. Thereafter, he acted with that singleness of purpose and simplicity of conduct which at all times, and especially in great times, ought to be a model for us all.

When he returned to duty a few weeks after a most severe operation, the bombardment of London and of the seat of government had begun. I was a witness during that fortnight of his fortitude under the most grievous and painful bodily afflictions, and I can testify that, although physically only the wreck of a man, his nerve was unshaken and his remarkable mental faculties unimpaired.

After he left the government he refused all honours. He would die like his father, plain Mr Chamberlain. I sought the permission of the King however to have him supplied with the Cabinet papers, and until a few days of his death he followed our affairs with keenness, interest and tenacity. He met the approach of death with a steady eye. If he grieved at all, it was that he could not be a spectator to our victory, but I think he died with the comfort of knowing that his country had, at least, turned the corner.

At this time our thoughts must pass to the gracious and charming lady who shared his days of triumph and adversity with a courage and quality the equal of his own. He was, like his father and his brother, Austen, before him, a famous Member of the House of Commons, and we here assembled this morning, Members of all parties, without a single exception, feel that we do ourselves and our country honour in saluting the memory of one whom Disraeli would have called an 'English worthy'.

Augustus John (1878–1961)
painter

by Lord David Cecil
(writer)

*Memorial Service at St Martin-in-the-Fields Church,
London, on 12 January 1962*

Today we meet in the presence of God to do honour to the memory of one of England's greatest painters. Yet to remember him only as a painter is misleading. Augustus John was no impersonal machine for the production of masterpieces. No one who knew him can disassociate the artist from the man. The grandeur of the one is the grandeur of the other. I remember taking a friend – who had never met him – to his house at Fryern Court. It was a fine July evening: Augustus and Mrs John were alone. We sat, for perhaps half an hour, looking out at the garden whose midsummer beauty, heavy with the sun-warmed flowers, seemed so appropriate a setting for the two magnificent-looking beings who were entertaining us there. Nothing very serious was spoken of. Augustus, genial, formidable, Jove-like, was in light-hearted mood and told us tales of his past picturesquely and also with a delightful mischief. But, as we drove away, my friend said to me, 'We have had a very rare experience, we have been with a great man.'

This was the impression Augustus always made. It was partly by the sheer scale of his personality. Everything about him – his strength and sensibility, his scorn and his affection, his imagination and his humour – was on a heroic scale and endured with an intensity of which ordinary mortals are incapable. So also was his independence of mind. Here was another aspect of his greatness. He was a natural king of men, born to lead and to command. He spoke and acted always with a superb indifference to vulgar opinion. To the end of his life, he always came forward to support what he felt to be the cause of right and justice, whether it was popular or unpopular. If he came across a new movement in art, he neither shrank from it nor hastened to approve it. He looked at it; judged it; and went his own way. Yet he was never 'out of touch'. Like the great Elizabethans of the sixteenth century, who in so many ways he resembled, he was a citizen of the world, partook of its life. How whole-heartedly he responded to the imaginative appeal made by historical events, historical figures, diverse cultures! How robustly he entered into the common basic joys of humanity – song, dance, conviviality! Robustly; but also romantically. For he saw them transfigured and enabled by the holy spirit of imagination.

Here surely we come to the secret of his unique quality both as man and as artist. For Augustus John was never a mere recorder of fact. In his most famous and characteristic pictures he shows us his vision of the earthly paradise, imaged in groups or single figures by sea or lake or mountain. As paradises should be, it is both real and ideal, appeals both to body and to soul. It is splendidly and unashamedly physical in the out-of-door earthiness, its full-blooded sensuous beauty. Yet it is spiritual too. A visionary gleam pervades these rocky shores, these wild wind-blown skies: through the eyes of the majestic figures, the soul gazes out lost in reverie.

This blend of the earthy and the spiritual in his art expresses the essence of the man who created it. I cannot say exactly what was Augustus's creed. Like everything else about him, it was independent and unorthodox. But it was also certainly the reverse of materialistic. Indeed, it was sacramental; that is to say, it was rooted in the sense that the spiritual is incarnate in the physical, that the body is the image of the soul. In Augustus John's vision of reality – perceptible alike in his art and his personality – we were made to see the rich life of earth in its fullness, touched for a moment by the shadow of a divine mystery.

For this vision we honour him today; and in gratitude commend his soul to the keeping of Almighty God, whose creation he did so much to glorify.

Vivien Leigh (1913–1967)

actress

by Sir John Gielgud

(actor)

Memorial Service at St Martin-in-the-Fields Church, London, on 15 August 1967

In the first shock of losing a very dear friend one does not feel able to talk of it to other people. Grief is a private and personal emotion, and, in some ways too, a selfish one – so many good times that will never come again, so many opportunities lost of expressing one's affection for the one who is gone, such bitter resentment against the suddenness – the sadness that was so unexpected and so final.

To talk of Vivien Leigh in public so soon after her death is almost unbearably difficult for me. Many of you here today knew her far more intimately than I did, but, since those most near to her have asked me to pay tribute to her memory, I will try, however inadequately, to do so.

What seems to me most remarkable, as far as her career was concerned, was her steady determination to be a fine stage actress, to make her career in the living theatre, when, with her natural beauty, skill and grace of movement, gifts which were of course invaluable in helping to create the magic of her personality, she could so easily have stayed aloof and supreme in her unique position as a screen actress. Of course she will always be remembered as Scarlett O'Hara, as Lady Hamilton, and later for her wonderful acting in the *Streetcar* film. But these screen successes by no means satisfied her ambitions, and she had a lifelong devotion to the theatre, and determined to work there diligently through the years in order to reach the heights which she afterwards achieved. Though in her first big success, *The Masque of Virtue*, she had taken the critics and public by storm, she knew that her youth and beauty were the chief factors of her immediate success, and she was modest and shrewd enough to face the challenge of developing herself so as to find the widest possible range of which she was capable.

Her marriage to Laurence Olivier was an inspiration to her qualities – not only as a devoted pupil but also as a brilliant partner. Her performances in their seasons together, not only at the St James's Theatre, whose untimely destruction she tried so gallantly to prevent, but also at the Old Vic and Stratford, and in tours all over the world in Russia, Australia, Europe and America added fresh laurels to her crown. Besides the classic parts, she delighted everyone too in the modern plays she chose, each of which made different demands upon her versatility – *The Skin of our Teeth*, *The Sleeping Prince*, *Antigone*, and later *Duel of Angels*.

She had a charmingly distinctive voice. On the telephone one recognised it immediately – that touch of imperiousness, combined with a childlike eager warmth full of friendliness and gaiety. But she was determined to increase the range of it for the theatre, and in Shakespeare's *Cleopatra*, in which I thought she gave her finest classical performance, she succeeded in lowering her whole register from the natural pitch she was using as the little girl Cleopatra in Shaw's play – a remarkable feat which few actresses could have sustained as successfully as she did. Her Lady Macbeth, too, showed an astonishing vocal power and poignancy of feeling – and it is a thousand pities that the project of filming her performance was abandoned, for I believe it would have created worldwide admiration.

Her manners both in the theatre and in private life were always impeccable. She was punctual, modest and endlessly thoughtful and considerate. She was frank without being unkind, elegant but never ostentatious. Her houses were as lovely as her beautiful and simple clothes. Whenever she was not entirely absorbed in the theatre she was endlessly busy, decorating her rooms, planning surprises for her friends, giving advice on her garden, entertaining lavishly but always with the utmost grace and selectivity.

I had never thought to become an intimate friend of hers. My first meeting with her was at Oxford in 1936, when she played the little Queen in *Richard II* with the students. I was acting in London at the time, and so only met her when I was directing the rehearsals. The part is not a very interesting one, though she managed to endow it with every possible grace of speech and movement, and wore her medieval costumes with consummate charm – but I never got to know her in these days.

A few years later, during the war, I acted with her in *The Doctor's Dilemma*, when another actor was taken ill, and from that time we began an acquaintanceship which slowly ripened into a deep friendship and affection, and it is a wonderful happiness to me that during these last years I had the joy of seeing her so often and came to love her so well.

Of course, she was restless and drove herself too hard. Although she seemed so astonishingly resilient, she often suffered from ill health and fits of great depression, but she made light of the fact and rarely admitted to it or talked about it to other people. Her courage in the face of personal unhappiness was touching and remarkable. She always spoke affectionately of those who had first recognised her talents and helped her to develop her natural gifts. She studied and experimented continually and always brought to a rehearsal a willingness and technical flexibility which was the result of unceasing self-criticism and devotion to her work.

As she grew older she acquired a new kind of beauty, without any need of artifice, and she seemed to harbour no resentment against the competition of younger beautiful women. She was always enormously interested in everything, people, places, changes of fashion – and she had friends of every different sort and kind in London, in her country homes, in America and Australia. How delightfully she would talk of her Japanese admirers, who wrote her such charmingly phrased letters, and of those in Russia, where her film *Waterloo Bridge* is still considered a classic. She had the most punctilious and gracious way of answering letters and of dealing with strangers, admirers and newspaper men and women, and she was loved in the theatres she worked in for her sweetness to staff and company alike.

Fortunately at the end she seems to have had no idea how ill she was – she was full of plans preparing to rehearse a new play – and one can only hope she slept away her life without pain. She will not be forgotten – for her magic quality was unique. A great beauty, a natural star, a consummate screen actress and a versatile and powerful personality in the theatre, she had a range that could stretch from the comedy Sabina in *Skin of our Teeth* to the naturalistic agonies of Blanche Dubois in *Streetcar*, and the major demands of Lady Macbeth and Cleopatra. Even in *Titus Andronicus*, when she had only a few short scenes, she contrived the most beautiful pictorial effects. Who can forget the macabre grace with which she guided the staff with her elbows to write in the sand with it, a ravished victim gliding across the stage in her long grey robe.

Now she has glided away from us for ever, and we who are so much the poorer for her passing must be always thankful for knowing and working with her, and salute her for all she gave the world, so generously and so gaily.

> Now boast thee, Death, in thy possession lies
> A lass unparalleled.

Sir Harold Nicolson (1886–1968)
diplomat, writer and diarist
and Vita Sackville-West (1894–1962)
*writer and gardener**

by John Sparrow
(Warden of All Souls College, Oxford, 1952–77)

Memorial Service at St James's Church, Piccadilly, London, on 16 May 1968

When someone we are fond of dies, our affection and our sorrow are naturally fused into an emotion – I know no other name for it than *desiderium* – a sense of emptiness, an indefinable longing, that nothing – nothing, certainly, this side of the grave – can fully satisfy. If that longing cannot be satisfied, it can, however, be assuaged. Time, we know, heals all things; but time assuages our grief in the wrong way, by teaching us to forget. The better way is by remembering. For if we can summon up an image of the friend we have lost, and keep that image undimmed before the mind's eye, then we shall not have lost him altogether. That, I take it, is the purpose, or one of the purposes, of a memorial service.

Let me then try to re-create, as best I can, an image that will serve that purpose for us today. Of course, this is something that each of us can do only for himself; for it is of personal impressions that any such image must be composed, and the impressions of no

---

* Although Vita Sackville-West died six years before Harold Nicolson, this eulogy was intended for them both.

two persons will be quite the same. And surely no one can have left upon those around him a richer variety of impressions than Harold Nicolson; he lived in so many worlds, he was himself so many-sided, he had so many talents, so many interests, so many friends.

How various are the settings in which memory presents him! Some will see him entertaining his friends in his Albany chambers or at the Travellers' or the Beefsteak or, in the old days, in King's Bench Walk; others will, no doubt, recall him in animated discussion in the smoking-room of the House of Commons, or presiding at committee meetings of the London Library or the National Trust or the Portrait Gallery or the Governors of the BBC; or at his ease on a Hellenic cruise; or at Sissinghurst with a pair of shears in the garden, or at the typewriter in his cottage study.

Each of us will have a string of personal recollections that must remain his own: I will not try to collect them all and make a unity of them.

Still less will I attempt to trace even the outlines of an official portrait, giving its due to his work as a diplomatist, as a historian and a biographer, as a literary critic and an essayist, as a broadcaster and a commentator on the social and political scene, and in many fields of public service. If I mentioned one of his books as a classic example of its kind, I should have to mention half a dozen. Synoptic sketches of this sort have been attempted, very successfully as it seems to me, in several obituary notices, and the frame for a full-length portrait surely awaits him in the *Dictionary of National Biography*.

All that I can do, in these few minutes, speaking from my partial knowledge — for I knew him only in the latter half of his life — is try and convey to you some of the things that evoked my own affection and admiration, that made him seem to me so valuable as a person and so lovable as a friend.

First of all, he was such good company; one enjoyed being in the room with him. He was as richly, and as naturally, amusing *viva voce* as he was when he talked on paper. He raised one's spirits, he diffused a sense of *bien-séance*. He enjoyed making fun of himself and, it must be said, of other people, especially if they were there to be teased. But, though he was invariably an entertaining companion, he never played the professional humorist, and it was not so much his wit that made his company rewarding as his perpetual curiosity about human beings, his interest in the interplay of personalities, and his delight in human problems and social predicaments. 'Those who do not observe cannot converse': he noticed everything, and half the charm of his conversation was due to his power of communicating to others the results of his own shrewd and idiosyncratic perceptions.

Any stranger or acquaintance could enjoy his ironical observations on his fellow-men; but those who got to know him better soon perceived that human beings were to him something more than a source of interest and amusement; he positively liked them. 'I can't dislike anyone I don't know,' he once said to me, 'and if I really know people I can't help liking them.' Here I think he deceived himself: he didn't like his acquaintances as much as he thought he did. He was in fact fastidious about people, and he did not always suffer gladly fools or bores. But to those he found acceptable, and especially to the young, no one was a kinder, a warmer, or a more faithful friend. 'The older I get,' he wrote in his diary, 'the more I like young people. They are the only source of wisdom.' A glance down the list of his younger friends – and it was a long one – does not suggest that it was always for their wisdom that they were chosen. But, wise or foolish, young or old, I don't think there is one of Harold's friends that would not testify to his sympathy and patience, his generosity and affection. Innumerable young writers, from the 1920s onwards, must have been grateful to him for the trouble he took for them about their work, reading and revising their manuscripts and introducing them to editors or to people it would be useful or interesting for them to know. Nor was it only writers that he helped; the list of his beneficiaries ranged from refugees from foreign tyrannies to young men down from the university and starting in life; he would listen to their plans and their aspirations, their problems and their perplexities, offering them the benefit of his own experience; giving them advice when they needed it, and not expecting it to be taken; giving them money when they needed that, and not expecting it to be repaid. If they came back for more assistance, as they not seldom did, they could rely, however great the demands they made upon it, on Harold's inexhaustible indulgence; his sympathy and help were proportioned always to people's needs and not to their deserts.

'The secret of influence is a consistent life': Harold helped his friends also by being, imperturbably, what he was. I don't mean, of course, by the ostentatious practice of virtue, nor am I thinking simply of his steadfastness as a friend. But he set an example of how it was possible, while taking things with apparent ease, to concentrate one's powers on the main business of one's life – in his case, the task of writing. He never wasted a moment: he was an unremitting and methodical worker; his joy was in the *difficulté vaincue*, the hard job well done; he despised idleness and inaction, particularly the intellectual dalliance, the reluctance to get things finished or even to get them started, that disguises itself, and excuses itself, as 'perfectionism'; with that, as I have cause to know, he had no sympathy at all.

His power of concentration was aided by certain exclusions: he had no time for games or hobbies, and no ear for music; he was not interested in philosophical speculation or in the minutiae of scholarship; the things that claimed his energies were life and literature.

He was, indeed, a much more serious person than he seemed; his air of *insouciance* was misleading. 'He didn't live his life,' said Arthur Benson about an Edwardian contemporary, 'he stayed with it and lunched with it.' Someone who never met him, and was too young to have known the beau monde that populates his diaries, asked me whether that wasn't true of Harold Nicolson. Of course, no description could have been less apt. No one more thoroughly *lived* his life than Harold, and no one's activities were more consistently directed by a serious purpose. True, the close-knit aristocratic society into which he was born provided him with luxuries that he relished and a way of life that he took for granted. But he set no store by rank or money, and it was a small part of his nature that was gratified by the external things of life.

He was a complex human being – a nineteenth-century character, one might say, living an eighteenth-century life in the middle of the twentieth century. He would have felt more at home in an age before the enfranchisement of the proletariat, the emancipation of women, and the discovery of England by America – an age when there was plenty of time for landscape gardening, and when politics was a family affair. His knowledge of history and literature might, one felt, have been derived, like Gibbon's, from his own library; his familiarity with the capitals of Europe might have been acquired on the Grand Tour; he had the versatile, unpedantic competence of an eighteenth-century country gentleman, whose school was life. But his beliefs, his ideals, his values, were Victorian: faith in progress, an incurable optimism, strong patriotic and family feelings, affection for institutions – the Foreign Office, his old college at Oxford – a lively social conscience, and a belief in the virtues of hard work. When he perceived that the world and the society he belonged to could not outlast the 1930s – and about that he had no illusions – these Victorian attributes of his helped him to accept the fact, and almost persuaded him that he did not regret it and it was these convictions that determined the uneasy position he adopted in the party politics of his day.

If in politics he did not achieve everything that he hoped for, that was due – as he himself ruefully admitted – to the fact that he was too kind-hearted; he wanted everyone – yes! everyone – to be comfortable. But if he lacked the ruthlessness needed for political success, neither did he assume the bland impersonal mask that is so often its concomitant: in public places his was always a private face. Nor did he ever regret his decision to enter politics; it took him into the centre of events in an epic period, and it gave him two memories he had reason to be proud of: he gained the *entrée* to Parliament by winning, against odds and in a hard-fought election, a victory that was a personal triumph; and he rose to a great occasion in the House of Commons by keeping his head, and also his seat, while all round him, except his friend Duff Cooper, sprang to their feet to cheer the news of Munich.

With his zest for life, his manifold interests and activities, and his host of friends, he could hardly have failed to be a happy man. And he was endowed with a natural buoyancy that kept him cheerful even when things were not going well. At the end of 1931 he noted in his diary: 'Of all my years this has been the most unfortunate. Everything has gone wrong.' He had left the Foreign Office, burning his boats, and a string of disasters had followed: he catalogues them almost with relish, and then concludes: 'Yet in spite of all this, what fun life is!' 'What fun!' – these were the first words that Vita Sackville-West remembered hearing on his lips twenty years before. Some people's 'fun' conceals an inner melancholy; Harold's was the natural ebullition of a deep-seated spring of happiness.

He was at his happiest at Sissinghurst, because there he was in the place, and with the people, he loved best in the world, at home among his family.

He was, I should think, the most devoted and the most under-standing father in England; and he was rewarded by the unalterable devotion of his sons. When they married and had children he prac-tised not only what the poet called *l'art d'être grandpère*, but the more difficult art of being a father-in-law; he did it perfectly; and here too he had his reward, in a devotion that comforted the last years of his life. But it was to Vita more than to any single other person – perhaps more than to all other people put together – that he owed his happiness. Husband and wife could hardly have been more different: dark, simple, reserved, in her veins the blood of the English aristocrat and of the Spanish gypsy, she was a deep, straight, slow-flowing river, with an irresistible current; he was fair, complex, extrovert, a rapid, sunny winding stream, with pools of unexpected depth. Vita hated London – she went there reluctantly, once a year for the flower show at Chelsea – she hated public life, and all that it implied; public life and London were the breath of Harold's nostrils. They were as different as poetry is from prose.

That two natures apparently so antithetical should have become complementary was a miracle – a miracle that required, to work it, the two strongest forces in the world: intelligence and love. The miracle happened: they led, in complete mutual dependence, their own two independent working lives. This cannot but have called for sacrifices from both of them; and if his were the greater, he would not have wished it otherwise. For 'sheer joy of companionship', she wrote, the early years of their marriage were unsurpassed; towards the end of his life he recorded, in four words, what he felt for her:

'immortal love, immortal gratitude'. Neither could well face the thought of life without the other.

'Have you and your wife ever collaborated in anything?' asked a foolish journalist, in hope of some literary titbit. 'We have two sons,' replied Harold, with a serious face. They impressed their image on another joint creation, Sissinghurst. At once a home and a work of art, that remains, with her poems and his books, a lasting monument of their individual talents and their joint life.

There, then, are my few touches towards a portrait of that warm-hearted, serious-minded, irresistibly amusing and intensely happy man. My picture is, of course, in several respects imperfect. But I can think of one person who might have drawn it perfectly – with complete understanding of the subject, full knowledge of its lights and shades, a humorous detachment, and a sure, firm, easy touch. I mean, of course, Harold Nicolson himself. How well he would have done it!

But he did do it. In the diaries that cover the second half of his life he has left for posterity not only a picture of the age and the society he lived in that will take its place with the classic English books of memoirs, but also a full-length portrait of himself, at work and at ease, at home and abroad, in peacetime and in wartime, in London in the centre of events, and in the country in the bosom of his family. There stands the daily record of what he thought and felt and did, movingly supplemented by passages from the letters that passed between him and Vita almost every day over long periods of their married life. It is fitting that on the first page of that book there should have been inscribed by himself and one of his sons, its perfect editor, a dedication to the other son. But every page of its text is in truth dedicated – as was the life it chronicles, *sicut omnia vitae* – to Vita. Six years ago, at her death, half of him died; to her his own death reunites him.

Sir Maurice Bowra (1898–1971)

classicist, Warden of Wadham College, Oxford, 1938–71

by Sir Isaiah Berlin

(Fellow of All Souls College, Oxford, and historian of ideas)

*Memorial Service at the University Church of St Mary
the Virgin, Oxford, on 17 July 1971*

We are here to commemorate the life of Maurice Bowra, our friend
and colleague; scholar, critic and administrator, the greatest English
wit of his day; but, above all, a generous and warm-hearted man,
whose powerful personality transformed the lives and outlook of
many who came under his wide and life-giving influence. According
to a contemporary at Cheltenham, he was fully formed by the time
he left school for the army in 1916. In firmness of character he
resembled his father, of whom he always spoke with deep affection
and respect; but unlike him he was rebellious by temperament and,
when he came up to New College in 1919, became the natural
leader of a group of intellectually gifted contemporaries, passionately
opposed to the conventional wisdom and moral code of those who
formed pre-war Oxford opinion. He remained critical of all estab-
lishments for ever after.

Bowra loved life in all its manifestations. He loved the sun, the
sea, warmth, light, and hated cold and darkness, physical, intellectual,
moral, political. All his life he liked freedom, individuality, independence, and detested everything that seemed to him to cramp and
constrict the forces of human vitality, no matter what spiritual
achievements such self-mortifying asceticism might have to its credit.

His passion for the Mediterranean and its cultures was of a piece with this: he loved pleasure, exuberance, the richest fruits of nature and civilisation, the fullest expression of human feeling, uninhibited by a Manichean sense of guilt. Consequently he had little sympathy for those who recoiled from the forces of life – cautious, calculating conformists, or those who seemed to him prigs or prudes who winced at high vitality or passion, and were too easily shocked by vehemence and candour. Hence his impatience with philistine majorities in the academic and official and commercial worlds, and equally with cultural coteries which appeared to him thin, or old-maidish, or disapproving. He believed in fullness of life. Romantic exaggeration, such as he found in the early thirties in the circle formed round the German poet Stefan George, appealed to him far more than British reticence.

With a temperament that resembled men of an older generation – Winston Churchill or Thomas Beecham – he admired genius, splendour, eloquence, the grand style, and had no fear of orchestral colour; the chamber music of Bloomsbury was not for him. He found his ideal vision in the classical world: the Greeks were his first and last love. His first and best book was a study of Homer; this, too, was the topic of his last book, had he lived to complete it.* Despite the vast sweep of his literary interests – from the epic songs of Central Africa to the youngest poet of our day – it is Pindar, Sophocles, the Greek lyric poets who engaged his deepest feelings. Murray and Wilamowitz meant more to him than scholars and critics of other literatures.

Endowed with a sharp, quick brain, a masterful personality, an impulsive heart, great gaiety, a brilliant, ironical wit, contempt for all that was solemn, pompous and craven, he soon came to dominate his circle of friends and acquaintances. Yet he suffered all his life from a certain lack of confidence: he needed constant reassurance. His disciplined habits, his belief in, and capacity for, hard, methodical work in which much of his day was spent, his respect for professionalism and distaste for dilettantism, all these seemed, in some measure, defensive weapons against ultimate self-distrust. So, indeed, was his

* Nine out of ten chapters were later found, and the book was published in 1972.

Byronic irony about the very Romantic values that were closest to his heart. The treatment of him at New College by that stern trainer of philosophers, H.W.B. Joseph, undermined his faith in his own intellectual capacity, which his other tutor in Philosophy, Alick Smith, who did much for him, and became a lifelong friend, could not wholly restore.

Bowra saw life as a series of hurdles, a succession of fences to take: there were books, articles, reviews to write; pupils to teach, lectures to deliver, committees, even social occasions, were so many challenges to be met, no less so than the real ordeals – attacks by hostile critics, or vicissitudes of personal relationships, or the hazards of health. In the company of a few familiar friends, on whose loyalty he could rely, he relaxed and often was easy, gentle and at peace. But the outer world was full of obstacles to be taken at a run; at times he stumbled, and was wounded: he took such reverses with a stiff upper lip; and then, at once, energetically moved forward to the next task. Hence, it may be, his need and craving for recognition, and the corresponding pleasure he took in the many honours he received. The flat, pedestrian, lucid, well-ordered, but, at times, conventional style and content of his published writings may also be due to his peculiar lack of faith in his own true and splendid gifts. His private letters, his private verse, and above all his conversation, were a very different matter. Those who knew him solely through his published works can have no inkling of his genius.

As a talker he could be incomparable. His wit was verbal and cumulative: the words came in short, sharp bursts of precisely aimed, concentrated fire, as image, pun, metaphor, parody seemed spontaneously to generate one another in a succession of marvellously imaginative patterns, sometimes rising to high, wildly comical, fantasy. His unique accent, idiom, voice, the structure of his sentences became a magnetic model which affected the style of speech, writing, and perhaps feeling, of many who came under its spell. It had a marked effect on some among the best known Oxford-bred writers of our time. But his influence went deeper than this: he dared to say things which others thought or felt, but were prevented from uttering by rules or convention or personal inhibitions. Maurice

Bowra broke through some of these social and psychological barriers, and the young men who gathered round him in the twenties and thirties, stimulated by his unrestrained talk, let themselves go in their turn. Bowra was a major liberating force: the free range of his talk about art, personalities, poetry, civilisations, private life, his disregard of accepted rules, his passionate praise of friends and unbridled denunciation of enemies produced an intoxicating effect. Some eyebrows were raised, especially among the older dons, at the dangers of such licence. They were wholly mistaken. The result, no matter how frivolous the content, was deeply and permanently emancipating. It blew up much that was false, pretentious, absurd; the effect was cathartic; it made for truth, human feeling, as well as great mental exhilaration. The host (and he was always the host, whether in his own rooms or those of others) was a positive personality; his character was cast in a major key: there was nothing corrosive or decadent or embittered in all his talk, no matter how irreverent or indiscreet or extravagant or unconcerned with justice it was.

As a scholar, and especially as a critic, Bowra had his limitations. His most valuable quality was his deep and unquenchable love of literature, in particular of poetry, of all periods and peoples. His travels in Russia before the Revolution, when as a schoolboy he crossed that country on his way to his family's home in China, gave him a lifelong interest in Russian poetry. He learned Russian as a literary language, and virtually alone in England happily (and successfully) parsed the obscurest lines of modern Russian poets as he did the verse of Pindar or Alcaeus. He read French, German, Italian and Spanish, and had a sense of world literature as a single firmament, studded with works of genius the quality of which he laboured to communicate. He was one of the very few Englishmen equally well known to, and valued by, Pasternak and Quasimodo, Neruda, and Seferis, and took proper pride in this. It was all, for him, part of the war against embattled philistinism, pedantic learning, parochialism. Yet he was, with all this, a stout-hearted patriot, as anyone could testify who heard him in Boston, for example, when England was even mildly criticised. Consequently, the fact that no post in the public service was offered him in the Second

World War distressed him. He was disappointed, too, when he was not appointed to the Chair of Greek at Oxford (he was offered chairs at Harvard and other distinguished universities). But later he came to look on this as a blessing in disguise; for his election as Warden of Wadham eventually made up and more than made up for it all.

Loyalty was the quality which, perhaps, he most admired, and one with which he was himself richly endowed. His devotion to Oxford, and in particular to Wadham, sustained him during the second, less worldly, portion of his life. He did a very great deal for his college, and it did much for him. He was intensely and, indeed, fiercely proud of Wadham, and of all its inhabitants, senior and junior; he seemed to be on excellent terms with every undergraduate in its rapidly expanding population; he guided them and helped them, and performed many acts of kindness by stealth. In his last decades he was happiest in his Common Room, or when entertaining colleagues or undergraduates; happiest of all, when surrounded by friends, old or young, on whose love and loyalty he could depend. After Wadham his greatest love was for the university: he served it faithfully as proctor, member of the Hebdomadal Council, and of many other committees, as Delegate of the Press, finally as Vice-Chancellor. Suspected in his younger days of being a cynical epicure (no less cynical man ever breathed), he came to be respected as one of the most devoted, effective and progressive of academic statesmen. He had a very strong institutional sense: his presidency of the British Academy was a very happy period of his life. Under his enlightened leadership the Academy prospered. But it was Oxford that claimed his deeper allegiance: the progress of the university filled him with intense and lasting pride. Oxford and Wadham were his home and his life; his soul was bound up with both. Of the many honours which he received, the honorary doctorate of his own university gave him the deepest satisfaction: the opinion of his colleagues was all in all to him. When the time for retirement came, he was deeply grateful to his college for making it possible for him to continue to live within its walls. His successor was an old personal friend: he felt sure of affection and attention.

Increasing ill health and deafness cut him off from many pleasures, chief among them committees and the day-to-day business of administration which he missed as much as the now less accessible pleasures of social life. Yet his courage, his gaiety, his determination to make the most of what opportunities remained did not desert him. His sense of the ridiculous was still acute; his sense of fantasy remained a mainstay. New faces continued to feed his appetite for life. Most of all he now enjoyed his contact with the young, whose minds and hearts he understood, and whose desire to resist authority and the imposition of frustrating rules he instinctively shared and boldly supported to the end. They felt this and responded to him, and this made him happy.

He was not politically minded. But by temperament he was a radical and a non-conformist. He genuinely loathed reactionary views and had neither liking nor respect for the solid pillars of any establishment. He sympathised with the unions in the General Strike of 1926; he spoke with passion at an Oxford meeting against the suppression of socialists in Vienna by Dollfuss in 1934; he detested oppression and repression, whether by the right or left, and in particular all dictators. His friendship with Hugh Gaitskell was a source of pleasure to him. If political sentiments which seemed to him retrograde or disreputable were uttered in his presence, he was not silent and showed his anger. He did not enjoy the altercations to which this tended to lead, but would have felt it shameful to run away from them; he possessed a high degree of civil courage. He supported all libertarian causes, particularly minorities seeking freedom or independence, the more unpopular, the better. Amongst his chief pleasures in the late fifties and sixties were the Hellenic cruises in which he took part every year. But when the present regime in Greece took over, he gave them up.

His attitude to religion was more complicated and obscure: he had a feeling for religious experience; he had no sympathy for positivist or materialist creeds. But to try to summarise his spiritual outlook in a phrase would be absurd as well as arrogant. As Warden he is said scarcely ever to have missed chapel.

The last evening of his life was spent at a convivial party with colleagues and undergraduates. This may have hastened the heart attack of which he died; if so, it was as he would have wished it to be: he wanted to end swiftly and tidily, as he had lived, before life had become a painful burden.

He was, in his prime, the most discussed Oxford personality since Jowett, and in every way no less remarkable and no less memorable.

Uffa Fox (1898–1972)
yachtsman and yacht designer

by Sir Max Aitken
(newspaper proprietor)

*Memorial Service at St Martin-in-the-Fields Church,
London, on 21 November 1972*

'Farewell and adieu' were the first words of Uffa's favourite song,
'Spanish Ladies'. And this remarkable gathering of his friends is a
great tribute to a fine man. Princes, princesses, Prime Minister of
our land, yachtsmen, fishermen, boat-builders are all here to do
honour to the man we love. He was a man of achievement. His
books, his seamanship, his draughtsmanship, his sense of generosity
and above all his friendship and his loyalty to his friends.

As a seaman, he was unsurpassed. He loved the sea; he respected
it; sometimes he was afraid of it, and, at sea, when one was with
him, he talked all the time not about the ship he was on, but about
the sea and the wind and weather, and the gales he had survived.

He was devoted to animals. To see Uffa riding over the downs
of the Isle of Wight on the mare Ffrantic, in his pink coat and
breeches, with Bruce, his labrador, galloping at his heels, was a
wonderful and stirring sight.

His books were quite unique, especially the early ones. He wrote
them in a style which was then unknown. If you read them now,
you will find how thrilling, and how wise they are.

As a draughtsman, and as an artist, he was meticulous, and he
was helped always by his devoted staff.

And his songs; they were really quite wonderful. One night he and I were sailing back from France in the schooner *Lumberjack*. When we got clear of Cherbourg it was blowing hard from the west and we snugged down. Uffa and I took the first watch, he started to sing, and we left all the other crew below right through the night. He sang all the way. As we took turns at the wheel, song after song came out. 'When we make landfall at the Isle of Wight,' I said, 'we must record those songs because they will be forgotten when you die.'

'I will never die,' he said. But he has.

His songs were, fortunately, recorded, and there they are for all of us to listen to.

His generosity was immense. He had no interest in money; he really never had any, and if he did get some, he gave it away.

And then his family. We mourn with Yvonne, and we mourn with all those who took such tremendous care of him over the last years of his life, when his heart was failing.

We mourn for Uffa, whose mind touched our hearts.

He was pure gold.

W.H. Auden (1907–1973)
poet

by Sir Stephen Spender
(poet)

*Memorial Service at Christ Church Cathedral, Oxford,
on 27 October 1973*

This gathering of friends to honour and remember Wystan Auden
is not an occasion on which I should attempt to discuss either
Wystan's personality or his place in the history of English literature.
It is, rather, one on which to recall his presence, and express our
praise and gratitude for his life and work, in these surroundings
where, intellectually and as a poet, his life may be said to have come
full circle.

He was a citizen of the world, a New Yorker with a home in
Austria, in the little village of Kirchstetten, where he is buried; and
for whom Christ Church, 'The House', had come to mean his
return to his English origins. For making this possible, the Dean
and Canon and students are to be thanked.

I knew Wystan since the time when we were both undergraduates, and saw him at intervals until a few weeks before his death. It
is impossible for me, in these surroundings, not to juxtapose two
images of him, one of forty years back, and one of a year ago only.

The first is of the tow-haired undergraduate poet with the
abruptly turning head, and eyes that could quickly take the measure
of people or ideas. At that time, he was not altogether quite un-chic,
wearing a bow-tie and on occasion wishing one to admire the suit

he had on. He recited poetry by heart in an almost toneless unemotional quite unpoetical voice which submerged the intellectual meaning under the level horizontal line of the words. He could hold up a word or phrase like an isolated fragment or specimen chipped off the great granite cliff of language, where a tragic emotion could be compressed into a coldly joking word, as in certain phrases I recall him saying. For instance: 'The icy precepts of respect', or 'Pain has an element of blank'. Or perhaps lines of his own just written:

> Tonight when a full storm surrounds the house
> And the fire creaks, the many come to mind
> Sent forward in the thaw with anxious marrow
> For such might now return with a bleak face,
> An image pause, half-lighted at the door . . .

A voice, really, in which he could insulate any two words so that they seemed separate from the rest of the created universe, and sent a freezing joking thrill down one's spine. For instance, the voice in which, one summer when he was staying with me at my home in London during a heatwave and luncheon was served and the dish cover lifted, he exclaimed in tones of utter condemnation like those of a judge passing a terrible sentence: 'Boiled ham!'

The second image of Wystan is of course one with which you are all familiar: the famous poet with the face like a map of physical geography, criss-crossed and river-run and creased with lines. This was a face upon which experiences and thoughts had hammered; a face of isolated self-communing which reminded me of a phrase of Montherlant's about the artist's task of 'noble self-cultivation'; a face though that was still somehow entertaining and which could break down into a smile of benevolence or light up with gratified recognition at some anecdote recounted or thought received. It was a face at once armoured and receptive.

It is difficult to bring these two images – spaced forty years apart – together. But to do so is to find reason for our being here to praise and thank him.

His fellow-undergraduates who were poets when he was also an undergraduate (John Betjeman, Day Lewis, MacNeice, Rex Warner and myself) saw in him a man who instead of being, like us, romantically confused, diagnosed the condition of contemporary poetry, and of civilisation, and of us – with our neuroses. He found symptoms everywhere. 'Symptomatic' was his key word. But in his very strange poetry he transmogrified these symptoms into figures in a landscape or mountains, passes, streams, heroes, horses, eagles, feuds and runes of Norse sagas. He was a poet of an unanticipated kind – a different race from ourselves – and also a diagnostician of literary, social and individual psychosomatic situations, who mixed this Iceland imagery with Freudian dream symbolism. Not in the least a leader, but, rather, a clinical-minded oracle with a voice that could sound as depersonalised as a Norn's in a Norse saga. Extremely funny, and extremely hardworking: always, as Louis MacNeice put it, 'getting on with the job'. He could indulge in self-caricature, and he could decidedly shock, but he did no imitations of other people's speech or mannerisms, though he could do an excellent performance of a High Mass, including the bell tinkling. His only performance was himself.

He was in no sense public and he never wanted to start any kind of literary movement, issue any manifestos. He was private even in public.

> Private faces in public places
> Are wiser and nicer
> Than public faces in private places.

We are grateful for a person who was so different from ourselves, not quite a person in the way that other people were. His poetry was unlike anything we had expected poetry to be, from our public-school-classical-Platonic-Romantic-Eng. Lit. education at that time.

He seemed the incarnation of a serious joke. Wystan wrote somewhere that a friend is simply someone of whom, in his absence, one thinks with pleasure. When Wystan was not there, we spoke of him not only with pleasure and a certain awe, but also, laughing. People sometimes divide others into those you laugh at and those you laugh with. The young Auden was someone you could laugh at-with.

I should say that for most of his friends who were his immediate contemporaries, the pattern of his relationship with them was that of colleague; with his pupils, that of a teacher whom they called 'Uncle Wiz'. During the years when he was teaching at prep school, he wrote his happiest poetry. But in those days of exuberance, merging into the vociferous and partisan 1930s, he almost became that figurehead concerning whose pronouncements he grew to be so self-critical later on: the voice of his generation. Or, rather, its several voices, under which his own voice sometimes seemed muted. For it was not true to his own voice to make public political noises. His own voice said:

> O love, the interest itself in thoughtless Heaven,
> Make simpler daily the beating of man's heart.

Nevertheless he did speak for the liveliest of the young at that time: those who wanted to throw off the private inhibitions and the public acquiescences of a decade of censorship and dictatorship and connivance with dictatorship, those who were impassioned by freedom, and some who fought for it. He gave to them their wishes which they might not have listened to otherwise. They were grateful for that. He enabled impulses to flower in individuals. All that was life-enhancing.

Thinking now of the other face, of the later Auden, a great many things about him, quite apart from his appearance, had changed. He now mistrusted his past impulsiveness and rejected in his *oeuvre* many lines and stanzas which had been the results of it. His buffoonery was now sharpened and objectified into wit. His eccentricities had rigidified into habit imposed according to a built-in timetable regulating nearly every hour of his day. This was serious but at the same time savingly comic. He never became respectable, could always be outrageous, and occasionally undermined his own interests by giving indiscreet interviews about his life. These tended to disqualify him in the eyes of members of committees dedicated to maintaining respectability.

He had also perhaps acquired some tragic quality of isolation. But with him the line of tragedy coincided almost with that of comedy. That was grace. One reason for this was his total lack of self-pity. He was grateful that he was who he was, namely W.H. Auden, received on earth as an honoured guest. His wonderfully positive gratitude for his own good luck prevented him from ever feeling in the least sorry for himself. Audiences were baffled and enchanted by this publicly appearing very private performer, serious and subtle and self-parodying all at the same time. They could take him personally and seriously, laughing at-with him.

He had become a Christian. There was a side to this conversion which contributed to his personal isolation. Going to Spain, because he sympathised with the Republic during the Spanish Civil War, he was nevertheless – and much to his own surprise – shocked at the gutted desolation of burned-out churches. Later, he had some signal visionary experiences. These he did not discuss. He was altered in his relations with people, withdrawn into his own world which included our world, became one of those whom others stare at, from the outside.

In his poetry Christianity appears as a literally believed-in mythical interpretation of life which reveals more truth about human nature than that provided by 'the healers at the end of city drives' – Freud, Groddeck, Homer Lane, Schweitzer, Nansen, Lawrence, Proust, Kafka – whom Auden had celebrated in his early work as those who had

> unlearned hatred,
> and towards the really better
> World had turned their face.

For throughout the whole development of his poetry (if one makes exception of the undergraduate work) his theme had been love: not romantic love but love as interpreter of the world, love as individual need, and love as redeeming power in the life of society and of the individual. At first there was the Lawrentian idea of unrepressed sexual fulfilment through love; then that of the social revolution which would accomplish the change of heart that would change society; then, finally, Christianity, which looked more deeply into the heart than any of these, offered man the chance of redeeming himself and the society but also without illusions showed him to himself as he really was with all the limitations of his nature. Christianity changed not only Auden's ideas but also in some respects his personality. Good qualities which he had always had, of kindness and magnanimity, now became principles of living; not principles carried out on principle, but as realisations of his deepest nature, just as prayer corresponded to his deepest need.

Of all my friends, Wystan was the best at saying 'No'. But if asked for bread, he never produced a stone. Young poets who brought him poems were told what he thought about them. (Though, in their case, if he gave them a discourse on prosody, they may have thought that, instead of bread, he was giving them a currant bun.) He no longer believed in the efficacy of any political action a poet might undertake; but that did not mean he had no social conscience. A few years ago I told him that some writers in Budapest had said to me that if he would attend a conference of their local PEN club, which was soon to take place, the name Auden would impress the authorities, and their lives perhaps become a bit easier. Wystan left Vienna almost immediately and attended their meeting in Budapest.

Still, he no longer believed that anything a poet writes can influence or change the public world. All a poet can do perhaps is create verbal models of the private life: a garden where people can cultivate an imagined order like that which exists irresistibly in the music of Mozart, and, perhaps really, within eternity.

Much of his later poetry was a long retreat from his earlier belief in the feasibility of healing literature, into the impregnable earthworks and fortresses of language itself, the fourteen-volume Oxford dictionary, the enchanted plots of poetic forms in George Saintsbury's book on English prosody, the liquid architecture of Mozart, and the solitaire of The Times crossword puzzles.

Wystan died a month ago now. How long it seems. In the course of these few weeks much has happened which makes me feel he may be glad to be rid of this world. One of his most persistent ideas was that one's physical disorders are reflections of the state of one's psyche, expressing itself in a psychosomatic language of spots and coughs and cancers, and unconsciously able to choose, I suppose,

33

when to live and when to die. So I am hardly being superstitious in joking with him beyond the grave with the idea that his wise unconscious self chose a good day for dying, just before the most recent cacophonies of political jargon blaring destruction, which destroy the delicate reduced and human scale of language in which individuals are able to communicate in a civilised and affectionate way with one another.

We can be grateful for the intricate, complex, hand-made engines of language he produced, like the small-scale machinery he so loved, of Yorkshire mines, or like the limestone landscapes of that northern countryside of hills and caves and freshets where he spent his childhood. He made a world of his imagination and had absorbed into his inner life our outer world which he made accessible to us in his poetry as forms and emblems to play with. His own inner world included his friends whom he thought about constantly.

He also had a relationship, which one can only describe as one of affection, with an audience, wherever that happened to be. He could project the private reality of his extraordinary presence and voice on to a public platform, when he gave a public reading. He provoked some uniquely personal reaction from each member of his audience, as though his presence had dissolved it into all its individual human components. The last time we met in America I asked him how a reading which he had given in Milwaukee had gone. His face lit up with a smile that altered its lines, and he said, 'They loved me!' At first I was surprised at this expression of unabashed pleasure in a public occasion. Then I thought, How right of him. For he had turned the public occasion into everyone's private triumph. One reason why he liked writing – and reciting – his poetry was that a poem is written by one person writing for one person reading or listening – however many readers or listeners there may be. So as a public, an audience, a meeting of his friends as separate individuals here gathered together, may each of us think separately our gratitude for his fulfilled life and our praise for his completed work.

H.E. Bates (1905–1974)
writer

by Sir Robert Lusty
(publisher)

*Service of Thanksgiving at St Bride's Church,
Fleet Street, London, on 22 April 1974*

A service of thanksgiving for a life and work is not an affirmation to be lightly given. And this is very especially so for a man so honest, and with so deep a reverence for words and what they mean as H.E. Bates.

Thanksgiving for a life? We each know of some it is hard to be thankful for.

Thanksgiving for the work? Again not always easy to sing loud in praise.

We are saying something here today that no formal memorial service could so fully express.

H.E. would want us to be very careful about this. If there were any mockery, and lack of deep sincerity, it is not difficult to picture the questioning of slightly raised brows and the quizzical look in those wonderfully clear blue eyes with which he surveyed the world.

And we can hear the unmistakable chuckle which attended much of its goings-on.

It is beyond reasonable expectation that words can be found wholly acceptable to H.E.'s penetrating analysis, and able to express within the brevity of minutes what is in our hearts.

It is inconceivable that H.E. could have been anything but a writer. There are few of significance to the literature of our time who have applied such instant and devoted and continuing dedication. He had no other vocation and he needed none.

But conviction and certainty are not for the faint-hearted. Courage there has to be, perseverance and determination to meet frustration and disappointment.

These are shining qualities and H.E. contained them. The man and his work were one.

Sadly the man has gone, but the work remains, and will abide to glorify the English language long after all who knew the man have gone as well.

In many lands and in many tongues can be heard the authentic voice of England as proclaimed by H.E. Bates. He understood and loved his country and its people as few writers of his time. Under the anonymity of Flying Officer X he wrote, when we were all in peril, of gallantry with gallant words. In the wider sense of Winston Churchill's great tribute he was one of the few.

It is interesting that in his teens H.E. wanted very much to be a painter. He loved, through all his life, the work of artists and especially that of the French Impressionists.

There exists a remarkable and touching affinity between the writing of H.E. Bates and the glorious compositions of the best Impressionists. Even in the choice of scene and subject and character can be discerned an identity of interpretation.

H.E. did not create portraits in any precision of formal realism. It was more a matter of suggestion; a hint here and there, an intentional blurring of detail which leaves something to the imagination and is so infinitely more alive than any exactitude can accomplish.

To obtain the best from H.E. Bates, to savour the richness of his quality demands contemplation and repeated readings. The texture of his prose, the limpid ease of his style, and above all the glowing depths of his compassion acquire new substance and new wonders from quiet reflection. So it is with the paintings of Renoir and others.

H.E. travelled far and enjoyed it, but he was a man of the English countryside to which he returned always with gratitude. He was no pastoral sentimentalist. His honesty was far too penetrating and forthright for that. He had a quality for earthiness. His humour had the rumbustiousness of a rural life far removed from the gin and Jaguar belt he so detested.

Walking around the present exhibition of the Impressionists in the Royal Academy is to find oneself face to face with many of the girls and women to be encountered in his writing.

In a curious way H.E. seemed ill at ease in London and when surrounded by the trappings and tinsel of sophistication. However congenial the occasions, and however attractive he might sometimes find the accolade of distinction and the material rewards of success, it was only in the honesty of nature's countryside, and particularly in his beloved Kent, that the quality of the man found illumination. H.E. was essentially an honest man without pretence. He looked very straight not only at his craft but at life as well.

If there were moments of failure I suspect that in the quiet hours he became his own harshest critic.

He was also a simple man who found his greatest happiness in the quiet of contentment. He loved to have his family around him; to hear their voices and their laughter, and to watch their steps into lives of their own. He talked to his grandchildren as equal friends. He saw no reason to put away all childish things. He retained always the best of innocence.

H.E. knew very well the immensity of his debt to Madge, his wife. It was Madge who created, with love, the tranquillity without which he was incapable of his best work.

There was, too, his garden, in which yet again was that affinity of magic it shared with the Impressionists. It, too, was never an exact formality, but rather a riot of colour and blossom concealing infinite care. H.E. would, in an odd way, consult his garden as he would his dictionary.

To watch him at work in his hothouse, or handling a flower, or in contemplation of the sweetness of early morning dew on grass saw the revelation of an artist, all the time in search of words to convey the sad still music of humanity and to arouse compassion for all its moods.

He was a man of essential stillness, not very easy to know or to converse with on all occasions. He could withdraw to some world of his own.

He needed to find what T.S. Eliot has called 'the still point of the turning world' to write the best of which his very real genius was capable.

This he found most readily in the countryside, in his garden and in his home.

The large world will read and remember the works of H.E. Bates, a writer of our time. But for most of us here and for many who cannot be, there is something more. It is H.E. the man; our friend whose lives he doubly enriched.

Sir Neville Cardus (1889–1975)
cricket writer and music critic

by Alan Gibson
(writer and broadcaster)

*Memorial Service at St Paul's Church, Covent Garden,
London, on 1 January 1976*

Since we are in a church, I thought it proper that we should have
a text. Hear then these words from the prophet Blake (I am not
sure whether Blake was one of Sir Neville's favourites, though he
has recalled how enthusiastically he would join in 'Jerusalem' in his
days with the Ancoats Brotherhood). Blake wrote, in *Auguries of
Innocence*:

> Joy and woe are woven fine,
> A clothing for the soul divine;
> Under every grief and pine
> Runs a thread of silken twine.

On an occasion such as this, joy and woe are inseparable companions: thanksgiving for such a life, sadness that it has ended. But
more than that: it was the mingling of joy and woe that made Sir
Neville such a writer – the sensitivity to the human condition, not
least his own; the ability to observe it, and to communicate what
he saw with detachment and yet with passion. His books are full of
humour: rich comedy, sometimes almost slapstick, and yet he keeps
us hovering between tears and laughter. For always he is conscious,
and makes us conscious, of the fragility of happiness, of the passing

of time. He loved the good moments all the more avidly because he knew they were fleeting.

There is no need to recite his achievement. His autobiographical books, the crown of his life's work, have done that already. His early cricket books gave him a reputation for 'fancy' writing. The words 'lyrical', 'rhapsodical', were sometimes applied to him, usually by people who would not know a lyric from a rhapsody. These terms were still jostled about long after they had any possible justification, to Sir Neville's wry amusement. His mature prose was marked by clarity, balance, and indeed by restraint, though he never shrank from emotion or from beauty. Perhaps George Orwell was as good a writer of prose or you may think of P.G. Wodehouse, or Bernard Darwin – everyone has his own favourites – but in this century it is not easy to think of many more in the same class.

I remember clearly how I was introduced to Cardus's writing. It was in August 1935. We were on holiday in Cornwall, at St Ives, and my father was buying me a book, because of some small family service I had done. I said I would like a cricket book, and the choice narrowed to two: a book of reminiscences attributed to Hendren, I think it was, and *Good Days*, by Neville Cardus. I doubt if I had heard of Cardus then, because it was difficult to get the *Manchester Guardian* in the south of England. I was inclined to Hendren, but Father was inclined to Cardus. Father won. We bought *Good Days*. Father read it before I did, though I have more than made up for that since. Most of us, perhaps half a dozen times in our lives, read books – not always famous books – which change us, change our thinking, books which open doors, revelatory books. That was one of mine. It was the essay on Emmott Robinson that did it – do you remember it? – when Cardus imagined 'that the Lord one day gathered together a heap of Yorkshire clay, and breathed into it, and said "Emmott Robinson, go on and bowl at the pavilion end for Yorkshire"'. And then the next bit, about how Emmott's trousers were always on the point of falling down, and he would remember to grab them just in time.

All cricket writers of the last half-century have been influenced by Cardus, whether they admit it or not, whether they have wished to be or not, whether they have tried to copy him or tried to avoid copying him. He was not a model, any more than Macaulay, say, was a model for the aspiring historian. But just as Macaulay changed the course of the writing of history, Cardus changed the course of the writing of cricket. He showed what could be done. He dignified and illuminated the craft.

It was, it has occurred to me, fortunate for cricket that Bradman and Cardus existed at the same time: fortunate for them, too, since the best of batsmen was recorded by the best of critics. Each was worthy of the other.

In the music of Sir Neville's time, at least in English music, there was never one figure quite so dominant as Bradman. Elgar, Delius and Beecham were, he wrote, 'the three most original spirits known in English music since Purcell, if we leave out Sullivan'. He said it with a shadow of a wink, as if to say 'and take it out of that'. You remember how he described Delius, when he met him in what now seem the improbable surroundings of the Langham Hotel: 'His attendant carried him into the sitting-room of his suite and flopped him down on a couch, where he fell about like a rag doll until he was arranged into a semblance of human shape. There was nothing pitiable in him, nothing inviting sympathy in this wreck of a physique. He was wrapped in a monk-like gown, and his face was strong and disdainful, every line on it grown by intrepid living.' There is a picture for you; there is a piece of prose for you.

As for Sir Thomas Beecham, he is always bursting out of Cardus's pages and making his own way. It was with some difficulty that Cardus stopped his splendid Aunt Beatrice from conquering his first autobiographical book. He never quite stopped Beecham, any more than Shakespeare quite stopped Falstaff taking charge of *Henry IV*.

Perhaps the most remarkable episode in the life of Cardus, going by what he said himself, and one to which we should refer here, was his conversion. I think the word is properly used: I mean his conversion to music. It was achieved by one of the minor saints: Edward German. He was watching a production of a light opera, *Tom Jones*, at the Prince's Theatre, Manchester. He had gone there because he was reading Henry Fielding, but, he says, 'the music of Edward German got past my ears and entered into my mind behind my back'. Only twenty months after that first experience he was listening to the first performance of Elgar's Symphony in A Flat, and wondering, with the other musicians in the audience, how Elgar was going to cope with such a long first subject.

He used to say that he was baffled that it should have been Edward German who had first revealed the light: yet he should not have been. It was all of a piece with the man and his thought. When Beecham and McLaren, and Bradman and Ranjitsinhji, and Elgar came within the experience of Cardus, he rose to them and did them justice – but he was capable of being moved, such was his sense of humanity, by men who were no more than good county bowlers, Emmott Robinson or Edward German.

'Joy and woe are woven fine'. They are not alien, they are complementary, 'A clothing for the soul divine'. And in another part of that poem, Blake says:

> It is right it should be so,
> Man was made for joy and woe,
> And when this we rightly know,
> Safely through the world we go.

I am not sure whether Sir Neville Cardus would approve of that as an epitaph: but he is probably too busy to bother just now, arguing with Bernard Shaw.

Lord Kinross (1904–1976)
author and journalist

by Sir John Betjeman
(poet laureate, 1972–84)

Memorial Service at St Mary's Church, Paddington
Green, London, on 10 June 1976

I feel honoured, moved and disturbed to think that I should have
been selected to speak at the funeral of my dear old friend of
over forty years, Patrick Kinross. He would have been moved and
disturbed and, I think, secretly delighted with the notices which
have appeared in the papers about his ability as a travel writer and
historian of Turkey. Patrick was so generous of his time and hospitality to his friends that we forget he was at the same time a conscientious journalist. He was a real professional and always had his copy
in on the day it was demanded. He never failed an editor and I
think he learned this in those hard days of working in Glasgow for
a daily paper, a sudden change after the luxurious Oxford of the
twenties. He transferred to London and became a gossip writer not
from choice but for money. Again he strictly stuck to his business
though he didn't much like it. I can remember how pleased he was
when his fellow-Wykehamist Kenneth Clark commended his book
Society Racket (1933), which was a most amusing and caustic summary
of doings of the Bright Young Things of the late twenties and the
stuffiness of their parents. K. Clark recognised then that Patrick was
not just a gossip columnist but a good social historian.

For all of us here Patrick was chiefly a friend and the mainstay of our happiness. A girl who loved him in the twenties has written to me and I can't forbear quoting her last sentences: 'Patrick was the kindest, most unmalicious, unpossessive man I have ever known.' She goes on to say how her old diaries of the years 1927– 30 bring back such comfortable memories and of his urbaneness with other people's 'dramas'. 'Oh I am so sad he is gone and so sorry for you.' And 'you' means everyone here in John Plaw's cruciform lantern-like church (1788–91), this Pretty Polly Perkins of Paddington Green, which was so beautifully restored by Raymond Erith in the early seventies thanks to the encouragement of its present vicar, Father John Foster, a friend of Patrick. Patrick was not an ardent church-goer. His parish church in Paddington had been demolished in favour of a block of flats. It is worth recalling that among the many battles he waged on behalf of the architecture of London, and Paddington in particular, the saddest defeat was his battle to preserve St Saviour's Church which had been designed as an eye-catcher and vista termination to several streets. Patrick very much disliked public speaking. He said he couldn't do it. And the only time he spoke in the House of Lords was in a long and reasoned defence of St Saviour's as a building. At the end of the speech he was congratulated by peers from all sides and they hoped he would speak again.

He was much better employed talking to all of us here in Paddington. He loved introducing congenial people, or rather people who would be congenial to each other. At his table I met friends I have known for the rest of my life. And at his table I met friends from the past whom I would otherwise not have had a chance of finding again. It was Patrick's gift to make people get on with one another. What was particularly endearing was his appeal for the young. He took them as seriously as they take themselves. He listened with the same patience that he listened to me over fifty years ago when I was a young man complaining about lack of sympathy. He supplied the sympathy, he entered into one's enthusiasms with a tolerant smile.

He was one of the earliest members of the Georgian Group founded by Robert Byron and Lord Rosse. I stress this architectural side of Patrick because it was through him that the side of Warwick

Avenue at its south end was left as an open space. There would otherwise have been developers' flats darkening the area. He wrote a letter to *The Times* in which he referred to Browning's residence in Paddington and who first called it 'Little Venice', and really Browning's cheerful lines exactly fit Patrick:

One who never turned his back, but marched breast forward,
Never doubted clouds would break,
Never dreamed, though right were worsted, wrong would triumph,
Held we fall to rise, are baffled to fight better,
Sleep to wake.

I never saw Patrick lose his temper though I often heard him argue. He enjoyed argument and he very much enjoyed life. I remember him telling me that he had the most enjoyable war. I recall no one else who said that. One of the reasons for his constant cheerfulness was his stern self-discipline in work. Every morning at the same time he could be seen through the window from the street writing at his desk in that flowing even hand. Everything about Patrick was calm and well-ordered. He was a rock and his affection for his friends never failed. I never heard of him turning on anyone though I often heard the sharp rebuke and the laugh that followed it. For that was what made Patrick so endearing – his keen sense of the ludicrous. He didn't mind being laughed at either. I think his happy temperament came from his happy family life; in Edinburgh where I came to stay he and his brother and three sisters lived in Heriot Row, in the house where R.L.S. wrote 'The Lamplighter'. I went to stay with Patrick's family in Skye and we danced reels. There was a Highland gathering at Braemar and Patrick, whose much loved mother was a Johnstone-Douglas, went to the gathering wearing a Douglas tartan. It was one of those terrible mistakes that only the Scottish understand. And I remember his father, whom he called the Baron, referring to Patrick as a Piccadilly Highlander. It is lovely to think of all the laughter and hospitality Patrick gave us and how his last years were made happy by the Paddington Set. And in particular Illtyd Harrington, the three Berkeley boys and Lennox and Freda. Patrick used sometimes to refer to a Presbyterian minister, an ancestor of his who was known in Edinburgh as

'Perpendicular Peter'. Perhaps that's why Patrick was called 'Pete' by his brother and sisters. 'Perpendicular Peter' may have been very strait-laced. That could certainly not be said of Pete.

Patrick was my idea of the great Christian described in one of St Peter's Epistles: 'And above all things have fervent charity among yourselves, for charity shall cover the multitude of sins. Use hospitality one to another without grudging.' That was what Patrick did. He was a great giver. He loved the beautiful. He gave generously of his wisdom to his colleagues in journalism; of affection to his friends; and loyalty and hospitality. I am thankful to have known him so long and so well.

Dame Edith Evans (1888–1976)
actress

by Bryan Forbes
(film director and author)

*Memorial Service at St Paul's Church, Covent Garden,
London, on 10 December 1976*

Like Lilian Baylis, Edith had a special relationship with God. 'God
was very good to me,' she said. 'He never let me go on tour.' This
was a slight exaggeration, of course, because God did sometimes
allow her to visit the colonies. But I think it is true to say that we
can literally thank God for Edith, for what man would have dared
to invent the fiction of her extraordinary life?

It would take a brave novelist to write a story built around an
unknown young Cockney milliner, with no theatrical background,
who is suddenly plucked from obscurity and plonked firmly in the
centre of the English stage, a position she did not relinquish for
over sixty years, becoming in the process the greatest English-
speaking actress of this century.

Such a story would be dismissed as *Peg's Papers*, a mere romance.
Yet romance is a good word, for romance it was, a romance which
existed on both sides of the footlights. Edith was in love with words,
in love with the theatre and with her audiences – and they in turn
loved her.

Unlike Dame Peggy Ashcroft, Miss Gwen Ffrangcon-Davies and
Sir Michael Redgrave, I was denied the pleasure of her company
and the warmth of friendship during those years when her star was

47

rising. I only had the great fortune to share the twilight – the glorious twilight of her last years. And what years they were! She once told us: 'I can't imagine going on when there are no more expectations.' Well, she went on, and there were always expectations to the end of her days.

She said so many wise things about acting, and about life itself. 'You have to be desperately unhappy,' she said, 'before you can play comedy, so that nothing can frighten you. And you can't do tragedy before you know absolute happiness, because, having known that, you are safe.' She defined happiness as 'an essence not a chunk'. Life was always 'larky' to Edith; even her oaths were somehow jolly: 'Crikey', she would say, or 'Crumbs!' She had a way of describing ordinary things and events that made them seem unique. 'When the sun hits the top of a building, I think: it must be marvellous up there.'

Ellen Terry, whom Edith revered, wrote in the copy of her autobiography that she gave to Edith: 'To a Girl after my own heart.' Edith had a big, if secret, heart in contrast to the public face she sometimes presented and which could easily be misunderstood. Since her death I have been amazed to discover how many private kindnesses she performed. There are many people – perhaps people in this church today – who had cause to thank Edith for helping them in hard times; always generously, with no outward show, no fuss, for she hated fuss; everything had to be done quietly.

She was a funny person with a delicious sense of humour, which could be acid when the occasion demanded. I am reminded of the young actor who had the temerity to approach Edith before the transmission of a BBC sound broadcast. 'Good luck, Dame Edith,' he said. 'With some of us,' Edith replied, 'it isn't luck.'

We honour Edith today in this, the traditional actors' church where so many of our colleagues are commemorated. We remember her great landmark performances: Millament, Rosalind, Mrs Sullen, Daphne Laureola, Mrs St Maugham and, of course, the lady she grew to loathe, Lady Bracknell, of whom she once said, 'I've played her everywhere except on ice and under water.'

A great gallery of portraits, for as Agate wrote: 'there has never been a more versatile actress.' She played old women, fat women, maiden aunts, even men in her early days. 'I had to do those first so that later I could play my beauties, my lovelies.' She played ladies and servant girls, the royals and commoners, for she was a woman for all seasons and we shall never see her like again in our lifetime.

At an age when most people are thinking of retiring she conquered a new world, the world of the cinema; and when it became sadly obvious to her that she could not wrestle with a major stage role any more, she took to the road with her one-man poetry readings.

She did everything with style and discipline, including playing in a variety bill with Ellen Terry at the London Coliseum, and for me, in the last year of her life, she sang and danced in a film musical. She refused to cut herself off from life. She loved television, and conquered that medium too, notably when she appeared with one of her favourites, Michael Parkinson. She was an avid watcher of *Match of the Day* and once told me she would have liked to have managed George Best. 'I could sort him out,' she said. I'm sure she could have.

I remember her first real illness – a major one which would have crushed lesser mortals. She asked for me and I went to visit her in a cottage hospital in Kent. I was told she had but little time to live. I fought my way past a somewhat fearsome matron and there was Edith at death's door. She recognised me and, amazingly, sat up in bed. 'Give me a mirror, Bryan,' she said. I found one and gave it to her. She looked at herself in it. 'They all think I'm going to go,' she said finally. 'But I'm not going to go looking like *that*! I'll have lamb chops for lunch.' Edith's wishes were most people's commands. She got her lamb chops and she recovered to make three more films and sustain a season at the Theatre Royal, Haymarket.

'I can't see myself dead,' she told me. 'I shall be cremated as soon as possible, and then I shall be renewed. But not dead. I shall not die.'

Towards the end of her life when it became obvious to me that she could not linger much longer, I felt that I ought to prepare our youngest daughter, Emma. Edith, although never blessed with children herself, had many godchildren and as with our two daughters, Sarah and Emma, she always remembered their birthdays. I did not want her death to shock Emma, so I returned home from my last visit to Edith and said to Emma, 'You know, one of these days, dear Dame Edith will have to die. She's very old and very tired, and I expect she'll just go to sleep and never wake up.' Emma pondered this for a few moments and then she said, 'No, I don't think she'll die. She's not the type.'

And that, dearest Edith, is the verdict of us all.

John Fowler (1906–1977)
interior decorator

by James Lees-Milne
(writer)

*Memorial Service at St George's Church, Hanover
Square, London, on 24 November 1977*

Sometimes, in the watches of the night, I try to induce sleep by
counting the virtues of my friends. It is remarkable how few vices
they seem to have. I honestly believe that John Fowler had none
at all. If he had a few shortcomings, they were inconspicuous. On
the contrary his virtues *and* accomplishments were almost legion.
Of the former he had courage, humility, industry, candour, kindness,
generosity, discretion, humour; and of the latter, the gifts of craftsmanship, painting, gardening, music and friendship in very full
measure. One could go on and on. Each one of us doubtless has his
or her cherished recollection of John's remarkable and memorable
qualities. I will touch upon a few that struck me.

I first met him in 1944 during the height of the Blitz – an
uncomfortable episode in London history which some of you may
recall. In those days he and I happened to be Chelsea neighbours.
I lived in a flimsy little house on the river. He in a flimsy little
house in a Regency terrace along the King's Road. John somehow
had managed to rig up a shelter in his back garden. He had implicit
faith in its resistance to bombs. It consisted of a not very deep hole
in the ground, covered with a few sheets of tin. There were bunks
in the shelter into which John liked to invite his friends, and also

any neighbours who, he decided, needed a respite from danger and a night's comparative peace. Nervous dogs and cats were not excluded. I often enjoyed the hospitality and cosiness which his shelter afforded, whether he was there or not. For I should explain that on several nights of the week he was absent on duty at Guy's Hospital, where he attended operations and dressed the wounds of badly mutilated victims of air-raids, without apparently turning a hair.

It did not take long for me to appreciate and admire the sheer goodness, the almost restless desire to help others, and the fun of this most lovable person. His sense of the ludicrous was very highly developed, and he was one of the few people I have known who would laugh, until he literally cried.

I never discovered much about John Fowler's early life beyond the fact that he came of an impoverished family. He had Irish ancestry of which he was proud. At an early age he lost his father. His mother, to whom he was devoted, was left extremely hard up. She underwent great sacrifices to have him educated, and her privations weighed heavily upon him ever after. This explains per-haps why he glossed over his childhood. While still a boy he became a bank clerk at some pitifully low salary. He once told me he knew what it felt like to go hungry. The work was uncongenial and he hated it. A kind relation, taking pity on him, got him a job with an antique dealer. There he learned the decorative arts of gilding, marbling and repairing old furniture; of resuscitating old fabrics; even of repairing damaged Chinese wallpapers. In fact, he learned the various tricks of craftsmanship at which he became so adept. For a time he worked on his own. From 1930 to 1933 he worked at Peter Jones. From Peter Jones he joined Sibyl Colefax, becoming her right-hand man, and eventually a partner in Colefax and Fowler, which he made into a firm of world renown. From comparatively modest beginnings he rose to achieve, in John Cornforth's words, 'a legendary name and influence in interior decoration'. Innumerable indeed are the houses of England, in private hands and those of the National Trust, which have been retrieved from decay and given new life by his magic touch.

Yes, his early life had been a struggle. And the fruits of that struggle were enhanced by extraordinary industry and powers of observation. Because he worked so hard himself, he expected his assistants to do likewise. He would go to endless trouble teaching those who were willing to learn. I have often watched the local builders visibly inspired by John's deft and lightning movements, as he mixed paints for them, climbed ladders and demonstrated how to wield the paintbrush in order to achieve some special effects he had in mind. He could be called a hard taskmaster. Yet I do not suppose any of his pupils, of whom several are in this church this morning, resented his severity. For one thing, they learned so much from him. For another, there was no task he might demand of them, which he himself could not do rather better than they.

Consequently, most of them became intimate friends, whom he would treat in his funny paternal manner as though they were his children. He delighted to share with them whatever he possessed. The little Gothic hunting lodge at Odiham, and the exquisite garden, entirely created by him in the French style, with its pleached horn-beam hedges, statues and pavilions, was just as much dedicated to his friends' pleasure as to his own.

John was of course a perfectionist down to the last detail. To get a thing right nothing was allowed to stand in the way. And it didn't. What made him unique among interior decorators was his strong historical sense. This led him to be conservative in his treatment of old buildings. He did not impose his own tastes, but endeavoured to reinstate what had existed originally. Through this restraint and humility he achieved greatness. He was reluctant to redecorate the walls or ceilings of historic rooms unless it was essential. He would scrape and scrape through the layers of later coats of paints and wallpaper, until he satisfied himself that he had come upon what the Caroline or Georgian architect had intended. Thereupon he reproduced the original colours or papers as closely as he could. He was a master of related tones, and his adoption of contrasting shades of white almost amounted to genius.

Old craftsmanship was sacred to John Fowler. Ancient artefacts were venerated by him. Even a simple Georgian nail was a thing to be cherished. Lifting his thick spectacles, he would hold the nail within a few inches of his large myopic eyes and scrutinise it with a tender devotion.

The eighteenth century was alive to him. By its standards of beauty he measured the achievements of the twentieth, usually to its detriment. If ever there was a conservationist he was one. He made it his duty to protect classical buildings; sometimes even from his own clients. He would threaten an offending owner with public obloquy, with letters to *The Times*, with questions raised in Parliament. Any other decorator, adopting such tactics, would have lost both job and client. But not John Fowler. His charm and authority were too compelling, and his services too much in demand.

It cannot be claimed that he was a good businessman. He cared not a hoot about big money. He found his fulfilment in being an expert, an artist and a fighter. All his life he fought, first, extreme poverty and loneliness, and then philistinism. To those foes yet another crueller one was to be added. The last ten or twelve years of his life he was threatened with a mortal illness. He fought it, as he fought all the other evils – valiantly to the end.

Henry Williamson (1895–1977)
writer

by Ted Hughes
(poet laureate, 1984–98)

*Memorial Service at St Martin-in-the-Fields Church,
London, on 1 December 1977*

As a service of mourning, this ceremony belongs properly to Henry Williamson's family. But as a memorial service and a service of thanksgiving it belongs to all of us.

We have come together today to remember the extraordinary vitality, the long life – productive and energetic almost to the very end – and the genius, of an extraordinary man.

When his daughter Margaret asked me to say something today, I was startled, because there must be quite a few people much better qualified to do this than I am. But after all there is a kind of logic to it. I hope I shall be forgiven if I speak now of my own feelings, and of my private acquaintance with his work and with him. But Henry Williamson has been such an essential and precious part of my life, in some ways a crucial part, that I can't really do otherwise. And in paying some of my own debt of gratitude, perhaps I shall speak for a great many others.

First of all, as for a very great number of his countrymen, he was for me the inspired author of *Tarka the Otter*. No doubt if he could hear me say that, he would howl with exasperation, because if ever a writer was hounded and hallooed by one of his own creations, Henry was hunted by the fame of that book. As if he had never written anything else. At the same time, he was passionately attached to *Tarka*. He knew just how important it was for him. In a very real sense, that Devon otter was his totem, sacred to him, deeply and mysteriously kin, and it remained so throughout his life. It may seem odd, but to me he always resembled a fierce otter facially – that fierce, fiercely alert, bristly look. However that may be, it was through his instinctive loyalty to the spirit of that animal that he wrote his most wonderful pages. And it was through that wild creature, too, that he arrived at much in his later beliefs, even much of what many came to regard as his later mistakes.

My own bond with Henry Williamson was made through that book. I was about eleven years old when I found it, and for the next year I read little else. I count it one of the great pieces of fortune in my life. It entered into me and gave shape and words to my world, as no book ever has done since. I recognised even then, I suppose, that it is something of a holy book, a soul-book, written with the life-blood of an unusual poet. Henry knew the same. I remember him describing the writing of those deeply engraved paragraphs – he called it 'chipping every word off the breastbone'. What spellbound me, as I read, was a sensation I have never felt so acutely in any other book. I can only call it the feeling of actuality. The icy feeling of the moment when you realise that things actually are just so.

On every page of *Tarka* was some phrase, some event, some glimpse that made the hair move on my head with that feeling. In the confrontations of creature and creature, of creature and object, of creature and fate he made me feel the pathos of actuality in the natural world. It was the first time I was ever aware of it. But I now know that only the finest writers are ever able to evoke it.

I tried to impose the weird atmosphere of those haunting sentences and episodes on my own doings. And a world I was already given to completely – my world of wild creatures in the South Yorkshire countryside – became a world of Henry's radiant language. In this way, *Tarka* put my life under an enchantment that lasted for years, and that gradually crystallised into an ambition to write for myself, and to fasten that strange feeling, that eerie sense of the moment of reality, in my own sentences. What I had responded to, and been awakened by, was the poetic intensity of Henry Williamson's vision and words.

It is not usual to consider him as a poet. But I believe he was one of the truest English poets of his generation. He was different from the others in that he never published any verse, and I don't know that he even wrote it. He was dedicated to the presentation of realities in prose — in the tradition of the Tolstoy he loved so much. But in those early books about wildlife, he created a genuine poetic mythology. He set it in an actual world, and he peopled it with actual creatures and men, but it is in fact an imaginative vision, intensely controlled at every point by imaginative laws, and it does the real work of poetry.

The poet of the natural world was the first Henry. The second Henry I encountered later in a book called *Patriot's Progress*. In its way, *Patriot's Progress* is as phenomenal a piece of writing as *Tarka*. It is a slightly fictionalised account of Henry Williamson's baptism of fire in the trench fighting of the First World War. We see there that spirit of Tarka — a wild supersensitive creature — hurled into the dreadful world of modern history. It is one of the very best records of trench warfare, and it certainly describes one of the key experiences in Henry's life.

We now know what a decisive effect that war against Germany was to have on him. In some ways he spent the rest of his days working out the implications and living out the consequences of what he had felt there. The illuminations and ambiguous revelations of that war are at the heart of all his later books. And out of them came the indignation that drove him along the razor's edge of his particular brand of political idealism.

The importance to Henry Williamson of his political ideas can't be ignored, but I don't think it is difficult to understand when we see how the ideas evolved. He was not two different writers — an inspired author of nature stories which everybody loves, on the one hand, and a political extremist full of unpopular pronouncements on the other. The whole system was really one system. If one ignores the superficial errors of judgement he seemed to make, in trying to adjust his ideas to the practical world of contemporary politics, and looks instead into the heart of his books, into the poetic vision which is the dynamo at the centre, one sees his consistency. At bottom he worshipped a small group of simple, related things. He gave them old-fashioned names, often enough, but they were permanent things, and it seems to me they were real and good things. Maybe they were the *only* real and good things.

First, he worshipped energy. And worshipping energy, he feared – with a fear that was always ready to become rage – inertia, disintegration of effort, wilful neglect, any sort of sloppiness or wasteful exploitation. Even here, we can see how a feeling for a biological law – the biological struggle against entropy – quickly sprouts its social and political formulations, with all the attendant dangers of abstract language. He worshipped natural creativity, and therefore rejoiced in anybody who seemed able to make positive things happen, anybody who had a practical vision of repairing society, upgrading craftsmanship, nursing and improving the land. He worshipped the clear, undistorted spirit of natural life, and this led him to imagine a society based on natural law, a hierarchic society with a visionary leader. It seemed to him that he had glimpsed the perfect society in the stable, happy world of some of the big old estates, where discipline, courtesy, tradition, order, community and productive labour flourished in intimate harmony with a natural world that was cherished. And this memory shaped his reaction to the worst side of democracy, the shoddy, traditionless, destructive urban emptiness that seemed to him to be destroying England, in its ancestral wholeness and richness, as effectively as the work of a deliberate enemy. Well, history played some nasty tricks on him, and gave his ideas strange bedfellows, but who is to say that the ideas, in themselves, were wrong? Everything I have described, in the real moral basis of his vision, springs out of the natural world, and a passionate concern to take care of it, in which he was quite a long way ahead of his contemporaries. He was a North American Indian dreamer among Englishmen. Given the extreme vehemence of his nature, it was almost inevitable that he should find himself entangled in other men's misunderstandings. But it is possible now to forget those, and see what he was really talking about.

A third Henry, the Henry who for me at least made everything about Henry Williamson very clear, was the man himself.

I got to know him in his sixties, when I was a little over thirty. Still spellbound by his magical book, albeit quite unconsciously, I had found myself living where I still live, on Tarka's river, the Taw, in the middle of Devon, and soon I made contact with Henry. It seemed very right to see that he too was still in a way spellbound by Tarka, working in a hut on that patch of territory he had bought with the prize-money Tarka had won for him long ago.

I remember our first meeting, among a group of young people, at the house of a friend, and I remember my astonishment. He had five times the vitality of anybody there. I remember thinking that he was like a young man – but of an earlier, more courteous, more confident age. And throughout our acquaintance that impression remained, that Henry was really a young man. I imagine he had changed very little from the time of the First World War, as if that experience had fixed him, and preserved him, but with all his activity and freshness and enthusiasm.

For several years I met him quite often. And gradually learned my way through his unpredictable moods. And gradually I understood what I liked about him most of all. We had noisy arguments about his politics, wonderful evenings when he told stories — with what seemed like microscopically detailed total recall, and an uncanny ear for Norfolk and West Country dialect, full of wit and drama. And he was always different, mercurial, emotional, outrageous, amusing. But in one thing he was constant, and constantly attractive. He was untamed, and he was free. What D.H. Lawrence would have called his Demon was still in full clear flame. Life and a full share of difficulties had not humbled or soured him in any visible way. The tremendous energy that had driven him through all those long books was still there, at any moment of the day, a torrent of surprises. His Demon had a black side, even a diabolical side, which gave him his bad times, but that was the powerhouse of his writing; it connected him to a dark world of elemental force. It was the beast on his back that drove him. It was also Tarka – still wild, alert, open to everything, ready for anything. It was what pulsed through the best of his writing, and it was genuinely him, and it was beautiful. Fascinating and beautiful.

Though he's gone now, I can't feel this is a time to mourn. He lived a long life, and lived it to the end with a gusto and courage and satisfaction that few men attain to. He was blessed with an intense vision of the world, and a genius for expressing it, which he harvested to the full. He added some masterpieces to the literature of his country, and he had fame, and it may be he now has the kind of immortality he would have wanted. What more might we have asked for, for him? Let us rest content in our gratitude, to his Maker, and to him.

Ginger Dennistoun (1911–1979)
racehorse trainer

by John Oaksey
(racing journalist)

Memorial Service at St Michael and All Angels'
Church, Lambourn, Berkshire, on 23 May 1979

I know that Ginger would be glad that so many of you, his friends, have come to remember him.

But I also know that the one thing he would hate – the one thing absolutely guaranteed to tilt the famous pipe at its most threatening, storm-warning angle – would be for us to meet and mope, long-faced, in gloom and grief to mourn his passing.

'Remember me if you please,' I can hear him saying, 'but for God's sake smile when you are doing it.'

I am convinced that would be his wish and I do not believe there can be a single person in this church who cannot, at this moment, without notice, call to mind a memory of Ginger which makes you want to smile. Most of us have hundreds, but the trouble is that they usually come complete with the sort of sound effects which are a little difficult to reproduce in church:

Ginger on the downs, shrieking in vain at some unfortunate runaway – probably me – disappearing out of control off the end of the gallop.

Ginger by the winner's enclosure after a selling race – bristling with ill-concealed anxiety and darting furious looks around the ring designed to paralyse anyone rash enough to bid.

Ginger at the card table playing his favourite seven card high-low and trying without much success to look as though he neither knew nor cared about the perfect hand he held.

Ginger and Guy Knight playing backgammon, each trying hard to make the other the first to lose his temper.

And latterly Ginger in his nautical disguise, pipe thrust skywards, rain streaming down those grubby macs, chugging across the Solent in a flat calm and diving below, keeping Tor and me and our children, who adored him, in helpless fits with the role he had chosen for himself afloat – somewhere midway between Ted Heath and Long John Silver.

All these and many more . . . Oh, how he made us laugh!

And of course the fact that the source of all that laughter has now suddenly dried up makes you want to cry as well. There's nothing wrong with that. But I'm still sure it's the smiles Ginger would want to see today. It is in them he would take pride.

Mind you, it would be even more ridiculous to make him sound like some ever-cheerful Pickwick figure surrounded by an aura of permanent good humour. Of course, he was nothing of the kind. 'The most infuriating man in Berkshire', someone once called him and he could, just occasionally, be all of that.

Soon after I had the good luck to meet and fall in love with his daughter he made very clear his view that a conscientious father-in-law's duty included a good deal of constructive – or, if necessary, destructive – criticism.

It didn't matter what you were doing – scribbling for the papers, blathering on the box or, as Ginger so gracefully described it, 'floundering about like an inebriated monkey on the back of some poor unfortunate horse' – you could count on him for a frank, unbiased review of your activities which cared much more for accuracy than for the feelings of the subject.

I think that was much the same for all his family, from his beloved Nancy down to his youngest grandchild. But if there was something to be proud of, no one could be prouder. Nancy's beauty and courage and patience, all the various exploits of Tory and Ginny and Christopher, Charlie's winners – especially when he backed them – and Sara's riding, helping with which, I'm glad and proud to say, he happily spent the last day of his life: all these gave him infinite pleasure.

Suddenly, amid all the shouts and howls of simulated rage, there would be a pause, a smile, a twinkle of the eye – maybe even a word or two of actual praise. And they, those precious moments, because we knew he really meant them, were worth a thousand times the glib superlatives of lesser men.

No such embroidery is needed to describe Ginger's various careers. A regular soldier before the war, he and his mules fought their way across the Middle East and pursued the Germans up Italy with such stubborn courage that Ginger was decorated not only by his own country but also by the Iraqis and the Poles.

> He either fears his fate too much or his deserts are small
> Who will not put it to the touch to win or lose it all.

Both as a fearless and particularly forceful amateur rider – I believe the least desirable place on the whole racecourse was between him and the rails if he did not think you ought to be there – and as a skilful, knowledgeable, infinitely hard-working trainer, Ginger lived his life in racing by those words of the great Montrose.

He was never afraid to put it to the touch and although not quite all his touches came off, many that did were memorable: two consecutive Imperial Cups with High Point when the Imperial Cup was far and away the most difficult handicap hurdle to win; River Trout, Sapphire Queen, Mintako, Fellhound, Barbizon.

Fred Winter and Fellhound looked so flawless one day over fences at Lingfield that a well-lubricated clubman watching on television rang up Ginger and asked him to buy a horse. The result was Barbizon, who cost just over a hundred pounds, trod on Ginger's foot when he got him out of the railway box at Challow station, and won us all a small fortune in that unforgettable Kempton seller.

Of all my countless arguments with Ginger, one of the very few which ended with a measure of agreement was about the probability of an afterlife. 'I reckon it must be better than even money,' he said, 'and in any case if you hope for a second chance, what is the point of betting against it? By the time you know the result it will be too late to pay.'

Well, now the numbers are in the frame and if, as I hope and believe, Ginger is getting his second chance – if there *is* another world – then for those who are there that world will, by reason of his presence, be more cheerful, less predictable, less dull and above all simply more fun. For he was a man who, in terms of pleasure, happiness and fun, gave far more than he took.

If he was here he'd be saying, 'Oh, do shut up, you have gone on much too long,' but at a service like this for Ginger's old friend Clive Graham I finished with some words from *Pilgrim's Progress* which I knew that Ginger liked because he told me so. The last of them, I feel, must certainly apply to him.

'Then,' said Mr Valiant-for-truth, 'I am going to my Father's; and though with great difficulty I am got hither, yet now I do not repent me of all the trouble I have been at to arrive where I am.

'My sword I give to him that shall succeed me in my pilgrimage, and my courage and skill to him that can get it. My marks and scars I carry with me, to be a witness for me that I have fought His battles who now will be my rewarder.'

When the day that he must go hence was come, many accompanied him to the river side, into which he went, he said, 'Death, where is thy sting?' And as he went down deeper, 'Grave, where is thy victory?'

So he passed over, and all the trumpets sounded for him on the other side.

Reynolds Stone (1909–1979)
engraver

by Dame Iris Murdoch
(writer)

Memorial Service at St James's Church, Piccadilly, London, on 20 July 1979

It is a privilege to speak about Reynolds Stone, and it is not difficult, since there is so much to say in his praise. Yet also it is hard to speak worthily, accurately, eloquently and briefly about so unusual a person, so modest, so talented, so unostentatiously refined and subtle an artist. The marvellous book of his engravings published two years ago contains a few pages of autobiography, an account of his childhood and youth, beautifully and simply written. We learn of how he grew up among scholars and bookish men, and took to book learning as a natural part of a life which contained many other things, and where painting too was taken for granted. Herein his love of the countryside, of craftsmanship, and of the physical being of books as well as of their contents found its felicitous beginning. Reynolds's art is in the happiest sense traditional, while it is at the same time like the man himself, quietly and strongly original and independent. We are constantly reminded of that intensity of imagination, precise, visionary and spiritual, which we associate with Thomas Bewick and with Samuel Palmer. At the same time Reynolds's early interest and experience in printing, his admiration of Stanley Morison, betokens a natural connection with the practical and public world which he retained all his life. He combined in himself, with a certain special grace and perfection, the roles of artist and of craftsman. We can still see his pure fine lettering, his strong clear images, in many ordinary and public places, on tombs and tablets, on Winston Churchill's memorial in Westminster Abbey for example, in churches, in streets, on trade signs and letter headings, and well-known armorial bearings. His art proceeded unself-consciously from an intense personal privacy into a public world where it has set enduring standards and has given a pure aesthetic pleasure to many who never heard his name.

Reynolds once said that he would be content to paint for the rest of his life within his own garden. Those of us who have been fortunate enough to know the garden, the paintings and the man can well understand that. The patterns of leaves, the live solidity of trees, the atmosphere of green light, the flash of water: his paintings have the charm and strength of truthful art which opens the eyes of the beholder and changes and clarifies his vision. Good art shows us reality, which we too rarely see because it is veiled by our selfish cares, anxiety, vanity, pretension. Reynolds, as artist and as man, was a totally unpretentious being. His work, seemingly simple, gives to us that shock of beauty which shows how close, how in a sense ordinary, are the marvels of the world.

Reynolds is of course better known as a stone carver and a lettering artist, best known as a wood engraver. In these fields he can I think have, and have had, few peers. Wood engraving, that extraordinary art, when practised by a master such as Reynolds, can produce in a tiny compass a masterpiece of authoritative imagination: details of botanical minuteness, scenes of sylvan charm, cities and rooms, vast landscapes, mountains, seas, skies that stretch into far distances of speculation. In his autobiographical note about his child-hood Reynolds mentioned in passing how much he liked insects and ships. And he once said to me sadly that some of the things he loved most seemed to be vanishing from the world: butterflies, whales and (already gone) Thames sailing barges. One thinks of him in connection with such things. He was a close observer and lover of separate particulars, well equipped to be a happy inhabitant of this planet. One associates him with leaves, stones, animals, the rigging of ships. I see him on the Chesil Bank with a great background of sea, picking up a small pebble and looking at it carefully.

We remember him too of course in his garden, in his house where in the corner of the drawing room he practised his minute magical art (it is hard to believe that he is gone from that place) and in the midst of his family, where he lived the happy good loving life of a true man, creating with his wife and children a serene and beautiful home which was a refuge and a joy to his many generously welcomed friends, a place of pleasure and spiritual refreshment.

Reynolds never ceased to view the world with a childlike attentive wonder, the equivalent in the artist of the perpetual wonder of the philosopher. And he was in his way a philosopher, a totally independent reflective being, unconventional, unworldly, generous in his admiration of others, and unambitious except for the true ambition which is a love of perfection. To say he was untouched by vanity is so much an understatement as to belong to another universe of discourse. He was, in the proper and the deepest sense of the concept, a free man. He was the kindest and most constant of friends. He was a gently humorous person with a sweet school-boyish sense of fun – and he was also in the quietest imaginable way a polymath.

I think of him as a profoundly religious person, though I do not know, and perhaps he never asked himself, what exactly he believed. As he belonged naturally in an English tradition, so he also belonged naturally in a Christian tradition. Although he was a private home-keeping man, his art, as I have said, reached out into ordinary life with its lesson of simplicity, truthful imaginative vision and pureness of heart. He has touched many people and will touch many more. We must be thankful for such a man, for the example of his life and the continuing joy of his work: the standard which he set by his art and by his mode of being. He had the good fortune to be able to go on working until the end. He was, and deserved to be, a happy man, and this thought, as we miss and mourn him, we can give to ourselves as a consolation. God rest his soul.

Lord Mountbatten, First Earl of Burma
(1900–1979)
Viceroy of India and First Sea Lord

by His Royal Highness the Prince of Wales

Memorial Service at St Paul's Cathedral, London,
on 20 December 1979

I still cannot believe that I am standing here in this pulpit delivering an address about a man – about my great-uncle – who to me, at any rate, always seemed reassuringly indestructible, full of energy and with enormous enthusiasm for a multitude of projects – even at the age of nearly eighty. Lord Mountbatten asked me to give the address at his funeral several years ago when he was planning the arrangements, but little did I think under what circumstances I would be making that address. Does it not seem a cruel and bitter irony that a man who served under Admiral Beatty in his flagship during the First War, who in the Second War was torpedoed, mined and finally sunk by aerial bombardment in HMS *Kelly*, who helped defeat the scourge of tyranny and oppression throughout Europe and the Far East and finally ensured that independence should be brought to the continent of India – that a man with such passionate concern for the individual and for progressive thought and action should suddenly and mercilessly be blown to bits with members of the family he adored through the agency of some of the most cowardly minds imaginable? What on earth was the point of such mindless cruelty? Without the heroic efforts of people like Lord Mountbatten this country, and many others like it, might even now be under the sway of some foreign power, devoid of the kind of liberty we take so easily for granted in this day and age. Perhaps the manner of his passing will awaken us – or is it too much to hope for? – to the vulnerability of civilised democracies from the kind of sub-human extremism that blows people up when it feels like it.

There is, I suppose it is true, a sense in which Lord Mountbatten died a hero's death – at sea and wearing his HMS *Kelly* T-shirt, given to him by the surviving members of that famous destroyer's ship's company. But with him died two members of his family – his son-in-law's mother, Doreen Lady Brabourne, and his grandson Nicholas Knatchbull – together with Paul Maxwell, the boy from Enniskillen who so enthusiastically looked after the boat during the summer. Today we remember them – two elderly people and two on the threshold of their lives – in this great cathedral which has witnessed so many stirring and sad events in the history of the nation. The fact that two of his family died with him would have appalled Lord Mountbatten. He was, above all, a family man. He was a devoted husband, a deeply affectionate and enlightened father, a wonderful grandfather and a very special great-uncle. He was a man for whom blood was thicker than water – a fact which helped to make him the natural centre of the family and a patriarchal figure who provided advice, frank criticism and boundless affection for all those members of his widespread family, with whom he kept in close touch. It was actually quite frightening how much he knew about his relations' breeding through his authorship of a most complicated genealogical tour de force, known as the family relationship tables.

These tables were one of the results of a constantly active brain which was never allowed a moment's rest. There was always a new challenge to be overcome, fresh projects to be set in motion, more opposition to be defeated – all of which were pursued with a relentless and almost irresistible single-mindedness of purpose. Sometimes the approach could be compared to that of a steamroller, where anything in the path tended to be flattened, but what distinguished him as a noble character was his ability to see the point and withdraw if you had the courage to stand up to him and he could see that you meant business. One of his greatest qualities was his willingness to listen to the opposite point of view, or several different views, and then make a decision based on what seemed to him to be the most reasonable course. In this he was helped by a progressive outlook, inherited from his parents, which influenced so many of his ideas and decisions. But he also made a conscious effort to listen to the more left-wing approach and made sure that there was someone on his staff, particularly in South-East Asia and India, who could provide him with such advice – even if he didn't feel obliged to take it.

Although he could certainly be ruthless with people when the occasion demanded, his infectious enthusiasm, his sheer capacity for hard work, his wit made him an irresistible leader among men. People who served under him or worked on his various staffs invariably adored him. And why? Because I believe that above all else he was honest. He was devastatingly frank with people. There was never any doubt as to where you stood: you always knew what he thought about you, whether it was complimentary or rude. That quality of real moral courage, of being able to face unpleasant tasks that need to be done – and yet to be fair and consistent – is a rare quality indeed. But he had it in abundance and that, I think, is one of the reasons why people would have followed him into hell; if he had explained the point of such an expedition . . . It is also one of the reasons why I adored him and why so many of us miss him so dreadfully now. Another reason was his unique capacity for open-mindedness. There seemed to be nothing he could not cope with or could not understand. This again is a precious quality, where so often people's judgement and wisdom seem to be clouded by various forms of prejudice. Lord Mountbatten was certainly a man of wisdom, of practicality and common sense, but he also had a wonderful flair for the unconventional and a gift for original thought – hence his enthusiastic support for some unusual ideas and inventions while he was Chief of Combined Operations. One of the most brilliant of the schemes he helped to inspire and fight for was PLUTO – or Pipeline Under The Ocean – a scheme which together with the Mulberry Harbours made the invasion of Europe a success. This imaginative and unconventional approach made it possible for him to appreciate the metaphysical aspects of the universe around us and to become fascinated in so many unexplained phenomena – particularly unidentified flying objects.

Perhaps one of the most distinctive features of his life was the way in which virtually everything he attempted was a success. He excelled – and he excelled because he was a true professional. Nothing he did was ever done without vast application and effort – perhaps *that* much more effort than most other people were prepared to make. As a result he was pretty nearly always right and didn't hesitate to say so. That apparent conceit and arrogance annoyed some people, but in a strange way he was big enough to carry it off because it was an adjunct of his honesty – above all his honesty to himself. The fact that he was such a civilised and humane character I am sure stemmed from his knowledge of himself. There is no doubt that in many ways he was a showman, but his genuineness always shone through in terms of his concern for the individual and his ability to communicate with anyone. There can surely be no finer tribute to a man than that so many people loved him, thought of him as a hero and admired him for his humanity to the 'ordinary' individual. I know this is true for I myself received over two thousand five hundred letters after Lord Mountbatten's death and so many expressed the feeling that he somehow belonged to them and understood them.

This sentiment formed a thread which ran through the whole tapestry of his life – from the Invergordon mutiny (when one of the chief ringleaders acknowledged that if more officers had been like Lord Mountbatten there would never have been a mutiny) to HMS *Kelly*, to the South-East Burma command and Asia, to India and finally to the United World Colleges movement which filled the last ten years of his existence. It is for his achievements in South-East Asia, in India and the United World Colleges that he most wanted to be remembered. In South-East Asia he brought, as Sir Winston Churchill said, 'a young and vigorous mind into this lethargic and stagnant Indian scene'. But above all it was through his far-sighted vision that he realised the aspirations of the Burmese for their independence when others were determined to bring them back under colonial rule. In the end he was bitterly disappointed that he had not been able to exert his influence enough to prevent the Burmese leaving the Commonwealth when they finally achieved independence. In India his achievement was immense and because he had plenipotentiary powers he was able to ensure that India remained within the Commonwealth in an atmosphere of trust and friendship instead of recrimination and bitterness. His personal success was exceptional. He brought a true sympathy and insight into the problems of the Indian people and won a lasting place in their affections by the informality and friendship of himself and his wife. The United World Colleges movement was a particular passion of his in the final years because he saw within the scheme a means of bringing peace and international understanding through students from many countries to a world that he had seen pull itself to pieces in twenty-five years. He worked long and hard to establish something special for which he held a passionate conviction.

. After fifty years of service to the Royal Navy that he loved and after defending his country in two world wars, they finally succeeded in murdering a man who was desperately trying to sow the seeds of peace for future generations. Rarely have the immortal words of Laurence Binyon been more appropriate: 'They shall not grow old as we that are left grow old. Age shall not weary them, nor the years condemn. At the going down of the sun and in the morning – we will remember him.'

Sir Cecil Beaton (1904–1980)
photographer and writer

by Richard Buckle
(ballet critic, author and exhibition designer)

*Memorial Service at St Martin-in-the-Fields Church,
London, on 6 March 1980*

It is not easy when you have been for half a century 'the glass of fashion and the mould of form' to resign yourself to isolation and idleness; when you have been the most industrious of men to find yourself unable to work. This was the fate of Cecil Beaton after his stroke in 1974. Of course he loved his house in Wiltshire; of course he was lucky to be at home and not in 'a home'; and of course he was cared for by Eileen Hose with a devotion which few men could inspire. Nevertheless, for the first year or so he battled with Giant Despair. He won the battle, but as Wellington said of Waterloo, it was 'a damned near-run thing'.

It is not easy, when your right hand is incapacitated, to learn to use your left. To the acquiring of this new skill Cecil applied himself with diligence. He began to answer all his letters every morning with his left hand, while Eileen addressed the envelopes. Nor was it only a question of writing letters. He needed to draw again. Like a child, he began by copying: he copied reproductions of drawings by Holbein. Later, on a visit to Majorca, he made studies of a gnarled tree; in Italy he sketched the house where he was staying; and he tried out many pen and watercolour drawings of interiors at Broadchalke. I thought these remarkable, and perhaps I overdid

73

the praise. If so, I doubt if Cecil was taken in. One day before dinner, I spotted on a stool by the library window an interior with a figure. 'You've done a portrait of Clarissa!' I exclaimed. 'And it's just like her.' It seemed to me little short of miraculous that Cecil's left hand had got the message from his eye by way of his brain, and that the great catcher of likenesses had scored a bull's-eye once more. Yet he was not really satisfied even by this. It is very hard to persevere when the results of your labour offer inadequate encouragement. Observing how he kept at it, I thought of Tennyson's 'Ulysses'.

> Old age hath yet his honour and his toil.
> Death closes all; but something ere the end,
> Some work of noble note may yet be done,
> Not becoming men that strove with Gods.

It is no pleasure, when you have been renowned as a wit and raconteur, and had so much to say, to be limited in your power of expression; to find, on trying to give a funny account of a party, that you cannot get out the names or make your point: but when this happened Cecil brushed aside his failure with a dismissing 'Oh never mind', and changed the subject. He was the most considerate, constructive, generous and loyal of friends. He always had very good manners, and I think both the strength and sweetness of his character became more evident as he grew older. Oscar Wilde said: 'It is not what you do that matters, it is what you become.' No, it is far from easy to improve and to rise above circumstances as Cecil did.

None of these things was easy: but then, it had not been easy for him in earlier years to capture the attention of the public and to hold it; to establish a pre-eminent position in the worlds of photography, fashion and stage design; to keep his end up during the war while serving his country in the way best suited to his powers, flying between Europe, Africa, India, Asia and America to take half a million photographs; to do several jobs at once, speeding from studio to dressmaker, then on to the theatre; to go back to school at the Slade when he was nearly fifty, and try to learn to paint in oils from scratch; to please with his sets and costumes such perfectionists as Binkie Beaumont, John Gielgud, Lincoln Kirstein,

Edith Evans, Rex Harrison or Margot Fonteyn; to gratify ten thousand sitters with their photographic likenesses; to 'fill the unforgiving minute with sixty seconds' worth of distance run'.

If there be any present who thought of Cecil Beaton mainly as a master of revels to the rich, it may strike them as odd that I should praise him for his heroic virtues. This was indeed my intention; for, however frivolous Cecil's beginnings may have appeared, I consider that when you have added up the sum of courage, generosity, loyalty, civility and perseverance you will find the total is nobility: and I think he ended as 'a very perfect gentle knight'.

At a ball at Wilton in October I noticed him seated on a sofa in the Double Cube Room, watching the dancers. Beside him sat his old friends Diana Cooper and Mary Pembroke and two other ladies who bore historic names. Above him stretched that huge canvas of Van Dyck depicting the younger of those brothers to whom Shakespeare's First Folio was dedicated, with his children and with his second wife, Lady Anne Clifford, the most famous woman to come out of Westmorland, where Cecil's own mother was born. More than any portrait painter in oil I thought that Beaton the photographer had been the Van Dyck of our day, and I realised he was already part of history.

I have buttressed with quotations from the poets my puny edifice of prose. Here are two quotations from people you do not know. A letter from New Jersey:

> It is winter. The Saturday morning news jolted me. That same week Sir Cecil wrote 'Many thanks for your sendings! They have a power of good.' Our relationship in letters started nearly eight years ago ... Although I often told my friends I was a 'friend' of Sir Cecil Beaton I knew it wasn't really so, but his kindness bolstered the illusion. I never met him in person.

A letter from California:

> I feel as if he had been a parent or my own brother ... The simple fact of his existence pleased me enormously, and added an incomparable lustre to life. I always cherished the unlikely dream that I would one day meet him in the flesh. Truly my greatest luck are his letters to me. I have set my course by his star.

Cecil liked to say that his own 'greatest luck' was to have been given a helping hand by the Sitwells. On the day he died he penned a letter to the last survivor of that glittering triumvirate. He wrote: 'Oh, what courage we all need!'

Courage he had; and of a quality which must have won the commendation of blind Milton, the author of these final words: 'I cannot praise a fugitive and cloistered virtue, that never sallies out and sees her adversary, but slinks out of the race where that immortal garland is to be run for not without dust and heat.'

Ann Fleming (1913–1981)

wit and grand hostess

by Lord Annan

(Provost of King's College, Cambridge)

*Memorial Service at St James's Church, Piccadilly,
London, on 20 November 1981*

We are here this morning to remember Ann Fleming – though none who knew her can ever forget her. Indeed history may not forget her because she captivated an extraordinary number of the most gifted spirits of her time, people who were quite different from her in taste, upbringing, beliefs and temperament but who were enthralled by her wit, her affection and her temerity. People speak of her as a great hostess but she bore no resemblance to the hostesses of the previous generation – to Lady Cunard or Lady Colefax. She was indifferent to celebrities, to the up and coming, to the famous. She did not exist to please, to flatter and cajole. She possessed the art, as every great hostess does, of mixing incongruous people together. But her particular gift was to sharpen people, make them more themselves, inject them with her own vitality; and this she was able to do because she was totally self-confident and cared not a jot for the opinion of others, still less if they were critics or detractors.

She said what she thought and she did not mind to whom she said it. She did what others did not dare to do and won through. When she was a young girl at a dance, she heard Shane O'Neill ask his partner to sit out the next one on the stairs. 'I don't want to do

77

that, I'll ruin my dress,' the girl said. 'I don't mind ruining my dress,' said Ann and plonked herself down on the stairs beside her future husband. In naval terms she was something of a privateer. She would move into a calm lagoon where barques and frigates were careening peacefully and suddenly loose off a broadside. The calm vanished, ripples spread across the waters, the whole harbour became animated, galvanised, expectant.

Most people, even those who want to change society, want peace and harmony and believe that the world will be a better place if we can loosen tensions and resolve conflicts. Not Ann. There is a passage in *Wuthering Heights* in which Cathy Linton explains how she differs from her sickly cousin, and, if I read it now as I did to Ann, it is because I think it reveals what her temperament was and incidentally describes so well her love of birds and of nature.

> He said the pleasantest way of spending a hot July day was lying from morning to evening on a bank of heath in the middle of the moors with the bees humming dreamily among the bloom, and the larks singing high up over head, and the blue sky and bright sun shining steadily and cloudlessly. That was his most perfect idea of heaven's happiness. Mine was rocking in a rustling green tree with a west wind blowing and bright white clouds flitting rapidly above; and not only larks, but throstles, blackbirds, and linnets and cuckoos pouring out music on every side . . . and woods and sounding water, and the whole world awake and wild with joy. He wanted to lie in an ecstasy of peace, I wanted all to sparkle and dance in a glorious jubilee.

Ann thought that life would be a very tame affair if everyone made conventional responses and had a conventional regard for rules and regulations. This belief is not pagan. Gerard Manley Hopkins in one of his great poems, 'That Nature is a Heraclitean Fire and of the Comfort of the Resurrection', pictures the world as a huge, self-fuelling bonfire which creation perpetually replenishes: where life is endurable only if we recognise that everyone and everything in it is produced by discord and strife. Ann lived by this principle. She herself was not above rolling an apple of discord in among the goddesses. She loved turmoil, she provoked, she led her friends on, she wanted movement, and hated the pale and the placid. She believed in a life to come. She told her grandchildren to think about eternity rather than ask themselves what exactly they believed.

Life's changes she took in her stride. In the thirties photographs regularly appeared of Lady O'Neill at Ascot or Lady O'Neill at Sandwich addressing the ball with her niblick in a bunker. In later years neither racing nor golf courses saw much of her. She vastly enjoyed, when married to Esmond Rothermere, the excitement of newspapers and the power which it gave to promote the careers of friends whose talents she admired. But when that world vanished, she had no regrets. She could entertain on the grandest scale at Warwick House, but Sevenhampton and the minute rooms of Victoria Square were to her as agreeable. Perhaps Stanway, the house of her childhood, was the one place for which she felt an unassuageable longing.

What then was the notion which governed her life? It was her sense of style. Of the difference between right and wrong she had virtually no understanding. To the consequences of her actions, even of their intrinsic value, she was sublimely indifferent. Perhaps she was like Tolstoy's Prince Andrei in *War and Peace* who at one point says: 'It is not given to man to know what is right and what is wrong. Men always did and always will err and in nothing more than in what they consider right and wrong.'

But if her sense and style gave no very clear sense of the difference between right and wrong, she knew the difference between good and evil. She hated corruption. Dishonourable motives, envy, being on the make, caginess and trimming, squirming and sucking up, weakness of character in facing a crisis for her were infallible signs of evil. She lived her life by a code, the code common to aristocratic families. She knew that people spoke of her as typical of her class and rather enjoyed it. She was proud of belonging to the upper class and never dreamed of not acknowledging it. Her mother died when she was eleven, and her father gave her a hundred a year and his blessing, so she learned to be self-reliant. To her, courage was the first of the virtues. She was a prey to nerves, for instance in a car or before a party; but she would not give in to fear. If at times she was reckless in what she said or did, she was never foolhardy. If Perry Brownlow lost his hat on the shark-infested side of the reef in Jamaica, no taunt of cowardice would induce her to swim out to retrieve it.

She admired generosity, gaiety, fortitude, stout-heartedness, personal beauty and charm. She appreciated the unique, the odd, the varied, and despised the safe and the orderly who never put a foot wrong. She was fierce in her loyalty to friends and – for her it was a consequence – was implacably dedicated to the discomfiture of enemies. Her warmth of heart was proverbial but she disliked the effusive. A kiss on one cheek was sufficient greeting. 'After all,' she said, 'we are not French generals.' Self-pity was totally foreign to her. In her last years misery engulfed her, she did not deny it; but not even when her son died, nor when death itself appeared to her, would she appeal for pity. She reeled under Caspar's death. It was meant, in the way that those who decide that life has nothing to offer, to inflict anguish. At one time her grief was so intense that it seemed as if even she might go under. But no, coming of chain-mailed families, she rallied, returned to the tournament and regained her zest for people – what they did, what they were, why they succeeded or failed, how they loved and lived. As we grow older some of us mellow and become soft like medlars. Others of us become hard like chestnuts and put truthfulness before nostalgia. Ann was a chestnut.

Her friends were her life, but they bore no relation to her opinions. She liked politics. Her political views were considerably to the right of the Tory Party, or, as she preferred to say, to the right of Genghis Khan. But if her views coincided on a number of points with those of her great friend, Evelyn Waugh, that was not the reason why the finest writer of his generation relished her company. Still less why Hugh Gaitskell, Roy Jenkins or Tony Crosland were her friends – nor for that matter Peter Carrington or Ian Gilmour whose conservative principles could hardly be said to be very near hers.

Her audacity endeared her to the great and the good. The great and the good often find that in conversation people are somewhat overawed, somewhat anxious to please, rather too anxious to plead a case, and they get bored by bland inoffensive exchanges. Ann refreshed them. She said things to her liberal friends which startled and challenged them, she said dreadful things to her nearest and dearest, she disdained ever to tack or toady. No one could tease with more deadly skill than Evelyn Waugh, but Ann enjoyed every minute of their encounters and gave as good as she got.

Thinking of Ann in Washington, Nicko Henderson wrote:

> As if by the light of nature, she sought to give pleasure. That is what she did from the time she woke in the morning to look out upon the lawn to the distant lake at Sevenhampton until she said goodnight to the last of her guests reluctant to tear themselves away from the sparkle of her salon ... giving pleasure to others was part of her being, part maybe of the way of enjoying it herself.

That is true. But she gave something else. She sustained her friends. She knew how to console; and you cannot console people truly unless they feel you love them. If any of her friends heard the hiss of the world in his ears, she would defend him. It was just and fitting that at the end of her life she, who had always backed up her friends, received in turn from those closest to her the support which until that day she had hardly needed.

Despite her genius for hospitality she was at her best as a lone companion. When she travelled she had imperturbably good temper and would fall in with any suggestion. She was an unselfish traveller. I remember her refusing to let her departure from Dumfries to catch the night train to London break up the party. The station was bolted and barred and she had two hours or more to wait. But to the manner born she broke into the stationmaster's office and was posted through the window like a parcel. She was a wonderful companion because like many girls of her class and age she seemed never to have been educated, and therefore her response to new sights or to works of art was fresh and direct as nothing impeded the play of her intelligence and sensibility. Never having been taught to like things, she found out for herself. No one would call her an omnivorous reader; but she never read trash. And she learned the secret so vital for us to discover, the secret of how to refresh our weary spirits. Ann took two pitchers to the well. Like the wisest she read or listened to poetry and gathered the poems which moved her into what she called the Gloom Book. Even more important she let nature speak to her on her solitary walks or as she swam alone to the reef in Jamaica.

Others who knew her far longer and more intimately would have spoken better than I. But this is what I recall. The sound of her laughter and the sight of those lovely, sparkling, mischievous eyes will remain with me until I too come to die.

Dame Rebecca West (1892–1983)
writer

by Bernard Levin
(writer)

*Memorial Service at St Martin-in-the-Fields Church,
London, on 21 April 1983*

The long and fruitful life of Rebecca West, which came to an end on the 15th March, makes it most appropriate for us to be marking it here today under the rubric of a service of thanksgiving. In truth she gave her friends, and the world, much to thank her for.

It is worth reminding ourselves of just how different is the world we live in from the world she was born into. The Boer War and two World Wars were in the future; Queen Victoria had nearly a decade still to reign; six men who were to be President of the United States had not been born; Einstein had not yet propounded the Theory of Relativity; Nansen had not set out for the North Pole; among those still living were Tolstoy, Brahms, Robert Louis Stevenson, de Maupassant, Gladstone, Oscar Wilde, Bismarck, Samuel Butler, Lord Acton and Louis Pasteur; the Paris Métro did not exist; the Klondike Gold Rush had not started; Sir Arthur Evans was yet to embark upon his excavations in Crete; Dreyfus had not been arrested; and among the familiar objects and substances of today that were still unknown then were wireless, aeroplanes, safety-matches, razor-blades, the Rolls-Royce, radium, aspirin and the zip fastener. Even Sir Robert Mayer was only thirteen.

It was a world that stood on the threshold of changes greater and more far-reaching than any in the history of mankind; and the woman who was born when the motor-car had just been invented lived to see men standing on the moon.

Into the emerging world around her, the young Rebecca flung herself, adopting as her own name that of Ibsen's intense and passionate 'new woman', the heroine of *Rosmersholm*. And there is a line in that play which might have been written to sum her up, the line in which Rebecca says to Rosmer: 'Live, work, act. Don't sit here and brood and grope among insoluble enigmas.'

Rebecca West did indeed live, work, act, and refuse to brood and grope among insoluble enigmas. And the active, outgoing principle enshrined in the words ran through everything she did. Her criticism, from the early work in radical and feminist magazines to the massively authoritative reviews she contributed in her last years to the *Sunday Telegraph*, was always expressed without ambiguity and without reverence for reputations she thought unjustified. Her reporting, in both its descriptive and its analytical aspects, has been unequalled in our time, perhaps in any time, and these gifts, too, came from her astonishing ability to find a striking analogy which would bring the scene vividly alive, and at the same time cut through all the concentric circles of distortion and evasion to get at her goal: the truth. Perhaps none of her novels is wholly successful as a work of art (though her short stories certainly are), but all are coloured with the same clarity and urgency, as of course is every line of the work for which she is probably most widely known, her studies, mainly through the medium of criminal trials, of treason both black and red.

Her qualities as a writer and a thinker are seen at their finest, however, in the book that is the crown of her literary achievement, and one of the bare handful of undoubted, and undoubtedly ageless, masterpieces of our century: *Black Lamb and Grey Falcon*. It is a book like no other; wherever it is opened, it spills out an inexhaustible flood of topography, history, architecture, politics, biography, even gastronomy and botany. It contains scores of portraits, of individuals living or long dead, which constitute a gallery that alone would make the book unforgettable; it includes the most dazzling and profound analysis of the force of nationalism ever written; its evocation of the European past sets out with an intense prophetic fervour what was to be the tragic European future; and in its depiction of the sights and sounds and people and occurrences of the journey it relates, it takes its place among the greatest travel books of all.

Black Lamb and Grey Falcon is Rebecca West's masterpiece precisely because it has more of her in it than anything else she ever wrote. Her eternal curiosity; her almost incredible capacity for assimilating knowledge and turning it into true understanding; her love of the brave and the honest, and her searing scorn for the shifty and the false; above all the quality that springs from every page of the book, as it sprang from every moment in her company: her rich, gleeful, heartfelt, insatiable zest and relish for life and all that life can offer – of pain as well as joy – to those sufficiently intrepid to seize it.

Just such a woman was Rebecca West, for the qualities of her work were themselves the reflection and the outcome of the qualities of her character. She knew better than anyone that nothing is wasted, that we can learn and grow from any experience, however sterile it may seem at the time, and she never sought to deny that truth even in the agony of her unhealing wound, the relationship with Wells.

Next to that enhanced and enhancing love of life was her directness. The workings of her formidable mind issued in formidable thought; and what she thought she said, driven by a kind of holy rage at those who sought to veil reality, to confound right and wrong, to talk manifest nonsense and get away with it. They did not get away with it if she was within reach; she knew that cant is no joke, and that too much of it will suffocate us all.

This quality was itself derived from her passion for the truth, increasingly beset by falsehood in our world of bloody and barbaric ideologies. Her zeal for truth, for justice, for freedom – and she knew that those three stand or fall together – was without any fanaticism but without any weakness, and she achieved a massive contribution, direct and indirect, to making the world a better and safer place for the truth to live in.

Her kindness, her invariably practical generosity, her wit, her

friendship given without stint – these were among the private qualities that supported and informed the public ones. She will be
remembered as a writer and thinker of genius, a woman of grace
abounding and courage undismayed. If we cannot hope to emulate
either the achievements or the qualities of this noble spirit, we can
at least resolve to remember and honour her, and to do what we
can, as the most fitting memorial possible, to strengthen and further
the great cause of true liberty for which she fought throughout the
decades of her glorious life.

There are some words by Alexander Woolcott, written after his
last meeting with Mrs Patrick Campbell, which seem very apposite
here today:

> I put her in a cab and thought as it went racketing off up the street
> how tremendous a woman she was, how negligible were most of us
> beside her, how many and how terrifying were the citadels she had
> stormed in her long and tragic day, how bright in the afternoon
> sunshine was the banner that flew ever in her heart.

That was also Rebecca West, whom we are met to thank and
celebrate. Though we grieve that she is dead, we rejoice that she
lived, and we know that she will live on. Her mortal body is
committed to the earth of the English countryside; her living
memory to the safe keeping of those who knew and loved her; and
her enduring repute into the hands of the countless generations who
will read her, and admire her, hereafter.

Alasdair Clayre (1935–1984)

writer, poet, singer, broadcaster and Fellow of All Souls, Oxford

by David Pryce-Jones

(author)

Memorial Service at St James's Church, Piccadilly, London, on 16 February 1984

Everyone here will have felt at some time or other that Alasdair was a most remarkable man and perhaps the most remarkable they were ever likely to know.

Superlatives for Alasdair come easily: 'Professor Lord Clayre', some of us used to tease him, with affection and with expectation. I can see him looking, quizzical at it, giving that unforgettable shout of a laugh, into which went all the emphasis and energy of his personality.

Alasdair was a very clever man indeed. 'Tell me, Alasdair, what's the point of this? What's being argued?' He would sweep his black hair off his forehead and tell you. His extraordinary capacity to absorb information and to synthesise ideas has never been better displayed than in his last book, about China.

He was also a perfectionist and a man of imagination, a moralist and a romantic. These qualities are not always or often compatible, the perfectionist collided with the man of imagination, the moralist with the romantic. As a result Alasdair lived in a continuous drama of many possible choices, and some would say too many. There was something Byronic about his gifts and his destiny. Alasdair came from an altogether exceptional family, consisting of several generations of people with unusual intellectual ability and a deep sense of purpose as doctors and lay missionaries.

Scholarships to Winchester and Oxford might seem to have been in the natural order of things for him, but always with that sense of purpose in him too, which might change in direction but not in idealistic intensity.

When I came to know him, I was struck that the best he could say in praise of something was 'good work', while the strongest criticism was 'bad work'. At the start of a journey we once made to Italy, I remember, I asked how he saw his future, and he replied that he was going to reconcile Wittgenstein and Christianity. I said that I hardly understood what was meant either by Wittgenstein or Christianity, so he told me, over the next twenty-four hours, on the train between Paris and Naples. At Naples station, within moments of arrival, the bag with our money and passports was stolen. For some days we continued as before, while Alasdair analysed the position in the approved Oxford manner in which he had previously been analysing Wittgenstein and Christianity, until on a beach an elderly English lady happened to overhear him and lent us money, to the chagrin of her children who looked as if they did not believe in logical romantics.

National service, of all unexpected things, had brought us together, in circumstances which show him harmonising the different elements of his character. On a February day, I arrived at a training ground on the Yorkshire moors at their most desolate. Snow had fallen heavily, and more was to follow. Visibility was almost nothing, but music was coming from a hut, and there was Alasdair inside it, playing Schubert on a flute. His bedside reading was Kant. It turned out that he was stationed there in command of the platoon which demonstrated to trainee Guardsmen the principles of the platoon attack. Even in that, he had been singled out as exemplary.

Those who knew Alasdair at Oxford often felt that he had a more formative part than the university at large in their education. It is hardy possible to exaggerate the impact he had on his contemporaries. Two compliments attached to him at that time were 'the Messiah of Peckwater' and 'the Clarifier'. It was not only that he was such entertaining and original company but also that he had a way of seizing particulars and generalising them. Here was the moralist side of him, moralist in the sense of explicating matters, to determine what was to be done. He showed us what a full life was like – and not merely the life of the mind. Human curiosity about everyone and everything brought him an immense range of friends and admirers.

It appeared to be only right and proper that he was elected a Fellow of All Souls, and no doubt Professor Lord Clayre could have been launched from there. The romantic in him would have none of it. Projecting other futures, he then realised them as a novelist, film-maker, writing journalism and broadcasting, active with the Open University, song-writer and singer. In between he had also been a gardener for the writer Richard Hughes in Wales, apprentice architect, businessman – involving barges, as I recall, from the days when he had lived down by the river at Limehouse. To express it in language used before this age of the specialist, he was an encyclopaedist, a man of parts, a free spirit.

What he achieved in his forty-eight years is astonishing enough. To wonder where his particular genius would have taken him, and what mark it would still have made, is truly to grieve for him.

J.B. Priestley (1894–1984)
writer

by Dame Diana Collins
(freedom activist)

*Memorial Service at Westminster Abbey, London,
on 2 October 1984*

J.B. Priestley, OM. Few people during the last seven weeks can have failed to be aware of the passing of a great man. Jack was a great writer, a great Englishman, and, perhaps transcending even these, a great man.

Much has been written and spoken about his work, but this is a personal tribute; I am a reader and a play-goer, but, more importantly, a friend. For me Jack is one of the really great masters of the English language. He creates unerringly those marvellous rhythms and cadences of English prose at its best; metaphors leap out at you one after another; he moves you to laughter – plenty of that – to tenderness, even to tears; his writing is alive with poetry in the widest sense; ripples and bubbles of humour are never far away, however serious his subject, and he can be very serious; he never loses his lightness of touch, his humour nor his power to entertain; he is always stimulating, and never, never dull. Considering the enormous amount that he wrote in so many different forms on so many different subjects, this, in itself, is amazing.

As a writer he is very much a whole man, one who harmonises his inner and outer worlds, who listens equally to his consciousness and to his unconscious, who writes – in his own words – 'out of a heightened ordinariness'. Anyone who wants a sane, balanced yet profound view of our tormented century should turn to the works of J.B. Priestley. I believe that his wise, entertaining and compassionate words and philosophy will remain when all our terrible ideologies and 'isms' have vanished into the murk of history.

'I am as English as steak and kidney pudding,' said Jack. He did like steak and kidney pudding, and he did love and understand England and the English. 'If I were compelled to choose between living in West Bromwich or Florence, I should make straight for West Bromwich'; and that was from a man who had travelled the world widely.

It was Jack's intuitive understanding of the English that enabled him to speak to us as he did in 1940. He understood us too well to give up hope, he spoke of what we really cared about, of what we were fighting for, of little ships, ducks on a pond, pies in an oven, everyday things, but symbols of so much more; his was the perfect complement to Churchill's splendid rallying rhetoric. The mastery and use of the English language by two such men did much to turn the tide in that perilous year.

Sometimes Jack felt that he could have done better work if he had not responded as he did to the pressures of external events. 'What is a writer to do?' he asked. 'If he shuts his mind and heart in order to concentrate on his own work, he cannot help feeling a self-centred and callous exquisite, fiddling while Rome burns. If he opens his heart and mind to the daily tidings of woe, to all the stresses and strains of the world, he finds it almost impossible to work properly.'

Jack never shut his mind nor his heart, though somehow, with his enormous creative energy, he still managed to do many times more work than other men, and much of it outstanding. He was always a citizen, warning us of the dangers of Fascism and Nazism, desperate to break through the crust of apathy, encouraging and sustaining us throughout the war, warning us again of the dangers and lunacy of nuclear armaments. He held up to his fellow-citizens a vision of English society – a liberal, tolerant, pinkish society, full of richness and variety, eccentricity, enterprise and opportunity, a home of freedom and of the arts, a society that had rooted out for ever 'the grey misery', 'the canker of injustice' that he had seen and described on his English journey.

So he would ride into battle with his full armoury of talent, but he had the rare quality, and this applied to his reviewing and criticism as well, of being consistently witty, amusing and hard-hitting without ever being malicious or personally wounding; if he dealt blows, he was always generous with praise.

Jack was a brilliant public speaker, a real spellbinder, but he mistrusted this particular gift; he deeply distrusted the crowd, and those who use it, and he was as mistrustful of those who work for and wield power over their fellow-men.

Jack was perhaps pre-eminently a man of the theatre, and acting was another technique that he could easily have mastered. Whoever doles out the talents is no egalitarian – they are heaped on chosen persons and denied to so many of the rest of us. Jack had them all, writing, painting, music, clowning and the supreme gift of creative imagination, all of which made him a marvellously stimulating and amusing companion, a great life-enhancer, and the most enormous fun.

Of course, he grumbled; but he did it with so much verve and humour that it could be as invigorating as a cold shower, except that nothing about Jack could really be called cold. He knew sadness and tragedy, and had his moods of melancholy and gloom – in fact the term 'Jolly Jack' was originally coined ironically. Jack relished irony – 'the whisky of the mind' – but he was irritated when 'Jolly Jack' was taken literally. In spite of what he used to call Jack's law (that everything gets worse and worse) he could not properly be described as a pessimist, even a life-enhancing one. He believed with Wordsworth that 'We live by admiration, hope and love.' And that, in his heart, was how Jack lived.

One of the things that impressed me as I got to know him was his self-knowledge. With himself, as with others, he was one of the most honest men I have ever known. He was his own most accurate critic. He paid attention to himself; knew all the tricks that the ego can get up to, all its little vanities, posturings and role-playings, and he kept them in order. So he never took himself too seriously, he never thrust himself at you, he listened, he was an excellent listener, and he gave you his attention. This had an effect on your own ego-activities: they were apt to wither rather quickly, not through anything he said; he was courteous and kind, and exceptionally sympathetic and understanding, but he could be a gentle and humorous pricker of pretensions. I once remarked how much I enjoyed *Kissing Tree House*, there were so many beautiful things to look at; Jack looked at me with a twinkle and said, 'Me for instance.' He was an immediate success with small children, not only because he was such a splendid funny man, and could enter so readily into their world of make-believe and magic, but because he also gave them his attention.

Magic: that is a word that is scattered through all Jack's writings: 'the hunger of the heart', 'the secret dream', 'the delight that never was', the desire for 'something more' than all the delights, for 'better bread than was ever made with wheat'. Jack created magic for others in his work and in his life – isn't laughter itself a kind of magic? – and he experienced magic in the arts, in love, in nature, and all those teasing and haunting intimations of immortality. Magic for Jack was a signpost on his lifelong quest for wisdom.

I once asked him what, in his experience, had been most important to him. 'The moments,' he said, 'the timeless experiences of joy and wonder.' Joy that is self-authenticating, outside the prison of cause and effect, and the prison of passing time.

Understandably, Jack was passionately opposed to any kind of reductionist thinking, any suggestion scientific or otherwise that man is a 'nothing but . . .'. And he was as fiercely opposed to any of what he called 'block thinking'. He had an open and wide-ranging mind that could never be constrained within any dogmatic system or intellectual strait-jacket. He stoutly defended the loose-enders, the so-called 'woolly-minded'. He was a firm upholder of feminine values which, in any healthy society, should be harmoniously balanced with masculine values, our own society being badly tilted towards the masculine. He quoted John Cowper Powys commenting upon a friend: 'He combined scepticism of everything with credulity about everything, and I am convinced that is the true Shakespearean way to take life.' That was certainly the way that Jack took life. 'A mind without credulity,' he wrote, 'would never learn anything new. A mind without scepticism would believe any nonsense'; and 'so long as a man guards against intolerance and anger, it is better to believe in too much than in too little.'

So Jack explored the frontiers of human consciousness; he was interested in dreams, in problems of time, and in the paranormal. He was ready to look at any new idea in science, philosophy, psychology or politics, but his realism and acute critical faculty never deserted him; he was always moving on, asking questions, forcing us to think.

He was fascinated by the discoveries of modern physics and astronomy. The vast spaces of the universe, far from terrifying him, excited and enthralled him. Black holes in which time runs backwards delighted him; all fed his intuitive conviction that life, both inner and outer, is infinitely and mysteriously complex.

Above all, Jack read and absorbed the depth psychology of Jung; it was this, I think. that was the most important and enduring influence on his thinking and on his life. He believed that it is in the development and increase of consciousness to an ever truer and deeper level that the way forward for human beings must lie, and he would quote Jung's words written on the outbreak of the Second World War: 'A man at peace with himself, who accepts himself, contributes an infinitesimal amount to the good of the universe. Attend to your own private and personal conflicts, and you will be reducing by one millionth millionth the world conflict.' For all his public life and public persona, this was the path that Jack followed.

I can convey only a fraction of what could and should be said about Jack. We could talk about him endlessly and there would still be more to say. When we read his books it is impossible not to hear that rich, warm, humorous, seductive voice, so resonant of Jack himself. 'Amiable, indulgent, affectionate, shy and rather timid at heart': his own words about himself, the right words. He was a most loyal and affectionate friend – and for all his restless intellectual and creative energy, he did take life easily. 'Ah wears life like a loose garment,' he used to say, quoting an old coloured woman. 'Affection' is an important word. Jack maintained that the best writing should come out of affection, and his certainly did. 'Affection not only brings warmth into humour, but also insight into character, so creating more humour,' he said, and even his strongest criticism has a ground-base of affection.

It is impossible to think of Jack without Jacquetta, whom he loved so deeply and devotedly for so long; who brought to their marriage her own brilliance, talent and independence; who made the second half of his life so deeply and peacefully happy, and who cared for him so lovingly through his older age. Our admiration and gratitude must go to Jacquetta, as well as our love and our sympathy.

At the conclusion of that giant of a book *Literature and Western Man*, Jack wrote: 'We live, under God, in a great mystery.' And that is where we must leave him, in the final and greatest mystery, the mystery of death. We leave him with those qualities he most valued, with admiration, with hope and with love. He helped and taught us to admire so much, and he gave us so much of his own for our delight and admiration. We can share his hope for the kind of England in which he believed, the vision he never abandoned – we can hope for it and work for it. And for that other hope, of personal survival, the great question mark – we can believe or disbelieve, we cannot know; but we can hope. Jack was open-minded, believing or doubting in his own highly individual fashion. I, for one, have a hope, and want to leave Jack with it.

And love – well, love is easy. Jack was a man who gave and received much love. He wrote: 'To create and sustain conscious love, against heavy odds, may be what this universe is all about.' Maybe it is. Maybe Blake, 'who understood so much' – Jack's words – is right that:

> We are put on earth a little while
> That we may learn to bear the beams of love.

But last words should be personal not general; the words of one of the young nurses who cared for Jack through his final illness. She wrote: 'He died peacefully, with dignity and surrounded by love.'

Charles Douglas-Home (1937–1985)
editor of The Times, *1982–5*

by Lord Home of the Hirsel
(Prime Minister, 1963–4)

*Funeral Service at Quenington Church, Gloucestershire,
on 29 October 1985*

If somewhere in the gatehouse of heaven there is a book which records the life and the exploits of man, across the title page of the biography of Charles Douglas-Home the word 'courage' will be written in letters of gold. For in the last years of his life he had to face trials and afflictions which were to the onlookers seemingly beyond endurance. Yet one after another he confronted them with a fortitude and a serenity which was almost beyond comprehension, and certainly beyond praise.

For us the words 'Death where is thy sting? Grave where is thy victory?' have taken on a fresh and very personal meaning. Charlie had to die, but it is clear that the spiritual and eternal values won the day.

He was equipped with many gifts. He had a clear mind; he was literate; he had a sense of history which gave him perspective and insight and judgement and wisdom in the affairs of men. He was unconventional when he thought the situation required it, and he had loyalty which is even now the greatest of all the virtues. He gave his loyalty to the profession of journalism to which he had devoted his life, and in particular to his editorship of *The Times* with which distinction he had crowned his career.

So we think of him as we knew him in happier and more carefree days. In his love of the countryside and all its pursuits which he loved to share. Today we are infinitely sad, but we need not be so for we know that the last of Charlie's gifts was faith in his Christian God. Today his trust is justified.

How apt are our hymn and psalm today. 'All things bright and beautiful, all creatures great and small; all things wise and wonderful, the Lord God made them all.' And, 'Goodness and mercy all my life will surely follow me, and in God's house for evermore my dwelling-place shall be.'

All of us, and especially Jessica and Tara and Luke, will grieve deeply at this parting, but they will have the inspiration of a life well lived, and they and all of us will share the comfort that all our memories of Charlie are good.

Charles Douglas-Home (1937–1985)

editor of The Times, 1982–5

by Sir Edward Cazalet

(High Court judge)

Memorial Service at St Paul's Cathedral, London,
on 25 November 1985

For a person who died so young, Charlie has received some of the most outstanding tributes that any of us has ever read. Naturally these have concentrated upon the remarkable achievements of his professional career. Of those achievements I intend to say little. Instead I want to say something of the Charlie we knew, and with whom so many of us felt that we had a special personal relationship.

My friendship with him started at Eton where he was a scholar. In appearance he was small, round and consistently scruffy. The fringe of hair which hung permanently over his eyes caused one master to describe him as 'Douglas-Home, a boy who maintains the grand tradition of Highland Cattle'.

History was his favourite subject. This apart, on more than one occasion he was taken to task for neglecting his studies through having 'too many friends' and 'too many diverse interests'. Typically he took no notice, and a diversity of friends and interests was the continuing theme that ran through his life. In all his qualities, Charlie was consistent: and ever present was that bubbling sense of humour which gave us all so much fun when we were at school, and which prevailed even to his last hours.

Charlie did not go to university. But, after an unruly spell as a national service subaltern, he was offered an alternative educational opportunity: that of going as ADC to Evelyn Baring who was then Governor in Kenya. It was there that he first became fully involved with political and diplomatic life and with individuals concerned in shaping world events. His book on Evelyn Baring (later Lord Howick) shows what a deep impression that man and that period of his life made on Charlie's thinking.

There seemed to be throughout Charlie's life – not surprisingly with his Scottish roots – an irresistible force which pulled him towards Scotland. He began his career as a crime reporter with the *Scottish Daily Express* and soon obtained a number of hair-raising scoops in Glasgow's Gorbals. The crucial landmark in his career came in 1965 when he became defence correspondent to *The Times*. This was the breakthrough to the higher ground of serious journalism which he had always been seeking.

As a journalist, Charlie had three outstanding qualities: he was a good listener, he could cut through complexity and confusion, and he was able to give a balanced and masterly exposition on any major subject on the political or international front.

Shortly after the start of his career with *The Times*, Charlie was married. To cope with the demands of his long journalistic hours and the wide commitments of his life, an exceptional person was needed. This he found in Jessica. She developed and broadened his interest in the arts and throughout their marriage brought him the happiness of family life which meant so much to him. In their latter days, never can a wife have given a husband more support in his hours of need.

An abiding memory is of Charlie with his family. He was such an enthusiast that it was inevitable that his family would become fully involved in all that he did. How thrilled he was that Tara and Luke have developed so many of his interests under his guidance and encouragement.

Charlie's idea of relaxation consisted of intense activity in numerous different fields. Writing books, lecturing, travelling, playing the piano, listening to music, reading, the arts, wildlife, sailing and, of course, hunting.

Hunting with Charlie used to resemble a military exercise on a grand scale: the terrain, the plan, the tactics were invariably analysed to the full. I know of no one who got more thrill from riding flat over fences despite the falls which he took. But although Charlie was one of those rare beings who combined courage with judgement, that judgement seemed to desert him over the simple matter of what his horse could surmount.

There are countless stories about Charlie's hunting exploits. I have one particularly vivid memory of a fast and desperate hunt in the Cotswolds on a bitterly cold January day. The hounds crossed a deep and strongly flowing river. Charlie and Lennox Hannay were to the fore and, as all others turned back for the bridge, Charlie uttered just one word: 'Forward!' he said, plunging deep down a steep bank into the river. Having swum the river on his horse, Charlie rode at a large hedge, only to sustain a heavy fall. Undaunted, he remounted just in time to see the hounds double back. Once again Charlie took on the river, but this time he and his horse parted company, providing the improbable spectacle of the defence correspondent of *The Times* and his horse swimming side by side, independently – but fortunately – in the same direction. Reunited on dry land, Charlie jumped two gates and joined the hounds, alone and triumphant.

The powers-that-be in the hunting world traditionally insist on conformity in dress; they reckoned without Charlie. Warned that he was not amongst the elite permitted to wear a red coat and black hunting cap, Charlie immediately soaked his father's ancient red hunting coat in blue dye, reducing it to the colour of mottled plum. He then sewed on the buttons of his former regiment and reappeared in the hunting field. At this stage he was noticed by a senior officer of the regiment who, outraged, wrote a strong protest to the colonel, as follows: 'Wherever in this dreadful coat a button happened by chance to coincide with a buttonhole, I saw, to my horror, the Regimental Crest.' In the high level of exchange of correspondence which followed, Charlie gave not an inch. He finally won the argument by pointing out to some unfortunate general, who had been drawn into the debate, that as the regimental crest was allowed to appear on beer mugs and place mats, it was surely preferable for it to be seen in a field of real endeavour, namely that of hunting.

Another side of sporting life he loved was sailing with his family in Norfolk. He was drawn there by the presence of his mother, Margaret, and other members of his and Jessica's family. But when Charlie arrived at Burnham Overy Staithe he became a sort of honorary harbour-master with scores of children hanging on his every word and plan. Then, after a careful analysis of wind and tide, a flotilla would set out with Admiral Home leading, like some nautical Pied Piper, a supporting cast of idolising children.

He played a similar role on the beach at Mothecombe, the Mildmay-Whites' beautiful estate in Devon, which for both of us was a second home for nearly forty years.

Whilst so much has already been said about Charlie's achievements as editor of *The Times*, recently I overheard a particularly fitting tribute. After the funeral I was standing near Mr Murdoch as he was being thanked for his loyalty to Charlie during his illness. Mr Murdoch looked surprised, and said quite simply, 'When you have got the best man doing the job – why should you be thanked for keeping him on?'

Yet on the occasions when Charlie was editing the paper from his hospital bed, we all know that both proprietor and editor found themselves in an unprecedented situation. And I know that Charlie would have wanted me to thank Rupert Murdoch and, indeed, many of the staff of *The Times* for the overwhelming support which they gave to him and his family during those last heroic months.

They do not need reminding – none of us needs reminding – of Charlie's lion-hearted refusal to surrender to his illness. Faced with obstacles and difficulties which to an ordinary man would have seemed insurmountable, he dismissed them with a cheerfulness which made them seem part of normal life.

His moral courage and will, supported by his Christian faith, were just as rock-like in empowering him to withstand hostile criticism with unflinching dignity. These same qualities, combined with a sound and resolute judgement, fierce loyalty to individuals and causes, and his natural ability as a leader of men, enabled him to bring to *The Times* a new sense of stability, purpose and success. The voice of the Thunderer is indeed now being heard again. And yet the more Charlie grew in eminence the more striking by contrast was his total lack of pretension.

Charlie cared passionately for individual freedom and he expressed this through an interest in people of all kinds which was immediate and deeply sympathetic. This explains why his death brought personal tributes from the Prime Minister and from the President of the United States and at the same time brought heartfelt tears of grief to the girl who looked after his horse, to his driver and to countless others in this country, not least to so many of our children whose hearts and minds he understood so well.

In our last conversations, it was always of his family that he spoke, speaking with deep feeling and with the greatest pride. Their happiness was his overwhelming concern; to leave them was for him the overriding tragedy. Yet in all these final conversations, of himself he said nothing.

But when all is said and done, courage – moral as well as physical – was the quality central to Charlie's character. He often spoke of 'the high ground'. In his last years he climbed an awesome mountain and planted a bright banner on its summit. And for us who look up to that banner with love and admiration, it is the word 'courage' that will for ever be blazoned across it.

Lady Diana Cooper (1892–1986)
stage and film actress and legendary beauty

by Nigel Ryan
(author and television journalist)

*Memorial Service at St Mary's Church,
Paddington Green, London, on 17 July 1986*

What is that special quality, that special radiance, that sets one human being apart from others?

Some people call it goodness. When talking of Diana I prefer to call it innocence of heart. It was not so much a virtue acquired as something never lost from childhood: the innocent heart that marks the child and, with it, the innocent eye that marks the artist.

When Diana loved she loved totally, as a child loves, and she was guilelessly blind to the faults of the loved one. And with her love came absolute loyalty. If trouble came she would say, 'Oh, trouble! That's all right. I'm all right with trouble!' And so she was: more than any other human being I have known. In a flash all her strength and skill and wiles were at your service – absolutely and unconditionally. It was never a case of too little; occasionally of too much – she tended to leave no string unpulled.

If she was a grande dame, a spectacular beauty, brilliant natural writer and wit, she certainly didn't think so herself. 'O for ordinary, that's me,' she would say. And of course, she was nothing of the sort. But then she did not really know what 'ordinary' was. She certainly was not ruled by ordinary conventions. Diana was ruled by her heart. And people who came in contact with her sensed it and loved her for it. And therein, I hold, lay her glory.

Henry Moore (1898–1986)
sculptor

by Sir Stephen Spender
(poet)

Memorial Service at Westminster Abbey, London,
on 18 November 1986

We are here to give thanks for the life of Henry Moore, a man loved by all who knew him for his work, and to those who knew him both for that and for friendship.

I cannot talk about Henry Moore without naming old friends of his, any one of whom, if living, would be better qualified to stand here than I: Kenneth Clark, Philip Hendy, Herbert Read and Colin Anderson.

Kenneth Clark once remarked to me that if the inhabitants of this planet found themselves having to send an ambassador representing the human race to the inhabitants of another planet, they could not choose better than to send Henry Moore. He doubtless meant that Henry combined in his personality the best qualities of the entire human being with those of the creative man of imaginative intelligence, the artistic genius. Perhaps Herbert Read was expressing the same thought at a deeper level of consciousness when, looking with me at a Henry Moore sculpture which seemed part animal, part human and part rock-face, he remarked, 'Henry is the only true Surrealist.' It was an essential part of Henry's extraordinary humanity that, without any desire to analyse or pry into his own psyche, nor any programmatic intent to make an artefact according

105

to the principles of the Surrealist movement, he could instinctively draw upon images of his unconscious or dream life and realise them in sculpture or drawings. In his best work the primitive unconscious material is transformed into the shared consciousness of the profoundly human. The coincidence in Henry of the artist of great originality with the man of great humanity suggests an ideal norm of individual man as creative, imaginative, responsible and, even in some sense, ordinary. At any rate, universally human and incapable of definition in terms of social class, simply a human being. The son of a miner, Henry told me that in his whole life he never had any sense of anyone being socially superior or, for that matter, socially inferior to him. All people to him were equals simply in being human.

I first knew Henry in the early thirties when he and his beautiful Russian émigrée wife Irina lived in a Hampstead studio adjoining those of Ben Nicholson and Barbara Hepworth, and with Herbert Read, Edwin Muir and Geoffrey Grigson as near neighbours. Often at the end of the day's work they would gather in Henry's studio, where there was gossip and laughter, and sometimes they would show each other recent work. Henry was for a time partly drawn into the pursuit of pure abstraction of Ben Nicholson and Barbara Hepworth, but he could never – he later said – make sculpture which referred to nothing beyond itself. 'Try as I might, my work always ended up looking like something, probably a Reclining Figure,' he told me. He felt that purist movements in art only succeeded in fragmenting elements which should be fused in the work. In 1938 he wrote: 'The violent quarrel between the abstractionists and the surrealists seems to me quite unnecessary. All good art contains both classical and romantic elements, order and surprise, intellect and imagination, conscious and unconscious.'

His own art unified these elements, and others, from civilisations remote in time and place beside, into his own unique modern vision which was certainly of his time. Like the poet W.B. Yeats who in 1912 walked round London with the words 'hammer your thoughts into a unity' ringing in his head, Henry Moore throughout his life had a unique capacity for bringing together diverse elements of his observations of nature and of art into a unity of his personal vision.

This vision, really a vision of greatness, was not in the least vague or vaporous. As any visitor to his smaller studios or living room at Much Hadham could observe, he had a fine eye for objects which were 'minute particulars' – flints, pebbles, small rocks, shells, bones – objets trouvés of every sort of shape and texture. His almost magical sense of scale made him have equal respect for the smallest and the largest things in nature, as in art.

Yet when he came to making works of art derived from observation of the many facets of nature – as also of other works of art from all times and places – what he sought to create as a unity in his own sculpture was what he admired in the work of the masters: spiritual greatness. His passion was for major art almost to the exclusion of the minor. The idea of a work of art having, within the context of its genre and scale, to achieve the overarching mysterious aura of greatness, means that Moore's works are dominated by themes which are, as it were, in the major key: the rhythms of organic form discovered in nature, the vitality of primitive art with its direct response to life and its expression of powerful magnetic beliefs, and above all the human figure, sacred in subjects such as the Mother and Child which preoccupied him from the first; and later on, after the birth of his and Irina's daughter Mary, the theme of family. Perhaps also he discovered the nobility of nature in its way of working, for millions of years, on stone – the wearing smooth of pebbles, the nervous rhythms of rocks, the upward twisting of tree trunks, the numinous quality of Stonehenge which he first saw when he was a student. The humanist organic element, he insisted, would always be for him of fundamental importance in sculpture. He wrote: 'Each particular carving I make takes on in my mind a human, occasionally animal character and personality which controls its design.' In art, energy released into form was more important to him than beauty. I quote: 'Beauty, in the later Greek or Renaissance sense, is not the aim of my sculpture . . . Between beauty of expression and power of expression there is a difference of function. The first aims at pleasing the senses, the second has a spiritual vitality which for me is more moving, and goes deeper than the senses.'

In his work – that is, almost every hour of every day – Henry was busy with material: clay or wax, stone, wood or bronze; and with all those details of workmanship which are inevitably the concerns of a great master of technique. He was always interested in talking about the workmanship in art, particularly about drawing. But beyond all this, what he discovered in great masters whom he admired was ultimately spiritual, and his dedication to his own art and the results of his dedication were ultimately spiritual also.

He was a wonderful friend, who made lifelong friendships, as many of you who are here will know well, because you are among them. In the fifty-odd years of our friendship he changed less than anyone I can think of, except in the outward external circumstances of his life, and they changed more than those of any other of my friends. He had the simplicity of his achievement and the happy well-being of unending work of the kind which is not just work but making things. His immense success brought with it public acclaim resulting in much travel. He certainly enjoyed all this, as though it were a holiday he shared with friends all over the world. But after these journeyings he was always glad to get back to his house and his studios. It was the life of making which mattered to Henry and to Irina also. His family was inseparably bound up with his own creativeness, flesh and blood and sculpture of his own ego. Of all this, he was extremely conscious.

To visit him was a delight. He paid friends the great compliment of assuming that they were interested in his work, and showed them round his studio and Irina's garden with the most lively and shared interest – his and theirs.

Sometimes one arrived to find him working in the small studio, drawing or making a maquette, releasing a form which seemed instinctive in his mind with hands which seemed to have a consciousness of their own. Wonderful hands which, throughout his adult life and until his strength failed him, continued working, drawing when he could no longer sculpt. At the end of his life when he could no longer even draw they were forever restlessly moving as though calling down invisible forms out of the air. His first sculpture was of hands and he once said that he found hands, after the face, the most obvious part of the body for expressing emotion. Hands also are for praying and for giving thanks that he lived the life and created the art in which his sense of the sacred was realised, so I am happy to end these remarks with the image of his endlessly creating hands.

Russell Harty (1934–1988)
television presenter

by Alan Bennett
(writer)

*Memorial Service at St James's Church, Piccadilly,
London, on 14 October 1988*

'I don't seem to be able to get started,' Russell wrote to me in 1966. He was a lecturer at a training college in Derby and at the age of thirty-two had just made his first foray into television, a catastrophic appearance as a contestant on Granada's *Criss Cross Quiz*. The only question he got right was about Catherine of Braganza. It was such a public humiliation that Myrtle, his mother, refused to speak to him, treating him, as he said in the same letter, 'like Ena Sharples treated the now late Vera Lomax'.

When he did get started, of course, there was no stopping him, and it was soon hard to recall a time when he had not been on television, though it was the capacity for provocative half-truths and outrageous overstatement that stood him in such good stead as a schoolmaster which now fitted him for a career on the small screen.

To me and his other close friends his career in radio and television was almost incidental. It furnished him with more stories, the cast of them more glamorous and distinguished and the attendant disasters and humiliations more public, but he never really altered from the undergraduate who had rooms on the same staircase as I did thirty-four years ago at Exeter College, Oxford.

He had learned then, by the age of twenty, a lesson it took me half a lifetime to learn, namely that there was nothing that could not be said and no one to whom one could not say it. He knew instinctively that everybody was the same (which is not to say they are not different), and he assumed instinctively that if a thought had occurred to him then it must have occurred to someone else. So by the time he got to Oxford he had long since shed youth's stiff, necessary armour, and the television personality who, in the last year of his life, introduced himself to a slightly mystified Pope wasn't very different from the undergraduate who invited Vivien Leigh round for drinks. 'You can't do that,' I would protest. 'Why not?' said this youth off Blackburn market. 'They can only say no.' And if one had to point to the quality that distinguished Russell throughout his life it would be *cheek*.

While cheek is not quite a virtue, still it belongs in the other ranks of courage, so that even when he embarrassed you, you had to admire him for it – and, of course, laugh. It came out in the silliest things. He was one of the first people I knew who drove. It was the family car – opulent, vulgar, the emblem of successful greengrocery – and driving through Leeds or Manchester and seeing an old lady waiting at a bus stop he would pip his horn and wave. She would instinctively wave back and, as we drove on, one would see her gazing after us, wondering who among her scant acquaintance had a large cream-coloured Jaguar. 'Brought a bit of interest into her life,' he would say, and that was as far as he got towards a philosophy: he understood that most people are prisoners in their lives and want releasing, even if it's only for a wave at a bus stop.

He spent his life fleeing boredom, and he had no real goal beyond that. He had various romantic notions of himself, it's true: the country squire, for instance, though he was never particularly rustic; the solitary writer, though he hated being alone. Half an hour at his desk and he'd be on the phone saying, 'Is the patch of wall you're staring at any more interesting than the one I'm staring at?'

'Private faces in public places,' says Auden, 'Are wiser and nicer/ Than public faces in private places.' For his friends he was naturally a private face, but for the public he seemed a private face too, and one that strayed on to the screen seemingly untouched by expertise. That was why, though it infuriated his critics, the public liked him and took him to their hearts as they never did more polished performers. And yes he fumbled, and yes one wished he would reach for the right word rather than the next but two, and yes his delivery could be as tortured as his mother's was answering the telephone, but it didn't matter. That was part of his ordinariness and part of his style.

Still, television magnifies some personalities, but Russell it diminished, and people watching him saw only a fraction of the man. He once had to do a promotion for British goods in Bahrain. Flown there on Concorde with a party that included a beauty queen and a town crier, they sat down to a lunch of roast beef and Yorkshire pudding in a temperature of 110 in the shade. They all got on very well, except that after Russell had stood up and done his bit and sat down the town crier leaned over and said, 'I'll tell you something. You're better off than on.' And of course he was.

One laughed more helplessly with him than with anyone else I know, but so much of his humour – immediate and throwaway and born out of disaster and humiliation – is hard to recapture. The worst meal I ever had in my life was with him, and, ironically, in France. After the soup he pushed his plate back. 'Well, that soup might be a big event in a day in the life of Ivan Denisovich but it didn't do much for me.' International figures had a habit of intruding on the domestic scene. 'I think,' he'd say, popping in another violet cream, 'the only person who must be more depressed than I am at this moment is Benazir Bhutto.' He took no interest in current affairs except in so far as they intruded on his immediate concerns. 'I think the pace of glasnost is too hectic. The next thing you know we shall have Mr Gorbachev on *Blankety Blank*.'

'I'm fed up with Agewatch and Childwatch. I'm thinking of founding a society against potential suicide called Wristwatch.'

Some random thoughts:

He loved Italy, hated Greece.

He liked families and was an *ami de maison* in half a dozen households.

He was uncensorious of himself and of other people.

He knew that there are no rules.

He never kept people in compartments, introducing and mixing one layer of his friends with another. If somebody new came into his life he expected his old friends to budge up and make room for them. Which, Russell being Russell, they generally did. And he would do the same for them.

He was unashamedly self-interested. He switched on Dennis Potter's *The Singing Detective* at the point where the naked Michael Gambon is having his psoriasis anointed by a nurse. In order to stop himself getting excited, Gambon recites a list of the most boring television programmes he can think of. Russell waited with bated breath long enough to make sure he wasn't on the list, and then switched off.

He would telephone in the morning to find out whether you were free for supper that evening, promising to call back later to confirm. When he didn't you knew he'd had a Better Offer. The principle of the Better Offer was respected, though complained of, by all his friends.

If you did manage a meal, a couple of hours would do it. 'I'm bored now,' he would say.

'But he's so silly,' pompous people would tell you, not understanding that that was why one loved him, that to be silly is not to be foolish.

The fourteen-year-old boy who had thought it worth while confiding in his diary that Princess Margaret had a slight cold remained all his life a sucker for royalty, and unashamed of it. A couple of years ago he arranged for the Princess of Wales to visit Settle and Giggleswick. At the end of the visit the Princess offered him a lift back to London in the royal plane. Notwithstanding he had to get into the plane with a plastic bag over his head to evade the attentions of the press, he accepted with alacrity. They had both of them got on very well and made each other laugh, and now spent a happy hour chatting as they flew south. Arrived at Northolt they said goodbye, the Princess sped off to Windsor while Russell flung himself into a taxi and rushed to Heathrow and a plane back. He hadn't wanted a lift at all, but just couldn't resist the offer. It was sheer cheek.

The spell of royalty persisted to the end. The last time I saw him I had gone up to Leeds for some function and met there Professor

Losowsky, the head of the team that fought so long for his life at St James's Hospital. At that time prospects were quite hopeful, and the professor told me how patient Russell had been under weeks of wearisome treatment, unable to speak, fed intravenously, rest impossible. 'I have,' said the professor, 'great admiration for his qualities of character.' Now this set me back, because it was taken for granted by all his friends that Russell had no qualities of character at all. How else could he have been such good company? But I went up to the hospital prepared for a change, expecting, in Larkin's phrase, to see a new man when I'd quite liked the old.

I need not have worried. I found him festooned with wires and equipment, a tracheotomy tube in his throat, monitored, ventilated. But underneath all this he had a message he wanted to convey. The nurse, who had got used to lip-reading him, thought it was something about sherry. Russell shook his head and closed his eyes in that familiar gesture of impatience, learned from Annie Walker in *Coronation Street*. We tried again, and he began to get agitated. Fearful of a relapse, the nurse thought we'd better find out what this vital message was, so she laboriously disconnected Russell from his machine, took out the tracheotomy tube, and pressed a pad over his throat so we could hear his faint voice and the essential words. They were: 'Ned Sherrin had supper with Princess Margaret last week and she asked how I was. Twice.' It was a triumph for the strength of weak character.

Russell never made any secret of his homosexuality even in those unliberated days when he was an undergraduate. He didn't look on it as an affliction, but he was never one for a crusade either. He just got on with it. He had never read Proust, but he had somehow taken a short cut across the allotments and arrived at the same conclusions. His funniest stories were always of the absurdities of sex and the ludicrous situations it had led him into, and if he was never short of friends it was because his partners knew that there would always be laughs, sharing a joke something rarer than sharing a bed.

In the succession of his friends he was happier than most people, certainly during the last five or six years of his life in his friendship with Jamie O'Neill, but with the gutter press systematically trawling public life for sexual indiscretion he knew he was in a delicate position. So when in March last year the *News of the World* set him up, then broke to an unstartled public the shocking news, Russell thought his career was over. One longed for him to say 'So what?' but here, not surprisingly, with his livelihood at stake, his cheek failed him. He expected the BBC not to renew his contract and that offers of work elsewhere would be bound to dwindle.

In fact this did not happen, and he began to work harder than he had ever worked before. So convinced was he that there would soon be no more, he accepted every offer that came his way. Thus at the same time he was making his television series *The Grand Tour* for the BBC, he was doing a weekly TV programme for BBC North West and presenting *Start the Week* on radio, besides doing a weekly column for the *Sunday Times*. In addition to all this he had to write the book of his television series. On the surface it seemed things had never been better. But his first instinct had been right. The gutter press had finished him because they had panicked him into working so hard that by the time he was stricken with hepatitis he was an exhausted man.

And it went on. Reporters intermittently infested his home village for more than a year, bribing local children for information about his life, even (there is a terrible comedy in it) trying to bribe the local vicar. Now as he fought for his life in St James's Hospital one newspaper took a flat opposite and had a camera with a long lens trained on the window of his ward – the nurses would point it out to you when you visited him. A reporter posing as a junior doctor smuggled himself into the ward and demanded to see his notes, and every lunch-time journalists took the hospital porters over the road to the pub to try to bribe them into taking a photo of him. One saw at that time in the tireless and unremitting efforts of the team at St James's the best of which we are capable, and in the equally tireless, though rather better rewarded, efforts of the journalists the worst.

As the days went on their fury mounted, and one had to sympathise. Russell, with his usual lack of consideration, was dying of the wrong disease. Even worse, for a time it seemed he wasn't dying at all and looked boringly likely to recover. The final touch, however, came on television when Russell was actually on his death-bed, and the woman who had written the original story in the *News of the World* could not be restrained from retelling the tale of her journalistic triumph. Some of you may think these kind of recrim-inations are out of place at a memorial service, and certain it is that Russell would not have approved of them. Had he recovered he would have gone on going to Mr Murdoch's and Mr Maxwell's parties and doing his column for a Murdoch newspaper. The world was like that. Or at least England is like that.

There was one more joke before he died. Many of you will know Russell's secretary and personal assistant of many years, Pat Heald. Pat maintained some order in his frenzied life; no one under-stood him better, and the efficiency – clairvoyance almost – with which she anticipated his requirements and outflanked his changes of mind never ceased to gratify and also to infuriate him. He did not like to think he was known so well. On the day before he died I rang his oldest friends, Hugh and Joan Stalker, to find out what the situation was, but they were already at his bedside. The person who answered the phone told me that in a last desperate gamble the team at St James's were going to try a liver transplant. 'But,' she went on, 'there's some confusion. The hospital hasn't been able to find a liver, but apparently Pat Heald has managed to put her hands on one.' It wasn't true, quite, but for both of them it would have been a wonderful apotheosis.

But it was the last joke, and the first that he was never going to be able to share.

God bless him.

Sir Frederick Ashton (1904–1988)

founder choreographer for the Royal Ballet

by Dame Margot Fonteyn de Arias

(prima ballerina assoluta)
Read by Michael Somes

Service of Thanksgiving at Westminster Abbey, London,
on 29 November 1988

It would take a poet of equal genius to do justice to the genius of Frederick Ashton. In ordinary words I can only say that he was a rare artist, comparable in his field to Shakespeare for his extraordinary understanding of the human heart and mind and his ability to illuminate through his own art form.

One has only to think of ballets like *A Month in the Country*, *Enigma Variations* and *La Fille Mal Gardée* to appreciate that his range of understanding covered every kind of human emotion.

He once said that he could not remember innocence, that he had always seen through people to their hearts, their motives and their characters since he was a child. How he came to be able to translate that insight into movement is a mystery which must be explained only by the word 'genius'. And one must say the same for the sheer beauty and musicality of his choreographic invention.

With the passing of time his perception and sensitivity deepened; his eye for movement was refined, and while he was creating a ballet, he eliminated everything that was not totally valid. You will not find a superfluous movement or gesture in his works.

As a man I see a paradox: on the one hand sophistication and

117

finely developed taste in all things, yet on the other hand a very simple person at heart. One might expect a highly sophisticated person to make an effort to conceal some emotions. Not Ashton; like a child, if he was hurt, angry or even jealous he made no pretence. He was, above all, a very *human* human being, and for that, as much as for his extraordinary talents, he was beloved by all. Yet with all these things he was ever modest. He always longed for what he called '*real*' success and was as delighted as a child when it came, for he never counted on it.

I remember so well how piteously nervous he was as he started on a new ballet. I can picture him coming into the studio pale and anxious, sitting down and shakily lighting a cigarette, then standing up again and saying, 'I haven't an idea in my head, I don't know what we are going to do. Well, let's hear the music anyway.'

Some two hours later the whole structure of a magical *pas de deux* would be there ready for the refining and polishing.

I must certainly recall his wit, which was very quick and sometimes cutting, and his humour, which was so warm.

One remembers him too as a wonderful stage performer, his Dago in *Façade*, his Carabosse, his Kotschei in *Firebird* and, above all, his unsurpassable Ugly Sister.

Having come late to ballet training he was not technically a great dancer but when he was creating his earlier ballets his suppleness and swirling, dipping movements were usually beyond the rest of us to imitate.

There seems to be no limit to the different facets of that truly remarkable man; but today, knowing, loving and remembering him as I do, I cannot help but feel strongly that he is looking down on us all and saying to himself, 'Ah, a packed house, much better than I expected.'

John Howard (1902–1989)
painter

by Elizabeth Jane Howard
(novelist)

Funeral Service at St Andrew's Church, Meonstoke,
Hampshire, on 19 June 1989

When one is a child, uncles are background. I can't remember ever not knowing John, but the earliest memory I record is of him playing the part of his father in a family play that we did for the benefit of our grandparents. I remember tears of laughter rolling down their collective cheeks at John's brilliantly accurate imitation of his father. As I grew older, I noticed that he had a number of unusually funny and interesting friends: Arthur Ford, Barry Craig, Charles Wright, Stephen and Mary Potter, Jean Varda and others. One became a slightly dazzled spectator of the jokes, the conversation and fun – some designed to please the young, some more sophisticated. I remember Barry Craig being a zoo-keeper and throwing rolled-up socks – herrings – to John who was a lounging sea lion on a sofa. Barking wildly, he would plunge after them; we never got enough of that one.

It was some time before I realised that he was a painter, but one day I admired a small picture that hung in my grandmother's drawing room and she told me that it was of a street in Paris: 'John painted that – it's always been one of my favourites.' I thought how extraordinary that he should have secretly been a painter all this time while pretending to be quite ordinary like the rest of us, but then

I thought that he must be a real painter or it would not have been in a frame. He acquired for me another – still general – dimension.

In some respects he was like all the Howards; he had many of the family traits: the disposition towards plain food, strong drinks and cold houses – draughts of any kind were deeply appreciated by our family; I remember my mother once saying that even if they opened a cupboard they preferred to find a draught in it, and the sight of even the smallest log fire damply hissing would send them flying to open windows. It was also *de rigueur* not to admit to being much good at anything, so how good a painter John was was never really acknowledged – least of all by himself. That painting mattered to him was only revealed to me when I was about fourteen, and he asked me to go for a walk with him. He told me that he had been invited to join the family timber firm, and could not decide whether he should or not. What did I think? He was the first person ever to ask a serious opinion of me and I was paralysed by the honour. Painting and being a businessman did not really go together, he continued, so he had to choose – what did I think? My naturally bossy nature asserted itself. Art was far more important than money, I said, knowing nothing whatever about either. 'How interesting you should say that!' he cried, and instantly I felt interesting.

John had the capacity to make anyone – even a priggish schoolgirl of fourteen – feel interesting. So many of us here must have experienced that: how his eyes, sparkling with amusement and interest, would fix upon your face; the way that he would throw back his head with a hoot of laughter and then lean suddenly forward and grasp your hand with some endearment. He was the most generous, creative listener in the family, but he also possessed to a great degree an ingredient, which, had they acknowledged it, the family would have regarded with great suspicion. He was a very very *charming* man: in fact I think he was the first person I ever got to know at all who possessed this rare and lovely asset too often castigated by those without it as a superficial trick of no real account. I always looked forward to seeing him and it was never disappointing; his charm, of which I think he was wholly unconscious, was an integral part of his nature and I suspect that everyone who knew him was warmed and lightened by it.

When the war came, and things in Sussex got rather strained by the Battle of Britain – fought over our heads – the bombing of London and the threat of invasion, John was the one who could relieve tension. I remember at dinner one night he suddenly became Goering planning the bombing of every Odeon cinema on the Great West Road, and his descriptions of his first weeks in the War Office, when he had to deal with the loquaciously disgruntled Polish officers who had come to complain that no women were provided for them in their camp (John would be the Poles, the interpreter and himself), would make us laugh till we cried.

Crying from laughter was the only approved crying in our family, and I remember with particular affection how, years later, John sobbed in the car with me when my father was dying. It was the most comforting thing that ever happened about that. John loved all his family very deeply.

John's nature, warm, anxious, indecisive, sometimes irritable, deeply emotional, generous, tender-hearted, appreciative, romantic and kind, was all transparently up front as they say. His sense of the absurd is so memorable and endearing because he was quite without malice.

Sometimes, we who are getting older feel that our lives are diminishing, dwindling, withering quietly on the stalk: it is lovely to remember that with John it was not at all like that. At the end of his life he went back to painting, had his first one-man show in a London gallery, and that after his sad loneliness when Kate died, he should have found someone who loved him and whom he could love so much. All of us who loved John – and who did not? – are grateful to Ruth for the wonderful happiness she gave him. I can think of nobody who better deserved such a blessing.

Lord Olivier (1907–1989)
actor

by Sir Alec Guinness
(actor)

*Memorial Service at Westminster Abbey, London,
on 20 October 1989*

When Larry Olivier died, some lines of Shakespeare came to mind:
'The star is fallen, And time is at his period. The long day's task is
done.'

And his life of eighty-two years had been a long task, filled to
the brim with hard work, great achievement and – during the past
decade or so – with his valiant and all-but-victorious fight against
constant wretched illness. His courage and determination were
phenomenal as was, even in old age (though I find it difficult to
think of him as old), his physical energy on those days when he
was not crippled by his disorders.

As an actor he stands alongside the acknowledged great – Burbage, Betterton, Garrick, Kean and Irving. Even allowing for violent
changes of fashion, I feel each of these tremendous actors of the
past would have recognised, applauded and welcomed him as one
of their own.

The theatrical profession is notorious for its extravagance both
in praise and blame. Quite minor or wayward acting, which only
catches like Osric in *Hamlet* 'the tune of the time', is sometimes
hailed as 'great'. It is a much abused word: but a vastly refreshing
one when it can be used with total confidence, as it can of Olivier.

I wouldn't be sure how to define it when applied to an actor, but it is easily recognisable when seen.

Perhaps it consists of a happy combination of imagination, physical magnetism, a commanding and appealing voice, an expressive eye – and danger. Larry always carried the threat of danger with him: primarily as an actor but also, for all his charm, as a private man. There were times when it was wise to be wary of him.

The danger was most evident in his comic parts. Not altogether surprisingly, as many comedians appear to have a quick eye and ear for not only what is funny but also for what is cruel. And Larry was a supreme comedian.

We all know of, or saw, his pinnacle performances in the classics – Romeo, Oedipus, Henry V, Richard III, Hotspur, Macbeth, Coriolanus, Othello and Lear. But side by side with these I would place the smallish parts of Justice Shallow, Captain Braze in *The Recruiting Officer* and Mr Puff in *The Critic*. The delightful, self-regarding, almost feminine way he removed the little tricorn that he wore as Mr Puff and stabbed it with a gigantic hatpin was a highlight of brilliant timing and mincing absurdity.

I don't know how he set about his work as an actor; probably very privately and from the outside in, so to speak. He quickly formed an image of what he wanted to look like in a part. That was an anchor for him. He needed all the practicalities to be clear and firm before he could infuse his spirit into what he was playing.

I have the impression that, when studying a script, his imagination would alight on a phrase or two which he would then emphasise extraordinarily. Sometimes I have thought: I don't believe that line is in the play. He must have made it up. But sure enough it was there. And he had been right to draw attention to it.

I am not altogether sure, though, that he was right in altering a particular piece of punctuation when playing Malvolio; but the result was undoubtedly funny. He changed the line – when Malvolio interrupts Sir Toby, Sir Andrew Aguecheek and Feste in their midnight carousal – from 'My masters are you mad, or what are you?' to 'My masters are you mad or what? Are you?' Of course in these days of some very peculiar productions that would pass unnoticed.

'To see him act,' Coleridge wrote of Kean, 'is like reading Shakespeare by flashes of lightning.' Some of us might prefer a steadier light. Larry Olivier provided the flashes often enough.

Sometimes we have read in the press over the past twenty years or so of a young actor being hailed as a 'second Olivier'. That is nonsense, of course, and unfair to the actor. If he is of outstanding talent and character then he will carve out his career in his own right and in his own name; he won't be a second anyone. In any case there may be imitators but there is no second Olivier. He was unique.

His first really big impact in the theatre was in 1935 when he appeared as Romeo at the New Theatre (now the Albery). He presented a beautiful, graceful, Italianate youth; gentle, passionate, highly strung and desperate with love.

His reading of the line towards the end of the play, 'Then I defy you, stars', was so searing it seemed to wither the world of romance. He could do that sort of thing boldly and alarmingly.

One of Larry's most moving performances, although it did not find much favour with all the critics, was his Lear in 1946. He spoke with the utmost simplicity the speech which begins, 'I'll pray, and then I'll sleep' and goes on, 'Poor naked wretches, whereso'er you are, That bide the pelting of this pitiless storm.' He knelt centre stage, facing the audience, and made no movement. He created an awful stillness.

It was a speech that appealed to his sympathies, his conscience and his religious sense. He had been brought up a High Anglican in a clerical household, and I don't think the need for devotion or the mystery of things ever quite left him.

We owe our National Theatre to his efforts, and also the companies he formed under his own management, at the St James's and elsewhere. He toured indefatigably, here, in Europe, the United States and Australia.

Hollywood beckoned when he was young and he enjoyed considerable success there but, thank God, he made his remarkable career in this country. His work in modern plays – modern in their time – covered a wide spectrum from *Journey's End*, *The Farmer's Wife*, *Private Lives*, *Becket* and *Rhinoceros* to *The Entertainer*. In all he acted well over a hundred parts in the theatre, directed about twenty-five plays and produced twenty. He also starred in twenty films.

Honours were heaped upon him. His knighthood came in 1947. He was made a life peer in 1970 and received the Order of Merit in 1981. He was an Officer of the Légion d'honneur, Commander of the Order of the Dannebrog, Grand Officer of the Italian Order Merito della Repubblica and a member of the Order of the Yugoslav Flag with Golden Leaf.

He also received honorary doctorates from the Universities of Oxford, Edinburgh and London. For many years he was president of the Actors' Charitable Trust, a cause which was near his heart.

Larry could justly say, with Othello: 'I have done the State some service, and they know't. We must obey the time.'

During the early part of the Second World War he served with the Royal Navy in the Fleet Air Arm, perhaps not one of his most appreciated roles – at any rate not appreciated by those in authority. He did, I believe, quite a bit of damage, but not to the enemy. With each take-off he scored an own goal.

A shrewd man, with an acerbic wit and great charm. Ambitious, determined, brave and daring. A full life, lived generously and shared with all of us. He has, I am sure, the nation's gratitude.

> Good night, sweet prince
> And flights of angels sing thee to thy rest.

George Gale (1906–1991)
journalist

by Paul Johnson
(historian)

Memorial Service at St Bride's Church, Fleet Street,
London, on 23 January 1991

George Gale had many virtues but five were outstanding. And at the head was courage. He always spoke and wrote his mind without fear for the consequences, often in reckless disregard of his own interests. He looked at the world, and into the future, with sombre realism and with an unwillingness to tell himself reassuring stories. Having renounced the Presbyterianism of his youth, he passed a life which was often stressful uncomforted by religious belief. He was always plagued by ill health, the chief reason why he was not able to make the fullest use of his marvellous talents. In the last two or three years he knew his existence was precarious. But he looked death in the face without flinching. He was capable of great physical courage as during those desperate days in the Congo of 1960, when, as he put it, 'I was bloody nearly murdered by the locals.' But I never admired him more than during his last, twilight phase, when he knew the fell sergeant was always at his elbow: he carried on regardless, working, arguing, laying down the law, not least laughing. We never had such good laughs as during the few days we spent together in Bournemouth, not long before he died. And George's courage was the reverse of unthinking. No one ever thought more deeply, continually and penetratingly about the meaning and purpose of life, and the finality of death. The huge work of political philosophy he wrote, which he allowed me to read, will one day be published and then the world will know the full breadth of his mind. But it was precisely because he thought so much, and so profoundly, that his courage under the shadow of death was so moving.

George's second great quality was truthfulness. That is not such a rare virtue in journalists as some people think. George had it to an unusual degree. I doubt if he ever wrote a word he did not believe to be strictly true. He was incapable of writing to a brief in which he was not wholly convinced. He insisted on truthfulness even in conversation, and often rebuked me for exaggeration, inaccuracy and hyperbole. That was one of the things which made talking with George so exacting and exciting; you could not afford to be slovenly in your thoughts or in the terms with which you expressed them. Like all men with powerful minds, he radiated authority. But it was an authority always exercised in the cause of truth.

His third great virtue was professionalism. He might have made a great headmaster or a firm, fair-minded judge. But he chose journalism because he loved it. He was the complete professional. He never missed a deadline or shirked an assignment. As a columnist he had that indispensable quality: his column not just reflected, it was his personality. The words on the page were the voice of the real man: as you read them you could hear George, roaring, expostulating, reprimanding; sometimes praising too, or touching a note of pure kindness. If you saw his page lying on a table and ran your eye over it, it was as though he himself were suddenly in the room filling it with the pungency and power of his presence. He not only loved words: more importantly, he respected them, moulding them carefully in pure, spare English, with no surplus adjectives or adverbs, so that when, on rare occasions, he chose to make a verbal flourish, it came with stunning effect. His mastery of English explains why he could write at every level of the market, and why four of the great editors of his time gave him free rein in their pages.

A fourth virtue may come as a surprise to some. George is usually portrayed as a rude and irascible man with a heart of gold. There's some truth in this, but it is by no means the whole truth. George could put down pretentious or objectionable people more firmly than anyone of his day, and there is no doubt that he got a certain satisfaction from performing a necessary duty so decisively. But the quality I most associate with him, and which helps to explain the heart of gold, is not so much righteous anger as sensitivity. This expressed itself in many ways. If George saw something impressive – a fine landscape for example – for the first time, he might describe it in words. But he might also paint it. His line drawings were extraordinarily subtle and expressive, and his use of colour unusual and full of art. Alternatively, he might write a poem. That happened when he visited the island of Iona, cradle of Christianity in which he could not believe. He jotted down some lines on the spot, and later worked them up into a fine sinewy poem. It was characteristic of George, who hated boastfulness in any form, that he thought little of these talents, and never mentioned them. But they were very much part of his character. Rough he could be, but there was also something almost feminine in many of his responses and judgements. He did not, as some supposed, have a complete set of opinions for every contingency, time-worn with use. Quite the contrary. He was always rethinking things and would come out with a thought so original as to make one gasp. And because he thought so deeply, he felt deeply too. He was often moved more than he cared to admit. Despite himself, he could shed tears, as well as roar. Compassion was something that came naturally to him, and often.

This brings me to his last outstanding quality. If courage is the greatest of virtues, a capacity for friendship is surely the most enviable of gifts. And George had it in royal measure. He collected, and kept, friends throughout his life. No one attended more assiduously to Dr Johnson's maxim: 'Sir, friendships should be kept in constant repair.' George's friends formed a mighty army. They came in every sort. He was as fond of the lame dogs as of the brilliant people whose company he relished. He loved eccentrics. He had a huge reservoir of affection for those down on their luck. He didn't say no to the odd millionaire or Prime Minister either. You might say that George's life was composed of friendships: interest in, concern and love for his fellow-human beings was the warp and the woof of his existence. He did not leave behind any great stock of wealth or possessions; no great shelf-full of books, either, to impress or possibly to bore posterity. He rarely even bothered to keep his articles, to grow yellow and collect dust. In material terms, he travelled light through life. But, as Churchill said of his old colleague Birkenhead, 'He banked his treasure in the hearts of his friends.' There it is in safe keeping, and we will cherish it until our own time is come.

Angus Wilson (1913–1991)
novelist

by Margaret Drabble
(novelist and biographer)

*Memorial Service at St James's Church, Piccadilly,
London, on 25 September 1991*

We are here today to celebrate the life and the work of one of the most loved and admired of British writers. He was also one of the most amusing and the task of evoking him as wit and mimic is an impossible one. Those of you who knew him well will have to sit there and hear for yourselves that strange, high, tumbling, chuckling, precise and fluent voice, those elaborately constructed stories, and those impromptu asides and decorative rococo digressions. You will have to conjure up for yourselves that bow-tie and that tossed mane of floating white hair, 1930s actor or 'old school southern state senator style', in his own words; you will have to see that startling, sudden and dangerous grin, those flashing eyes, those sudden and disconcerting switches from geniality to fierceness. He may or may not have fed on honey-dew and drunk the milk of paradise but he certainly intoxicated his audiences and he also enjoyed his food. His company was exhilarating. Students, friends and colleagues, even fellow-members of worthy public committees, would look forward eagerly to his next appearance. You could see the excitement that he generated from afar. A Japanese professor, greeting him on his 1957 PEN visit to Tokyo, writes that Angus Wilson looked so cheerful as he stood there in the hotel foyer that he was unable to prevent himself from rushing up to him and blurting out, 'Hail to thee, blithe spirit! Bird thou never wert.' A similar emotion overcame the Indian gentleman who, moved by Angus's eloquence in a British Council lecture, cried out admiringly, 'He has got the gift of the gab that one.'

Angus was a wonderful ambassador. He loved to travel and he collected travellers' tales to regale us with back at home. He would bring us stories of maharajas from Mysore and matrons from Mississippi, of Italian intellectuals and Singhalese scholars and Australian æsthetes. All these stories backed up by a well-informed and sympathetic appreciation of the different social and political problems of each country he visited. He prided himself with justice on knowing what was going on in all the troubled corners of the world. But his sharpest eye was for us, his own. The darling dodos of Britain never ceased to delight, distract and at times depress and infuriate him. He attracted eccentrics and had the keenest relish for the oddities of our strangely persistent class system. As the Auden poem that we have just heard suggests, he was equally at home with duchesses and with cloakroom attendants, with professors and with publicans. So much at home indeed that I hear he had to be restrained from singing loudly in the bath at Chatsworth a song which I wish I could render, I wish I had the theatrical talent present in this room, but according to a well-informed friend the song went:

> Now hearken you dukes and duchesses
> Now listen to what I've to say
> Be sure that you own all you touchesses
> Or you'll join us in Botany Bay

Angus noted with pleasure all the finer gradations of rank. For instance he relished the short, spare and military colonel who ran a nursery garden in Suffolk and who came to advise him about a windbreak for his cottage at Felsham Woodside. Angus, as we know, was a keen gardener and loved his wild garden and when the colonel advised laurustinus for the windbreak, Angus replied, 'Oh dear no, too terribly suburban,' to which the colonel replied, 'Oh really, I'm afraid I don't know the suburbs.' One of the choicest items in the

Wilson archives is a mysterious postcard from an admirer addressed, clearly after Angus's elevation to the knighthood, to Sir Felsham Woodside. Ah, what a Wilsonian character that conjures forth. Sir Felsham Woodside, a pleasant country gentleman, surely, whose favourite terms of endearment, I'm told, were owl and duck and who had a special devotion to cats, to pigs and to badgers; and who was always keen to save small creatures from a watery death. He would save spiders, hornets, cockroaches, scorpions and mosquitoes.

Angus had an eye not only for the idiosyncrasies of time past, for *Flies in Amber*, for *Colonels* and for *The Old Men at the Zoo*, he also observed the changing contemporary scene with unsparing sharpness and some of his novels have a prophetic ring. They are not cosy reading. He disliked the cosy novel. 'Cosy' was one of his rudest words, followed closely by 'comfy'. Felsham Woodside, as one of his more elegant and choosy guests pointed out, was not comfy; it was picturesque but it was not comfy and Angus himself was not a cosy or a comfy person. He could fly into unpredictable rages and he could take one up sharply on small points; he was often unsettling. I myself have an infuriating habit of agreeing over-enthusiastically with people by using the phrase 'that's right'. One evening, goaded beyond endurance by my excessive civility, he snapped, 'I do wish you'd stop saying that's right all the time, of course it's right, if it wasn't right I wouldn't be saying it, would I.' Yes, he could take one aback and his books could and still do shock. He dedicated his macabre and futuristic fantasy *The Old Men at the Zoo* to his brother Clive and his sister-in-law Lucy who were then living in Torremolinos. Clive rang up to say, 'My dear Blond, both Luce and I are delighted with the dedication but friends here who take the English papers say the book has rude bits in it and that could make things a bit difficult with the expats here. So Luce and I wondered could you undedicate it for us please?'

The Wilson or Johnston-Wilson family was itself rich in characters about whom Angus loved to speak and to whom he remained affectionately loyal. He dined out on some of them but he was very faithful to them all in times of trouble. This church is a peculiarly appropriate meeting place for us today, for it was here, or so one of the rumours that he sometimes endorsed held, that his grandmother,

Matilda Barnes from the Haymarket, was married to his grandfather, Thomas Johnston-Wilson, without, it is also rumoured, the blessing of the regiment, a wonderfully Wilsonian fine point. Fate and Freud and Marx and history dealt Angus Wilson a strange hand, as much the youngest brother of six brothers of a *rentier* family of dwindling fortunes. And he played that strange hand of cards with courage and with panache. He also, which is perhaps more rare in a star performer, always displayed great kindness and great generosity to others. When celebrating him as we must as a talker and as an orator, we must also remember that he was one of the great listeners. He loved to do his turn, or so it always seemed to us. Was it sometimes, one now wonders, at times an exhausting strain to himself and to those nearest to him? But he also was generous with his appreciation of the turns done by others, and students, family, friends in trouble, young writers, found him attentive and helpful. He became the recipient of confidences about broken marriages and delinquent children, about failed hopes and failed degrees. He also received heaps of unpublished manuscripts, many of which he read and tirelessly tried to get published. He supported the neglected, both published and unpublished. From a brilliant *début* as an *enfant terrible* of letters he became the benevolent, but never institutionalised, grand old man.

Time does not permit us to rehearse his many public services but one has to include the British Museum, the University of East Anglia, PEN, the Royal Literary Fund, the British Council, the National Book League, the Royal Society of Literature and the Literature Department of the Arts Council of which he was a most innovative chairman. I got to know him myself on the first Arts Council tour of North Wales where his stunning charm and wit amongst bewildered Welshmen was something to be admired.

Nor can we mention all the good causes he supported, and not all of them, despite his Oxford education, were lost causes. They ranged from homosexual law reform to anti-apartheid, particularly dear to him because of his South African mother, and also to the reputation of neglected writers like John Cowper Powys. Women owe him a particular debt because of the sympathetic way he portrayed their lives in the vanguard of the women's movement of the

1960s. We think of Sylvia Calvert in *Late Call* and Meg Eliot in *The Middle Age of Mrs Eliot*. Angus Wilson listened to all voices and all causes and he missed nothing, but we shall all miss him. His presence so vital, so invigorating, was like none other. It cheered us and it entertained us and it made us laugh and it made us think. Nothing could replace it and nobody could ever imitate it. But we are left with consolations.

One is the inspiring image of his happy life with Tony Garrett, his companion of more than forty years, who looked after Angus in good times and in bad and who watched over him in his last long illness with such exemplary care. It is a tribute to them both and to the climate of opinion that they bravely did so much to change, that we are able now here to celebrate their life together with the blessing of the Church and of the literary establishment, with the gratitude of friends and family, indeed of all the regiments, sacred, monstrous and profane. It is no exaggeration to say that to know Angus was to love Tony. He must be tired of hearing people describe him as a saint but he has only himself to blame for this excusable hyperbole and we are only trying to thank him.

The other consolation is, of course, the work. Angus himself can no longer speak to us but his voice can be heard for future generations through his books and it is good to know that all the novels are to be republished by Penguin. His unique voice – wise, brave, humane, witty and tolerant – will continue to make itself heard. The books have been a great joy and inspiration and they will endure. They are books written for adults and they continue to satisfy through a lifetime.

I want to end by quoting from a letter from one his students, now himself a successful writer, who wrote to me after Angus's death, saying: 'I liked Angus very much. Although I did not know him well, I look forward to knowing him better.' And so indeed, thanks to that hard-won magic by which Angus transformed difficulty, despair and depression into joy and creation, so may we all.

Sophie Lichfield (Mrs John Irvin)
(1942–1992)
photographer

by David Dimbleby
(broadcaster)

Memorial Service at All Saints Church, Putney,
London, on 27 February 1992

The photographs of Sophie and John's wedding in Los Angeles in
1970 are a period piece. The wedding was held by the swimming
pool. There was a sitar player. Women in long flowered dresses
with a hint of the caftan. Men with moustaches and white suits,
John included. Imported to conduct the service was an elderly judge,
chosen by Natalie Wood. He was trying desperately to come to
grips with the culture shock he was experiencing by marrying old
and new. He launched into a long homily on the theme that though
men were now able to fly to the moon, marriage remained as it
had always been: something that had lasted for hundreds of years.
He went on like this, rambling away, until he was interrupted by
a sharp rebuke from the bride in that voice we all remember so
well, 'Oh, for God's sake. Get on with it!' I feel it's an injunction
I ignore at my peril here today. Sophie may interrupt at any moment
to say, 'He's got it all wrong!' And if I try, by way of explanation,
to explain, as is true, that I've talked to many friends and shared
impressions with them since her death, she'll simply stand in the
middle of us and say, 'John, they've *all* got it wrong!'

It isn't difficult to summon back that distinctive voice and that fierce manner which so alarmed strangers and so endeared her to her friends. There was a side of her that liked to shock, that was amused by the impact she made. It became her style, saying what to everybody else was unsayable and saying it with wit and fearlessly. I suppose it was seen at its most flamboyant in the most flamboyant places, in restaurants, at parties. A stream of complaints, each apparently more exaggerated than the last, would pour from her lips and would often end in memorable exit lines, as to a New York hostess, 'I'm taking my friend home, he's having a horrible time.' It combines everything. Unerring truth, the protection of her friend and practical steps to resolve the problem.

People see us in different ways. One friend said, 'She was the artist of the complaint.' Another that complaints were Sophie's way of starting a conversation. Another, that the great thing about Sophie was that 'she did your bad behaviour for you'.

But of course, if it was just outrage and complaint and making difficulties, she wouldn't have attracted and kept the wide range of close friends both here and in America who mourn her today. And who owe her so much, for always being there when she needed them, for never bearing grudges, for staying even if there'd been gaps and for never changing when the rifts were healed. Her old friend Earl McGrath told me that he had a terrible rift with Sophie. It lasted he thinks a year (John says three) over something called a Luxury Scrabble set, which had apparently been taken by Sophie and lost. Sophie hadn't shown sufficient remorse. Three years passed. A number of intermediaries tried to heal the rift and in the end Earl McGrath turned up at her apartment. There was Sophie, Luke at her breast, Emily clinging to her thighs and she just looked at Earl and she said, 'Earl, you really are the most tiresome man.' And Earl said, 'I thought we were trying to make it up, Sophie.' And she said, 'We are, but I just wanted you to know you really are the most tiresome man.'

But beware. Underpinning all of those characteristics of outrage and the ability to shock were distinctive qualities which made Sophie unique. There was an honesty which prevented her ever being other than totally truthful. There was a courage that would not admit evasion and there was this loyalty to her friends that led her, for their sakes, to say exactly what she thought, to ask any question until she was satisfied that she'd been told the truth.

One of these friends wrote to John after her death and said, 'She wasn't intimidated by anyone. Even if you tried to silence her, she wouldn't be silenced. She merely looked you in the eye and repeated the question, confident that eventually you would answer it, and eventually we did.' It was a technique of confrontation, which forced others, or perhaps freed others, to confront themselves. A directness that sometimes made heavy demands on the people around her, but that was always tempered with a sense of mischief, with a twinkle in the eye that made her exhilarating and wicked company. She had a love of gossip but no malice and no desire, even in her frankest moments, to hurt. And in her deadpan way, she was, of course, very, very funny.

I think the most touching tribute I heard paid to her is this: 'You could be yourself with Sophie and not regret it.'

The other great quality she had, and perhaps it's the one people talk about the most, is the power to love. It spread outwards from her family who were her true passion, to her friends and her friends' children who were often surprised that someone who filled them with awe when they first met her would, when they ran into difficulties, encourage and invigorate them with the same directness with which she treated adults, so that they too came away with their thoughts a bit clearer and their faith in themselves restored.

And then there were the animals. No portrait of Sophie would be complete without them. The hapless dogs on Malibu beach, running cheerfully hither and thither in their innocence until captured by Sophie and taken into the house for a shampoo and a brush-up and a good meal. Dogs that she assumed were strays but that very frequently weren't. One which she had, as she thought, rescued she kept for a day or two in the house on the beach. She was taking it out for exercise when its distraught owner spotted it and came running across to claim it back, objecting vociferously to the kidnap saying, 'It knows its way home!' 'Well,' said Sophie, quite unabashed, 'it looked very lost to me.'

Or the turtles. John was shooting *The Turtle Diary*, the story of turtles being freed from captivity and allowed to swim back into the ocean. He had hired or borrowed three forty-year-old turtles, enormous animals, procured from the Morecambe aquarium. To Sophie's horror she discovered, when she went on location, that far from being freed as the cameras rolled, each turtle had a rope tied to its back legs, so that after being launched off the north Devon beach on its supposed odyssey, it could be pulled back for a retake. She was so outraged by this that she insisted John promise that at the end of the filming these turtles should be freed, otherwise they were all a bunch of hypocrites, making a liberal film about freeing turtles and then returning them to captivity. She threatened to ring the press if nothing was done. John's version was inevitably slightly different. He said, 'The turtles were so old and feeble that in fact, on being propelled into the chill waters of the English Channel, far from seeking their freedom, they turned round and scuttled back up the beach in search of the comfort and the warmth of Morecambe.'

Life deals savage blows, and none more savage than the kind of illness that Sophie suffered from. Its second onslaught came at a particularly cruel time, just as she was embarking confidently on a renewal of family life and on her work as a photographer. She'd taken photographs before her marriage professionally. When her children were growing up, they were mainly restricted to pictures of the children and occasional portrait commissions. But recently, she'd picked up her old career, working for the arts pages of the *Sunday Times* and the *Observer* and the *Sunday Telegraph*. And I think it would be good to see an exhibition of her work. It is, as you would expect, powerful. The images are dramatic. It has her own stamp very much on it because, as always where her own talents were involved, she was meticulous and painstaking, always doing her own printing and reprinting until she got exactly the image that she wanted.

But none of that was to be. She went back into hospital once again to submit herself to painful and exhausting treatment. And all those who visited her there were struck by her bravery. She didn't lose her humour. She didn't lose her directness. If anything it increased. She complained, as ever, when she was right to complain. She wanted to know the truth about her illness and she grumbled sometimes because she thought the doctors were keeping it from her.

But there was something else which she revealed in these last months, particularly to her family, which can only be called a kind of grace. It's not a word you would immediately associate with her. But grace it seemed to be. An acceptance of what was happening to her and a serenity that sprang from that acceptance.

There's one last thing I think she would have wanted me to say and it's about her family and particularly about John. 'You have no idea,' she said to a visitor, 'how wonderful John is being.' And wonderful he was. His dedication to her was total. He was always there at her side, trying to make her more comfortable, prop her up better, help her into a chair. And always with a reassuring kiss at the end of each painful manoeuvre. He was in control, calm, never showing his fear, and it must have made her very happy.

Our hearts today go out to him and to Emily and to Luke and to Amy and to Viggie, so gentle, and to Mark and to her mother and father. In the words of John's family motto which is written in the order of service: 'Who loves, lives.'

In the love that she gave and by her love of life itself, she will live for all of us always.

Sophie Lichfield (Mrs John Irvin)
(1942–1992)
photographer

by Jilly Cooper
(writer)

*Memorial Service at All Saints Church, Putney,
London, on 27 February 1992*

I loved Sophie. I loved her beauty, her warmth, her passionate
loyalty, her wonderful, wonderful sense of the ridiculous. Like
Yorick, she was a person of infinite jest, of most excellent fancy.
She also had the ability to ginger up any occasion.

After we left Putney, I wrote a book describing our life on the
Common and one of the most endearing and glamorous characters
was called Rosie. She was an amalgam of several people, but she
had in her very much of Sophie. Several of Sophie's escapades were
Rosie's and here is one of them:

Wednesday, November 1st 1978
Go to Hallowe'en party with the children. Tremendously impressed
at how hard the hostess had worked. Apple bobbing, however, was
not a success as the children keep leaving their loose teeth in the
apples.

Fortunately a diversion is provided by a ghoul arriving. It is Rosie,
dressed in a white sheet with a skeleton mask stuck on the front. It
is wonderfully spooky, and all the little girls have the vapours and
scream with terror.

Later Rosie and I drink a little bit too much wine and I take her, in her ghoul kit, out on the Common. First we accost two middle-class, middle-aged women, who start to walk very fast away from us, then break into a high-heeled run. Then they hear me say, 'Really Rosie, you mustn't frighten people.'

So they creep cautiously back like little calves, and start to giggle and say, 'We really think you're rather wonderful. What a se-uper idea,' etc.

Then two simply ferocious punks come up, and so Rosie jumps on them. They are quite unmoved and say, 'You don't look well, dear, do you want us to call the doctor? There's a lot of flu about.'

Rosie and I get totally hysterical with giggles.

I can't help feeling very envious that now with Sophie there, heaven must be a much jollier place.

Frankie Howerd (1921–1992)
comedian

by Barry Cryer
(comedian and writer)

*Memorial Service at St Martin-in-the-Fields Church,
London, on 8 July 1992*

Just make myself comfy . . .
Once more unto the speech, dear friends, once more
And sing in praise of Howerd, Francis
the tight-rope walker who always took chances
Always wobbling, never falling
Captivating and enthralling
Confiding, chiding, but never crawling
Fearful confident of his ability
Positively arrogant in his humility
Making every line a sonnet
Please yourselves – don't take a vote on it
A true friend but not a sentimental man
He was, to each lady and gentle-man
Who enjoyed his friendship which always lasted
Steadfast, never has my flabber been so gasted
I was amazed! when I realised how long it was in reality
He had beguiled us – such whimsicality
That face – someone called him King Leer and like Lear he
    depicted

To his audience of mad fools — a world where it was wicked
    to mock the afflicted
A world where pianists opined that it was chilly
With which he agreed, apparently willy nilly
While confiding to us he was sweating like a pig
Frank was always in for a penny infra dig
He could also inform us it was bitter out
Followed by a plea to get each titter out
That we could muster — oh folly, folly!
Such irrelevance — nolle prosequi? Not on your nellie!
That face — he defined as like a milkman's horse
To which my reaction was neigh, thrice neigh, of course
Crying: 'No don't laugh, it could be one of your own!'
This stand-up comedian stood alone
St Francis of Assisi — 'A Sissi?' 'I heard that' I can hear the
    retort
'How very dare you!' never was haughty quite so haught
Such haughty culture   Bottom crossed with Puck
Yet ever reminding us 'Common as muck'
If that was common, say we all be so
He had common ground with us and we all know
With respect to E.M. Forster, there is no Howerd's End, that
    is not the case
At the risk of being naughty, shut your face
At this Eisteddfod, I shall go the whole hog
No epitaph, no epilogue. No. I joyfully conclude
The prologue.

William Douglas-Home (1912–1992)
playwright

by Brian Johnston
(cricket commentator)

*Thanksgiving Service at St Martin-in-the-Fields
Church, London, on 5 November 1992*

I had always hoped that William would do for me what I am sad but honoured to be doing now for him. I especially wanted *him* because I knew that he would be kind, generous and witty.

He would, I'm sure, have been delighted, though modestly surprised, to see the House Full notice up here today. I suspect that there are many here who, like myself, claimed that William was their best friend, and we've all come to thank him for that friendship, his kindness, his generosity and unfailing good humour and wit.

It may sound like a cliché but I personally never heard William say an unkind word about anyone, nor did I hear anyone say an unkind word about him. Of course there were criticisms of, and disagreements with, some of his more eccentric campaigns or beliefs. But there was never any malice against him personally. He got on with everyone, whoever and whatever they were, and he was marvellous with children.

We, his friends, have suffered a great loss. But how much greater is the loss to Rachel and his devoted family. William and Rachel had such a happy partnership for over forty years. Rachel gave him her unfailing support, offering steadfast defence at one end, whilst William was the David Gower playing strokes at the other. So far as I know

William never had a diary. Whenever one asked if he was free to do something, he always said, 'Ask Rachel.' He relied entirely on her and in return was a loyal and loving husband. I must say I wouldn't have minded having him as a father either; he was so tolerant and kind. So our love and deep sympathy go out to Rachel and the family, and we thank them for having shared William with us.

He was unique, a one-off, a lovable, slightly eccentric aristocrat. To the public he was a highly successful playwright who wrote a succession of light comedies, with many of the plots drawn from his own experiences or those of his family. His great strength was his flowing witty dialogue and his flair for making his characters likeable, sympathetic and amusing. What a contrast to some of the modern plays today.

Pauline and I must have gone to all his first nights, and shared in the successes and the not so successful. Sometimes the critics appeared suspicious or even jealous of his background. But he stood up to them and was not afraid to match blow for blow.

He pretended not to be, but he was in fact, a very hard worker.

It's not for me in front of such a distinguished congregation – many from the theatre world – to analyse his theatrical achievements.

Of the sixty or so plays which he wrote, *The Chiltern Hundreds*, *The Reluctant Debutante*, *The Secretary Bird* and *The Kingfisher* were perhaps the most outstanding. But there were many others like *Lloyd George Knew my Father*, *The Jockey Club Stakes* and *The Dame of Sark*, the latter being one of several with a more serious message. He also loved to act. I first saw him in the late thirties in Dodie Smith's *Bonnet over the Windmill*. He always jumped at the opportunity to take over a part in one of his own plays. I saw him in Brighton in *Aunt Edwina* as the Master of Foxhounds who came back from a trip to Paris changed into a buxom lady. The play, in spite of William's brave efforts to salvage it, was a flop. It was before its time. It might have been a smash hit today!

He and I first became friends at Eton over sixty-five years ago. It was there that he penned his famous short essay in an exam. When asked to write as briefly as possible on the future of coal, he wrote just one word: 'Smoke'. And I believe he was marked seven out of ten for it.

In the holidays I used to stay with him in Scotland and enjoyed meeting his lovable eccentric father – Lord Home – the wee Lordie as he was called. When he visited London he was given just £20 spending money by his agent. By the time he had reached Brown's Hotel, half of it had gone in tips to porters and the taxi driver. He was hopelessly generous – just like William always was.

His mother was a tower of strength and especially loved William. Lord Home treated her like a permanent invalid, and packed her off to bed every night at ten sharp. After he died, she used to stay up and watch the midnight movies on television. It was a very happy family, with his four brothers and two sisters.

At New College we used to take it in turns to breakfast in each other's rooms – and you *do* get to know people at breakfast. And my goodness he ate large quantities of marmalade! William didn't work too hard and was more often at a debs' dance in London than at a tutorial with his tutor in Oxford. As a result in the end he was sent down for a short time, but was allowed back to take his Schools. But by then his licence to have a car had been taken away by the city authorities. So he hired a horse and carriage and drove round Oxford in that. The horse was a mare called Lily – by a strange coincidence the name of the Lady Mayoress at the time.

Everyone knows William's moral courage in standing up for his principles during the war. I myself have always felt guilty that I deserted him in his time of trouble.

But he also had physical courage. He had always shot and fished but never ridden a horse. For some reason in our last year at Oxford he decided he wanted to ride in a point-to-point and persuaded me to join him. I at least had hunted as a boy. Anyway we hired two horses. His was a roan called Nero. Mine was a half-brother of the April the 5th Derby winner and was called Tip Top. We used to practise riding the horses but never dared to see if they could jump – or whether we could stay on. It's here that William and I had a lifelong difference of opinion. I say that Nero refused at the *second* fence, William always maintained it was the *fourth*. No matter. It was a very plucky performance and inspired the local tipster to say: 'There are jockeys here today who couldn't ride in a railway carriage unless the door was locked.'

Before the war we shared a house in South Eaton Place kept by a wonderful couple called Mr and Mrs Crisp. Gert had a lisp and was a second mother to William. Mr Crisp used to dress up as a butler in a wig and knee breeches when he had people to dinner. One evening when he was handing round the vegetables, William said, 'Anyone here know of a good butler? We are thinking of making certain changes here.' On cue Mr Crisp promptly upset all the peas into the lap of one of the guests. It was that sort of house – a crazy, happy home from home.

On Sunday, September 3rd 1939, William, his brother Henry and I were filling sandbags at Westminster Hospital when that famous siren went off just after Neville Chamberlain had announced that we were at war with Germany. William immediately joined the Fire Service, and I went off to join the Guards.

I caught up with him immediately after the war, and have been in regular, often daily contact with him ever since. How I am already missing those telephone calls when we would swap jokes, many of which he used to repeat to his friends. I shall always remember the last one I told him just a day or two before he died. I think he would have liked me to tell it to you today, as I doubt if he had time to pass it on to his friends.

Tramp Story

A dirty old tramp knocked on the door of a very posh house. A lady answered: 'What do you want, my man?'

'Please Mam, I'm very hungry. I'd like something to eat.'

'Very well. Do you like *cold* rice pudding?'

'Oh yes, Mam, I do – very much.'

'Well that's all right then. Come back tomorrow. It's still hot!'

And believe it or not he had the grace to laugh.

Someone else who will also be missing his telephone calls to William is his brother, Alec, with his daily racing tips. They once had a big coup and went right through the card at Ascot, but otherwise the only winners seemed to be the bookies.

In fact if anyone has shares in either British Telecom or Ladbrokes, I should sell them both. Their profits are bound to plummet!

William had so many interests. Politics, his frequent witty letters to *The Times*, the daily crossword, his golf, which he played regularly. It could be a bit hazardous playing with him, as just as you were stooping to putt, he would very likely tickle you from behind between the legs with his putter.

Then there was his bridge, in which his bidding was highly optimistic and always worth a double. And his racehorses which seldom won but gave him great pleasure – especially Goblin who finished tenth in the Derby. William always said it would have won had it not caught its tail in the starting gate. A likely tale!

William was also an inveterate leg-puller. He once got me to dress up as a clergyman and pretend to be deaf, in order to embarrass one of his aunts. He would ring up Alec when he was Prime Minister pretending to be some important statesman from abroad. There was also the occasion when his brother, Henry, was recording birdsong for the BBC from the woods at the Hirsel. Both Henry and the Beeb were thrilled at the brilliant recording they got of an owl hooting from the depths of the wood. The recording was used as a sound effect in quite a few BBC plays. It was only discarded when William admitted to Henry that it was *he* who had given the hoot.

What a rich life William enjoyed in his happy family homes in the Meon Valley, with his family, the garden and the birdlife. But he was never a man of Great Possessions. His cars always seemed to have done two hundred thousand miles. Nor, except for his occasional bow-tie, was he a natty dresser. He had an old favourite anorak in which he would garden in the morning and then put it on over his dinner jacket when he went to dine with the Other Club at the Savoy. It must have shocked the cloakroom attendant. But knowing William he probably tipped him a fiver.

I mentioned *Great Possessions* just now. That was the title of his very first play, which I saw at the Q Theatre just before the war.

I remember it had a very sad ending, and the dear old nanny walked across the room, and looked out of the window. Outside it was raining hard. 'I think,' she said, 'that God must be crying' – and the curtain fell.

Well, the curtain has fallen now but, unlike God, *we* mustn't cry.

William wouldn't like that. Somehow the loss has made the thought of dying oneself that much easier. If ever I get there I can look forward to being greeted by William at the gates of heaven, asking for the latest joke, which he will then promptly tell to the angels.

God bless you, William. We all loved you, and thank you for your friendship, and the happiness and laughter which you brought into all our lives.

Sir Kenneth Macmillan (1929–1992)

principal choreographer of the Royal Ballet

by Dame Ninette de Valois

(dancer, teacher and founder of the Royal Ballet)
Read by Sir Anthony Dowell

Memorial Service at Westminster Abbey, London,
on 17 February 1993

Kenneth Macmillan. When one thinks of the English ballet scene and its startling youth next to the much greater age of Russian, French, Italian, Danish and German schools we have to reflect on those to whom we owe so much. The achievement of the English scene is something we are entitled to regard with gratitude towards those whose names who have made it possible and high on this list stands the name of Kenneth Macmillan. Our country's national ballet with its worldwide acceptance is the youngest. Choreographers are the core, the solidity of such achievement, and we have in Kenneth Macmillan a wonderful example of this.

How is such an achievement assessed? By that simple yet frightening word: success. Macmillan ballets are in the repertoire of most international ballet companies of any importance. His is now a great international name – England rather accepts this with true down-to-earth British understatement. If we are not careful to assess the position from time to time in the long run such an attitude can appear to be ungrateful.

This is a sad occasion for any form of assessment to be made but we are all filled with memories of intense pride and admiration for what Kenneth Macmillan achieved for the English ballet scene. In the end his worldwide recognition does as much for his country as it does for him.

I hope that in the future his ballets will remain in the English repertoire as classics of the English scene. They are great ballets and have an international renown which is not surpassed at the moment by any other choreographer.

We should all be grateful for his loyalty and devotion to his own home scene and fulfil our duty in seeing that his repertoire is kept alive.

Sir Kenneth Macmillan (1929–1992)
principal choreographer of the Royal Ballet

by Nicholas Hytner
(director of the National Theatre)

Memorial Service at Westminster Abbey, London, on 17 February 1993

I met Kenneth for the first time about three years ago to try to persuade him to choreograph the National Theatre's production of *Carousel*, which I was directing. I was greatly in awe of him, but he listened courteously as I talked on and on; until – desperate to make an impression – I blurted out: 'The point about this musical is that it's about sex and violence.' Kenneth slowly raised an eyebrow, and said: 'Well, that's what I do.' He agreed to do the show, and I soon discovered that what Kenneth did was often hidden behind a veil of mordant wit, or an ironically raised eyebrow. As we prepared *Carousel*, I knew that the climax of the show would be what turned out to be one of Kenneth's great *pas de deux*, so I floated the idea that the prologue might start with a ghostly pre-echo of it. Kenneth was mildly interested – although you sometimes couldn't quite tell – but when we began to talk about starting the show with a line of mill girls working a loom, he sprang into action. He said that a factory seemed to him to be *exactly* the right location for a ballet: he wanted real girls, rooted in the earth, who through his gifts bore witness to a spirit which transcended the meanness of their circumstances.

I never got to talk to him about spiritual transcendence. He just did it, claiming much of the time to be doing something easier. I remember him firmly telling the assembled National Theatre on the first day of rehearsal that we were using classical ballet in the production because it was the best way of telling a story. And then – just in case anyone might spring to the defence of the spoken word – he added, 'And it's sexier that way.' Nobody argued.

The last thing he ever created was the outburst of joy and naked libido for the number 'June is Bustin' out All Over'. The excitement after he first ran it through was overwhelming, but he seemed rather weary of the compliments. He was thrilled, though, when the dialect coach told him it was like an orgy on speed. He kept repeating it, to everybody.

I think he was a little daunted by the ever-growing band of people who used to crowd into the rehearsal room pretending to be on official business whenever he was working. But he didn't chase them away, and I hope he knew that what drew them in was a sense of wonder. He was the master of a language largely new to us at the National, but familiar I guess to most of you here, which dazzled us, and spoke to us of passion and pain, and about the connection between them; and made poetry of it.

What Kenneth did was life, experience, everything. And he made you rejoice to be part of it. And if that's not worth giving thanks for, I don't know what is.

Dame Freya Stark (1893–1993)
traveller and writer

by Colin Thubron
(traveller and writer)

*Memorial Service at St James's Church, Piccadilly,
London, on 28 September 1993*

Some ten years ago I remember Freya Stark wondering what attributes people might carry with them into the afterlife. Would we take our compassion, she wondered, would we take our sense of justice, would we take our courage? She entertained only vague ideas about the hereafter, she said, since it would be a poor secret which would yield itself up to any human imagination; but I was reminded then – as we all must be now – of the extraordinariness and distinction of her own qualities.

I, personally – and I think most of us who knew her – was never in her company without feeling in some way enhanced and challenged. Life simply seemed to be richer and grander because of her. It was an incomparable gift, and can only be ascribed to that indefinable quality, stature.

She had a trust – almost an innocence – which, I think, conveyed itself even to the wildest people among whom she journeyed: a woman alone in a man's world, perhaps with a single guide. Although she was a famous admirer of the British Empire, she was the least conventional and condescending of travellers. She accorded to the societies through which she moved an open-minded curiosity and a respect for other values. It suffused her books with a remarkable alloy of tenderness and grandeur. Allied to this was something which most of us who knew her sensed instantly: a serenity, an inner resolution, which perhaps came from a conquest of self. She seemed, in some magic way, to have overcome fear.

This could be embarrasing to her friends. I remember in Italy she had the most appalling fibreglass car, which was covered in dents and lacerations from innumerable road accidents. She was, without exception, the worst driver I've ever known. When this machine appeared in her home town of Asolo, the streets would magically clear of their inhabitants. She would reprimand nervous passengers by saying that the only security lay in accepting danger — as she shot up another one-way street. Some mutual friends had a go-cart in Sussex. At an advanced age Freya clambered into it and roared up and down the drive, only returning to announce: 'I may not be a very good driver, but I *am* a *very* fast one.'

I wish I could reproduce for you that extraordinary contralto voice, with its distinctive timbre — how it would lift an octave in emphasis or descend to a rather naughty chuckle — or convey something of the charm of her rounded figure and friendly hawk's face. Then there was her extraordinary polyglot learning. Her unconventional background — she had almost no formal schooling at all — equipped her wonderfully for the life that she was to follow. She kept a touch of continental Bohemia about her, and in spite of the wisdom of her views and the breadth of her values, a sense too of mischief and wonderment.

I think the gypsy existence that took her through so many worlds was absolutely natural to her. Yet from the wilds of Anatolia or Arabia she would reappear, surprisingly, among the statelier families of Britain and Italy. Her work in Allied propaganda during the Second World War she stamped with her own individual mark; and always she would return to her haven in Asolo; to her famous circular writing-table which she designed herself, and her eighty-seven yards of books. For she was, in spite of all the other business of her life, exceptionally well-read, especially in the classics. She spoke, with varying fluency, at least six different languages. Yet she always denied any claims to originality either as an explorer or as a scholar.

But she would be angry if I painted her as an angel. She was nothing so insipid. She was exacting, could be quite brilliantly manipulative and she expected the same generosity from her friends as she would often bestow herself. She was, of course, profoundly lucky in her beloved and much put-upon publisher Jock Murray, who died just a few weeks after she did, as if she had summoned him impatiently to edit the manuscript of her latest travels.

Patrick Leigh Fermor said that if Freya Stark had been born a boy, she would most certainly have been a general. Yet she was famously feminine. Her hats were notorious. Lord Wavell – not a man for demonstrative behaviour – said in 1941 that he had to pass through Baghdad in order to see Freya Stark and her seven new hats. And what the Parisian couturier Madame Grès felt goes unrecorded when Freya ordered an elaborate ball-gown for a function in Tehran, but added that it should be of uncreasable material since it would have to be folded into a saddle-bag.

Whatever qualities Freya Stark has taken with her into the after-life, she has left them behind abundantly for us in her books: a handful of the most beautiful and distinguished travel books in our language. She has left, too, a plenitude of remarkable published letters, which celebrate her gift for friendship – a gift which scarcely needs emphasising today, when almost all the friends of her own generation are dead, yet this church is full.

She also left behind – lesser known – a superb library of photographs. She was an artist with the camera as well as with the pen.

The books, of course, are peculiarly her own. She had a jewelled way with words. They shine, I think, with that combination of the visionary and the particular which permeated her own life, as if the great riches of time and space sat cheek by jowl with a wonderful intimacy of observation, so that often history, people and landscape interfuse in a seamless unity.

This concept of the unity of things came to absorb her more and more as she grew older, and into her early nineties she contemplated – quite unmorbidly – on death. She saw it simply as the elimination of time and space, and the start of the next great journey. She wrote – and I want to leave you with her words rather than mine – that 'for every journey, imagination only is needed – and an awareness of the rim beyond which the world is made new. And if one were asked which, of all sights in nature, is the most lastingly satisfying, would one not choose the horizon?'

John Murray (1909–1993)
publisher

by Patrick Leigh Fermor
(writer and traveller)

*Memorial Service at St James's Church, Piccadilly,
London, on 6 October 1993*

A hundred and one years and two hundred and four days ago, a service just like today's was being held in this very church for another John Murray, the third of the dynasty. Three years before Waterloo, the famous publishers had migrated from the City to 50 Albemarle Street – the family home and the publishing headquarters were then under one roof – and St James's Piccadilly was only a couple of minutes away. It became their parish church for well over a century and, in a sense, it still is.

As a boy of seven, this earlier Murray saw the first of the many meetings between Sir Walter Scott and Lord Byron. After hours of talk in the drawing room, he watched the two great men, both lame, stumping cheerfully downstairs side by side. In the same surroundings and at the same age but over a century later, his great-grandson Jock, whom we commemorate today, was running about those splendid Regency rooms and peering up into the glass cupola and sliding down the banisters. It was an amazing place to grow up in. Hung with portraits of the famous, it was an Aladdin's cave of relics and mementoes. Archives were stacked to the ceiling, japanned boxes were crammed with old letters, locks of hair, sometimes whole tresses – Byron's scalps indeed – were coiled in drawers and the Corunna pistols of Sir John Moore lay casually about. There was hardly a stick of furniture without its anecdote. Did Jock ever have a flicker of apprehension about the traditions his father had married into? If he did, we must be grateful to the shade of Sir Arthur Conan Doyle for exorcising it: he bumped into him coming upstairs with *The Casebook of Sherlock Holmes* under his arm in manuscript. 'He greeted me with great courtesy, just as though I were a grown-up,' Jock recalled, 'and I fell under his spell. If this is an author, I said to myself, what fun to be a publisher.'

And what luck for the rest of us!

I don't know what share Eton played in his early years but the high point at Oxford was his friendship with John Betjeman, ironically sent down for failing Divinity. In the end Jock duly joined the firm, added his maternal 'Murray' to his paternal 'Grey' and served, as he put it, as a general dogsbody under the august shadow of his uncle, and every aspect of his calling, however menial, specialised or abstruse, proved a fascination. His early days were only interrupted by war service as a gunner, when he was decorated for his help in organising the air transport for Arnhem. By the late sixties he was running the whole firm.

He was the ideal, the quintessential publisher, and his success was rooted in his total and passionate devotion to literature in general and to books in particular, and, hence, to the people who wrote them. All through his reign, whenever you closed the door behind you in Albemarle Street, the outside world faded away as if by magic. Everyone there, from the receptionist to the night-watchman, was a friend, on your side, and in league. How could so much activity, you wondered, go hand in hand with apparently so unhurried a pace? Upstairs, behind a desk with its orderly maelstrom of papers, Jock would be sitting in scarlet braces, lop-sided bow-tie and undone cuffs flying loose like fins, brimming over with enthusiastic suggestions, and going through galley or page proofs with a captivating process. They might be pushed aside for a moment to look at Freya Stark's latest Anatolian instalment, or a chapter of Ruth Jhabvala's from Old Delhi, or tidings of Dervla Murphy in Peru. Towards lamplighting time, drinks would appear – Chambéry for Jock – and

Osbert Lancaster might wander in after his daily cartoon, full of wonderful gossip; or Kenneth Clark with an armful of illustrations; or Betjeman, with news of a huge Early English church in the Fens, where an aged vicar preached a long sermon studded with Latin and Greek to a congregation of one reed-gatherer. Could they talk about it with John Piper?

Inevitably, Byron pervaded the premises, and on his anniversary, rain or shine, Jock laid a wreath on the statue in Hyde Park. One evening, with glasses in hand after dinner round the famous fireplace, Jock was carefully unfolding the poet's letters and reading them aloud to Peter Quennell and Harold Nicolson. A book was being planned: they knew his life backwards − or almost. But after an hour, at the mention of a date, Harold Nicolson's lowered eyelids suddenly sprang open. 'Ah!' he exclaimed. 'So that's what he was up to that Thursday night.'

Days with Jock and Diana at Cannon Lodge − poised above all London between the Heath and a kestrel-haunted steeple − had an invincible charm: pages for final revision, brought uphill in Jock's great slung postman's satchel, were spread out under a tall plane tree. One knew of his fondness for music, the part he played in learned and bibliophile societies and his involvement with the Royal Geographical Society, but it was here that one learned of his love for trees and his skill as a tree surgeon. A split in the trunk or an ailing growth would send him shinning up into the branches and setting all methodically to rights with a saw and twine and bast and a tin full of tar. Perhaps it was akin to the astringency, care, advice and encouragement that he brought to bear on his authors. 'I don't mind tuppence about the overshot deadline,' he said to an author long overdue with the last volume of a sequence, 'I just want to see how it ends before I die.' A few months ago, discussing the banes of advancing years with a friend, he said, halfway between a laugh and a sigh, 'Yes. Old age is not for sissies.' Now, as the weeks pass, we see even more clearly what a gap he has left. Two thoughts offer a sort of consolation. Firstly, the line of the Murrays, thank heavens, is flourishing; so are the traditions that Jock inherited and fostered and made his own. Secondly, all the trees and many of the books he tended with such care will spread their shade and give pleasure for long years to come. But the kindness, the comic sense, the wisdom, the thoughtful response to life, the enthusiasm and good repair in which he kept his friendships can never be replaced.

Anthony Burgess (1917–1993)
writer

by William Boyd
(writer)

Memorial Service at St Paul's Church, Covent Garden, London, on 16 June 1994

I want to begin by quoting a sentence – one sentence only – from *Enderby Outside*. Enderby – the middle-aged poet hero – is leading another life, for reasons too complicated to go into, as a barman in a large London hotel. At a grand banquet, where he is serving drinks, Enderby encounters an American poet. The man approaches, not recognising him, and orders a drink. Enderby smells the mouthwash on his breath and remembers a time when they had met before, at another banquet. It's designed to be read, rather than heard, this sentence, but I hope I can do it full justice. 'Then – instead of expensive mouthwash – he had *breathed* on Enderby – bafflingly – (for no banquet would serve, because of the known redolence of onions, onions) onions.'

I believe this sentence, tucked away in chapter two, part two, was a response to a challenge someone had made to Anthony. Namely, could he write a single sentence where the word 'onions' appears three times, one after the other, in a manner that made perfect sense and was not simple repetition. Well, of course he could, and with perfect poise and a great deal else besides. I don't think it's being unduly fanciful to see in this sentence, in microcosm, many of the facets that made Anthony Burgess the writer he was.

It's funny, it's clever and it exhibits that typically Burgessian zest for the English language: its nuances, its idiosyncrasies, its remarkable malleability – aspects that Anthony exploited and exulted in all his writing life.

And what can one say confronted with a body of work like Anthony's? Over fifty books, ranging through every category and genre – short stories, verse epics, screenplays, biography, criticism, textbooks, translations, libretti, travel writing, musicology and one of the great literary autobiographies of the century – the polymorphous abilities are genuinely amazing. And to his peers, to his fellow-writers, Anthony was a prodigy, a daunting and awesome one. The myths and apocrypha that sprang up around him: that he was a brilliant and inspirational cook, that he could read – and probably speak (for all we knew) – every European language including Finnish, that he would compose a string quartet in the ten minutes he allowed himself between finishing a novel and writing a monograph on James Joyce and – this is the one that really got to us – that in his capacity as literary journalist he always read *and* reviewed the book that was sent to him *the day it arrived in the post*. These legends about Anthony are tributes to the real admiration which he inspired and a proof of the affectionate recognition we felt that he really was one of a kind.

And amongst those fifty-odd books are thirty-one novels. I said that the sentence I quoted from *Enderby Outside* was 'funny' and it's worth reiterating now that Anthony was a comic novelist, one of our great comic novelists. The comic form – at its most serious – uncovers the absurd truths about the human condition and the utter insignificance of our lives on this small blue and green planet; it does not flatter mankind's pretensions about our place in the scheme of things or nurture or cosset our dignity or self-importance. When you consider Anthony's body of work, when you look through the extraordinary range of novels from *Time for a Tiger* in 1956 to *A Dead Man in Deptford* in 1993, you not only marvel at the abundant richness of his genius and inspiration but also at the well-nigh incredible energy and the sustained quality of the writing. Anthony's last novel is one of his best. His imagined life of Christopher Marlowe is as dense, inventive and pyrotechnical as his imagined life of Shakespeare was thirty years earlier: as humane, wry and fiercely intelligent as everything he wrote.

When Charles Dickens died his great friend John Forster was away in the country. Thomas Carlyle wrote to Forster to commiserate and sympathise: 'I am profoundly sorry for you,' Carlyle wrote, 'and indeed for myself and for us all – a *unique* of Talents suddenly eclipsed.'

Anthony Burgess was a 'unique', a unique of talents like Charles Dickens. And the comparison is just and worth celebrating and not simply because they shared the same boundless energy and rapt fascination with language. It's fitting, then, to let some words from Dickens's will stand as Anthony Burgess's testimonial.

'I rest my claims,' Dickens said, 'to the remembrance of my country upon my published works, and to the remembrance of my friends upon their experience of me.'

We have our personal remembrance of Anthony, our experience of him, and we have his published works. As the last line on the last page of his last novel says: 'That inimitable voice sings on.'

Robin Cavendish (1930–1994)

responaut

by the Right Reverend Lord Runcie
(Archbishop of Canterbury, 1980–91)

*Memorial Service at the Abbey Church, Dorchester,
Oxfordshire, on 30 September 1994*

There was no one like him. I don't mean there was no one quite
like him. I mean there was no one like him.

As Robin grew weaker in the summer, it became clear the end
could not be long delayed. He was asked about a memorial service.
He was not too keen. But others persuaded him it was inevitable.
He began to plan things with characteristic gusto. 'Jonathan, get
hold of the Yellow Pages. Find the best undertaker. Make sure it
is not a rip-off. You know how they are – like garages with women.
Diana's always being ripped off at garages.'

Some suggestions he blackballed. Others he greeted with enthusiasm. 'Leave the music to Diana.' One visitor on the day before he
died was waved off with the words, 'Keep the end of September
free. There may be a memorial service.'

A prepared draft obituary was sent to Jonathan for checking. He
decided to try it out on his father who enjoyed it immensely –
gurgling away and disowning its superlatives. 'Oh how absurd, how
absurd, how ridiculous.'

It is no conventional piety to state that Robin is with us. He has
been party to this celebration of his life. When I was told that out
of the sometimes hilarious debates about this memorial service,

Robin had insisted (I don't know the strength of the opposition) on my giving the address, I felt more honoured than when Margaret Thatcher asked me to be Archbishop of Canterbury. I suspect it may have been a feeling on his part that the service should not get too religious. It is an awesome responsibility to attempt to articulate the affection and gratitude and sense of privilege felt so deeply by us all. But at least I know that no preacher ever had a congregation so completely on his side.

Robin was a light-hearted character, not, we were to discover, light-weight; but Robin seemed to be born gloriously light-hearted and gifted − not even Winchester could dent that and brilliantly gave him his head as the intelligent all-rounder and graceful games player instead of treating him woodenly as if he were a potential Wittgenstein. In Derbyshire he was already the young man with whom all the girls wanted to dance at Christmas balls. He emerged from Sandhurst a natural, effortless leader, not in a macho way but competent, dependable, great fun − adored by his men, the originator of mischievous plots to send up the pompous. Signals officer, he became knowledgeable about all the technology. In the days when our feet danced to the tunes of *Oklahoma* or *Annie Get Your Gun* Robin made the easy transition from popular young officer in Germany to man-about-town in London.

He had charm but he was one of those rare characters who give charm a good name. For it was not carefully polished smoothness. Nor was it manipulative. He was devastatingly attractive to women of all ages and seldom uninterested in them; but he never ever gobbled up people or destroyed those who were devoted to him.

In 1957 he married Diana. They met in Berkeley Square which was romantic enough − certainly more so than the way in which his mama on one meeting with Diana gave her approval. 'She will do. She is fit, strong and doesn't smoke.' It seemed the most perfect match and of course we know that it was so, quite beyond words or any expectation. The young tea broker and his stunningly beautiful wife set up house in the Ngong Hills in Kenya. Jonathan has told of what Robin was later to describe as the happiest days of his life.

I have told this tale to remind us, and perhaps to challenge us −

though challenge was not a word often on Robin's lips – with the thought that he did not change as a character through the terrible disaster of 1958. Of course he went down into the depths of despair and the agony of the total stripping of all his physical gifts. Into that darkness it is hard for us to enter; but the miracle is that he emerged not changed but with all the essential parts of a clearly etched character firmly in place. And so they remained until his dying day: light-hearted, practical, wise, charming, humorous, courteous, convivial – all those things but with depth and amazing achievements in the infectious and creative use of them.

I plead to add a few personal impressions.

We first met on a cricket ground. The Squire's Match at Garsington in 1961. A little south Oxfordshire period piece to which we were both then strangers. I was warned, 'He's not very keen on clergymen.' I pushed my wife up front. It worked a dream. I spoke to Diana and discovered we had enough in common to head me off improving sympathy, moral uplift or chatting her up.

It was well timed. The early sixties were not easy for those in charge of theological students. Furloughs became far and away the best refuge for the restoration of spirits. Our car breasted the Chislehampton hill and made its eager way far too fast round the curving lanes in high expectations which were never disappointed. The usual distribution of energies as soon as we arrived. Lindy sitting beside Robin always noticed the way his eyes began to sparkle and roll a little when the conversation was clearly about to disgorge a delicious morsel of gossip. At the same time he always felt real sorrow when he heard that a friend's marriage had broken up, or a student had committed suicide, or a friend once entertaining had become a bore, or barmy or a fanatic. He could express outrage at human folly or massive injustice. Irritation about an idle or creepy vicar. Fascination at the mixture of monkish austerity and liberal bad conscience that he thought to reign in my college. I billeted upon them a carefully chosen star couple and of course nobody has watched their subsequent career with more pride than Robin. We fed him our students for his opinions. Time has proved him an astute bishop-spotter.

Each little gasped nugget that came out of him was cherished – that was because he listened and he pondered. I cannot honestly claim he had the safest ear in Oxfordshire but there was never anything malicious or hurtful in his indiscretions. He always said what he meant and never said what he didn't mean. That's why his approval counted for so much.

The range of his conversation was immense. Stocks and shares to government policies. God-talk was robust; but never concluded. There was usually a point at which it was a case of 'Let's have another drink' and 'I know that girl over there wants to come and talk to me.'

These were the days of his greatest public achievements. The days of the amazing partnership with Geoffrey Spencer and Teddy Hall. What a trio of ability and commitment to go with the trio of affection that Mark Baring so strikingly spoke about.

There was the design of a respirator chair and the beginning of his control system at home for radio, television, telephone and alarm. There was the money he raised that others might share his achievements. The minute particulars with which he tracked down and listed responauts in Britain. 'If I can get around and enjoy life, so can they. Of course I have Diana. I have a little money and I have inventive friends; but we must help others to get out and discover what is possible with money, love and invention.'

He encouraged me to open an exhibition for aids for the handicapped in Hatfield and asked to see one of the industrial enterprises in my diocese of St Albans. I chose the headquarters of the Wine Society at Stevenage and they have never forgotten the whirlwind trip of the cellars, the unyielding palate down which Diana gently poured some of their finest wines.

At the same time to holiday with them was to discover the knife-edge on which he lived, the appalling indignities that were laughed away and the cost of constant vigilance which Diana so effectively masked with such serenity and grace.

The work for Refresh and his design and raising money for the home on Southampton Water and the establishment of the Lane Fox Unit in St Thomas's all engaged his mixture of energy, diplomacy and sheer bloody-minded push.

Handicap for him was no excuse to fail in the duties of friendship. If he possibly could he would always turn up. He rather enjoyed my cathedral occasions, consecration or enthronement. Trumpets and ceremonial were to his taste, provided he was not at the centre of them.

Equally fascinated he was about the Byzantine intricacies of Church finance and what they got up to in the Church Commissioners. He regularly watched the religious television documentaries of the eighties and formed his own independent opinion of the issues. He was never taken in by the label, the cliché, the predictable quote.

He came to some of our establishment parties because he was our friend and endured cheerfully the attention of those who sought him out, thinking him the representative disabled character. Nobody could ever have been less chippy with the insensitive, the ponderous or the patronising.

He was an unashamed elitist. I remember with what pleasure he heard me say one day, 'I wonder why it is that Jonathan looks so much more aristocratic than my own son.' But nobody was less of a snob. People were put at their ease because he enjoyed their company and he was totally incapable of talking down to them or scoring points off those who could not answer back.

He chose this lovely abbey at Dorchester for our service today because it would be convenient for as many as possible of all his friends.

His final public appearance was the retirement party for Geoffrey Spencer in St Thomas's Hospital. It was an amazing achievement that he got there – a final illustration of the dynamism that pushed the team spirit of Robin, Diana, Jonathan and Lesley to the utmost. I shall never forget their dramatic appearance and look of feigned puzzlement and sheer delight that we should be so pleased to see them and welcome them without the embarrassment of cringe-making speeches.

One of the most memorable sentences for me in the obituaries of Robin was this: 'It is a strange irony that though professing to be an unbeliever himself, he had a capacity for making others feel closer to God.'

There is a charming story of his days as a young officer. Several of his platoon were discovered to be unbaptised and a keen chaplain persuaded them to rectify this omission. They were all won over but they all insisted that Robin should be godfather to every one. He could do that then. Later he declared simply that religious faith did not work for him.

But as he was popular with the young because he never made them feel guilty about their good health, so he was a friend of many clergy because he never made them feel guilty about their faith. He expected robust exchange in response to his outraged 'But surely you can't believe tosh like that.'

His life brought many abstract doctrines alive for puzzled believers. If you had been taught that providence was something that made God responsible for all the major disasters of the world you might well despair. But if you discovered it meant there was no human tragedy so terrible that it could not be redeemed and turned to good effect – well, here was a living example of it.

If you held that the indissolubility of marriage was a dogma concocted by medieval celibates you might resent its imposition. But if you saw in Robin and Diana how bonds of affection could grow stronger and deeper through the years of shadows and darkness, you might think again.

I have a friend who says that joy is a word which is only used by clergymen and when they use it they put on a funny tone of voice and sagging jaw and say 'joy'. But though he might not use the word Robin was the most amazing expression of this central Christian virtue. Happiness is different. It is a matter of harmony. When the body works well and we are healthy. When a family gets on without friction. When there is enough money to pay the bills and no anxieties.

The trouble is that there are not so many neat harmonies in life and they don't last long. The deepest experiences are those which have tension in them – where things are askew and where what is askew is transfigured and something richer emerges. The Bible talks a lot about joy and sorrow – not much about happiness. Christianity is the only religion which has at its heart not an eternal calm but a cross. These are the mysteries which for a believer take us closer to God and these are some of the mysteries we touched as we loved Robin and Diana.

I believe that if anything is sacred their story is sacred. Nothing could be more appropriate than that we should come to this sacred place in order to express our joy and our gratitude for someone who will always be around and a living part of us whatever our beliefs. How can we ever stop treasuring titbits to share with Robin, or pondering what he would say about what we intend to do, or how he would laugh at the amazing tangles in which human beings ensnare themselves.

Robin was the last person on whom I would want to project faith. Perhaps he would forgive us for wanting to have faith on his behalf.

I once remember him saying, 'If there should be an afterlife I should be delighted but astonished.' It was characteristic and I remind you that the capacity to be astonished is part of the childlike faith which is Our Lord's qualification for those who enter the Kingdom of Heaven.

I know there is not a believer in this church today who would want to enter any heaven which excluded Robin Cavendish. So with affection and gratitude and the firm hope for which this Church stands that there is always a future for our deepest loves, let us praise God for the blessings we have known in the most courageous, lovable and gracious of friends and for an inspiration that will never fade.

For us, there is no one like him.

Lord Bonham Carter of Yarnbury
(1922–1994)
publisher and Liberal Democrat politician

by Lord Jenkins of Hillhead
(writer and statesman)

*Memorial Service at St Margaret's Church,
Westminster, London, on 27 October 1994*

I regard this as perhaps the most difficult as well as the most heartfelt address of my life. Mark Bonham Carter was not only, as I summed it up a few years ago in deliberately cool terms, 'my closest all-round friend'. He was also a brilliant memorialist. His tributes to John Lyttle, to Michael Swann, to Jo and Laura Grimond, will be forgotten by few of those who heard them. In addition, he was commemorated at his Wylie Valley funeral on that September afternoon of slanting sunlight and piercing sadness, now six weeks ago, in an address of exceptional warmth and penetration.

Mark was born and educated into the Liberal purple, but at a time when purple, at any rate Liberal purple, was a less fashionable colour than it had been. As a result those great openings which his grandfather had so effortlessly seized were not as open to him, and he was never able to exercise what would undoubtedly have been his high quality in government. Yet although his talents exceeded his opportunities, it would be a mistake, and one to which, with his continuing zest and gaiety, and sense of ever opening windows, he never succumbed, to see his life as one of frustrated promise. To make a natural comparison, his actual achievements far exceeded those of his legendary uncle Raymond Asquith, to whom he bore many resemblances of wit and verve, and this was by no means only because his life lasted nearly twice as long.

Every opportunity which presented itself to Mark, from Torrington to the Race Relations Board to the BBC to Anglo-Polish relations, to making a major one-man contribution to the modern reputation of the House of Lords as a chamber of critical iconoclasm, he developed to the full. And he did so in a way which was never pedestrian, sometimes acerbic to those of whom he disapproved, who were invariably the grand rather than the humble; and always exciting rather than depressing. How anyone could see him as priggishly judgemental, I cannot imagine. He was the least priggish man I have ever known.

In personality he was a Cavalier, although with a few Roundhead views. In the phrase Churchill is supposed to have used to Mark's mother about himself – he was a *glowworm*. His life, from early childhood summers alongside Margot, Oxford's glittering Wharf – glittering because of the company not the architecture of the house – through his exceptionally dramatic war with a murderous Tunisian battle and a five-hundred-mile walk to freedom down the length of the Apennines, and his subsequent period of youthful fame and fashion, leading into his being a publisher who was as adventurous as he was discriminating, and one of the last in that now fickle profession to maintain a connection with one firm for nearly four decades. And then there were his public service jobs, and they were jobs of real service, carrying far more benefit to the public than reward to himself.

Yet anyone who attempts to sum up Mark mainly through his public *persona*, fine though that was, will get him wrong. Although he was intensely gregarious, articulate, argumentative, never bored, never boring, always the last to want to go to bed, he was very much a private person in the sense that his relations with people were of transcendent importance. He banked his treasure in the hearts of his friends; and there was a great store of non-material treasure, a lot of friends, and now a vast void of deprivation, relieved by peculiarly strong memories.

Mark's friendships were wide-ranging and he was better than

anyone else I know at spanning the generations. And he did so not just with benevolence, still less patronage, but with a spontaneous empathy which, I would guess, means that in the twenty-first century, say in the year 2030, he will be far more alive in the hearts and memories of his young friends, then grown old, than will many of us who wrote more books, occupied more offices, received more baubles. That will be, if not exactly immortality, at least a major compensating extension to a life which although just over the allotted span, seems to many of us to have been cut off horribly soon.

However, unlike some people who have a devoted band of friends, which Mark most certainly did, he was not a coterie man. As with any person of sensibility he was of course most at ease with those who were most at ease with him. But he drew people the right way rather than pushed them the wrong way over this borderline. Some people who had received, and mostly deserved, the lash of his tongue, believed that Mark had bad manners. I think that in what really counted he had the highest of good manners. He was, for instance, the best of fellow-guests to have with someone whose chicness did not glisten and who needed a little drawing out. He was the reverse of the man who at a party is always looking over a shoulder for someone smarter to talk to. If by chance he moved to such a figure it would almost certainly be to excoriate him. But on balance he did more of the building up of the meek than of the putting down of the grand. He was very good at both.

As well as being highly gregarious he was also intensely *familiale*, although not at all in an enclosed way. His family he saw as a core for wider friendships and not as a shuttered fortress against the surrounding countryside. His marriage to Leslie came relatively late in his own life at the age of thirty-three and lasted for thirty-nine years. She was then a twenty-five-year-old Anglo-American peeress with a family background of international fashion magazines whose first marriage had ended. This bald combination of fact could create a brittle picture, which could not be more misleading about the woman of exceptional warmth, sense and kindness who is Leslie Bonham Carter. Their three joint daughters, Jane, Virginia and Eliza, together with Laura, Leslie's previous child to whom Mark was equally close, constituted a remarkably cohesive and refulgent family.

Nowhere did their light shine more brightly than at Bussento, the fine house in the south of Italy which Leslie's mother most adventurously built in the late 1950s. From his long march of 1943 right through to the end Italy was a recurring background to Mark's life, although I cannot say that, any more than with me, this led to a total mastery on his part of the nuances of the Italian language. It was there in the Gulf of Policastro that Mark during thirty or more holidays brought into the most happy confluence his love of family and his love of friends, his love of life and his love of beauty, both natural and man-made, his love of books and jokes and well-lubricated argument. And it was of course on a short expedition from there, on a serene late summer Sunday evening, that he died, brutally suddenly for others but without pain or any gradual darkening of the horizon for himself.

Ironically, but with typical considerateness, he had decided that my health this last summer was temporarily too fragile for the Mezzogiorno medical services and we did not make our planned journey down the peninsula with him and Leslie. We had parted at Florence railway station, where I last saw him rolling a suitcase towards the entrance. That memory will never fade, but nor will a thousand others.

Kathleen Tynan (1937–1995)
writer

by Angela Huth
(writer)

*Memorial Service at St Paul's Church, Covent Garden,
London, on 27 February 1995*

When I went to see Kathleen a few days before she died, her first
question was: How are *you*?

But then that was always her first question to a friend, one
which her own approaching death could do nothing to dislodge.
Always she wanted to know the real answer, and if the friend
in question was in any real kind of need, next would come the
familiar help, the good ideas – why don't you call So and so? Why
don't I call and see if *I* can arrange whatever? In the practicalities
of friendship, as in so many other ways, Kathleen was a very rare
creature.

She and I met when she was eighteen, and one of Oxford's most
glorious Zuleikas. That was a role, happily, she never outgrew. Only
a few years ago she and Matthew often came to Oxford to try to
decide which college he should apply to. I can vouch that at least
four heads of college were unusually eager to offer their advice,
thereby winning an hour or so of her company and attention.

Among Kathleen's many strengths was the fact that material
changes meant little to her. She loved the heydays of wonderful
parties she would brilliantly organise both before and after Ken died.
But she was unfazed by the rather trying time when the house in

Thurloe Square was on the market, and she was living in the basement. She hardly seemed to notice the change. Indeed, beneath her lower ceilings, her generosity as a hostess was sometimes, endearingly, out of all proportion to her actual circumstances.

'Come to lunch or dinner,' she would say.

'Surely that's a nuisance when you're so busy,' I would say.

'Oh no, I've employed a chef.'

'A chef? Just for yourself in the basement?'

'Only a *daily* chef,' she assured me, as if that explained everything.

Behind the magnificent style, the glamour, the fun − God, how we laughed about men, mistakes and other matters − Kathleen the talented writer was rather more elusive, private. She worked with prodigious energy, but always made light of her work. The huge regret we all feel, of course, is that having come to the end of the Tynan industry, as she called it, she was denied the opportunity to return to her own planned fiction. But given that time was running out, finishing her memorial to Ken was how she wanted to spend it. She was never in any doubt about priorities.

To me, Kathleen was as much an enigma as an inspiration − I once put this to her and she professed not to know what I was talking about. But the sense of mystery, that some women assume, came naturally to Kathleen. We all knew our own bits of her, but areas outside our range she left hazy with, I always felt, a certain glee. She would whiz off to America, Paris, Rome: on return, although she would roughly describe what she had been up to, you felt you never *quite* knew and could never *quite* imagine. Tantalising. And this meant, mercifully, she was not a cosy friend, but something more stimulating than that − an intriguing friend.

Always a brave optimist, in the last two years of her life her courage and her silence were extraordinary − but also very typical. She would not presume to burden others with a problem of an insoluble nature. Though God knows what she would have done without the support of the children she was so devoted to, Roxanna and Matthew, whose constancy and comfort we can only wonder at.

In the years to come without her I think the reflections I shall most often turn to are these: for all her beauty she was entirely without vanity, for all her talent she was genuinely modest. As a wife, mother and friend she was a life-giver of the highest order.

'Nonsense,' I can hear her say.

But for once, we have to disagree.

Angus Macintyre (1935–1994)
historian

by Ben Macintyre
(writer)

*Memorial Service at Magdalen College Chapel, Oxford,
on 25 March 1995*

This is a joint memoir by Kate, Magnus and myself. It is inadequate, I know, for the very simple reason that the one person we would always have turned to for advice in writing it is not here.

I don't think my father was ever bored. Indeed, I'm not sure he knew how to be bored. Boredom was the failing he most disliked in others and enthusiasm the one he most admired, and one he most consistently displayed. As children in Oxford and Scotland, Dad somehow managed to imbue even the most mundane moments of growing up with gaiety, excitement and enquiry.

In Oxford he channelled his energies into the college, university administration, his pupils and his family. But it was in Argyll that the inquisitive boy in my father, never far below the surface, seemed to bloom most happily. He approached every aspect of our shared lives there with a resolute determination to have fun, and to give it. Whether the task was mounting a fishing expedition, building bonfires (he had strong pyromaniac urges), or organising a scratch game of cricket on the beach with a broken oar and a sock full of sand, my father always brought with him a sense of occasion, a *brio* that was intoxicating. He was often the prime mover in our childish pursuits: if there was a burn to be dammed, a rhododendron to be demolished or a sand rampart to be built against the marauding redcoats, he was always there to co-ordinate the troops and, wherever possible, compound the mischief.

Scotland provided an antidote to the rigours of our parents' Oxford lives. After a term spent wrestling with Peel and Proust, Dad was only too happy to wrestle sheep and immerse himself in the mysteries of ovine obstetrics. I have a vision of him, leaning on his stick and wearing one of any number of preposterous and ancient hats, casting an eye over the ruffianly flock of blackface ewes he referred to, with heavy irony, as his 'woolly fortunes'.

Dad immersed himself in Argyll life with the same determination he brought to his scholarship. The quarry on our fishing trips were not so much the trout (although he was the most elegant of fishermen) as adventures in shared fellowship. Dinner parties in Achaglachgach would often culminate by Dad suggesting, with a twinkle, that we load up with nets and whisky and go down to the loch for some splash netting, a bizarre sport which involved all members of the party leaping into the water, fully clothed, and shouting. Or, if the water was particularly cold, screaming. As I recall we never caught a thing, except Dad's infectious laugh floating across the water.

When Kate and I were ten and eight years old, and Magnus was not much older than my own baby son is now, Mum and Dad took us out of school for six glorious months to educate us themselves in Argyll while my father took a sabbatical to work on editing the Farrington diaries. A strict academic *régime* was imposed, at least in theory, but I recall those months as a series of family expeditions loosely termed 'environmental studies' which meant exploring every inch of the landscape, from the islands, to the birds to nautical knots and, of course, the life cycle of the blackfaced sheep. He loved to read to us aloud, most memorably from P.G. Wodehouse – he would spot the joke several paragraphs ahead and become convulsed with laughter in anticipation.

Dad taught us all, all his life, gently, and with boundless good humour. I don't feel we were ever pressured in any particular direction, although it was surely no coincidence that we all read Modern History, and all at Cambridge. He adored Oxford, but he would not have us walk the ground he had already trodden. He believed deeply in the benefits of exploration, and delicately but emphatically prodded us always to look in the unexpected direction, to fish in unlikely pools, to cast upriver and against the wind. Having now met and talked with so many of my father's former pupils, I discover that literally hundreds of people were inspired by the same methods, of which we were, perhaps, the luckiest beneficiaries.

If enthusiasm was the quality most highly prized by my father, then laughter and love of friends were the others. Dad also had that rare talent, a wit that could be irreverent but never mocking, except towards himself.

He made friends with consummate ease and, once made, he never lost them. He loved to entertain, and he insisted on keeping an open mind, an open door and an open bottle for whoever might chance along. In his company, people suddenly found themselves to be more amusing and remarkable than they had ever quite realised. His extrovert nature often bubbled over into delicious farce: every Hogmanay he would, after much unnecessary persuasion, juggle three raw eggs. The eggs would fly higher and higher until his giggles became too much, his timing evaporated, and he would send two eggs crashing to the floor and, as a finale, whisk out his *skein-'dhu* and try to skewer the third. I don't know if any of you have ever tried to stop a raw flying egg with a small sharp dagger. It isn't possible, but the effect is truly remarkable.

He was particularly solicitous of our friends, most of whom promptly became his. Perhaps it was partly a reflection of his childhood, which was not always a happy one, that made my father so attuned to the needs of the young and the agonies of adolescence, so ready to put one at ease with wisdom and sympathy.

Watching my father dance Highland reels was an unforgettable sight. Arms akimbo, and emitting strange whooping noises, he would whirl his partner around with great panache, graceful courtesy and studied incompetence. In fact, my father knew only too well how to dance those complicated jigs, which can leave the unwary feeling hopelessly humiliated and in mortal danger, but it was part of his style to feign ineptitude in order to make his invariably nervous partner feel more confident.

That was, I think, my father's approach to the Big Dance: he could not bear to behold a wallflower. Life, like the loch on those hilarious summer nights, was something you plunged yourself into. He relished people with natural talent and confidence, his star pupils, but even more, perhaps, he loved to help those who would otherwise have held back. In a way he made it his mission to pluck wallflowers and bring them, with generosity and tact, into the dance.

My father's own dance ended far too soon. Long before the music stopped. There was so much that he was looking forward to doing, as a historian, as Principal of Hertford, as a grandfather. But there was also so much that he had already done, for us, for others and for himself. His was a crowded life, a merry reel, full of thought, laughter and profound affections, and an enduring love in marriage, that spanned forty years.

There is a poem, by the eighteenth-century poet Thomas Mordaunt, which my father often quoted. It is about enthusiasm, optimism and purpose; the belief, even the premonition, that every hour should be made to count as if it were the last; and the truth that a man's own history is, in the end, the one that matters:

> Sound, sound the clarion, fill the fife!
> Throughout the sensual world proclaim,
> One crowded hour of glorious life
> Is worth an age without a name.

Peter Cook (1937–1995)
satirist

by Alan Bennett
(writer)

Memorial Service at Hampstead Parish Church,
London, on 1 May 1995

It is thirty-five years, almost to the day, since I first set eyes on Peter, at lunch in a restaurant, I think on Goodge Street, with Dudley Moore and Jonathan Miller, the meeting arranged by John Bassett, whose idea it was that we should all work together writing the revue that turned into *Beyond the Fringe*. Having already written while still an undergraduate a large slice of the two West End shows *Pieces of Eight* and *One Over the Eight*, Peter was quite prosperous and it showed. He dressed out of Sportique, an establishment – gents' outfitters wouldn't really describe it – at the west end of Old Compton Street, the premises I think now occupied by the Café España.

There hadn't really been any men's fashions before 1960 – most of the people I knew dressed in sports coat and flannels, as some of us still do – but when I saw Peter he was wearing a shortie overcoat, not quite bum-freezer jacket, narrow trousers, winkle-picker shoes and a silk tie with horizontal bars across it. But what was most characteristic of him, and which remained constant throughout his life, regardless of the sometimes quite dramatic changes in his physical appearance, was that he was carrying, as he always seemed to be carrying, a large armful of newspapers. He had besides a book on racing form, and I remember being impressed not merely that this was someone who bet on horses but that here was someone who knew how to bet on horses, and indeed had an account at a book-maker's. But it was the newspapers that were the clue to him. He was nurtured by newspapers, and there's a sense that whatever he wrote or extemporised, which he could at that time with a fluency so effortless as to make us all feel in differing degrees costive, was a kind of mould or fungus that grew out of the literally yards of newsprint that he daily digested. Newspapers mulched his talents and he remained loyal to them all his life; and when he died they repaid some of that loyalty.

In those days I never saw him reading a book. I think he thought that most books were a con or at any rate a waste of time. He caught the drift of books though, sufficient for his own purposes, namely jokes, picking up enough about Proust, for instance, to know that he suffered from asthma and couldn't breathe very well; he decided in the finish, according to Peter, that if he couldn't do it very well he wouldn't do it at all, and so died – this is one of the gems from the monologue in *Beyond the Fringe* about the miner who wanted to be a judge but didn't have the Latin. How Proust had managed to work his way into the sketch I can't remember, because it was less of a sketch than a continuing saga which each night developed new extravagances and surrealist turns, the mine at one point invaded by droves of Proust-lovers, headed by the scantily clad Beryl Jarvis. Why the name Beryl Jarvis should be funny I can't think. But it was and plainly is.

In those days Peter could tap a flow of mad verbal inventiveness that nothing could stem; not nerves, not drink, not embarrassment, not even the very occasional lack of response from the audience. He would sit there in his old raincoat and brown trilby, rocking slightly as he wove his ever more exuberant fantasies, on which, I have to admit, I looked less admiringly then than I do in retrospect. I had the spot in the show immediately following Peter's monologue, which was scheduled to last five minutes or so but would often last for fifteen, when I would be handed an audience so weak from laughter that I could do nothing with them.

Slim and elegant in those days, he was also quite vain, sensing instinctively as soon as he came into a room where the mirror was and casting pensive sidelong glances at it while stroking his chin, as if checking up on his own beauty. He also knew which was his best side for photographers.

There were limits to his talents; one or two things he thought he could do well he actually couldn't do for toffee. One was an imitation of Elvis Presley and another was to ad lib Shakespeare. Both were deeply embarrassing, though of course Peter was immune to embarrassment – that was one of his great strengths.

What makes speaking about him a delicate task is that he was intolerant of humbug: detecting it (and quite often mistakenly), he would fly into a huge self-fuelling rage which propelled him into yet more fantasy and even funnier jokes. So it's hard to praise him to his face – even his dead face – that quizzical smile, never very far away, making a mockery of the sincerest sentiments. So he would be surprised, I think, to be praised for his strength of character, but in his later years when some of his talent for exuberant invention deserted him I never heard him complain. It must have been some consolation that the younger generation of comic writers and performers drew inspiration from him, but he never bragged about that either. Nor did he resent that Dudley had gone on to success in Hollywood and he hadn't. The only regret he regularly voiced was that at the house we rented in Fairfield, Connecticut, in 1963 he saved David Frost from drowning.

In later years I saw him quite seldom, though if he'd seen something you'd done on television he'd generally telephone, ostensibly to congratulate you, but actually to congratulate you on having got away with it again. There's a scene in *Brideshead Revisited* where Charles Ryder has an exhibition of his worthy but uninspired paintings which is a great success. Then Anthony Blanche turns up, who knows exactly what's what. 'My dear,' he says, 'let us not expose your little imposture before these good, plain people; let us not spoil their moment of pleasure. But we know, you and I, that this is all t-terrible t-tripe.' And sometimes what Peter was telephoning about had been tripe and sometimes it hadn't, but you didn't mind because there's always a bit of you that thinks it is anyway, and it was to that part of you that Peter spoke. And since he did it without rancour or envy it was a great relief. I suppose it was partly this that made him in his latter days such an unlikely father-figure for younger performers.

In the press coverage of his death one could detect a certain satisfaction, the feeling that he had perhaps paid some sort of price for his gifts, had died in the way the press prefer funny men to die, like Hancock and Peter Sellers, sad and disappointed. I don't know that that was true, and it certainly would not have found much favour with Peter. Trying to sum him up in his latter years – the television in the afternoon, the chat shows, the golf in Bermuda – one thinks of one of the stock characters in an old-fashioned Western: Thomas Mitchell, say, in John Ford's *Stagecoach*, the doctor who's always to be found in the saloon and whose allegiance is never quite plain. Seldom sober, he is cleverer than most of the people he associates with, spending his time playing cards with the baddies but taking no sides. Still, when the chips are down, and slightly to his own surprise, he does the right thing. But there is never any suggestion that, having risen to the occasion, he is going to mend his ways in any permanent fashion. He goes on much as ever down the path to self-destruction, knowing that redemption is not for him – and it is this that redeems him.

As for us, his audience, we are comforted by the assurance that there is a truer morality than the demands of convention, that this is a figure from the parables, a publican, a sinner, but never a Pharisee. In him morality is discovered far from its official haunts, the message of a character like Peter's being that a life of complete self-indulgence, if led with the whole heart, may also bring wisdom.

Sir Fred Warner (1918–1995)
diplomat

by Lady Antonia Fraser
(historian and biographer)

*Funeral Service at St Mary's Church, Stoke Abbott,
Dorset, on 6 October 1995*

When I think of Fred – and lately I've thought about him, and his family, all the time – I have an immediate image. It's a picture with two panels to it, both starring Fred. In one of them, he's racing up a mountain, his long, long legs emerging from his incredibly short shorts; way ahead of us all, energetic, enthusiastic. Like pilgrims, we pant to follow him far below. In the other panel, Fred is digging down with equal enthusiasm, planting a tree or shrub, as I remember him doing so often and so happily, at Laverstock and Inkpen. He is however still wearing those shorts and little else.

But I should say that when I first met Fred, June 1953, coronation year, he was attired like a Regency buck; and that was definitely his other sartorial side, an elegance unsurpassed. Like Hamlet as described by Horatio, 'the glass of fashion and the mould of form'. Except that Fred was nothing like Hamlet, he was much more fun. And that was the point. I met him at a lunch given by George Weidenfeld, at which it was understood that George was looking me over for a job. The idea was that I should shine in conversation, display wit and sparkle, and if I did, I would get the job. I was twenty, just finishing at Oxford, and hardly knew London. I was intensely nervous. Somehow Fred knew this. So throughout lunch, he regaled us all with the most extraordinary tale about taking his nephew to the coronation naval review at Spithead, something which involved Wodehousian mishaps of all sorts. In short it was Fred who made the lunch party full of wit and sparkle. The results of this were twofold. George decided I was a good egg, although I had not opened my mouth. And I decided, I want to see a lot more of this amazing man.

I'm very glad to say that I did, over the next forty years, in many different situations, and many different countries: I did see a lot of that amazing man. Even when Fred was abroad, he would suddenly come across with a letter, recreating a completely different world, as it were Laos, with that immediacy and vitality of which he was a master. With his great love of sightseeing, he was of course always the perfect person to arrange an expedition; not only something exotic, but even a humble expedition to Antwerp, when he was in Brussels and I needed to see a crucial portrait of Mary Queen of Scots. I asked him if he knew anyone in Antwerp. 'One doesn't *know* people in Antwerp,' he wrote back. 'All the Belgians I have approached were amazed by the suggestion. Fortunately there are many nuns in Belgium who were acquainted with Mary Queen of Scots. There are some in Bruges who remember her exceptionally well and I will take you to see them.'

But of course the high point was a visit to Japan, and unforgettable memories of dinner parties, picnics, swims in lakes and of course hikes up mountains for the unwary. Only by this time, Fred had turned into Fred 'n' Simone, and by degrees Fred 'n' Simone and Valentine and Orlando and of course Alexa.

It was a wonderful chance for Hugh and myself that Fred and Simone and Alexa were able to come to Christmas in Scotland when Valentine was on the way. Simone had just heard that being eight months pregnant meant – to her amazement and Fred's – that they could not go on some typically exotic and adventurous Christmas journey: Bangkok, the moon, whatever. So Scotland it was. I say it was wonderful because it enabled us to witness first hand the immense joy that Fred was experiencing in his new family life. For with Alexa there, he had an instant family life which got him ready for the arrival of the two boys he loved so much, and of whom he was so immensely proud. In our rumbustious household, Fred's tenderness towards the little Alexa's happiness was typical of that side of him, which made him shortly afterwards such a marvellous and true father.

As for Simone, I will offer just one vignette of Fred's feeling and admiration for her – her spirit which matched and complemented his own. In Scotland, we were driving on a winding road in a remote glen with a mountain on one side and a chasm on the other. Simone – never mind the advanced pregnancy – was driving with her usual panache; she was also singing – with the same panache. As we came round the corner – we *were* in the middle of nowhere – a post van hurtled towards us on the wrong side of the road. Without turning a golden hair, or even missing a note of her song, Simone simply swung across, avoided the chasm and, still singing, drove imperturbably on. We had missed death by a whisker. In the back, Fred and I were too shaken to speak. Until Fred whispered to me: 'Now you see what I married her for.'

I have stressed the wit, the elegance and the sense of adventure. But there was of course an extremely serious side to Fred, which was his profound patriotism. Fred loved his country. Was it patriotism which animated his love of nature and conservation? The desire to plant trees: something his family are commemorating? Or was it the other way round? At our last lunch together in late July, we argued about protected tigers taking human lives versus the extinction of the species, you know the sort of thing. Fred, in high spirits, defended the tigers, in order to tease me. So the next day I sent him a cutting about some pumas in California which were marauding and eating inhabitants. No one dared shoot them since it was against the law.

Antonia, that was shocking news you gave me about the California cougars [he wrote]. But worse happenings are afoot. I learnt recently that a group of carnivorous Giant Pandas has been uncovered somewhere in China. Apparently maddened by local shortages of bamboo shoots, which have been overcropped by Chinese restaurants, they have taken to killing ducks and goats. Surely it is only a short step from this to eating Sir Fitzroy Maclean or Lady Egremont on their wanderings. Yours apprehensively, Fred.

Patriotism in Fred also led to a strong sense of service. This expressed itself first in the navy, and later in the Foreign Office and the European Parliament, as well as other ventures including the National Trust, and Anglo-Japanese relations. What I always felt lay at the bottom of this was not so much worldly ambition but a real wish to serve and help his country. Perhaps it was rooted in his boyhood and his early life in the navy. At our last meeting, we had a long talk about the navy because I had been to the *Fighting Téméraire* exhibition at the National Gallery. Fred, a week before he died, was amazingly and characteristically erudite about the early nineteenth-century navy and the changes in his own day.

At the sight of *The Fighting Téméraire*, that great and noble ship being tugged away into the sunset, inevitably I had thought of Fred. Turner famously wrote of his sunsets: 'Extinction follows.' But that is not true and can never be true of Fred. He's gone up one of his mountains ahead of us and we shall never ever forget him.

Sir Fred Warner (1918–1995)
diplomat

by Robert Kee
(writer and broadcaster)

Memorial Service at St Peter's Church, Kensington
Park Road, London, on 26 February 1996

Freddie he was, as I first knew him, when we both first went up to
Magdalen nearly sixty years ago, and the same Freddie exactly he
always was, even when he also became Fred – even *Sir* Fred –
when, after many gaps in our acquaintance. I was again lucky enough
from time to time to enjoy his marvellous, intelligent, friendly,
humorous company

Every time that happened – and I think many people who saw
him only from time to time will have had this experience – it was
instantly as if one had been seeing him a lot *all* the time. And this
was a relief because though 'fragmented' is not a term one could
possibly use about such a stylishly consistent and integrated personality as Fred, his life certainly was one lived in many compartments.

This was partly because of the nature of his career; but also
perhaps partly, I think, because of something in his own nature too.

For all the engaging openness that was the essence of his delightful
friendship, his wonderful sharing of his intelligence, curiosity,
enthusiasm, knowledge and sense of fun – was it just the career
compartments that made there seem sometimes something a little
elusive about his personality?

This was in fact part of what made him attractive. Fred fitted no stereotype. Certainly you'd be mad to try to describe him as 'a reserved character' but he did have great private reserves, as powerful as his wonderful spontaneous empathy, and in his disciplined way he could keep these reserves to himself for as long as he wanted. But, goodness, how much at the same time he did give too!

When he came up to Magdalen at the age of nineteen in 1937, for his fellow-freshmen he certainly had some air of mystery about him at first − momentarily disconcerting almost. Momentarily.

Where *we* might talk of the Sadler's Wells opera he had actually been at the Met. in New York the week before (his mother was American). Where *we* might have been taken to the châteaux of the Loire and seen Chartres, Freddie, already bilingual in French, had two years before visited every Gothic cathedral of importance between Abbeville and Salzburg on a car journey to Austria he'd planned himself. He'd regularly travelled alone across Europe to take a small boat from Syracuse to Valletta in Malta where his stepfather was a Royal Navy captain. (Fred's father had also been in the navy and had been killed in the First World War before Fred was born.) In Valletta Freddie had frequently dined with a hostess who'd danced with the Prince of Wales, and in England he'd learned all about Freddie Ayer and logical positivism. In England too in his beloved West Country − where last 6th October the darkened hills and swirling black rain clouds mourned him in the wild winds − he had in the 1930s been cutting a dashing dancing figure at country house balls, dressed in the short jacket, gold buttons, boiled shirt, white tie and kid gloves of a Dartmouth naval cadet.

More awe-inspiring still: while we fancied we knew something about the Spanish Civil War, he had actually been a midshipman on a British cruiser anchored off Barcelona as the Communists there turned bloodily on their fellow-Republicans of the POUM.

However, his sophistication and knowledge of the world were already a natural part of his presence. They were worn stylishly but not arrogantly − and with a generosity that made him want to share them with friends in the joint pursuit of further interest and pleasure. He and his great friend Oliver Breakwell became for us enlivening mentors in that pursuit.

(Stern, sometimes, of course: 'You really must take this dreadful picture off the wall'; or: 'You're listening to those Scarlatti sonatas far too much.' But much laughter too.)

Fred had loved the navy and viewed it with satisfaction and pride, but he had got himself out of it because he saw such satisfaction as too limited for the way he wanted to live. As he put it: 'much wider horizons were opening up for me.' There's a whole great world out there, he thought, that is much more interesting, and he started to explore it by going to a university. He never stopped. He was to have been in Antarctica this week.

When war came he made a point of not rejoining the regular navy but the Volunteer Reserve because he knew he could get out of that easily at the end of the war, *if* he survived – which he very nearly didn't. His armed merchant cruiser was sunk in 1940 off Northern Ireland and he went into the sea – elegantly of course; he had been asleep when the torpedo hit and was wearing black silk pyjamas.

A routine listing of Fred's versatile public activities and achievements is something of a fanfare: the foreign postings: Moscow, Rangoon, Athens, Laos, NATO in Brussels, UN in New York, Japan; six years as Conservative Member of the European Parliament; serious West Country farmer speaking perfect French, perfect Italian, excellent German, fluent Greek, fluent Russian and some Japanese which he read and in which he could make some polite conversation though he always made a point of saying he didn't speak it; Oxford lectures on Japanese finance made the basis for a book of high distinction and scholarship; business directorships in companies in need of his bright powers of intellectual analysis; administrative posts – in some of which he was happy, in some less so – but this is all just great sound – and only a little fury – signifying his public activity. What was really important about Fred was Fred himself – the extraordinary qualities of his personality such as listed by one of his dearest friends in a letter to Simone – 'the virtuosity of his intellect . . . his marvellous physical and mental energy . . . his wonderful capacity for enjoyment . . . and the store of an ever curious mind, on which there was a base of deep seriousness and commitment to the highest values'.

Fred wrote, not long ago, that his whole life had been in the main an intensely happy one. I think he had an innate gift for happiness, though he couldn't perhaps always reconcile it with peace. And when in Laos, he'd had an initiation of sorts into Buddhism which did seem to help him find a peace he could reconcile with the intellectual excitements of his mind.

But there is no doubt about what made the most important contribution to his happiness.

When leaving Laos he characteristically gave an enormous leaving party to which everyone who was everyone – the Laos royal family, the lot – was of course invited. He was ready waiting, alone, for them to arrive, not perhaps without some anxiety at the thought of receiving so many hundreds of guests, when he was told a holy man had come to the door to see him and wanted to tell him about his, Fred's, future. Typically, instead of saying as most would have done in the circumstances, 'Oh for heaven's sake, this is hardly the moment, tell him to come back tomorrow', Fred saw him and one of the things he asked him was: would he, Fred, ever get married? Yes, said the holy man unhesitatingly, to a blonde lady much younger.

Fred had already once met Simone. Years before that, his inexhaustible curiosity had ensured that he had become one of the first members of the Interplanetary Society. He met Simone again, a year or two after leaving Laos, at the end of the sixties. It was a time when much talk of further exploration of space was in the news. On the day she told him she was pregnant he told her not only how incredibly happy this made him, but that nothing in life had ever made him so happy before. A little later he added: 'I do have to say, however, that while at this moment I can think of nothing more exciting in life than to be a prospective father, if asked tomorrow to join a new team going into outer space I would have to go.'

Valentine was born. There was no more talk of wanting to go into outer space when Orlando was on the way. To Fred's great love for, and sense of pride in, his two sons and his dear stepdaughter, Alexa, his curiosity now had to take second place – though of course it could now be shared with them: Simone once came into a room where Fred had been telling, I think, Valentine one of the great stories from Homer. Which he'd done so poignantly that she found them both in tears.

And what about Fred and what Walter Pater called 'the last curiosity'?

Everyone who had any contact with Fred from the time he'd learned that he only had a very limited time to live, and had made up his mind to make the most of life throughout that time as he had always done, will know and never forget what an amazingly extending experience it was to see or hear him then.

Simone has a wonderful photograph of Fred, at the top of his form and looking in the prime of life, which was in fact taken on a train going to Scotland for a great party for her god-daughter only three weeks before he was going to die. Papers are all over the table in front of him, including the *Financial Times*, and he has a magazine in his hands, but he is looking straight at the camera, upright as ever, with a happy smile, tie slightly awry, and his right hand raised to his forehead, perhaps to keep out the light.

When Simone, who took this picture, showed it to him a few days later he said, 'Well, you see the irony, don't you?'

'What do you mean?' she said. 'You're reading a magazine which you don't usually do?'

'No,' he said. 'The salute: *Morituri te salutant* – those about to die salute you.' (The cry of the Roman gladiator.)

Fred, Freddie, we salute *you*.

Molly Keane (1904–1996)
writer

by James Roose-Evans
(theatre director and writer)

*Funeral Service at St Paul's Church, Ardmore, Ireland,
on 26 April 1996*

The last time I saw Molly was a few months before she died. I had driven over to Ardmore for lunch. Dressed in greys, blues and silvers, she was at her prettiest and most flirtatious.

'Darling,' she said, 'I don't want to be like a heavy rosary around your neck!'

I remember accompanying her to the funeral of her friend Patricia Coburn. The church was very dark and gloomy, and the service lugubrious. As we came out, she clutched my arm, saying, 'Darling, promise when my time comes it won't be like that!'

And I said, 'Molly, when your time comes I promise that the church will be ablaze with candles and flowers in celebration of your life!'

And so it is for, as you can see, Sally and Virginia have filled every space with flowers and lit many candles. Although there was much sadness, pain and disappointment in Molly's life yet, as Blake observed, 'Joy and woe are woven fine', and so in Molly's life there was also much joy, friendship and, above all, fun!

Perhaps that last is the key word.

Once I went with her on a visit to Mount Melleray Monastery and there in the shop was the nearly blind Brother Gerard, then

ninety, a decade older than Molly. When he realised who it was
he greeted her with such delight that everyone in the shop turned
to stare. He then insisted on taking us on a tour of the abbey, but
it was in the smaller of the two churches, in front of a statue of the
Blessed Virgin Mary, that, slipping his arm around Molly's waist,
he said, 'Oh, Mrs Keane, to think what fun we'll have in heaven!'

I do not doubt but that there is laughter today in that country
beyond the stars.

Richard Cobb (1917–1996)

Professor of Modern History, Oxford; Fellow of Balliol College, Oxford, 1962–72

by Maurice Keen

(Fellow of Balliol College, Oxford, 1961–72)

Funeral Service at St Helen's Church, Abingdon, Oxfordshire, on 4 May 1996

We are here today to say goodbye to Richard Cobb, and to give thanks to God for his life. I say, to give thanks for his *life*. Here among so many of his friends, I am not going to dilate on its marks of achievement, the Chair of Modern History at Oxford, the honorary fellowships and doctorates, the CBE. Though of course these things brought gratification to Richard, as they would to anyone, I do not think that – with the exception perhaps of the Légion d'honneur – he cared about them in any profound sense. They were not what mattered to him about his living.

I want, though, to stress that word '*life*', in a different way. I remember Richard coming into lunch in Balliol about eighteen months ago, just after his discharge from the John Radcliffe Hospital – where Bill Williams, coming in to visit him, overheard the nurse's immortal remark: 'Richard, you must try to drink more.' Richard had done his best to follow the nurse's instructions and was talking to a group of us: 'I'm not worried by death,' he said, 'but what I simply can't imagine is not being alive.' Indeed, it is impossible to imagine Richard except alive, because he had a unique and exuberant gift of living, and with that a unique and exuberant capacity for sharing that gift with others. 'Don't forget to stress my frivolity,' he told Philip Mansel: in saying that he at once did himself justice and injustice. He had indeed an unmatched sense of the absurd, but there was very much more to it than that. He knew how important it was for people to see and taste the fun and zest of life – of all of life, of scholarship, of reading in the archives, of good meals and good tippling, of exploring the streets and the people of Paris or Leeds or London, of gossip. And he knew how to convey that taste and zest to those with him. He was never dull company; in weal or in woe – and Richard knew plenty of woe as well as weal – he was an enlivening force.

One reason why Richard was never dull company was that with him the unforeseen happened so easily, especially, of course, when, as the Irish put it, there was drink taken: you might find yourself, as his friend John Romilly did in Paris in the 1930s, 'chasing a mythical camel at 2 a.m. round the Place du Panthéon'; or as I, on a Balliol balcony beside him, listening to him as he addressed, in faultless French and in the assumed *persona* of Charles de Gaulle, a *clientèle* drawn by curiosity from the kebab stalls of St Giles (for me I must admit that is only the tip of the iceberg of a saga of hazards and *glissades*). A much more important reason why he was never dull company was that he was such a meticulous observer and such a wonderful raconteur. He could evoke eloquently the office atmosphere of the British consulate and the precision of the intonation of the official saying to him, 'Mr Cobb, in Vienna people do not just *lose* their passports'; he could recall exactly the civic insignia weighing down the Mayor of Hastings as a guest of honour at the banquet in Rouen to celebrate the ninth century of the victory of William the Conqueror, and the beads of sweat starting from his face as he was plied with yet another calvados. There were so many scenes that were favourite master-pieces of re-creation, from Shrewsbury, from the army, from Aberystwyth – above all from Paris, scenes of bathos and of pathos, of tragedy, high comedy and low farce, with which he delighted us. His breadth of reading too, and his intimate knowledge of things and people – especially of French things and people past and present – seemed inexhaustible. That made him a great hand at monologue; for the same reason his monologues were never boring.

Richard was a passionate person, warm-blooded, generous, quickly and easily moved – be it to anger or laughter or to sympathy in trouble. That often made him, in the management of his own affairs, too quick, thoughtless – especially over money. Generous and open-hearted to a fault, he was incapable equally of sustained wealth or sustained stealth, and very capable of infuriating the pompous, the protocolaire – and bank managers. In denunciation his anger could positively cascade. Richard was as prone as the rest of us to err, as he was more than free in admitting, but he was quicker than almost anyone I have known to forgive. And of one of the deadly sins he was I think almost incapable: that which is called *accidie*, self-absorbed melancholy. That was why, wherever he went, and however he outraged, he always drew friends, in troops: he was never depressant. I only knew him from the time he came to Balliol in 1962; but this body of us here is testimony that it was so everywhere, in the army in the war, at Aberystwyth and Manchester and Leeds and in France, just as it was at Worcester and Merton and Balliol and through all the Oxford which he came so to appreciate and which came so to treasure him.

Above all Richard was perpetually interested in people, alive or dead: sometimes it could seem that he hardly noticed the difference. That was the chief secret of his greatness and of his individuality as an historian. Curiosity, he told us, was important for the historian, 'the enjoyment of gossip, the desire to read other people's letters, a reasonable degree of cynicism'. So was imagination and a degree of intelligence – but not much, he added. Above all things, though, what was vital was sympathy, and here I must use his own words.

Perhaps the most important requirement of a historian is to feel sympathy . . . we are fortunate, for we are dealing with human beings, albeit dead ones, not with concepts but with individuals: and we would not be much good if we could not *abide* the (dead) people we are attempting to live with: we are better at our job if we like them, better still if we feel affection for them. Even rulers are deserving of *some* sympathy. And for historians of popular history, I mean for the history of the poor, the ordinary, the obscure, the unfamous, the hopeless, the underprivileged, but *never* unimportant, for that sympathy is an absolutely essential attitude.

To this deeply humane principle, that even if the historian has to be impartial he must never be indifferent, Richard was consistently true and it made him a unique figure. As Patrick Wormald, who was an undergraduate at Balliol in the sixties when Richard was a tutor, put it in a letter to me, this was why 'he will be counted among the great scholars of the century, and (still more) one of the immortal personalities of our profession.'

Patrick said another thing in the same letter. 'He was a phenomenon: the sort of presence whose departure can only leave a large hole in the world he so enlivened.' As we contemplate that hole, that gap that is there for all of us, our hearts go out above all to Margaret, his wife of thirty-four years, and to his children, Nicky, Richard, William and Lucy. Married bliss, as that is normally thought of, Richard could not have borne. It would have suffocated him to have his slippers warmed every night, and besides, on too many nights the slippers would have been toasted to cinders before he came home. Margaret brought him something that was much more important than that and that was vital to him, without which he would not have achieved what he did: partnership with someone who was very like him – who could share his joy in his second French identity, and much else too – but who was also very different from him – and he needed difference – partnership underpinned by dauntless, feckless, loyal love. There I must stop: blessing on you, Margaret, and your children in this sad time, and blessing, Richard, on the memory of you and thanksgiving for the life you gave us.

Sir Kingsley Amis (1922–1995)
writer

by Martin Amis
(writer)

*Memorial Service at St Martin-in-the-Fields Church,
London, on 22 October 1996*

Good afternoon and thank you all very much for coming. I'm going
to begin with a couple of brief extracts from my father's forthcoming
book about usage: *The King's English*. This little section is called
'Gorged-snake construction'. Gorged-snake construction happens
when the supposed writer can't be bothered to put his rag-bag of
facts into any logical order. Here is Kingsley's parody of it:

> Briton Chris Mankiewitz, twenty-six, has been named to lead Eng-
> land's soccer squad against Ruritania next month.
>
> The Warsaw born father-of-two said at his recently rebuilt
> £150,000 Deptford home, 'My attractive blonde wife Samantha,
> twenty-four, and I are just over the moon with the news.'
>
> Success has come just in time for the whiskered former schoolboy
> hurdler champion star of Clapton Occident's injury-stricken squad.
>
> The much-photographed hat-trick specialist and avid sports-car
> driver, a familiar local figure in his blood-red Halberstadt D-VII . . .
>
> 'Looks like we are out of the woods for a bit,' laughed the tall dark
> sun-worshipper as he dubbined with his own hands the boots that . . .

Here is a section called '*Déjà vu*':

> This expression has perhaps been done to death by now. I certainly
> hope so. Its original application was to a transient psychological state,

not uncommon among those under about forty, in which the subject feels that he has seen before some place where he has provably never been in his life. The journalistic contribution has been to apply this feeling to some event or situation a person *has* witnessed before; it's just another way of saying that, for instance, a governmental apology for one thing is reminiscent of the same government's apology for another. This added to the world's stock of verbal garbage but it also provided the needy with a useful and quite posh looking alternative to 'This is where we came in'.

I read *The King's English* soon after Kingsley's death and it was an enormous relief to me to hear my father's voice. In the last weeks of his life Kingsley was suffering from, among other things, nominal aphasia, loss of speech. He was capable of formulating only commonplaces or tautologies. You'd ask him how he was and he'd say, 'I feel a bit you know.' This sounded very strange coming from the most articulate man I have ever known; since when did Kinglsey let others speak for him? Anyone who has the slightest acquaintance with him or his work will feel the force of that terrible delegation.

You'll notice that this memorial occasion is pretty well entirely secular. But Kingsley's relationship with the Christian God was not frictionless as I was reminded by the Reverend Nicholas Hilton who welcomed us to his church today. In 1962 the Russian poet Yevtushenko asked my father, in King's Chapel, Cambridge, 'You atheist?' and Kingsley replied, 'Well yes, but it's more that I hate him.'

He explored this disposition most fully in the novel *The Anti-Death League*. But it is also beautifully encapsulated in the poem 'A.E.H.', where Kingsley emulated Housman, using a light verse rhythm, to tell the mournful tale of a soldier's loss of faith.

> Flame the westward skies adorning,
> Leaves no like on holt or hill;
> Sounds of battle joined at morning
> Wane and wander and are still.

> Past the standards, rent and muddied,
> Past the careless heaps of slain,
> Stalks a redcoat who, unbloodied,
> Weeps with fury, not from pain.

Wounded lads, went to renew them
Death and surgeons cross the shade,
Still there cries, hug darkness to them;
All at last in sleep are laid.

All save one who nightlong curses
Wounds imagined more than seen.
Who in level tones rehearses
What the facts of wounds must mean.

Kingsley, I think, wrote very well about dreams with an alert and
wary precision. He knew that dreams were elaborate jokes played
on the dreamer, and he knew too that dreams provide the only
sanctuary where the dead can visit us and where they can rediscover
their vigour. At first I used to dream about my father dying or, at
any rate, ailing. Very soon though he grew younger and after a
while he fully reassumed his paternal role of protector and rescuer.
Now it is all in a night's work for Kingsley to flip a few polar bears
over his shoulder and then come thundering through the hostiles
on his charger to lift me on to the saddle. What happens is that the
patient in the hospital bed, 'the old devil', recedes and the whole
man emerges. This is what will happen in general memory. It is a
process which this afternoon we have acknowledged and hastened.

We are now going to listen to one of Kingsley's famous imitations
of Franklin Delano Roosevelt but this is F.D.R. with a twist,
addressing his British allies across the North Atlantic on a faulty
short-wave wireless in the dark days of World War II.

Philip Larkin once described *Lucky Jim* as 'miraculously and
intensely funny'; so it is and so was he. His humour was unbelievably
dynamic, as a man he was a great engine of comedy. He held
nothing back and in his set pieces he seemed almost to be putting
his life on the line. The F.D.R. imitation is posthumous, so I feel
I can ask him to repeat it and you need to hear it twice to get the
beauty of it and the satire of it. The tape will run a little longer this
time. You will hear the radio interviewer's incredulous laughter,
and anxious laughter, before he asks his final question. Kingsley
answers that question but in his voice I detect an inconvenienced
tone as if he is being hurried into an approximation.

Kingsley always used to say that the good opinion of posterity would be of no use to him because he wouldn't be around to enjoy it. But he is around whether he likes it or not, survived by his three children; his four grandchildren – Jessica, Jacob, Louis and Delilah – and by a fifth grandchild who couldn't make it today but will probably be along next week; survived by his fellow-practitioners, his publishers, disseminators and critics; survived by a tremendous body of work; and survived, most crucially, by his readers, the majority of whom, I believe, are also as yet unborn. Thank you all very much for coming. We will have some of Kingsley's jazz as we file out.

Nico Colchester (1946–1996)
journalist

by Robin Lane Fox
(undergraduate at Magdalen College, Oxford, 1965–9;
ancient historian and Fellow of New College)

Memorial Service at Southwark Cathedral, London,
on 13 November 1996

There are those of you here, much in our thoughts, who knew Nico for all or most of his life. Many more of you knew him in one of his later phases. Towards the end of this beautifully planned service, I feel it is for me to emphasise a cardinal fact about his remarkable character: essentially, he never changed. We all knew where we were with him, and he knew where he was with life.

I know this fact because I first met Nico in autumn 1965 in the cloisters of our Oxford college, Magdalen. At once I was amazed (should I say 'bounced'?) by the ebullience, the humour of word and gesture – one moment a debate, and the next something nearer to a cabaret turn – by the optimism, the boldness, not least the boldness of the check pattern of those shirts, the lifelong absence of serious creases in the trousers. He seemed to have little or no self-consciousness in that highly self-conscious setting. Aged nineteen, he had already relished life's inside stories, evidently the journalist in the making. He reached so easily for the Christian names of elders and betters, not all of whom perhaps immediately remembered meeting him.

At times he overreached. Before long, at an Oxford party, he

206

took it for granted that the future Professor of English Literature agreed with him that James Joyce's later writings were a con trick. The man looked a little surprised. It took a fellow-guest to point out afterwards that Nico had told this to the man whose life's work had been devoted to the genius of *Finnegans Wake*.

These overreaches were due in part to his extraordinary mental range. I have known and taught many minds since, but never one quite like his. Nico made a nonsense of that era's argument about two cultures, the arts and sciences. Already he was self-evidently the ideal editor, but only for that ideal newspaper, never published, which gives everything serious equal space.

At Oxford he chose to read Engineering, with no prior training except his own innate practicality and the value set on it in his early years at Oxford's Dragon School, always his ultimate home from home. He combined it with a degree in Economics, then too a most unusual choice, but it could as well have been English Litera-ture, which he profoundly wished to return to read as yet another degree in his sixties or seventies. He read widely, he acted well, he directed excellently: some of his most successful castings I can see here in the congregation. He was intrigued by word-play and by poetry. He wrote brilliant heroic and mock-heroic verses to friends and family, and above all he relished the modern and the recent. To me, he represented the shock of the new: T.S. Eliot, Pinter, Beckett, Ionesco. Yet he could perfectly well have read as yet another degree my own Latin and Greek, which he knew already, confirmed by his family's years in Greece, a country whose resource-fulness had always appealed to him.

But could he at that age have been a modern linguist? The great European of the future loved to massacre French. '*Frapper la route*' was always Nico for hit the road, and '*essuyer le plancher*' for wiping the floor with an opponent in an argument. He remains the only person I know to have tried to say thank you in Italian to a railway compartment of Italian travellers and caused them all to hunt ner-vously for their passports.

If he was cast down sometimes, it was only for a moment, because then, always, he was ever confident and wonderfully encouraging. Unusually for someone even of his generation, he was encouraging to female colleagues at work or in discussion as much as to men. Throughout his life ran a constant thread of winning innocence, rare among journalists, let alone those in a financial world. It was not Nico's way to be artful or even devious. He bore no grudges, and he of all people feared no guile because he meant none. In life and debate, of course, he admired seriousness, and serious argument remained his strength. He made constant ironic fun of dullness, even greyness, which could have swamped others and might have swamped him. His time at Oxford was the era of the Gnomes of Zurich, the era of grey technicians, but Nico added a new note to the theme song of Walt Disney's Seven Dwarfs: 'Heigh-ho, Heigh-ho,' he would sing each morning on leaving our household, 'as off to the labs I go.'

Above all he loved stories, stories of people, met, observed, dramatised and relished throughout life. Here he had the most singular eye. It says so much about him that what he relished was others' tenacity. He loved to tell of their determination to live on by self-imposed goals or standards, which appealed to him too because they mattered so much to them. There was ample material in his own family: his grandmother, Lady Medhurst, ever economical with the small change; his Uncle Jock, boldly fox-hunting into his eighties; but also the experts and the specialists at any level whom he met in the labs, or later in the newspapers of the world. A particular Nico speciality was the world of exiles and émigrés, holding fast to their earlier life in New York or Germany or Japan. He stood outside them but engaged profoundly with them, because he was never above them, even when they came at him from odd angles. The odd angles made the best stories, like the occasion when his Oxford Engineering tutor told him that his planned research programme was to make the roads of rubber and the car wheels of concrete, or those evenings in the Oxford University Air Squadron, where Nico quickly gained a pilot's licence, and throve on tales recycled from the group's squadron dinners. He always revelled in jargon, never more than in the squadron Mess, whose after-dinner games culminated in the dreaded 'Bomber Run'. At the very moment when the Mess was resounding to the theme music of the film *The Dam Busters*, one of Nico's colleagues (at least in

Nico's version) turned to him and said, 'Nico, Mozart wrote such wonderful marches.'

Where, we began to wonder, could he ever settle down in life? Then, twenty years ago, he brought a female visitor, someone who discreetly corrected his economics, who took that frightful French in hand, who had seen even more of the world already than Nico had, and then nearly outpaced him on the shared journeys of marriage, from Ladakh to South America. New small centres of tenacity joined the old ones. Soulages, with Fernand and then with Jerome, and Laurence's own family and above all her parents, deeply appreciative of Nico, as he of them, and of their tenacious patch in life.

From an early age he did believe in God, but in his own way. He was, however, far from sure that Jesus was quite what the Gospels had tried to say he was. There were times in his own family when he began to feel encircled, but he delighted many of us and them with this version of his father Halsey's calling to the Church. Halsey was ordained, I think I can fairly now say, after a distinguished career in intelligence work abroad. In Nico's version the bells of the country church were dying away at his father's ordination, when a dark car drew up at the gate. Three men in grey suits came out of it, walked up the church path and took their seats in the back pew. When Halsey came down the aisle, now a fully ordained minister, so Nico claimed, one of the men in suits leaned forward and muttered, 'Deep cover, Colchester.'

There was no deep cover about Nico. He loved to simplify, to make abstract argument clear and vivid to us all, sitting maybe with a cushion on his head and explaining as editor, or just as a family friend, all the complexities of the World Bank. Singularly true to his own well-formed youth, he was entirely at one with children, the supreme test of a person, both his own children and others, many of whom are here today. Perhaps they will go on to share his enduring love for *The Wind in the Willows*, the subject of Nico's most memorable stage production. Among its many charms, Nico particularly appreciated the scene in which Mole returns after a long absence to his old home, Mole End. In the Water Rat's company he revisits the forecourt with its deeply personal mementoes, the plaster busts of Garibaldi, the infant Samuel, Queen Victoria and other heroes of modern Italy. Nico appreciated the Garibaldis in our own lives, but he also had a definite touch of rattishness. Ever cheerful like the Water Rat, he was supremely able in a crisis, and an excellent man with whom to bring a darkened house back to life.

At the other end of human time I, like many of you, was looking forward to Nico as the person with whom to survey a lifetime, try to make sense of it and still look forward to something new, as yet unvisited or untried. He was an exceptional person, exceptionally gifted, whose like we will never see.

It is, however, easy for me to know how to end. I had not known him long before a shared fondness for Tennyson's 'Ulysses' emerged, that poem of a wandering hero, now old and back at home, yet still restless and supremely crunchy, in Nico's famous use of the word. Thirty years later, I still see him, as you may, between this specially adapted selection of its lines.

> Much have I seen and known; cities of men,
> And manners, climates, councils, governments,
> Myself not least, though honoured of them all.
> I am part of all that I have met, yet all
> Experience is an arch wherethrough
> Gleams an untravelled world . . .
> How dull it is to pause, to make an end . . .
> When this grey spirit's yearning in desire
> To follow knowledge like a sinking star
> Beyond the utmost bounds of human thought.
> These are my sons, my own Max and Felix,
> To whom I leave my sceptre and my isle,
> Well loved of me, discerning to fulfil
> Our labours . . .
> The lights begin to twinkle from the rocks;
> The long day wanes; the slow moon climbs; the deep
> Moans round with many voices. Come, my friends,
> 'Tis not too late to seek a newer world . . . My purpose holds
> To sail beyond the sunset and the baths
> Of all the western stars, until I die.
> It may be we shall touch the Happy Isles
> And see the great Achilles whom he knew.

Though much is taken, much abides, and though
We are not now that strength which in old days
Moved heaven and earth, that which we are, we are,
One equal temper of heroic hearts,
Made weak by time and fate, but strong in will
To strive, to seek, to find and not to yield.

Already the young Nico loved to quote that last line, but always with apt irony. For even then, he had that intelligence, humanity and singular kindness which knew that such high aims do not always come quite so easily.

Denis Compton (1918–1997)

cricketing genius

by J.J. Warr

(cricketer, and President of the MCC, 1987–8)

Memorial Service at Westminster Abbey, London,
on 1 July 1997

Denis died on April 23rd this year, which, by amazing coincidence, was the same day in the year that his great friend and contemporary, Bill Edrich, also died. It is, of course, St George's Day and also William Shakespeare's birthday – and you would need a Shakespeare to do justice to his life and career.

Known universally by his friends and admirers as 'Compo', I remember his *This is Your Life* programme, hosted by Eamonn Andrews. We all met in secret in a studio in Teddington, to be briefed on the format. Eamonn asked me what I was going to say. I said I was going to go over to him and say, 'Compo, I love your programme, *The Last of the Summer Wine!*' That put me back in the chorus with a non-speaking part.

He was born in Hendon on May 23rd 1918 and in May 1967 he announced an enormous celebration to mark his fiftieth birthday. His mother got to hear of this, phoned him and pointed out that he was only forty-nine. It must have been one of the very rare occasions when he was early for anything.

Educated at Hendon's Bell Lane Elementary School, I am sure that they didn't know there that they had a genius in their midst. He did represent the London Elementary Schools at cricket in their annual match played on the nursery grounds at Lord's. He opened the innings with a young Arthur McIntyre, later of Surrey and England. He ran Arthur out. It was the start of a great career of run-outs, culminating in his running out his brother, Leslie, in Leslie's Benefit Match at Lord's, bringing his tally for the innings to three. He was the only batsman I encountered who called you for a single and wished you good luck at the same time.

Compo left school and went on to the ground staff at Lord's. He played his first game for Middlesex in 1936 and by 1938 was saving a Test Match for England against Australia on his home ground. He also joined the staff of the Arsenal at Highbury, and it is interesting that both Denis and his brother, Leslie, stayed loyal to Middlesex and the Arsenal throughout their playing careers.

In cricket Denis scored 38,723 runs (averaging over 50), 122 centuries, took 613 wickets and, when he was looking, held 415 catches. In football he earned a Championship medal and an FA Cup winners' medal, and played numerous internationals. You have to remember that five of his peak years were denied to him owing to the war. How would his statistics have read without that?

After the war he was one of the prime figures to light up and rejuvenate a nation exhausted and strictly rationed. He was the great symbol that times were getting back to normal. In 1947 he scored 3,816 runs and 18 centuries, averaging 95.85, and from hoardings all over the country his handsome face smiled out at you, advertising Brylcreem. I have to say, though, that I didn't see too many pots of Brylcreem next to where he changed in the Middlesex dressing room.

As with all geniuses it is impossible to analyse his technique as a batsman. It was a brilliant mixture of the unexpected spiced with a large measure of showmanship and improvisation. Totally untutored, if he ever read a coaching book he must have been holding it upside down.

His bowling was a glorious concoction of good and bad. For a man of his wonderful gifts he was amazingly modest and self-effacing. His stories were all about the moments of humour and minor sporting crises. He loved relating how the late Duke of

Norfolk, gout-ridden, over fifty and with fading eyesight, had hit him for six when Compo was trying to bowl him the unplayable ball in a charity match at Arundel – though I don't suppose for a moment that he was. His Cup Final appearance began with a bad first half. The great Alex James gave him a good slug of brandy at half-time and he played the game of his life in the second half.

I am afraid he did have a reputation for being in the wrong place at the wrong time. He also had a rather archaic filing system, which consisted of stuffing all invitations on the back seat of his car and forgetting them. When he stopped playing and went into advertising, journalism and TV commentating, he told me his image was suffering because he had become boringly reliable. When Edward Heath introduced the three-day week, I asked Compo how he was going to cope. He said, 'I am not going to work an extra day for anyone.'

Of the people outside his family he most admired, top of the list would be Keith Miller, although he spent most of the time when they played cricket together trying to knock Compo's head off. Keith symbolised for Denis two of the great strands that have held cricket together: courage and chivalry. How nice that Keith has come over from Australia for this service. Two others here for whom Compo had a special admiration, which was no doubt mutual, are Lord Runcie and John Major. After the Brian Johnston memorial service here in the abbey we gathered for a reception. A stranger came up to Compo and offered to fetch him a drink. 'Don't bother,' said Compo, 'the Prime Minister is getting me one.'

Of his many clubs, he was President of Middlesex, and Honorary Life Member of MCC and the Arsenal, a member of the Royal and Ancient, a long-serving member of the Denham Golf Club and also the Saints and Sinners Club of London. How pleased he would be to see them all so well represented here today.

If he had a cavalier approach to money he was equally unimpressed with honours. His CBE was last seen acting as a temporary lead round the neck of Benjy, his Old English sheepdog.

One final thought. In the last few weeks of his life a comet appeared in the sky over Britain. It is said to appear every four thousand years. Well, Compo was a comet in his own right, and we must all pray that it isn't another four thousand years before we see another like him.

Sir Isaiah Berlin (1909–1997)
Fellow of All Souls College, Oxford, and historian of ideas

by Lord Annan
(Provost of King's College, Cambridge, 1956–66)

*Memorial Service at Hampstead Synagogue, London,
on 14 January 1998*

When I heard that Isaiah Berlin had died, I sat down and read the letters we had written each other since 1950, and he lived again. He wrote as he talked, and he was the most dazzling talker of his generation. Strangers might hardly understand a word because his tongue had to sprint to keep up with the pace of his thoughts. Ideas, similes, metaphors cascaded over each other. His talk was sustained by a fabulous memory for names, events and the motives of the particip- ants in his stories. It was like watching a pageant. As Dr Johnson said of Richard Savage: 'at no time in his life was it any part of his character to be the first of the company that desired to separate'. At New Col- lege and All Souls he talked until his exhausted guest tottered to bed, only to find Berlin sitting on the end of it, unwilling to bring the evening to an end. On the historic occasion when he called on Anna Akhmatova they talked straight through the night.

No one else was remotely like him. Of course he had charm, but he had more than that. He was a Magus, a magician when he spoke, and it was for his character and personality as much as for his published works that so many honours fell upon him. The *Evening Standard* spoke truth when it said: 'the respectful sadness that met his death and the enormous regard in which he was held shows that intellectuals can still be prized as civilising influences in Britain.' He was loved by people with whom he had nothing in common – millionaires, obscure writers, world-famous musicians, public figures and young unknown scholars to whom he listened. Whatever the circle, he civilised it; and the world is a little less civilised now that he has left it.

Generosity came naturally to him. He was never sneaky or malevolent as a critic. Indeed he tried too hard, perhaps, to avoid giving offence. 'I enjoy being able to praise,' he said. He never intrigued to meet the geniuses of his time – Freud, Einstein, Virginia Woolf, Russell, Pasternak, Stravinsky – and he had no shame in admitting that he was greatly excited when he did meet them. His oldest friends, Stuart Hampshire and Stephen Spender, were especially dear to him. Yet he had an eye for human failings and noted feet of clay, even of people he esteemed. He did not censure, but he did not condone ungentle behaviour or sexual exhibitionism. 'I feel acutely uncomfortable,' he wrote me, 'in the presence of Beaverbrook, Cherwell, Radcliffe or Driberg.' People who rejected equality as a goal were deeply unsympathetic to him. Equality had to give way often to liberty but so did liberty sometimes to equality. For instance, he thought that the price England paid for the public schools was too high.

Nicolas Nabokov accused him of liking bores too much. But then Isaiah was meticulous in obeying the obligations of a scholar. No one was ever turned away who came to him genuinely wishing to discuss a problem. To watch him at Mishkenot She'ananim in Jerusalem, spending hours with those who queued to seek his advice, was to realise that he honoured anyone in search of truth. Those who have never believed, he wrote of the days when the young Oxford philosophers met with Austin and Ayer, that they were discovering for the first time some new truth that might have profound influence upon philosophy, 'those who have never been under the spell of this kind of illusion, even for a short while, have not known true intellectual happiness'.

Very few people are able to write unforgettably about liberty. Rousseau did; John Stuart Mill did; and in our own times, Schumpeter and E.M. Forster did. But, as Forster once said of himself in a parody of Landor: 'I warmed both hands before the fire of life,

And put it out.' Isaiah made it blaze. He took the unfashionable view that liberty meant not being impeded by others. He distrusted Rousseau's and Hegel's theory of positive freedom as a perversion of common sense. To deny free will – to believe in the inevitability of an historical process; to portray man as imprisoned by the impersonal forces of history – that ran against our deepest experience. He believed the creation of the state of Israel proved that history is not predetermined. Israel owed its existence to Weizmann, yet all Weizmann's schemes were swept away by fortuitous events. And what could be less inevitable than the survival of Britain in 1940? To Berlin, the very methods that Marxists, economists and sociologists used prevented them from discovering what is at the heart of men and women. He distrusted technocrats in government and sapient reports with their self-confident proposals for restructuring institutions. That was why he did not pontificate on daily issues. Monetarism, social security schemes were not for him. He disappointed President Kennedy by not advancing views on the number needed of ICBMs.

But there was one public issue on which he left no one in doubt. Above all, Isaiah was a Jew, and never forgave those who forgot to conceal their anti-Semitism, the nastier ways of snubs, pin-pricks, acts of exclusion which we Gentiles inflict upon Jews, and in so doing defile ourselves. He was a Zionist precisely because he felt that however well Jews were treated and accepted by the country they lived in, they felt uneasy and insecure. That was why they needed a country of their own where Jews could live like other nations. As he lay dying, he declared the partition of the Holy Land was the only solution to give Palestinians rights to their land and give Israel Jerusalem as its capital with the Muslim holy places under a Muslim authority, and an Arab quarter under UN protection. He never felt the smallest difficulty in being loyal to Judah and loyal to Britain. When he worked during the war in Washington, he told American Zionists that he was the servant of the British government – but its servant, not its conscript. At any time, he could resign if he decided British policy was unforgivable. He was proud to belong to Britain, to the country which Weizmann had praised for its moderation, dislike of extremes, a humane democracy.

There was another claimant for his loyalty – Oxford. He thought he owed it a debt. He paid that debt when, against the advice of his most intimate friends, he agreed to become head of a new Oxford college. Who can doubt that it was Isaiah's personality that convinced Mac Bundy of the Ford Foundation and Isaac and Leonard Wolfson, renowned for their princely generosity, to build and endow a new college with Isaiah as President? President, not Master. The Master of Wolfson sounded to Isaiah too much like a Scottish laird, and he did not fancy himself in a kilt. Many of the chores he left to the faithful Michael Brock; but it was Isaiah who negotiated the deal with the university and strangled some dingy proposals for shackling the new place. And it was Isaiah who travelled four thousand miles to interview architects, select materials, and convince the sixty Fellows with barely a dissenting voice.

He was a man of invincible modesty. But for Henry Hardy we would never have had his collected works. He genuinely believed that he was overrated and deserved few of the honours he was given. 'I have a pathological dislike of personal publicity,' he wrote me. 'It is like a terror of bats or spiders. I am not a public figure like A.J.P. Taylor, Graham Greene, Arthur Schlesinger, or Kenneth Clark. Nor an ideologue like Tawney, Cole, Oakeshott. Perhaps not as bad as Crossman and a good many others thought me to be, a well-disposed amiable rattle.' For years he had no entry in *Who's Who*, until he found the entry form he had left lying around had been filled in by Maurice Bowra, with scandalous fictious achievements. Then he gave in.

To have lived without music would have been to him a nightmare. Unthinkable to live without Bach, unendurable without Beethoven and Schubert. He loved Verdi for the uninhibited tunes and for Verdi's hatred of aristocratic brutality and tyranny. No one, he thought, had ever played the Beethoven posthumous quartets like the Busch ensemble. He admitted that Toscanini was not the man for the thick brew of Wagner; but when one saw Toscanini as well as heard him the authority was such that, so he wrote me, 'this and this only was the truth – the intensity, the seriousness and the sublime *terribilità* totally subdued you'. Walter, Klemperer and Mahler and the luxuriant valleys of Furtwängler, yes – but Toscanini was Everest;

compared with him he said the rest were not fit to tie his shoelaces, mere Apennines covered with villas. Yet in his later years he found a friend, an intellectual as well as a profound musician, in Alfred Brendel; and he and his old friend Isaac Stern have honoured him today.

He was at his happiest in a small group of intimate friends in Oxford colleges or sitting in a corner of the Russian Tea Room on 57th Street a few blocks down from the offices of the *New York Review of Books* with Robert Silvers, Stuart Hampshire and the Lowells. In Oxford as a bachelor – in the days before the war he was always called Shaya, renowned as the most amusing young don in Oxford – in those days his door was always open. Colleagues, pupils, friends from London dropped in to gossip. He loved gossip. An election to a chair in Oxford or Cambridge would inspire him to give a dramatic performance of the proceedings. The treachery of Bloggs, the craven behaviour of Stiggins, the twitterings of the outside electors, and when it came to the vote, the *volte-face*, the defection of those you had imagined were your closest allies. Brought up to imagine that such proceedings were sacred and secret, priggish Cambridge visitors such as myself reeled.

What made these excursions into fantasy all the more enchanting was Isaiah's irrepressible sense of humour. It was not English humour. It came from the Russian part of his make-up; from Gogol, from Chekhov. He loved jokes. He loved games. Who was a hedgehog, who was a fox? What is the difference between a cad and a bounder? When others were maddened by the perverse, egoistic, self-satisfied speeches in a college meeting, Isaiah revelled in them; to him they revealed the perennial eccentricity of human beings. Let none of us, however, be deceived. The lot of human beings, he saw, was tragic. And why? They are made of crooked timber.

As the years pass, bachelor life in college becomes exhausting, and in 1956 the greatest stroke of good fortune that ever befell him occurred. He married Aline. She transformed his life without changing it – if the contradiction be permitted. She gave him what he had always needed: love. As solicitous as she was beautiful, she caressed his existence in Albany, in Portofino and in Headington. Like him, she disliked ostentation. Aline had been a great competitor when she was golf champion of France, but she never competed with Isaiah. She was there as the setting in which he shone – perpetually anxious that all should go well for him, not for her. She brought him a family, her children Michael Strauss, Peter and Philippe Halban and her young Gunzbourg cousins, for whom he was a new uncle. To the delight of Isaiah's friends, they created a new *persona*, calling him 'Ton-ton Isaïe'.

And now he is gone. If I have not spoken sufficiently of his defence of liberty or pluralism, or his detestation of cruelty and ruthlessness, it is because I speak of him as a friend. Political thinkers and intellectuals, so I believe, have not yet understood how disquieting is his contention that good ends conflict. Isaiah Berlin was original, and he is as hard to come to terms with as Machiavelli or Hume. All I can say is that he seems to me to have offered the truest and most moving interpretation of life that my own generation made.

And I must add this. I owe everything to my teachers. They taught me to learn and, if I got above myself, how much more I had to learn. I was never, of course, one of Isaiah's students, but I never failed to learn from him. He taught me to think more clearly, to feel more deeply, to hope, and to put my trust in life.

James Lees-Milne (1908–1997)
writer and conservationist

by Nigel Nicolson
(writer)

Memorial Service at Grosvenor Chapel, South Audley Street, London, on 12 March 1998

We all know the purpose of a memorial service. It is to bring together in collective affection the people closest to a friend who has died, and to record in the best way we know, by our attendance here, our gratitude for all he gave us.

There would be many others here had Jim not outlived them, for he was eighty-nine when he died, and few people had a greater gift for friendship. He preferred his friends to be like himself – energetic, cultured, well-mannered and with a touch of eccentricity. He once said that he preferred houses to people, but that was only because houses last longer, and what really delighted him was the company of people whom he loved in delectable surroundings, as when he had Alvilde to himself at Alderley, Bath or Badminton; or take this scene from his diary of 1973:

> Yesterday I spent at Uppark with the National Trust Arts Panel. Sitting round the dining-room table, on which incongruously Emma Hart once danced, there were some of the most understanding, cultivated, earnest men of good sense and taste it was possible to find: Robin Fedden, Brinsley Ford, Johnny Walker of the Metropolitan Museum, Roddy Thesiger, Lord Plunket, Bobby Gore, young

Martin Drury, Gervaise Jackson-Stops and Merlin Watersen. Could there be a better lot? No, there couldn't.

Some of those he named have died. Some are here with us today. I believe that they would all have felt about him what he wrote about them: mutual affection, mutual regard, mutual trust and a shared commitment to save for future generations irreplaceable treasures from the past.

James Lees-Milne was not an aristocrat by birth, but he was by nature. I think he was aware of this, but he never traded on it. I once asked him where he had spent the past weekend, and he replied, 'With friends in Derbyshire,' when he had been staying at Chatsworth. Once he wrote, 'I am acutely conscious of, and amused by, class distinctions, and hope they endure for ever', but his critics, if he had any, in quoting this with relish, would always omit the next sentence: 'Class *barriers* are a different matter, which no sensible person would advocate.' He admired people for their gifts and dedication, whatever class they came from. There was an affinity between him and the thousands of craftsmen who, centuries ago, built the houses and filled them with works of art for the few who could afford them, and the thousands more who care for them today.

Jim's delight in the past sometimes made him contemptuous of the present. He had a breathtaking disdain for fashionable ideas, but nobody was less supercilious, nobody less arrogant, nobody more candid. He must be the only Englishman to have expressed publicly his regret that he never fought for Franco in the Civil War. He was given to self-reproach, but never to self-pity or self-praise. Few people were capable of rising to such heights of exhilaration or sinking to such depths of despair. For someone who was apt to say that the country was going to the dogs, he extracted a great deal of pleasure from it, both in his private life and in his work.

I remember a passage in his diary when Alvilde fell and slightly grazed her knee, and Jim wrote in the privacy of his room: 'It makes me realise how precious she is to me, more and more as the years roll by, and I dread ever losing her.'

That was one side of his nature. Another was his love of literature, and his own contribution to it. He was an art historian of great imagination and scholastic gifts, a biographer who included among his subjects the parents or forebears of some of us here today. He was an autobiographer of superlative merit, even if he sometimes cast himself as a character in an Evelyn Waugh novel. But perhaps he will be best remembered for his diaries, which he never intended for publication, and as the most successful house-hunter that the National Trust has ever had.

'I was not born in the heroic mould,' he wrote, but his achievement as a young man was truly heroic. As the executor of Lord Lothian's and Lord Esher's concepts, he toured the country before, during and after the war in an unparalleled pilgrimage of grace. He was not always successful. Having failed to add Longleat to his day's bag, he heard Lord Bath courteously suggest that it might be time for Jim to ring for his chauffeur and have his car brought round to the front door. Jim had to confess that he had no chauffeur; indeed he had no car. So a footman was despatched to the stables, and returned, smirking slightly, with Jim's battered bicycle, on which he rode away, casting over his shoulder a last, lingering, regretful look at that incomparable façade.

On another, less melancholy, occasion when he and Eardley Knollys went fishing for Dyrham Park, their host grew bored with their exclamations of delight at his wonderful possessions, and turned to his wife to say in his dreadful French, 'My dear, *pensez-vous qu'il faut les inviter* to dinner?'

But what a catch resulted from these trawling expeditions! Jim's houses – let me be excused for calling them that – read like battle honours: Dyrham itself, Charlecote, Blickling, Montacute, Stourhead, Knole, Polesden Lacey, Cliveden, Lacock, West Wycombe, Gunby, Cotehele, Petworth, Osterley, Nostell Priory and many others. When you consider that the Trust had almost no money of its own, and a minute membership, it remains a miracle how it was done. Indeed Jim often wondered himself. 'If the N.T. knew what I was up to, what promises I am making in their name,' he confided in his diary, 'they would be shocked by the extreme zeal of their servant.'

They are shocked no longer. He preserved an essential part of our history and inheritance. He was the most civilised of Englishmen, and we have come here to celebrate the excellence of his life, character and achievements, and to express our gratitude for what he has bequeathed to us.

Molly Baring (1911–1998)
countrywoman and racing enthusiast

by Candida Lycett Green
(writer)

Memorial Service at Holy Trinity Church, Ardington, Berkshire, on 14 April 1998

Moll wouldn't want us to be sad today. She would want us to remember her in sparkling form.

Making everybody happy that was her great gift – she could lift your spirits like no one else.

She personified gaiety;

She was gregarious in the very best sense, because she was genuinely *concerned* about people;

Her heart was as generous as all get out;

She was one of the cosiest people I've ever known;

She was my friend and my counsellor and she was the best listener in the world. You could tell her everything lock stock and barrel and if things were bad she made you feel safe and all right.

She *never* talked about herself unless I pressed her to. She was inordinately proud of all her children and grandchildren – they told her all their secrets and she kept up with their every move.

As everyone here knows she was utterly besotted with Dessie.

I can't really talk about Moll without Dessie being in the same breath. To me they are indivisible.

Theirs was one of the great love affairs of all time and in retrospect

I know that's why Ardington was such an extraordinarily happy place to come to.

For fifty years I have known and loved the Barings and I thank God for organising it. Something needed to be done to the church clock and Dessie, who was the churchwarden, had to go and see my dad who was on the Diocesan Advisory Committee.

Moll said to Dessie, 'Now for God's sake don't go and talk about racing and hunting because John Betjeman's not that sort of person. He likes poetry books – not form books.'

Of course the rapport was instant and Moll and Dessie and my parents were friends for ever. They felt utterly relaxed in each other's company.

Moll and Dessie had that magic about them and I'm sure you all know what I'm talking about. It's an ability to make people feel perfectly and utterly at home.

My brother Paul became thick with Peter and Nigel; and Tuffy and I became BFs. I spent far more of my childhood at Ardington than I did at home. I almost lived here.

In those far-off fifties I remember when Mr Higgs ruled the stableyard and Winnie Sprules ruled the kitchen in that huge dark world of brown lino on the north side of the house.

Shifting images return – Moll in a sunfrock bottom up in the herbaceous border;

Dessie making mysterious telephone calls in what my dad called 'the betting room', with the Lionel Edwards and Snaffles prints and always the desk behind the door and the two armchairs either side of the fireplace – ever the same (and once in that betting room, *entirely* egged on by Moll who could never abide people putting on airs and graces, she encouraged Peter Walwyn to ring up Mrs Poole. She'd just added Croker to her name to give it a bit of gravitas and Peter said he worked for the *Evening Standard* and he'd just heard that her daughter Sally was engaged to the Duke of Kent, which wasn't true at all. Mrs Poole went into paroxysms of excitement. We were all in hysterics);

Moll flirting mildly with Dick Poole who used to advise her on plants;

Moll in a snazzy bathing suit lying by the pool at Henwick Country Club where she used to take Tuffy and me;

Moll sitting very far forward on the driver's seat of the diesel Land-Rover with her nose almost on the windscreen;

Moll cutting a dash out hunting on Sinbad or Willy Can in Lord Burghley's day (Moll told me and some of her grandchildren that she'd jumped Rosey Brook but Peter isn't so sure);

Moll chatting to Betty Berners on the edges of woods and copses around Baulking and Sparsholt and Goosey and giving me her sandwiches because my feet were freezing off;

Moll saying good morning to Angela Walker and Angela Walker waving back, rippling her fingers (Tuffy and I used to call it the Lady Walker wave and we used to practise it from our ponies);

Then there was Moll's walk-in clothes cupboard, beside the pale green-coloured bathroom – dark from the big cedar tree outside. It was an Aladdin's cave for Tuffy and me: rows and rows of size two shoes, very high; a lot of white and navy blue and hats on stands on the top shelf out of our reach; and the silver-framed mirror in the bedroom and the shock horror when Dessie once found a grass snake curled up under Moll's pillow. It had climbed up the Virginia creeper. Moll never knew about it and we were sworn to secrecy.

And do you remember sitting on that terrace with the wonderful view across the lake to Larch's downs, or coming into the hall with Moll's flower arrangement on the round table; their friends flowing in and out, like the Todds and the Johnson Hortons and the Christies and Beebys and Collingses and Wigans?

Driving to Newbury races on Dessie's special back route is now part of my life. He was never one to wait in traffic and he had back ways to every racecourse in England except Lingfield. He never could work that one out. The stopping off on the way back at Rotherwood, the big tile-hung villa on the edge of Donnington with its dark oaky rooms and the warm welcome from Moll's heavenly parents, Pipey and Gran to us. Moll's father was Ben Warner, the legendary professional backer. I felt safely encompassed there. They were the real stuff of racing. I remember Tuffy saying to Pipey once, 'Can't you talk about anything but racing?' and Pipey replying, 'No, why the hell should I, it's the only thing I know anything about.'

Newbury Races was never such fun again without Pipey and Gran to visit on the way home.

Parties at Christmas with the huge tree between the double-flighted stairs with Pipey and his best friend Sam Long and good claret flowing and Moll's RADA training (don't forget she went to RADA with Vivien Leigh) shining through and her singing 'If I were the only girl in the world' and my dad doing the Charleston with Gran and Dessie smiling silently – the more he drank the more silent he got – and us children mortified by our parents showing off.

Then always Kempton Races every Boxing Day in our new gloves and my brother being taught to bet.

Dessie always said Moll was born on a racecourse. She was certainly well trained.

When Moll was fourteen she was sent to Donnington Post Office to send sheaves of telegrams to different bookmakers minutes before the off to get the money on Oyster Maid, a rank outsider running at Tenby. Meanwhile in Monmouthshire a certain Helen Walwyn had been sent by *her* father down to Raglan Post Office on her pony to do exactly the same thing. All the while Ben Warner, on the course at Tenby, was seen having a bet on the hot favourite also trained, like Oyster Maid, by Ben's friend David Harrison. Oyster Maid trotted up at 100 to 9. Moll and Helen didn't meet until years later and it was only when they were recalling childhood reminiscences that they discovered they'd been in on the same coup.

By the time she was twenty Moll was racing four or five days a week. One day she cadged a lift to Lingfield with her father's trainer George Beeby. He was a bit reluctant and said, 'Well, it's a bit difficult actually because I've got this owner staying.' Moll thought it would be some stuffy old geezer and in walked Dessie, twenty-three years old and dazzling.

Ben Warner encouraged the romance because he thought Dessie worked in the bank. Dessie said he only married Moll because he thought she'd be a walking form book. In fact she'd never opened a form book in her life.

They went to Paris for their honeymoon.

Everyone knows Moll loved a good frock and after Dessie had taken her shopping one morning they got back to the hotel and there was this telephone call from George Beeby.

'This horse of yours that's about to run,' he said. 'It still hasn't got a name – what are we going to call it? It's by Link Boy out of Boulevard.' And Dessie said, 'Well, I've just had the most expensive walk of my life so we better call it Rue de La Pay.' It went on to win five races. And Moll continued to like expensive clothes.

She told me, 'Dessie used to say, "I don't want you to be the second-best-dressed girl on the racecourse, I want you to be the best."' She had all her suits made by Digby and Morton at La Chasse and her hats were made by Swerlings. 'I used to say to Dessie, "Which one shall I have?" and he'd say, "Have both."'

Moll and Dessie owned some good horses: Spin Spin and Potters Bar and Gremlin which won the Queen's prize at Kempton.

Dessie told me that Sandown was his favourite course but I've got a feeling that latterly Moll and Dessie had their best times at Goodwood.

There was the time she told me about when they were staying with the Herns at West Wittering and everyone was getting ready for dinner and Dessie was having a bath and Moll was standing at the mirror chattering away. 'I was completely nude, duckie, and I said to Dessie, "Don't just lie there, say something," and Dick Hern who was *actually* lying in the bath said, "Well, the thing is, Moll, I don't quite know what to say."'

They played a lot of poker at West Wittering.

Moll loved her cards but it wasn't until she took in this mysterious lodger called John Hamner that she began to learn the finer points of bridge.

She soon became the heroine of the famous Lockinge Sunday Four or sometimes five. No outsider ever knew what went on at these games. I suppose Heck did but she never let on. Moll was known as Chesty and Guy Knight always used to say, 'Pray *God* I don't cut to play with Chesty,' but I have it on the best authority that Moll was a more reliable player than Guy or Jeremy Tree (who implied he was brilliant at bridge) and was always the biggest loser.

Kath Walwyn was a bit of a dark horse and Hamner was presumably a cut-above. Bridge is a game when you can have confrontations but Moll never took anyone on. Even if she was right she'd never contest anything. It wasn't her style.

After Dessie died a bit of Moll died too.

She missed him like billyo but true to form she cracked on. She never ever felt sorry for herself and she never complained.

Gregarious to the last, you had to book her weeks in advance. She'd say, 'I'm sorry I can't come to lunch, duckie, I'm having lunch with Larch.' And if you asked her to supper she'd be playing poker with the Franks and the Dicks and Helen.

At eighty-five Moll could still light up a room and she was still John Oaksey's favourite dancing partner.

She was in fine voice at John Dunlop's party for Dick Hern not long ago and sang her famous rendition of 'Won't you come home Bill Bailey' together with Dick and Tom Jones. Friday night happy hour in the pub next door which she introduced me to earlier this year won't be the same now . . .

But Moll and Dessie *will* always be at their loved Ardington and my God how they loved the place.

Sixty years of their passionate happiness won't evaporate over-night

I'd just like to end by praising Tuffy for her extraordinary strength of mind in letting Moll die so quietly and beautifully. Anyone less brave would have had her whisked to hospital. Instead she died in the heart of her family and it was the most perfect, noble and peaceful death imaginable. Just as it should be.

Life is about continuance and Moll knew that better than anyone. She carried her parents' torch through life and her and Dessie's spirit is here today in all their children and grandchildren who are the next chapter. Richard didn't do too badly by Moll yesterday, when he rode a winner, did he? But then that's only to be expected.

Sheila Hern told Moll that she was looking forward to seeing Dessie in heaven and now Moll is in heaven with them both and I'll bet she's got a glass of champagne in her hand and saying, 'Aren't we having a lovely time.'

John Wells (1936–1998)
writer and actor

by Richard Ingrams
(editor of the Oldie)

Memorial Service at St Paul's Church, Covent Garden, London, on 30 April 1998

The fact there are so many of you here today is proof of the great affection that John inspired. And the fact that I don't know who most of you are is proof of the many different lives he led – writing, acting, performing, directing, translating and teaching – as well as leading a very active social life in London and in Sussex.

The John Wells I knew was a fellow-member of a rather notorious gang – that gang which produced *Private Eye*, TV satire shows and various books and plays – a gang which made a nuisance of itself in a variety of ways over the years. Basically we were a group of friends who had had fun at school and university and wanted to go on having the same sort of fun for the rest of our lives. And by and large we succeeded – despite being asked by our elders and betters well into middle age, 'And when are you going to get a proper job?'

That gang still survives today, though in rather depleted form. In fact, it doesn't seem very long ago that John and I were both standing in this spot bidding farewell to Willie Rushton. And not long before that we lost Peter Cook. Not surprisingly, I am beginning to feel a bit lonely.

Though I first met John some forty years ago at Oxford, we had seen each other some time before that when we were both doing our national service in Korea – he as second lieutenant at the sharp end (the 39th parallel), I as an Education Corps sergeant at the slightly more civilised blunt end at Inchon. It was here that John spied me playing the harmonium in the garrison chapel, later describing 'an incongruous baboon-like figure, eyebrows raised and hands moving straight forward over the keys with apparent disregard for any little musical infelicities more sensitive spirits might deem to detract from the overall impression'. John could hardly imagine *then* that the same baboon would be performing in similar fashion at his funeral over forty years later at the little church in Sussex where he is now buried.

At Oxford I first heard of John when Peter Usborne, later the business brains behind *Private Eye*, said to me one day, 'I want you to come and meet the funniest man in Oxford.' It was a true description as I was soon able to confirm – visiting John at his digs over a newsagent in St Giles or meeting for a beer and darts at Oxford's smallest pub, the Duke of Cambridge in Little Clarendon Street. He was a brilliant mimic, one of those people who had only to make minuscule changes to his facial expression to have you laughing. His voices were legion. He could turn himself into a smug vicar, a camp antique dealer, Maurice Chevalier, John Betjeman, Field Marshal Montgomery – all in the twinkling of an eye.

All this, with a natural charm and a great gift for friendship, made him a natural collaborator. Over the years he worked with an extraordinarily varied bunch of people. He wrote a novel with John Fortune, a play with Claud Cockburn, another play with Robert Morley, he worked with Leonard Bernstein on a revival of his musical *Candide* – the list is endless. My own most successful collaborations with John were two long-running serials in *Private Eye*: the first was 'Mrs Wilson's Diary', launched in 1964 at a time when after long years of Tory government we had a young Labour Prime Minister keen to show how young and dynamic he was, a Labour Prime Minister who befriended big businessmen, who liked to be photographed with pop singers and who sucked up like anything to the American President. *Plus ça change.* As with 'Dear Bill', I think we wrote the diary according to the advice of Claud

Cockburn who once said that if you were a political journalist you should assemble all the known facts about a given situation and then try to imagine the most disastrous thing that the government could do – given those facts – and then write it up as if it had actually happened. In the case of Harold Wilson, nothing we could imagine was too improbable, as I was reminded recently when the government papers were released detailing his proposed plan to foil the Great Train Robbers by withdrawing all banknotes from circulation. As for 'Dear Bill', John was reliably informed that after we described a ferocious row involving Mrs T and her foreign secretary Lord Carrington, the security at Number 10 had been tightened up to prevent any further leaks.

Like husbands and wives, collaborators often fall out because they come to resent their reliance on one another. I am glad to say that John and I never did. There is nothing like a legacy of shared jokes to keep friendships together. Besides which, we tended to revere the same people – Claud Cockburn, Malcolm Muggeridge, John Betjeman, Joan Littlewood and Spike Milligan. John was always the easiest possible person to work with. He would come into the *Eye* office, his canvas satchel bulging with scripts, make phone calls to various (to me unknown) agents and producers and then we would retire to a cubby-hole to do 'Dear Bill'. John would turn himself into Denis for the duration and in spite of interruptions for gossip, it seldom took more than an hour to complete. If ever I didn't find one of John's jokes funny, I would repeat what Robert Morley used to say in similar circumstances when they were writing a farce about a transvestite judge: 'Put it in another play, my darling.'

All of us who visited John in the last months of his life, when his hopes were raised so often only to be dashed, were deeply impressed by the courage with which he put up with it all.

During one of my talks with him he began to reflect rather gloomily on whether anything he had done in his life had been really worth while. This type of gloomy reflection is perhaps quite common amongst those of us who deal in the very ephemeral business of journalism, television and entertainment, when most of what we produce is forgotten after about twenty-four hours.

But what I thought about Peter Cook and Willie Rushton applies as much to John. We owe a tremendous debt of gratitude to people who make us laugh. Never mind if afterwards we find it hard to remember what was so funny. Usually, the funnier it was the harder it is to remember.

Speaking personally, 1 know that I never enjoyed anything half as much as those sessions writing 'Mrs Wilson' and 'Dear Bill' with John. We often had to fit it in at the end of a long day – it was the equivalent, for me, a teetotaller, of a large gin and tonic or, as Denis would say, a mega snorterino.

Daniel Massey (1934–1998)

actor

by Sir Ronald Harwood

(playwright)

Memorial Service at St Paul's Church, Covent Garden, London, on 16 June 1998

There was an evening spent with Dan that seems to me to capture some of the unpredictable flavour of his personality. It took place in the Ivy, when he, Michael Pennington and I were asked by Sally Greene to have dinner with Virginia Bottomley, the then Secretary of State for National Heritage, after the theatre. To begin with Dan was charming, polite, almost humble. After a few glasses of wine, he suddenly launched into a long lecture, aimed, of course, at Mrs Bottomley. His face glowed as he told her in long, eloquent and, I have to say, sometimes incoherent sentences, that if she wanted to solve all the problems facing her and the Conservative government she must do one thing and one thing only: attract young people to the theatre. I can't remember in detail the thrust of his argument but I can remember the glazed look in Mrs Bottomley's eyes, her surreptitious glances at her wristwatch, her relief when Dan drew just enough breath for her to be able to say, 'I must go now.' When she'd left, Dan stared into space with a lost, sad look. I asked him if he was all right. 'Yes, darling,' he said. 'It's just that she reminds me of the matron at my prep school. She used to bath me. Lovely.' And then he laughed: that extraordinary laugh, when he threw back his head, opened his mouth out of which no sound came for about three seconds until a great guffaw erupted. It's how I like to remember Dan: I like to remember him laughing.

When somebody we know and love dies, it seems to me imperative that we do not try to appropriate a place for ourselves at his death that we never occupied in his lifetime. So, I have to say at the outset that I only knew Dan really well for the last four years of his life and if I put too much emphasis on those last years, and my tiny part in them, I ask for your understanding. Believe me, I do so not because of any desire for self-assertion, nor, as I have just said, because I want you to think I was closer to him than was the case, but because I feel the need to make this clear and because I happen to believe that those last few years, painful, triumphant, unbearable, glorious years, represent a magnificent summation, the climax, reached, of course, unjustly too soon, to the life and career of one of the most talented, courageous and lovable men I have ever known.

When Harold Pinter suggested Dan for the role of Wilhelm Furtwängler in my play, *Taking Sides*, I knew at once that there could be no better casting. There were concerns, of course. He had been ill but, we were told, he was now fully recovered. We lunched, Harold, Michael Pennington, Dan and I, to celebrate our coming together. A few weeks later, Harold telephoned to say that Dan had had a relapse and asked me what I wanted to do. Recast? Wait? What? Independently, Harold and I came to the same conclusion that we should wait. And thank God we did. Not, believe me, just because of the play but because, as Dan told me later, the knowledge that he would work again the moment he was well, playing a part that greatly attracted him, was an enormous incentive to his recovery. And recover he did because, I believe, work was Dan's true therapy, physically and mentally, when his concentration, his entire being was consumed by the task in hand.

Dan was not so much a man of the theatre as a child of the theatre. There was something wonderfully innocent about him and that innocence made him vulnerable and thin-skinned, which was at odds with his physique, his splendid voice and a kind of cragginess which could be misinterpreted as insensitivity. Dan was happiest in the theatre, it was where he felt most at home. And no wonder, given his background: the son of actors, Raymond Massey and Adrienne Allen. One of his godfathers was Noël Coward and Dan's impersonation of the most impersonated figure of his time was easily the best – the clipped diction, the wagging forefinger and, not often heard in public, the foul language at which Dan was especially expert. Yet, despite that background, and a talented younger sister, Anna, there seems to have been a hope that his education, Eton and King's College, Cambridge, would perhaps have pointed him towards a different career. But the pull of the theatre was too strong. I don't believe he had a choice in the matter.

As an actor, Dan had a rare gift, rare in England, at any rate, and that was power. He had genuine power not only because of his height and his mighty voice, but also, and chiefly, because he had the courage to express himself with uninhibited gusto. He did not seem to temper his style to popular or critical taste. Having seen him in a good many roles over a long period, it seemed to me that his power grew and began to flourish on a grand scale in these last few years. He gave what I thought was one of the best performances in 1994, as General Burgoygne in Bernard Shaw's *The Devil's Disciple*, directed by Christopher Morahan at the National Theatre.

But to say Dan was a powerful actor might suggest simply a sort of flamboyance or ranting or thrashing about. This would be quite wrong. Power requires stillness, too, and Dan could convey, effortlessly it seemed, crude energy under control, but the control, one knew, was fragile, which is why he was so dangerous on stage. And I use the word 'danger' with care because it is much overused in relation to leading actors and so becomes meaningless, just as the word 'timing' becomes meaningless when used in relation to comedians. Dan was truly dangerous, and when I used to see him stalking from one side of the stage to the other, bearing down on a fellow-actor, there inevitably came to my mind Coral Browne's description of what it was like to act with Donald Wolfit. She said it was like being a piece of fluff on a carpet at the approach of a vacuum cleaner. I think acting with Dan might have been a bit like that.

And yet I have to say that what I really think made Dan fascinating on stage were his personal qualities which perhaps he didn't even know were in play when he was acting. He could be charming, difficult, amusing, vulgar, sentimental, ruthless, eloquent, loving and sometimes just plain barmy. He was, as a person, often deeply troubled but also amazingly carefree. He could seem totally crazed one moment and bewilderingly rational the next.

And he could be witty and perceptive, especially about his fellow-actors. I had been told that during rehearsals in New York, Ed Harris, another very dangerous actor, playing the American major, frustrated with himself for not getting the lines right, had picked up a chair, hurled it at a wall and smashed it to pieces. I asked Dan if that had really happened. 'No,' Dan said. 'It wasn't like that at all. What actually happened was that the chair saw Ed approaching and decided to disintegrate.'

There was the night, too, when Elisabeth Furtwängler, the conductor's widow, attended a performance at the Criterion Theatre here in London. Being too cowardly and fearing lawyers' letters, I did not go that night. But I was told afterwards that Frau Furtwängler had liked the play and was especially admiring of Dan's performance. She was taken round to see him. Dan was, apparently, at his most charming, not to say unctuous. He bowed, he smiled, he listened. She said, 'I have two criticisms.' 'Oh,' Dan said, 'yes, please, I'd love to know.' Pointing to the sides of his wig, she said, 'You have too much hair over the ears. Wilhelm did not have so much hair in this place.' 'Oh, thank you,' Dan said, bowing even lower. 'I shall talk to the wig-maker and have it corrected at once. What was the second criticism?' Frau Furtwängler thought for a moment and then said, 'Your lips are not quite right.' 'Ooh,' Dan said. 'I don't know what I can do about that.'

I mentioned his courage as an actor but his true courage was as a human being. Rarely can anyone have faced their final, desperate months with such fortitude. My last conversation with him took place just before he went in for his final horrendous treatment. His voice was strong, he joked, sounded confident and prepared. We talked of future plans. It may all have been put on for my benefit, I don't know. But even if his optimism was assumed, the very effort it must have cost him points to a man of extraordinary bravery and, dare I say, nobility. And he could not have approached what was in store for him in the way he did, without the love and wondrous care of Lindy and all those who were close to him until the very end. Daniel Massey was a rare and inspirational spirit. He was larger than life and he is certainly larger than death.

Ted Hughes (1930–1998)
poet laureate, 1984–98

by Seamus Heaney
(poet)

Funeral Service at St Peter's Church, North Tawton, Devon, on 3 November 1998

No death in my lifetime has hurt poetry or poets more than the death of Ted Hughes. No death outside my immediate family has left me feeling more bereft. As a fifteenth-century Irish bard said of the death of his brother, the master poet, Fergal Rua O'h-Uiginn: 'A stave of the barrel is smashed/And the wall of learning broken.' Ted was simply beloved. He was a tower of kindness and strength, an arch where the least of poetry's children could enter and feel safe. We have to go back to the death of Dylan Thomas or García Lorca to find an equivalent moment, a moment when the poet's death is experienced as a rent in the veil of poetry itself.

Ted was taken from us too soon. Even on the eve of his seventieth birthday his creative power was, as Shakespeare might have said, still crescent. His loss to the language and to the art gives new force to W.B. Yeats's indignant phrase about 'the discourtesy of death'.

Ted himself experienced the unfairness and peremptoriness of death's arrival; and so, in order to echo that sense of unfairness – and our own sense of it – I would like to read, at the request of Carol and the family, Dylan Thomas's 'Do Not Go Gentle into that Good Night'. And after that, to celebrate our sense of Ted's ongoingness as a poet, his at-oneness with Caedmon and

Shakespeare, with the land and the river, I'll read two of his own poems.

Do Not Go Gentle into that Good Night

Do not go gentle into that good night,
Old age should burn and rave at close of day;
Rage, rage against the dying of the light.

Though wise men at their end know dark is right,
Because their words had forked no lightning they
Do not go gentle into that good night.

Good men, the last wave by, crying how bright
Their frail deeds might have danced in a green bay,
Rage, rage against the dying of the light.

Wild men who caught and sang the sun in flight,
And learn, too late, they grieved it on its way,
Do not go gentle into that good night.

Grave men, near death, who see with blinding sight
Blind eyes could blaze like meteors and be gay,
Rage, rage against the dying of the light.

And you, my father, there on the sad height,
Curse, bless me now with your good fierce tears, I pray.
Do not go gentle into that good night.
Rage, rage against the dying of the light.

The first poem by Ted is called 'Go Fishing' and it embodies effortlessly the hereness and nowness of his genius as a man and a poet.

Go Fishing

Join water, wade into underbeing
Let brain mist into moist earth
Ghost loosen downstream
Gulp river and gravity

Lose words
Cease
Be assumed into glistenings of lymph

As if creation were a wound
As if this flow were all plasm healing

Be supplanted by mud and leaves and pebbles
By sudden rainbow monster-structures
That materialise in suspension gulping
And dematerialise under pressure of the eye

Be cleft by the sliding prow
Displaced by the hull of light and shadow

Dissolved in earth-wave, the soft sun-shock,
Dismembered in sun-melt

Become translucent — one untangling drift
Of water-mesh, and a weight of earth-taste light
Mangled by wing-shadows
Everything circling and flowing and hover-still

Crawl out over roots, new and nameless
Search for face, harden into limbs

Let the world come back, like a white hospital
Busy with urgency words

Try to speak and nearly succeed
Heal into time and other people

The second poem is one Ted wrote in memory of Carol's father Jack Orchard, a man who was the guardian spirit of the farm at Moortown and indeed of Ted's England — which was and is the England of Cacdmon and Langland, Shakespeare and Hopkins. The poem is about loss, but it leaves us with a strong sense of something enduring. The keeper has in his turn been kept. All of Ted's human kindness and spiritual understanding and visionary apprehension are here. Although we now 'stand in new emptiness', the one consolation is that he will be with us always in the land and the language.

The Day He Died

Was the silkiest day of the young year,
The first reconnaissance of the real spring,
The first confidence of the sun.

That was yesterday. Last night, frost.
And as hard as any of all winter.
Mars and Saturn and the Moon dangling in a bunch
On the hard, littered sky.
Today is Valentine's day.

Earth toast-crisp. The snowdrops battered.
Thrushes spluttering. Pigeons gingerly
Rubbing their voices together, in stinging cold.
Crows creaking, and clumsily
Cracking loose.

The bright fields look dazed.
Their expression is changed.
They have been somewhere awful
And come back without him.

The trustful cattle, with frost on their backs.
Waiting for hay, waiting for warmth,
Stand in a new emptiness.

From now on the land
Will have to manage without him.
But it hesitates, in this slow realisation of light,
Childlike, too naked, in a frail sun,
With roots cut
And a great blank in its memory.

Lord Hunt of Llanfair Waterdine
(1910–1998)
mountaineer: leader of the 1953 Everest expedition

by George Band
(youngest member of the 1953 expedition)

Memorial Service at St George's Chapel, Windsor Castle, on 26 January 1999

Where to begin?

'Everest – the Crowning Glory' was the headline greeting the crowds outside Buckingham Palace on 2nd June 1953. Four days earlier Hillary and Tenzing had reached the highest point on earth for the first time. But it was to the leader of this British expedition, Colonel John Hunt, that the greatest credit was due. Even though he had climbed over twenty-seven thousand feet in support, it was his battle-hardened powers of leadership and skilful planning that were the hallmarks of the expedition's success.

Henry Cecil John Hunt was born in 1910, the elder son of an Indian Army officer, who died in World War I when John was only four. John also chose the army, passing first into Sandhurst and passing out first with the King's Gold Medal and the Anson Memorial award, setting a personal standard of performance which he maintained throughout his life, as a soldier, as a mountaineer and, latterly, in an exceptional record of public service.

But in this special service of thanksgiving, his dear wife Joy has asked me to speak about his mountaineering, which was a major passion in his life.

He had a lucky start. From the age of ten he was taken by his mother for summer and winter Alpine holidays and he climbed Piz Palu at fourteen. Remarkably, his first six climbing seasons were only in the Alps. Not until he was twenty-three did he start climbing guideless at home, and discover the particular joys of leading on steep rock which he was then able to test with friends on the Aiguilles above Chamonix, which became a kind of second home.

I first met John at the Royal Geographical Society when he interviewed me for a place in his 1953 Everest team. I might have expected a brusque and conventional military man. I was wrong. He was a very sensitive and intensely human person. With his engaging blue eyes and confident handshake, and by his warmth and sincerity, he immediately put one at ease.

John had been appointed leader of the expedition unexpectedly at short notice after the Organising Committee decided that he should replace Eric Shipton, despite his enormous experience. Coming fresh from Montgomery's planning staff at Fontainebleau, John seemed the leader more likely to ensure success. But it was also greatly to his credit that he was able to win over the best climbers from the previous year's expedition to Cho Oyu who had understandably remained loyal to Shipton. With the strength of his personality and determination, he was able to mould a group of strong individualists into the happy team we have remained ever since.

John came to Everest with impressive credentials despite having been outside the mainstream of Himalayan and Alpine climbing during the immediate post-war period. While serving in India, he naturally gravitated to the Himalayas. His attempt in 1935, with James Waller's party on Saltoro Kangri – when they reached twenty-four thousand five hundred feet – was among the more audacious Himalayan exploits of the 1930s. After that he was elected to the Alpine Club, but he was turned down for Ruttledge's 1936 expedition to Everest, so the story goes, after the doctors detected a heart murmur and told him to be careful going up stairs! So he married instead, and with his new wife Joy and friend Reggie Cooke in 1937 they reconnoitred the eastern slopes of Kangchenjunga and climbed the Zemu La where they came across strange tracks which his Sherpa Pasang firmly declared were those of a Yeti.

Everest changed his life. He gave up a brilliant army career to become the first director of the Duke of Edinburgh's Award and became a role model and inspiration to youth, influencing thousands to take up and enjoy challenging outdoor pursuits. But he kept on climbing, sharing experiences with young people, or doing more ambitious Alpine routes with friends like Wilfrid Noyce, David Cox and Mike Ward; major expeditions to the Caucasus and Pamirs; and a twentieth-anniversary trek across east Nepal.

He was elected president of both the Alpine Club and the Royal Geographical Society. He wrote the bestselling *Ascent of Everest* in an astonishing thirty days. He loved his fellow-men – and women – and called his autobiography *Life is Meeting*. The last chapter recounts some of his favourite climbs and concludes:

> There have been breath-taking moments, not only when I have been afraid, but also for the sheer joy of movement in rhythm up steep and sensational places; of balancing warily along some blade-like crest of snow, of dangling airily down some rock wall at the end of an abseil rope. Nor are difficulties and sensations the only mountain memories. To step upon the summit of the Matterhorn, when the crowds have been deterred by the mist and wind and falling snow, and find it bathed in sunshine above a sea of cloud; to reach the top of the Grand Combin in a tearing gale, when the weather has done its utmost to deter you – these are the experiences on easy climbs which I would not change for many a much more difficult one.

At last beginning to show his age, it still gave him enormous pleasure last May to preside with Joy over the extended 'Everest family' at our forty-fifth anniversary reunion in Snowdonia. Among the numerous press tributes last November, a sentence by Lord Longford struck me: 'In my eyes, Lord Hunt was the greatest Englishman of his time.' He was certainly the greatest that I could call a friend. Let us thank God for his wonderful life in all its rich diversity.

Nicholas Budgen (1938–1998)
Conservative MP

by Charles Moore
(writer and editor)

Memorial Service at St Margaret's Church,
Westminster, London, on 3 February 1999

I am glad to be following hard upon John Biffen's reading from Surtees, though not quite as hard as Nick Budgen followed hounds. One old friend's instant reaction to Nick's death was to say, 'The front field of the Meynell Hunt will now be a safer place.' Nick was what in hunting is known as a thruster. Indifferent to his own safety and, it must be said, to that of others, he liked to take the biggest fences at the greatest pace. The casualty departments of several Midlands hospitals bore painful testimony to the consequences. One Budget time, Madeleine approached the ward just as Nick was about to have a general anaesthetic so that the doctors could wrench his knee the right way round. 'Well, you'd better do it pretty damn quick,' she heard her husband say, 'I'm on the box tomorrow.'

Hunting, as its devotees know, is a metaphor for life, so I think it is worth saying a bit more about Nick's relationship with horses. From his earliest years, he loved riding. It certainly was not a love of show. His clothing was often in the last extremities of decay. Once, when he arrived at a particularly smart meet, late as usual, he was still in his suit from the House of Commons. Seventy pairs of eyes swivelled away in horror as Nick stripped down to his underwear and pulled on his moth-eaten breeches.

No, his love of horses was love of competition and of risk. Nick was never happier than when persuading a cheap nag to jump a fence which a rich man's thoroughbred had just refused. In point-to-pointing, too, he rode any old thing available in the hope of winning, with the result that he won almost nothing. Once, when his spectacles broke in one race he simply borrowed a pair from his old friend, Richard Matson, for the next. Needless to say, unable to see through someone else's glasses, he fell off, splitting his cap in two. He was matchlessly brave.

Horses offered Nick the false promise of commercial success as well. He had a small farm in Staffordshire and bred them. By last year, there were twenty-eight of the beasts, not selling. Nick rang a friend: 'You don't think horses could get BSE, do you?' he said, a faintly hopeful note in his voice. More desperate still, he rang again: 'Couldn't we recreate the Boer War?' he asked. 'That used up five hundred thousand horses.' As he was dying, it was his young groom who paid him a particularly touching tribute. 'You're such a brilliant boss,' she said. 'I couldn't have had such rows with anyone else.' Nick is buried with the whip he took hunting.

I have spoken of his love of competing and of danger. I think this drove Nick's approach to politics too. There was ambition, certainly, but I doubt if it was ever primarily an ambition for office or power. Nick's only experience of government duty – as a whip – was quickly ended by his own resignation over plans for devolution in Northern Ireland. Although he might occasionally complain that some worthless time-server got promotion while his telephone obstinately failed to ring, for the most part he was happy as a backbencher. His ambition was to make a mark, to carve his own way. He did this triumphantly. In conversation, he was argumentative, in a semi-rude, semi-humorous way, particularly when fuelled by a drink somebody else had bought him. In the House of Commons, he was the master of the telling intervention and the mischievous point of order. No one was better at putting ministers on their mettle. In the course of the famous Maastricht debates, which led to Nick losing and then, despite not giving in, regaining the whip, he rebelled against the government sixty times. It is a record of which he was almost indecently proud.

But if I am giving the impression that Nick was a show-off seeking notoriety and crossing the street to pick a fight, that is quite wrong. For someone who played down his intellectual gifts and liked to describe himself as 'thick', he was very reflective. He was an extremely good observer of, as well as participant in, the Westminster world. Indeed, it was his gifts of observation that first drew me, then a young political journalist, to Nick Budgen. He was fascinated by people, and by power, and by the interaction between the two. He was a connoisseur of great political characters like Willie Whitelaw or Margaret Thatcher, both of whom he teased a little and admired a lot. People's backgrounds, education, class, wealth and so on came under his minute gaze. 'So-and-so,' he would say of some colleague, 'son of a haulage contractor who got rich, went to Harrow, no university, married a toff, nice man but desperate for recognition. The whips can always get him,' and his description would be right. Sometimes – usually over a lunch I was buying him – his analysis would extend to myself. I came away from such sessions a sadder and a wiser man.

Although Nick loved combat, he entirely lacked partisanship: he was fair-minded and clear-headed in his assessment of politicians of all parties. His talk moved easily from hilarious gossip to discussion of power games to more philosophical thoughts about politics. He had a natural feel for the many layers of that strange occupation as good as any I have found. This feel was the better for not being clouded by an ex-minister's obsession with his own record. In thinking about politics, as in everything, he was a completely honest man.

The other reason why Nick was not a mere gadfly was that he had very strong beliefs. They were close to those of Enoch Powell, in whose footsteps at Wolverhampton South West he trod admiringly, but somehow more English, less mystical. From his background among the rural, well-educated but cash-strapped middle classes, and from the sad fact of his father's early death at Tobruk, Nick had learned, he told me, a hatred of inflation, a desire to control public spending, and a love of British institutions such as the armed services and Parliament. To him it was axiomatic that the people who paid the taxes should elect their parliamentary representatives who, in turn, would compose the government from their number. Anything that interfered with this broke the necessary and traditional compact between people and rulers. In Nick Budgen's opinion, the European Union interfered with it very badly indeed.

For Nick, these beliefs were visceral, but they were not bigoted. It is misleading to think of him as typically 'right-wing'. He was opposed to capital punishment and his call for strong immigration controls was not animated by racial prejudice. Once, I telephoned Nick, pretending to be a racist constituent. He told me that he supported a firm immigration policy. Acting in my invented character, I said that wasn't good enough – I wanted them all sent back. Nick was characteristically curt and direct. He was entirely opposed to compulsory repatriation, he said, and he offered me no warm words. His distance was palpable. I can think of many, far more ostensibly liberal-minded MPs who would have given much more ambiguous answers to someone they thought might vote for them.

And because Nick really did believe in our parliamentary system, he cheerfully accepted its disadvantages. He opposed salary increases for MPs, though he had no money. He rejoiced in physical discomfort and unsocial hours. He even liked the whips whom he persecuted, and recognised the need for them. He expected frequently to disagree with his constituency association but he readily acknowledged their right to tell him their opinion as brutally as he gave them his.

Nick's attitude and career were a living embodiment of Burke's often misapplied dictum about the responsibilities of an MP: 'It is his duty,' said Burke, 'to sacrifice his repose, his pleasures, his satisfaction to his constituents; and, above all . . . to prefer their interest to his own. But his unbiased opinion, his mature judgement, his enlightened conscience, he ought not to sacrifice to you . . . your representative owes you, not his industry only, but his judgement; and he betrays, instead of serving you, if he sacrifices it to your opinion.' This is a difficult and noble doctrine, and, more than almost anyone else today, Nick lived by it.

You could say that he died by it too. He was immensely distressed at losing his seat in the 1997 election. He felt lost and alone, and cast about rather desperately for the right way to respond. His sudden, fatal illness, though certainly not desired, seemed in a strange way unsurprising – a physical reaction, as it were, to a dreadful mental shock. For what Nick had lost was not only position and employment, but also, though he wouldn't have wanted to say this publicly, something that he truly loved. Like many who affect a humorous cynicism, Nick was a romantic – about our countryside, our history, our institutions. Both in political and family life, his words could be brusque, his criticisms severe, but his affections ran very deep. Outside of Parliament, he felt bereaved.

But when the end approached, all his disorientation disappeared. In September of last year, he learned that he had only months, perhaps weeks, to live. Nick reacted with his matter-of-fact honesty. It was going to happen, and the thing to do was to prepare for it with common sense and dignity. This he did.

I went to see him on his farm in Colton on what turned out to be his last good day. It was like a scene from a George Eliot novel. Farmers were coming and going in the yard, inspecting the horses Nick was trying to sell. He told me he was getting his affairs in order, his will made, his funeral planned, and he presented me with a battered old copy of Gilbert White's *Natural History of Selborne*. He said he was glad of the chances twenty-five years in Parliament had given him. 'I've tried to stop our servicemen being killed unnecessarily,' he explained, 'I've tried to defend our country's independence. I'm grateful to my constituency for putting me on the spot. Now I have thrown myself upon the intellectual comforts of the Church of England.' He was ready for his last ride.

Death came ten days later, with the family by his bed. Both Philippa and Rupert have told me how superb his courage was.

Madeleine spoke to me on the telephone afterwards: 'I found him almost impossible to live with,' she said, 'but we were very fond of one another.' That rather describes Nick's relationship with the Conservative Party too.

All of us here were very fond of Nick. He might be surprised at that, and he would be even more surprised to learn how much we shall always admire him. He was a true original, a true Tory and therefore a true Englishman.

Quentin Crewe (1926–1998)
writer and traveller

by Bamber Gascoigne
(author)

Memorial Service at St George's Church, Hanover Square, London, on 18 February 1999

For once it is easy to know how to start. Quentin was the bravest person I have known. And I suspect many of us in this church can say the same.

It would have been brave to go through life with his disability without ever grumbling. It would have been brave to do all the amazing things he did and to grumble all the time. But to go where he went, with never a hint of self-pity, not even letting his readers know until the last few years of his life that he had any particular difficulty – simply amazing.

I have known him all my life because he was my uncle. In that respect I felt that I should not be making this address. There are many here who could describe Quentin as well as I can and with more evident objectivity. I said as much to Angela when she asked me to do this. But she answered, unanswerably: He wanted you to.

The reason apparently was Quentin's seventieth birthday party. I made a speech at a family dinner and began by saying, 'Few nephews can have an uncle who has given them so many wonderful . . . aunts.' This brought a satisfied smile to the face of the guest of honour. Afterwards he beckoned to Angela and said, in Lew Grade style, 'Get that man.' 'What for?' 'My memorial service.' So here I am.

I began with Quentin's bravery. Bravery brings admirers. But it does not necessarily bring friends, at any rate in the number gathered here today. The talents that have drawn us all together to remember Quentin, with affection as well as admiration, are immediately recognisable as one pictures him in the mind's eye. They are his curiosity – curiosity about everything, but above all about people and their strange ways. His genius for friendship, both starting and maintaining it. And of course his wit, and his love of it in others. And these are the very qualities which made him such a good travel writer, with an eye for the arresting detail – and an unerring ability to get into conversation with the most intriguing local character.

In this respect I have always felt that the wheelchair must have been a help. There is something essentially unthreatening about a person in a wheelchair – and of course something irresistibly intriguing if you happen to bump into such a person in the middle of a desert. The natural way to talk to a man in a wheelchair is to sit down beside him. A relaxed and intimate tête-à-tête seems implicit in the scenario – just as Quentin wants. And just as a writer needs.

I am not going to list his books and achievements. Most of us here know them well, and I feel we have gathered to celebrate the man even more than the career. But for any of you who sometimes ponder your obituaries, Quentin has left an invaluable lesson. You must write, not too long before your expected demise, a delightfully informal autobiography – typically in his case called *Well, I Forget the Rest* – in which you list your numerous achievements in rich and telling detail but in sufficiently self-deprecating a fashion for the obituarists to plunder them without feeling put upon.

Quentin's magnificent obituaries enumerated with all his accustomed vigour the gastronomic highlights of twenty years as a mould-breaking restaurant critic for the *Evening Standard*, the extraordinary journey across the Empty Quarter of Saudi Arabia, and then the great adventure in the Sahara with its highlight of getting lost and driving over a land mine – with the result that Quentin flies through the air, as helpless as a large parcel, and lands in the sand ten feet from the vehicle, an experience which he described as 'even more provoking than losing the way'.

The books and articles went on coming, from India, Africa, South America, the West Indies. And I know it was a special pleasure to him that Susan Hill published in book form, in the last few months of his life, the delightful *Letters from India* which he wrote on his last travels there, only a very few years ago, with his son Nat.

And incidentally how proud Quentin would have been of Nat's great forthcoming adventure – motorcycling the whole length of the American continent in memory of his father to raise funds for muscular dystrophy (details on your seats). There is already a website – www.amchallenge.com – where one is greeted by a delightful photograph of Quentin and where there will be regular reports and photographs from Nat on his journey. Quentin loved his e-mail and the net. He would have revelled in this – a hi-tech adventure of just his kind.

For all his literary productivity, I think one of Quentin's most impressive creations has been his family. If you have, as he did, a serious affection for the role of bridegroom – and if you add his ability to get on with everybody, remaining close friends with departed wives and with the five children of three families – you become the centre of an extremely interesting group of people. In the middle of the twentieth century most of us grew up in tight nuclear families, viewing with misty romanticism the extended families of the past. Well, I can tell you there is nothing quite like a Crewe family occasion. Even Tolstoy might eye it with bewildered admiration. In this, as in transcending his disability, Quentin was among the pioneers of a modern way.

I will end, as I began, with his extraordinary relationship to that disability. When he was six, the doctors said he would die at sixteen. When news of this prognosis reached Quentin, some years later, he conceived his famous determination to prove such opinions wrong. And he fought this personal battle in such wonderful style. If I remember rightly the last time he danced was at his first wedding. The last time he walked was down the aisle at his second. And this fierce obstinacy stayed with him to the very end.

At the start of last year, when he was suddenly very ill, he passionately wanted to live long enough to see another grandchild, Candida's baby. The medical view was that he would be lucky to do so. But he was safely around to greet Erskine in July. By November he was extremely ill again, in hospital. It was said to be a matter of days, perhaps hours. The family gathered over a weekend. And suddenly, with a string of people appearing beside his bed, Quentin made an amazing recovery, or should I perhaps say a predictable recovery. He was out of bed, in a chair, chatting and telling jokes – in an extremely weak voice which made one huddle close. We made him a challenge, which I remember thinking was almost impossible: to get back to his flat in Bliss Mill in time for his birthday in a week's time. He was back there in two days. With that achieved, out of hospital and back in his own world, he lived a few more days and died an hour or two after midnight – on his birthday. Another year completed. Another how-about-that to the doctors.

To the very end, he did it his way.

William Brown (1898–1998)
farmer

by Ronald Blythe
(writer)

Memorial Service at St Peter and St Paul's Church,
Little Horkesley, Essex, on 23 February 1999

A phenomenon of twentieth-century East Anglian farming is that some of its best land fell into disuse and wretchedness until it was brought back to life – by young Scots. I called these adventurers 'the Northern invaders' in *Akenfield*. Down they swept from their Lowland farmtouns, with their poor soil and poverty, to the rich clays of Norfolk, Suffolk, Essex and Cambridgeshire. Not only did these Scots bring back to life our farms, of which they became tenants before owning them, but they breathed new life and vitality into our villages. The Scots are the most powerful emigrants which these islands have produced, and they are certainly the most heart-sick-for-home travellers, never entirely integrated where they choose to settle, and so they stay, like our old neighbour and friend, distinctive.

William Brown was born on an Ayrshire farm on Michaelmas Day just a hundred years ago. And he could say – indeed, he did say, for he was wonderfully articulate about what happened to him all his long life – that he had witnessed the whole history of modern agriculture, from the kind of dairying which we read about in a Thomas Hardy novel to that of today's Common Agricultural Policy. All of it had passed before his eyes and through his hands.

I remember once needing to know how they reared the sheep on Romney Marsh before the last war, and it was 'Ask Mr Brown'. He would ask me to look up the meaning of certain Gaelic words in the glossary to my Robert Burns poems, because when you leave home aged three some of its meaning gets left behind. But very little of what he had seen and heard in a century of fields and meadows had slipped out of his memory, and so he was good to listen to. For many years he and Mr Gray, another ancient Scotsman, sat together at the back of this church in what they liked to call 'Farmers' Pew', and I often found myself thinking of the struggles and triumphs, like 'a tale that is told' that had brought them to Wormingford and Little Horkesley.

In 1901, when William Brown was a little boy, his father and two Ayrshire dairymen neighbours hired a special train for ten pounds, filled it up with everything which they possessed, their ploughs, their stock, their chattels, their families, and came to eastern England. The Browns eventually settled on a farm at Beacon Hill near Ongar. It was four times the size of the one which they left behind in Scotland. And there they worked with new hopes. It would be seventy years before William saw Ayrshire again but his parents, his mother especially, kept in touch with their roots. She was a Highlander and was never reconciled to our modest scenery.

Here there had been an abandonment of the farms. It was called 'the flight from the land'. The depression which had set in during the 1870s had created a bankrupt situation. Before the First World War farms were almost given away or fell into ruin. It was not only the Lowland Scots, but their wives and daughters who pulled them round. William told me that, for all this, we East Anglians would mock them for their efforts and dub them 'cowkeepers'. Of course, what these hardworking incomers challenged was rural inertia. But it was a tough time and William saw bankruptcy, distress, suicide. He would also see the second agricultural revolution which, beginning with the 'War Ag.' as it was called, brought about the prosperity and mechanised farming which we have today, a farming without farm-workers. We – he and I – would talk about this rollercoaster of an industry, all ups and downs.

There was a certain wholeness of William's experience of country life which made him a natural philosopher. Sitting with me about once a week in my old farmhouse, I used to marvel at his memory and the extent of his knowledge. He drove his car well into his nineties, his dog leaning out of the window. And he took to sitting in it when he came to a beautiful view, particularly in the Stour Valley.

His father remained at Beacon Hill until 1905 then moved to a five-hundred-acre farm called Wyfields. It was from there that William walked to Orsett school. It was a magnificently wooded Essex, deeply rural still. In it the 'Northern invaders' formed their own community. They became in fact a kind of East Anglian-Scots clan – as can be proved by their descendants now filling this church. So great was the attraction of our farms to the Lowlanders that young farmtoun men – some of your grandfathers, no doubt – would walk from Ayrshire to Suffolk. William told me that one of the reasons why they remained clannish was because the locals looked down on them. I have always believed that they found the determination of these arrivals rather upsetting.

When William returned to Ayrshire after seventy years he took his grandsons with him. They went to look at a memorial to a Covenanter ancestor who had been executed by Claverhouse which had been set up on a lonely moor. William was amazed when I sang him the old song 'To the Lords of Convention 'twas Claverhouse who spoke'. We had been taught it at school but I can't remember why. Fragments of poem, scraps of tunes hang around in all our heads, making small connections but little sense. Something of his stern Presbyterian faith certainly hung around in William's head.

In 1917 with agriculture subsidised because of the war, the Browns moved to Maldon Hall, where William drove his first tractor, a Fordson. When the war was over he got a job as a factor to Sir George Watson, who founded the Maypole Dairies. Sir George had himself begun life as a Northamptonshire farm boy. He and William got on well together and stayed with each other for twenty years. In 1949 he came into our orbit here at Little Horkesley, already over fifty, but with nearly fifty more years to come. In fact he arrived at Michaelmas, the classic date for a farm move, and on his birthday. He loved the hilly acres of Malting Farm and the glimpse of the river below. He was amused when his next-door neighbour, the artist John Nash, called this landscape 'the Suffolk-Essex Highlands'.

Our memory of William is of 'Grandpa', whether we were related to him or not. He spent his last days with Colin and Zoë in his big East Anglian 'long-house', Dairy Farm, Colin so skilfully rebinding ancient books, although, said Grandpa, he never started work until halfway through the morning. 'But just think,' I said, 'how long Colin works when he does get up.' William died in his own bed with his children and grandchildren around him, just as a farmer-patriarch should. He took with him a whole history of farming such as one would now only find in a book. I was too old to call him 'Grandpa', so goodnight, Mr Brown.

Bobby Corbett (1940–1999)
countryman and bon viveur

by Alexander McEwen
(country gentleman)

Funeral Service at Stair Church, Ayrshire, Scotland,
on 10 March 1999

To say anything about Bobby is to say too little. There is so much to say that the task is almost impossible.

I first got to know Bobby well as my younger brother David's best friend. Together and with others they shared houses and flats in London, culminating with their flat in Inverness Gardens (to give it its proper name). The chaos and eccentricity of Inverness Gardens can be judged by the fact that when they moved into it, the previous tenant had left a large fridge in the kitchen. Neither Bobby nor my brother had very much interest or use for fridges, and so it wasn't until several months had passed that one of them opened the door to find that the interior had come alive.

The door was hastily closed and a long leather strap was bought which they pulled as tightly as possible around their fridge, where it stayed for the duration of their tenancy.

It was about this time that Bobby took his first, and what turned out to be his last, job. This was organised by the Keswick family in Jardine Matheson. Bobby turned up on his first day and, come the lunch break, went off to have lunch in Claridge's. Emerging from the Causerie at three thirty, he realised that he had no idea of the name of his new firm, only that of the Keswicks. He had to ring up my aunt Mary Keswick to ask her what the name of her husband's firm was.

Jardines and Bobby parted company with a mutual sigh of relief shortly afterwards.

Bobby had the great misfortune to have two of his best friends die very young – Pips Royston and my brother David.

This, I think, encouraged him to keep busy and to set a yearly routine which, although never written into a diary, once established was repeated throughout his life.

His great love was hunting, and particularly the Eglinton, of which he was master for so long. About hunting he was enthusiastic, conscientious and extremely knowledgeable and it dominated all his years.

A rough outline of the routine went like this:

January: Hunting and a visit to the Waterfords in Ireland.

February: Hunting and the Waterloo Cup with the Heskeths.

March: Cheltenham.

April: Easter with the Keswicks.

May: Chelsea Flower Show and lunch, provided latterly by a long-suffering Hannah Cranborne. In an earlier period these lunches took place at the Mirabelle or Wiltons, both of which masqueraded as bookshops for the benefit of the trustees. Also in May the start of the Puppy Shows.

June: MFH meeting and lunch in London. Ascot and Wimbledon and the Eglinton Puppy Show and lunch. This was very much a loaves and fishes affair, as Bobby catered for twenty-five and asked ninety.

July: More Puppy Shows and an annual highlight: his visit with Cindy and Houston Shaw Stewart to the Queen Mother at Royal Lodge for the King George and Queen Elizabeth Stakes at Ascot.

August: The 12th would find Bobby with Mary Keswick at Glenkiln, where he was wont to wear his amazing corduroy shorts. Cub hunting begins.

September: Cubbing and, until quite recently, stalking at Invermark with the Ramsays.

October: Cubbing.

November: Hunting and occasionally shooting, usually at Ardgowan.

December: Hunting. Christmas at Lillburn with Duncan and Sarah Davidson. New Year with me and Cecilia, without fail, since 1967.

All of this would hardly have been possible without Linda, who drove him, and Sarah, his housekeeper.

Many people had great difficulty in understanding Bobby. This was partly due to the speed of his delivery, but also because of his use of verbal shorthand, combined with an inspired and inventive use of the language.

It would be impossible to sustain an imitation of Bobby, but some examples of his favourite shorthands and phrases might bring an echo of his delivery.

Nicaraguan; Rangoon Rangoon; in the confusion; the cake; immereffing; gravel sweeping; Shiite Muslims (used as an expletive); sharpen up, sharpen up, shuch wooch; a huge one; nothing in the world to worry about; and an angel straight from heaven. The last two, just to add to the confusion, meant the exact opposite. So 'nothing in the world' etc. probably meant the boiler had caught fire and the house was about to burn down, and 'an angel straight from heaven' he usually used to describe someone who no one else could stand.

Having learned the shorthand and re-tuned your ear, what Bobby said was magic — witty and erudite. He had a brilliant brain. You need one to get a scholarship to Christ Church, Oxford, as he did. His reading was wide and deep, and he retained the information. His knowledge of families, their houses and their contents was en-

cyclopaedic and in my memory, never at fault. He served on the
Curatorial Committee of the Scottish National Trust since its
inception.

He had unerring taste, with the possible exception of the 'gardening trousers', the 'primrose suit' and the corduroy shorts, which left
a little to be desired. He was already collecting Pre-Raphaelite
drawings while still at Eton.

Bobby's hospitality was legendary and endless, and he indulged
it to the full wherever and whenever he could. It came into full
flower at Stair, of which he was rightly proud.

To his adored sister and to all his family, may I offer our sympathy,
love and prayers, and say that, in losing Bobby, we haven't just lost
a friend, we've lost an institution and all of us are diminished.

In the Highlands after the '45 there was a saying: 'There is no
joy without Clan Ranald.'

I would say for us there is no joy without Bobby Corbett.

Ernie Wise (1925–1999)
comedian

by Michael Grade
(chairman of the BBC and chairman of Pinewood and Shepperton Studios)

Memorial Service at Slough Crematorium, Buckinghamshire, on 30 March 1999

There is an overwhelming sense of sadness that hovers over any funeral. But today, the tears are not just confined to this chapel, to the family and the friends who have come to mourn. Today there is a sadness across the whole nation as we all have to say our last farewell to Ernie Wise, the last half of a beloved British institution: the Morecambe and Wise comedy legend.

He was born Ernest Wiseman, seventy-three years ago in York-shire, in the humblest of circumstances and went on to achieve what is given to very, very few of us: by dint of his God-given talent, his hard work and his intelligence, he managed to leave an indelible mark on the rich cultural history of his country. In the process, he found a place in the affections of millions of its inhabitants through his professional achievements.

The nation's hearts go out today to Doreen as she faces a future without the man who was her devoted partner for forty-six years, through thick and thin, and let it not be forgotten just how much thin there was in the early days. I doubt anyone here could imagine a couple more devoted than Ernie and Doreen. They made and kept friends easily, they laughed together and, no matter what success came Ernie's way, they remained inseparable and unspoiled by the trappings of his glittering career. They delighted in each other's company both at work and at play.

The written tributes of the past week have gone some way to redress a rather unfair imbalance in the appreciation of the genius of Morecambe *and* Wise which has tended to concentrate more on Eric's dazzling contribution and not enough, in my opinion, not nearly enough on Ernie's. Let us be clear, they were equal partners in the comic.genius department.

I am talking here about the commentators and the critics – not the public who adored them both equally, except, that is, for the woman who spotted Ernie a year or two ago with the words, 'Don't see much of you on TV these days.'

'I have retired,' replied Ernie with that easy, boyish smile of his.

'Too bad,' said the woman. 'There are people on TV today much worse than you.'

Ernie loved telling that story – a mark of his enduring humility.

I suppose the reason Ernie has not yet had the fullest recognition he deserves is simply that he was so good at what he did, it didn't look as if he was doing anything. Singing, dancing, acting, clowning and joking – he made it appear effortless and second nature, such was his dedication, his precision and his mastery.

Why were Morecambe and Wise more successful at making the whole nation laugh than anyone before or since?

To me the answer is rather simple: there was Eric and there was Ernie and when you mixed the two together they created a comedic chemistry that can only be explained as a divine process that defies analysis. The results of this combustion was a great gift for the British nation, a gift that will be remembered so long as people want to laugh.

Nobody who did not enjoy the privilege of working closely with Morecambe and Wise can possibly understand the importance of the one to the other. Wise without Morecambe, Morecambe without Wise? Unthinkable – like trying to create a table without legs, short fat and hairy or not. Even their voices blended and matched. You really *couldn't* see the join.

They worked together for over forty years, learning their craft the hard way, until finally the world recognised their combined talent. The rest, as they say, is truly the stuff of legend.

Watching them night after night, performance after performance in Blackpool, Bournemouth or wherever, as I did back in the days when I was learning my trade from their agent Billy Marsh, I learned to read their individual moods. If Ernie went on stage feeling a notch or two below par, you could detect Eric working that bit harder to lift Ernie's spirits on their first appearance.

Ernie was just as good at getting Eric's juices going with an ad lib, a surprise gesture or moment that was certainly not rehearsed. Ernie was just as capable of making Eric laugh. It was a marriage of a kind, in fact, two of a kind.

They shared virtually all of their working lives together. They respected each other's talents, they shared the same ambition to succeed, the same fear of failure. What they particularly shared was a determination not to end up hating each other like most double acts before them. They worked hard, very very hard at their own relationship.

If they started life as a traditional comic and feed (Ernie: 'The invisible man's outside.' Eric: 'Tell him I can't see him') by the time Eddie Braben joined them at the BBC, there was a lot more to them than that. Their individual attitudes and personalities, frailties and conceits were exquisitely delineated by the scripts, and delicately performed on screen to great comic effect.

If Ernie had been just a straight man, Morecambe and Wise would still have been good – but not *that* good.

One of my outstanding memories of Ernie was a sketch written by Syd Green and Dick Hills – a Spanish dancing sketch. The whole routine depended entirely on Ernie's ability, or rather inability, to sing flamenco folk songs to a Spanish guitar accompaniment through sporadic fits of coughing.

That was just one memorable, brilliant sketch in which Eric was truly little more than Ernie's stooge. The audience howled with laughter as Ernie wailed and coughed and choked falteringly through some high screeched notes.

It was clowning of the highest order. I remember Eric coming off the studio floor at Elstree after the sketch and being blown away with laughter himself at Ernie's comic brilliance.

Off stage and out of the rehearsal room, Ernie was a shrewd businessman. Together they would agree what work they wanted to do; they never argued about it: if one wanted something and the other didn't, that was it – they didn't do it. It had to be a unanimous decision, then Ernie would be left to get on and drive the negotiations. And very good at it he was, too.

I remember we had opened negotiations for a further series for Lew Grade at ATV. 'They want how much!' exclaimed Lew. 'Let me talk to them.' We duly paraded early one morning with Eric and Ernie.

Ernie opened the conversation and, through a cloud of Lew's finest ten-inch Havana smoke, said, 'We bought you a present, Lew,' and from his inside pocket he produced a tiny packet of cheap Mannekin cigars. Eric, Billy and I collapsed with laughter, Lew had a rare sense of humour failure and Ernie never blinked. He got the deal.

John Ammonds, who produced so many of their great shows, offers testimony to how Ernie enjoyed his role as the businessman of the duo. He tells this story of the time they were rehearsing with Vanessa Redgrave. 'They both wound Vanessa Redgrave up,' he reports. 'She was excellent, but every tea break at rehearsal she'd be off outside selling the workers' revolutionary stuff – the *Morning Star* and all that.

'Well, we were with her in the BBC restaurant, and she tried to sell Eric and Ernie a copy of the paper. They just said, "No thanks, love – we're capitalists." Undeterred, she then said, "But do you own the BBC?" and Ernie glanced around and said, "No – but we're willing to make them an offer!"'

He was also, like his partner, a very nice man, truly a gentleman. I don't think I ever heard him swear. He always listened to what was being said to him. The professional pressures on him were always immense; it was one thing to reach the summit but staying there took real nerve.

In living with the pressure, both Eric and Ernie were blessed in their choice of partner. Doreen understood the pressures on Ernie and provided a haven away from the public arena. Boats, dogs, big band music, and peace and quiet were the shared escape for Ernie and Doreen. Peace and quiet, that is, until Ernie's cheque book came out. Ernie used to laugh because every time he tore out a cheque the dog growled menacingly. In the last fourteen years or so since Eric died, they had time as never before to enjoy each other's company without distraction – this they did to the full.

How proud Ernie must have been to see the collected works of Morecambe and Wise enjoyed by new generations as the repeats continued to earn their place in the schedules, attracting millions of viewers.

The last few months were clearly very difficult as Ernie, seemingly the indestructible one, succumbed to serious illness. Doreen's devotion and caring were called on as never before. She spared no effort to make his last months as comfortable as possible, suppressing her own feelings of despair as nature took its toll.

For us, his public, we have the video tapes to keep us in touch with the genius that was Morecambe and Wise. For you, Doreen, the tapes are not enough. Our hearts go out to you today and I hope that our thoughts and prayers and our love, and the memories of that very special human being we were all privileged to know as Ernie, will, somehow, offer some comfort and in time soothe your grief.

Let us all, then, say farewell to Ernie Wise – and let us give thanks for the sunshine wot *he* brought us all.

George Clive (1940–1999)
countryman

by Thomas Pakenham
(writer)

Memorial Service at St Peter's Church, Wormbridge, Herefordshire, on 23 April 1999

> The trees are coming into leaf
> Like something almost being said.
> Their greenness is a kind of grief.

This week Larkin's poem seemed to strike unbearably close to the bone. We know what those unfurling lime leaves on the lawn at Whitfield are saying, and for whom they are grieving: George.

George, who kept his pink cheeks and his pelt of fair hair and his sweetness of character while the rest of us became grey and bald and bad-tempered. George, who could walk as fast as most of us could run, and could carry a boulder under each arm, wading like Gulliver in the ponds he had created. George, who had more energy for each day than we could find for a week. George, the prince of hospitality, the landmark of good sense and good humour. George, the young oak destined to live for a thousand years, the rock on whom we all depended – suddenly, shockingly, he has gone.

Two hours ago I stood in George's private garden – the one to the right of the pond – watching the rain varnish the leaves of the great willow-leaved magnolias he had planted. Last year I was there at his side soon after the leaves unfurled. George explained every nuance of the garden, as though introducing me to intimate friends.

He probed into that Himalayan jungle of fern and rhododendron and blue poppies (and I had sent him seed for some from Tibet), set off by the fangs of the snake-bark maples. This was his own private arcadia, a garden he had designed and built and planted. The garden had begun quite unassumingly, and now it had burst out into fruition, and joined a grand vista of ponds running down the skyline. One sensed the passionate pride of family — sensed only, for George would never have had the swagger to put this in words. He had marked out his territory, added his own grand vision to the vision of earlier Clives. Here was a salute to the past, to the Clive squire who had planted the ginkgo two hundred years before, to Archer Clive who sowed the great oaks and the even greater sequoias — above all to his mother to whom he was devoted like no one else's son. She had rescued Whitfield from ruin, snatched it back from the grave. Here was an act of homage expressed in a grand vision, a huge hug from George stretching out all the way to the skyline.

Did I say grand vision? The word 'grand' brings me up short. Was George really a grandee or a bigwig — as somebody said, 'the most up to date of eighteenth-century squires'?

Somehow the words don't seem to fit the George I knew. (And I know he would have told us, gently, that we were talking rot.)

To see him in his mud-stained Barbour by the library fire, after a hard day's shooting, one knew that he had less personal vanity, less self-importance than anyone who ever owned a grand staircase or planted a great avenue.

His calmness and gentleness presented a strange contrast to the character of his cousins and friends, many of whom were extremely noisy. 'You just can't make Clive cross,' said one outraged small boy at Sunningdale, his prep school.

Did George ever raise his voice in anger? I believe it only happened once. The pheasants, blast them, flew the wrong way out of the wood!

Kindness and sympathy were second nature to him. Like all truly sensitive people he was exceptionally sensitive to the feelings of others. He knew what they felt and how to help them. Sometimes he said nothing, but the silence said it all.

Two days ago his mother told me this story about him which she wants you to hear.

Before he was born, I decided to call him George. You see, in those days, when somebody stopped to get help – say, a lorry driver who had broken down or lost the way – well, he would stop and say, 'Hi, George', meaning help me. So I decided that, if I ever had a boy, I would call him George, so that, when someone called for help, George would run forward, and everyone would know he was kind and helpful.

George's talents were as rich as his gifts. Indeed he had a surplus. Sometimes I wonder if he was afraid of becoming a dilettante and spreading his talents too thinly. He could do most things better than most people. (True, he couldn't sing a note. But that was the Pakenham side of his inheritance.) He could act; in fact there is a film of him acting in drag at Eton. He could draw and design. At school he had drawn subversive caricatures of the masters. He could write. But there was the danger. Whitfield and country life plus a literary career in London might have proved a fatal intoxicant. Years ago one used to see him in front of the fireplace in the reading room of the London Library. The clubmen snored; George scribbled, with a mysterious smile on his face. He wrote first a play, then a novel. Perhaps these early works were brilliant. But George must have decided that writing books was a family failing – like alcohol in other families. So he kicked the habit.

Instead he concentrated his talents on three subjects where he could carry most weight and authority. These subjects became his ruling passion: trees and gardens, farms and the countryside, conservation of all kinds.

For an expert, George was extraordinarily self-effacing. The most knowledgeable depended on him for advice. But some of his London friends never understood what he did. 'Why doesn't George do something with his life?' I remember being asked at a London party. In fact George did everything. He was a hands-on-the-plough farmer who knew every corner of every field and forest on the estate. Locals looked up to him as the very type of the best landowner. His sense of public service impelled him to join every kind of committee in Herefordshire and beyond. For ten years he dominated one of the key committees of the National Trust, felling rotten trees, restoring great gardens, building follies and gazebos. He ruled the Herefordshire branch of the RHS with what one of his friends described as 'a rod of iron'. 'One always liked sitting next to George,' she said later. 'He was so reassuring. He didn't say much – a good chairman doesn't – but he knew what he wanted and he got it, and usually he was right.'

Sometimes he got what he wanted by stealth. He loved Hereford and its eccentric treasures. One day he heard that the famous chained library at All Saints Church was coming on to the art market to pay the church's debts. George was shocked. How dare they sell their patrimony! Within a few weeks he had raised the large sum – more than a hundred thousand pounds – needed to save the library, and it was rumoured he had paid for much of the rescue himself.

People who didn't know George could be misled by his extreme gentleness of manner. By nature and upbringing he was competitive. If challenged, he could prove a dangerous adversary. To play any game against George could be alarming. Not that he served a hard ball at tennis if he knew you were no good; he was far too kind-hearted for that. But if he thought you were up to his game then you were in for it. George did not exactly cheat. Shall I say that he had intimate knowledge of the terrain which he exploited with a stubborn will to succeed.

It was the same if you challenged George to an argument over dinner. George did not like small talk (unless it was gossip), but he adored a real argument, and expected to win. Usually he did. The soft voice and the hesitant manner concealed a powerful intellect, an iron will and a dangerously retentive memory. Sometimes you thought you had George on toast; and there was the book on the Whitfield shelves to prove it. But George had read it too and remembered it better. His knowledge was encyclopaedic. He seemed to have read and reread every novel from Defoe to Vikram Seth. Indeed his range was wider still – from vintage cars to Homer. It was typical of him to reread the entire *Iliad* when in hospital last month in Hereford.

George's illness brought to a tragic end what must have been the happiest eighteen years of his life. He had taken a long time to find the right companion. But in Penny he found her. This was a golden age for Whitfield, and for George a long-delayed spring. Penny's dazzling style exactly complemented George's lack of it. His shyness and awkwardness fell away as his life fell into place. They shared the same books and the same jokes. They were a hilarious couple at parties and private views. Penny shared and reawakened his own artistic gifts. Both loved foreign travel. They roamed Mexico, Guatemala, Tibet. Everywhere they had friends. No one blighted with shyness ever told funnier stories or broke free to make so many friends.

Then the unthinkable happened.

To die of a painful illness that the doctors could not diagnose would have tested the character of a saint. Characteristically, George was sweet-tempered and cheerful to the very end. He was loved by the nurses at St Thomas's who said they had never met a patient who cared so much about them. Of course he was worried about the pain his illness brought to others, especially to Penny, Alice and his mother. He hardly thought of himself – except to remark wryly to a friend that, if this was lung cancer (and tragically it was) then it was ironic that he should have it, when he had never smoked a cigarette in his life.

My own last conversation with him, a fortnight before he died, was hilarious. He laughed at the latest gossip. Then he told me a story about six huge, old trees at Whitfield – the giants of more than twenty foot in girth. He had measured them all when he had first come into Whitfield. When he went to re-measure them recently they were all dead – for one reason or another. 'But the odd thing was' – and George gave his famous gurgling chuckle – 'that I found six more giants of more than twenty feet girth, and I must have missed them the first time round. You see, out in the park they looked so unassuming, that you had no idea of their size, until you came close.'

George, too, was so unassuming that you could have no idea of his stature until you came close.

We were privileged to know – and love – such an extraordinary man.

Ted Hughes (1930–1998)

poet laureate, 1984–98

by Seamus Heaney

(poet)

*Memorial Service at Westminster Abbey, London,
on 13 May 1999*

At Ted Hughes's funeral in Devon last November his coffin was lifted out of the church by his daughter Frieda and her husband, by his son Nicholas and by members of his wife Carol's family. They carried it by the handles. It wasn't shouldered but held at knee level, and moved past us steadily and buoyantly, as if the aisle were a river where the bearers waded and the coffin rode towards the door on a clear channel of light and air.

The poet's removal was happening very close to us and yet at that moment we all felt part of a long perspective. What came into my mind was a poem by Wilfred Owen about a hospital barge appearing round a bend of the River Somme, sunk to its gunwales under a load of wounded men; and then in my mind's eye I saw what Owen had also seen in his mind's eye, eighty years before. I saw the image of King Arthur's twilit passage towards Avalon, the hero on his barge being translated into memory – 'renewed, transfigured, in another pattern'.

And this expanding of love is, as T.S. Eliot wrote, 'the use of memory' – and the use of a memorial service. At this moment, in this abbey where kings and poets lie translated into legend, it is impossible not to think of Ted Hughes as one of the figures in the tapestry, one of the valiant and the destined, a permanence who would be as much at home with Caedmon, the first English poet, in the seventh-century monastery at Whitby, as he would have been with Owen and his doomed men in the trenches by the Somme. He has become another 'genius of the shore', a guardian spirit of the land and of the language, as vigorous in the afterlife of his poems as those thistles he once compared to 'the gutturals of dialect'. His death has rendered his work utterly clear, like the water he wrote of, the water that wanted to live.

Utter sympathy with everything that wanted to live came naturally to Ted. He was the born poet in so far as his first impulse was to give glory to creation and through his glorification allow it to be more abundantly itself. But he was also the made poet, the poet schooled by deep learning in his art, marked by personal and historical sorrows, and by a kind of soothsayer's awareness that facing a destiny was bound to involve a certain ordeal.

One part of Ted believed in the gene and its laws as the reality we inhabit and are bound to adjust to, since there issues from the genetic code the whole alphabet of our possibilities, from the alpha at the start of the evolutionary journey to the omega at the end. But another part of him looked through the microscope and telescope into the visionary crystal, and could see Dante's eternal *margherita*, the pearl of foreverness, in the interstices of the DNA. This is the part of him that recognised that myths and fairytales were the *poetic* code, that the body was a spirit beacon as well as a chemical formula, that it was born for ecstasy as well as for extinction. And it is this believing and envisaging part of him which made a difference to the culture he was a part of, and made him a focus and an education in every company he entered. It also makes his death a heartbreak for all who knew and loved him.

Ted was a great man and a great poet because of his wholeness and his simplicity and his unfaltering truth to his own sense of the world. That sense of the world was epic and stern in that it constantly beheld, behind the business of the usual, a sacred drama being enacted. In this drama, everything that wanted to live, whether it was a cell or a salmon, was hurling itself over the top in wave after gallant wave, only to encounter the black fusillade of everything that was deadly and undoing. And from this perception of the struggle at the heart of things – a struggle in the soil as well as in the soul – the abiding at-oneness of all his work derives.

This instinct for wholeness made him a great poet laureate as well, for he had an almost Indo-European sense of the necessary consonance between the good of the land and the good standing of its bard. In the end he was fulfilling the role of the representative poet, answerable to the shade of Shakespeare, having to live up to the spiritual standards set by Blake and Dickinson and Hopkins.

'Merlin-like' is how one of his friends has described Ted's mes-meric accuracy in making a cast with a fly-line, but there was also something Merlin-like about his presence among us while he lived. He internalised the historical crises of the British nation and the ecological crises of planet earth. He took on the grief of the genera-tion that preceded him, the generation bound to the dead of the First World War, and transformed it into a healer's vision. And there was something homeopathic about his celebration of plants and creatures, since the poems were essentially reminders that we are all part of the same fabric, woven out of and into the palpable, mysteri-ous universe.

His ultimate gift was for setting experience afloat upon that pure river of the water of life which was revealed to the evangelist. And it was, as the scripture says, 'in the midst of the street of it' that he was carried away from us, down the aisle.

Lord Menuhin (1916–1999)
violinist

by Professor George Steiner
(Fellow of Churchill College, Cambridge)

*Memorial Service at Westminster Abbey,
London, on 3 June 1999*

He would have said it so simply. Directness was his genius.

He would have rejoiced in the presence of so many of his friends, colleagues and admirers from across the whole world. Above all, in that of his students. He was an incomparable teacher of being.

Yehudi Menuhin would have smiled at the high magnificence of this setting and occasion. Such magnificence, such shared radiance, was his from childhood on. He accepted it with sovereign ease. To honour those by whom one is honoured, to make of their acclaim a reciprocity, a donation in return, is the rarest of generosities. A Menuhin performance, overwhelmingly public or intimate, left everyone directly addressed, directly enriched. There is here a mystery of modesty, of luminous acceptance. Yehudi spoke, with totally unaffected wonder, of the relative effortlessness with which he had mastered early elements of his virtuosity, with which he had been given access to a range of music and musical tradition far beyond those of other performers, interpreters and teachers. He touched with the observant gentleness of the very strong on what he felt to be his good fortune. How could he not give utterly to others when so much had been given to him?

He would, one hopes, have delighted in this morning's

ceremonial splendour (the bond with Elgar was real). But Lord
Menuhin's rapid eye would have noted in our assembly some old
friend out of private life, some guest from a troubled part of the
planet, some beginner in the arts of music. And that single presence
would, one ventures, have brought him a pleasure as vivid, as great
as that of this eminent company. I do not know how to put this
adequately: never has there been a figure of world fame, a household name in the awareness of millions, who could make of his
public glory and impact a more individualised, a more private
encounter. To meet Yehudi, even briefly, was to be trusted. There
is hardly a homecoming to oneself at once more flattering and more
demanding.

Hence his capacity to reach out to men, women and children of
virtually every race, religion, nationality, ideology or social standing.
Hence his self-confessed ambassadorship to the human condition.
(Again, he would have said it so much more simply.) Generations
to come will marvel at his travels, at Menuhin's immersion in Asian
and African settings, at the rapport he established with 'princes and
potentates' on the one hand and the humblest, the most victimised
on the other. An untiring missionary of hope, of sometimes incensed
decency and protest in the face of the inhuman, Yehudi Menuhin
embodied the fusion of two legacies, of two legacies in so many
ways opposed: that of Judaism, with its thirst for justice, with its
messianic investment in futurity, with its fierce commitment to
teaching, and that of an ecumenism at once rooted in the Enlightenment and in an anguished clairvoyance as to the dangers which now
surround us. His was that most singular of visions: a Judaism of the
ecumenical.

This universality inheres in Menuhin's conception and practice
of music. He identified the performance and reception of music
with that of a universal language. This language had diverse dialects
– oriental and western, classical and popular. But it embodied the
only medium immediate to all mankind; a unifying imperative of
life-giving communication, of indefinable but also palpable truth
underlay its worldwide spectrum. Lord Menuhin was a fluent linguist. But what mattered was the unison within him, within utter-
ance and performance, of music and of any other mode of articulate

expression. To perform to others was, for Menuhin, a 'speech-act' as charged with significance, with person-to-person meanings, as any in speech.

This, I believe, accounts for the vocal, voiced quality – how else is one to put it? – of his playing and recordings. Consider Yehudi Menuhin's recording of the first violin concerto by Bartók, and of Bartók's concerto for viola. The instrument becomes a human voice. Its intensity and nuances of address are such as to abolish the distinctions between music and discourse, between musical phrasing and that in spoken grammar. The local inflection is wonderfully audible, as if it rose directly out of Hungarian, with its particular warmth and syncopation. But this particularity, this *vibrato* of intent in its historical, national setting broaden into universality. It enacts the ancient intuition of an Adamic tongue, which underwrites, which ultimately makes possible, the passage from one language to another, from one civilisation and legacy to another, across the manifold variousness of a world after Babel. As in only a handful of virtuosi, music, when performed by Menuhin – listen to his playing of the Beethoven romances – is made focused speech.

What is said is as prodigal and various as was Menuhin's career, as richly specific to occasion and place as were his performances and spoken interventions across the globe. But after 1945 – and there can be no overestimate of Lady Menuhin's, of Diana's, indispensable role in this crucial encounter with human catastrophe, with the death-camps for whose barely surviving inmates Menuhin performed – the central message became more and more urgent. It was that of a man compassionately but very firmly possessed by the ideal of peace, of reconciliation between ideologies, nations and political systems. Had we not the genius of the musician and educator in music, we would be bearing witness to the visionary advocate for mutual understanding.

The phone rang, very late one night. Yehudi's voice was at once anguished and strongly serene. The Six-Day War was raging. Ten of us must go at once to the Middle East and camp between the lines. This would initiate an immediate cease-fire. I ventured the thought that nine of us would be swiftly done away with, leaving his own illustrious self in intact solitude. The sadness in Yehudi's tone as he rang off made me regret what hint of cynicism or of levity there may have been in my objection.

His innocence − though that may be the wrong word − was measureless. It was a persistent reproach to one's tawdry, perhaps lazy, realism. It was axiomatic to Menuhin that human beings, brought face to face, made cognisant of their shared humanity, precisely as music makes us all aware of that fundamental bond, would come to mutual understanding and forgiveness. The pragmatic mysticism of tolerance, of millennial patience characteristic of certain oriental faiths and philosophies, appealed to him profoundly. As did the universalism of social justice, of moral equity in the Hebrew prophets. Menuhin could draw from within his own disciplined body and empathies of spirit on exceptional resources of tranquillity and of hope. How was it that other men and women could yield so readily to self-devouring fanaticism, greed and cruelty? Yet no soul was finally damned. 'If I believed that God could not forgive Hitler . . .' It was the one and only time I asked Yehudi Menuhin to leave a sentence incomplete. In Diana's eyes I caught a spark of amused malice.

It has been given to very few to live, to illuminate so many of the representative motifs in our dark century. The Menuhin background was one of immigration and refuge. Yehudi's training and early triumphs reflect the generosity towards great gifts characteristic of American society and idealism. Giving some five hundred recitals for Allied troops in the field, Menuhin saw the sufferings of war at close range. Yet his controversial decision to be the first to play amid the ruins of Berlin placed him at the very forefront of the dream of European renascence and pardon. Lord Menuhin's understanding for and assistance to his fellow-musicians struggling for breath under Soviet despotism were unstinted. His support became legend. But he lived to see the iron gates open and the restoration to the mainstream of music of that immense Russian contribution, particularly in the domain of the virtuoso string-players.

Menuhin's first gramophone recording is dated 1928. Thus he fully experienced and participated in the revolution of electronic means which has led to present-day criteria of fidelity and sonority.

It is possible that his own preference lay with warmer, technically less crystalline registers; Menuhin did not, so far as I know, perform or record much *avant-garde* experimentation. But he was never closed to the world around him.

This openness becomes exemplary after 1962 and the foundation of the Menuhin School for young musicians. Together with a deepening involvement in Indian music and holistic thought, Menuhin's turn to education was a wager, humane and joyous, on the future. We hear that wager, its dynamic lift, in the sixteen-year-old's unsurpassed interpretation of the slow movement and scherzo in the Elgar concerto; in Menuhin's lifelong dialogue with Mozart. Where that future for man and for music was concerned, Yehudi was never prepared to lose.

Perhaps it is that which makes Yehudi Menuhin so vividly present to us this morning. Which makes almost irrelevant where he and his work are concerned any resort to the past tense. For us, for millions beyond this gathering, Menuhin simply *is*.

Linford Cazenove (1974–1999)
actor, writer, director

by Julian Fellowes
(actor, writer, director)

*Memorial Service at St Paul's Church, Knightsbridge,
London, on 17 September 1999*

Of course, that it should fall to me, fat and bald and middle-aged
as I am, to give an address at the funeral of Linford Cazenove is to
spit in the eye of the natural order of things. But I am here because
many years ago Linford did me the honour of asking me to be his
godfather, an honorary godfather. Now most of us have to tolerate
the godparents that have been chosen with small regard to our taste
and it struck me then and it strikes me now that to be selected for
the job by the child in question was probably one of the finest
compliments I could ever receive.

I have many memories of Linford like all of you. I start young,
watching him at play in the fortress his father created at Vardens
Road or the rather more streamlined model he created at Boling-
broke Grove. I remember decorating a birthday cake for Linford.
He was very exacting as you know and this one had to be precisely
in the shape of a busy swimming pool. This required Chris and I
to spend an entire morning cutting little plastic figures in half at the
waist so that both their heads and their feet should stick out of the
water. I remember giving a house party in Sussex, where I used to
live, for bonfire night. He can't have been very much more than
nine and he came to me and said, 'I've got the most fantastic idea.

Let's stuff the guy with rockets. When it falls forward into the flames they will all go off but – this is the best bit – no one can have any idea what direction they are going to go off in.' This plan, happily, stayed on the drawing board.

And I remember him older, more sober, in evening dress in our dining room, waiting to go to Annabel's and celebrate my niece's twenty-first; and older still: at university, hard-working, committed and serious, but not, as we have heard, so serious as not to celebrate his Finals by running round George Square naked or by taking the clothes of the girls lucky enough to have joined in this prank and throwing them over the nearest wall.

And then suddenly he was a man. He had grown up as children are wont to do when you are not looking. But the danger of these nostalgic trends is, I think, they seem to lead inextricably to a point to where one sobs out the tragedy of a wasted life or a potential cheated of fulfilment and in this case, at least, I believe that would be quite wrong. I don't think Linford's was a wasted life. He was living his life and I don't think his potential was cheated of fulfilment. No doubt had he lived longer he would have done much, much more, but the fact is he achieved an astonishing body of work. His was not a spirit to linger at the garden gate of life wondering which way to choose. He was off and running from the very start. Even with his dyslexia, which I thought he always wore very gracefully, more as a tiresome nuisance than a great drama, as soon as he had realised all it meant was that he had to work three times as hard as everybody else, he got down to it and very soon first of all caught up with, then outstripped most of his contemporaries. His years at Edinburgh and Cambridge were full of triumphs, not just in his chosen field of philosophy but in the theatre, the revue, the Lyceum, the wonderful praise from the critics, the nominations, the awards, in his acting, in his directing, in his studying, in his writing, in his travelling, in his everything.

If we must judge a life, surely it should be by its quality and not its quantity. How many men and women in their dotage would cheerfully exchange those empty years for just a trace of the glory that was Mozart or Emily Brontë or Chatterton or Rupert Brooke, or any of those other bright stars that illuminate our sky for one brief shining moment, and so with Linford. It is too soon to say if any of his work will live on, although I believe it will, not least as an influence on the work of others. But it is not too soon to say that he has left a lasting legacy in the lives that he has touched. This was an extraordinary number given his twenty-five years and not just family and friends, but chance acquaintance and even strangers. He touched them both by what he did and by what he was. Of course today our hearts are with Angharad, Christopher and Rhys William who have lost not just a son and brother but their best friend. But I would like to leave you with one more thought. It is true that Linford Cazenove's life on earth is done but let us all give thanks that while he lived it he made it such a marvellous success.

William Whitelaw (first Viscount Whitelaw of Penrith) (1918–1999)
former Deputy Prime Minister

by Lord Carrington
(Foreign Secretary, 1979–82)

Memorial Service at the Guards Chapel, Wellington Barracks, London, on 27 October 1999

Willie was one of the most respected and successful public men of his generation. A courageous soldier in a remarkable battalion of the Scots Guards, followed by a long career in politics in many important positions. A quite outstanding chief whip who had the trust and affection of his party and, incidentally, in that and in another capacity, was an important factor in the appointment and election of two Prime Ministers; Home Secretary and Leader of both Houses of Parliament; above all, he was the shrewdest of men, an oasis of common sense. No wonder he was the man on whose wisdom and advice so many of his colleagues relied.

Both to those of us here this morning and particularly to those who knew him for fifty years or so, he was much more than just a politician and statesman. He was both physically and in character larger than life. He had a very loud voice and though most of his widely publicised indiscretions were intentional, a number were due to his mistaken belief that he was whispering! When Willie came into a room you knew he had arrived. He was an extrovert, he liked people and they liked him and became and stayed his friends and admirers.

He was a serious and thoughtful man, whose political philosophy stemmed from his upbringing in the thirties at a time of mass unemployment and deprivation, as well as his wartime experience. He was, in addition, a considerable operator. He had, for instance, a remarkable capacity to calm a fractious House of Lords, as much by his instinctive understanding of people as by his political skill.

He did not believe, however, that public life and politics had to be taken too glumly. Life was there to be enjoyed and as a result he made life more enjoyable for all of us. For example, it was most enjoyable to watch him, when irritated by a particularly foolish action, get into a tremendous rage and shake with fury; whether the rage was real or simulated, it always had the desired effect and he certainly didn't have a poker face, and to look at him, when a colleague was putting his foot in it, or when he was listening to an interminably boring speech, was unrivalled entertainment.

He had the sunniest of dispositions and to be in his company was as relaxing as it was fun. The gales of laughter, the hoots of protest, the No No Nos and Yes Yes Yeses, the exuberance of it all will be a lasting and cherished memory.

In a period of increasing conformity and political correctness, Willie was a shining exception. How fortunate for us that he dedicated his life to public service; how lucky we were to be his friend.

Sir Hugh Casson (1910–1999)
architect

by John Julius Norwich
(writer)

*Memorial Service at St Paul's Cathedral, London,
on 19 November 1999*

I was first conscious of Hugh's genius when, at the time of the Festival of Britain, he seemed effortlessly to transform the whole of London; but I got to know him only many years later in the National Trust, where we both served on the Properties Committee. Never without a pencil in his hand, he doodled constantly; I would make a point of always trying to sit next to him, watching over his shoulder as one exquisite little drawing after another would appear all over whatever paper we happened to be considering – at the top of the first page, at the bottom of the last, in the left- and right-hand margin, sometimes even between the lines of the typescript. Once, I remember, we were discussing an unexpected windfall from a lady who lived somewhere on the south coast. Nobody had ever heard of her; nobody knew what she was like. I heard the familiar sound of Hugh's scratching pencil and glanced across; there, sketched in about five seconds, was an enchanting little girl of about five, wearing a huge sun hat, crumpled ankle socks, clutching a bucket and spade and staring with the gravity of a small child at the sea in front of her. After the meeting Hugh left it – as he always left all his doodles – on the table. I collared it, as I had collared many in the past and was to collar a good many more in the future, and it still hangs on the wall of my study. The mimeographed words '8 – Any other business' and '9 – Date of next meeting' in the sky above her have always seemed to add to, rather than to detract from, the *ensemble*.

The speed of his hand and the certainty of his line left one astonished. There was a wonderful week – by now it must be a good quarter of a century ago – when a prodigiously rich Canadian foundation asked me to pick a team to attend a three-day seminar on the High Victorian period in the University of Guelph, after which we could all travel anywhere we liked in Canada as the foundation's guests. To my joy, I managed to enlist John Betjeman and Elizabeth, Asa and Susan Briggs – and Hugh and Reta. I have seldom enjoyed a week more. When the seminar was over, we flew to Calgary, drove to Lake Louise, and there picked up the overnight train through the Rocky Mountains to Vancouver. The moment I remember best is when we were all standing in the Lake Louise station, accompanied by some fifty Japanese – who were presumably attending some convention or other – all of whom were ranged down the platform, very seriously practising their golf swings. I thought John Betjeman was going to die of laughter; but Hugh rose at once to the challenge. Since it took him rather less time to produce a completed drawing than most of us needed to take a photograph, by the time the train came in he had a whole notebook full, each more acutely observed – and more dazzlingly executed – than the last.

That incredible eye of his: it missed nothing. Again and again the Fine Arts Panel of the National Trust would visit a room in one of the properties that was somehow lacking in charm or atmosphere; again and again Hugh would put his finger unerringly on what needed to be done to give it a lift – to repaint the chimney-piece, perhaps, or to switch round a couple of pictures.

But it's no good just talking about his draughtsmanship, or his eye for a room or a building; the real point about Hugh was his own inner magic. Oddly enough, I think his size may have had something to do with it. Large men can dazzle too, in their own way; but they can't twinkle as he did – still less can they be Puckish. Twinkle, Puckishness: do they suggest something shallow, or superficial? I think perhaps they do, but Hugh – heaven knows – was neither. There was mischief in him, certainly, and he was seldom reluctant to put the cat among the pigeons; but quite right too – every flock of pigeons is immeasurably improved by having a cat among it. And it was just that marvellous twinkle that enabled him to disarm opposition and to Get Things Done.

What he actually got done was a very great deal; but I'm neither an architect nor an Academician, and I'm not here this morning to discuss his achievements, superb as they were. I want only to talk of Hugh as a man and as a very dear friend – whom I admired, certainly, barely this side of idolatry, but whom I also loved. And, since the tragic news of little more than a fortnight ago, I must also talk briefly of Reta – an immensely distinguished designer and teacher in her own right, but also the perfect companion and help-meet to her husband. A moment ago I used the word 'tragic', which all deaths must be for those who are left behind. But when her own time came she, I suspect, would not have complained. Hugh had gone; she was ready to join him.

For us, too, it's as if the sun had gone in; the world is a duller place. But we shall all treasure our own memories of Hugh and Reta, of him with that twinkling eye and that black silk frock coat with its PRA badge, of her with that shy, faintly conspiratorial smile and those beautiful caftans. And yet somehow, whenever I think of them, there also comes into my mind a third, unforgettable figure: that little girl on the sands with her bucket and spade, staring solemnly at the sea.

Sonia Heathcoat-Amory (1921–1999)
war widow, married two cousins

by Sir Ludovic Kennedy
(writer and broadcaster)

*Service of Thanksgiving at St Michael's and All Angels
Church, Kington St Michael, Wiltshire,
on 21 January 2000*

Sixty-two years ago last autumn, that is in 1938, at a house party
in Ayrshire I was introduced to one of the prettiest girls I had
yet seen. This was Sonia Denison aged seventeen, and for me the
beginnings of a friendship which only ended last Christmas Eve
with her death. Nor was my assessment of her a biased one because
after war had broken out, there was a photograph of her in a Red
Cross nurse's dress on the cover of a magazine with the caption
'BEAUTY IN UNIFORM'.

Sonia's father was a retired naval captain. Her mother, Betty
Denison, was like her daughter a lively opinionated woman who
lived to the ripe old age of ninety-six. This enabled her granddaughter Amanda, who like her mother married at nineteen and had a
son at twenty to achieve what must be a unique record, of being
both a granddaughter and a grandmother at the same time.

The war treated Sonia and her parents cruelly. In 1940 she married
her first husband, Gerald Heathcoat-Amory, who I remember at
Eton as being a highly professional Master of the Beagles. In 1944,
after the birth of her son Michael and when Sonia was already
expecting Amanda, Gerald was killed within a week of landing in

France. Then, just a year later, her brother Philip, an Eton friend of mine, very brainy and rather dapper, also met his death, though in the most tragic circumstances. He had been captured in the retreat from France in 1940, and for the next five years was a prisoner of war. Then in the spring of 1945 when he and his fellow-prisoners were marching out of their camp on what they believed to be the road to freedom, some American fighters, mistaking them, as Americans often seem to, for the enemy, opened fire; and Philip was among those killed. Sonia met these devastating double blows with the same courage and stoicism that was to characterise her whole life.

Yet if fate had brutally brought to an abrupt end one very happy marriage, another rather different, though in the end no less happy, would soon begin. In 1947 Sonia married Gerald's cousin Roddy Heathcoat-Amory, then still in the army. One newspaper, perhaps short of space, reported the occasion in somewhat truncated and enigmatic form. 'On 28th April 1947 at St Mark's North Audley Street, Major Heathcoat-Amory married Mrs Heathcoat-Amory. They were attended by Master Heathcoat-Amory and Miss Heathcoat-Amory.'

In the course of his long life I got to know Roddy pretty well, as I'm sure many of you did, and being here today reminds me of the occasion two years ago – though it seems like only yesterday – when, as his coffin was being borne out of the church, the organ broke into 'Do you ken John Peel', a surprising yet wonderfully apposite and moving farewell to a lifelong sporting man. I always thought of Roddy as being the nearest thing to the perfect gentleman, not in the class sense but in his whole bearing and attitude to life and other people.

He was also one of the funniest. I'm sure I'm not the only one here to have dined out on some of his anecdotes, though none of us could tell them in the seemingly hesitant, carefully crafted way that he did. One of my favourites concerned his time with the British Army of the Rhine. In his office one day the telephone rang, and Roddy answered it. The caller seemed particularly obtuse and Roddy gave as good as he got. Finally the caller said, 'Do you know who you're talking to?' Roddy said he didn't and the voice said, 'Well, I'll tell you. It's Philip Keightley, the Commander in Chief.' 'Oh,' said Roddy, taken aback, 'and do you know who you're talking to?' 'No,' said Keightley, 'can't say I do.' 'Thank God for that,' said Roddy, and slammed the phone down.

Roddy's last army appointment was in Yorkshire and he and Sonia had come to love it so much that on his retirement they bought a delightful house in the village of Oswaldkirk. They stayed there thirty years, enjoying hunting, shooting and a full social life, both there and at the family's Scottish estate in Perthshire, stalking, pursuing grouse when there were any to pursue and fishing. Sonia also bred spaniels and Jacob sheep. She was gregarious by nature, loved entertaining and whenever any of the children brought home unexpected guests, a bed or a place at table could always be found for them. In all her relationships she was fiercely loyal and once you had found favour with her you were hers for life. She was particularly fond of young people and young people were equally attracted to her. All her children praise her qualities as a mother. As one of them put it to me: 'She made life so much fun for us.' She was also a splendid godmother to our youngest daughter who told me on the telephone from Sydney how disappointed she is not to be here.

In some ways she was so delightfully old-fashioned, believing that women's principal role in life was to see to the welfare of their men. But not all men. Not Germans for instance and not those from ethnic minorities whom Dame Edna Everage calls tinted people. Asked to describe a quite close friend, she used to reply, 'Jewish but nice.' Yet if ever she met a German or a Jewish or tinted person, which didn't happen all that often, no one could have been more friendly, more considerate, more charming.

For someone so socially conventional, one might have assumed she would be a staunch monarchist. In fact she was an ardent republican. She also had, at least with some people, one odd eccentricity in that if you said something on a particular subject, she would sometimes reply by referring to a totally unrelated subject. This could be quite disconcerting.

Sadly the last years of her life were clouded by illness, which she bore with her usual fortitude. When asked how she was she would invariably reply, almost brusquely, 'The same,' which pre-empted, as indeed it was meant to, any further enquiries on the matter. Yet when I saw her for the last time in her nursing home only a few weeks ago and asked her how she was, she said with disarming frankness, 'I've had enough. I'm exhausted, and I want to die.' And when I kissed her goodbye, knowing that what she had said was true, I said, 'I hope your wish is granted very soon.' And it was because Sonia had willed it. She had recognised the truth of the passage from Ecclesiastes which Patrick Cairns read us earlier that there is a time to die; and we should be glad of it because it meant an end to her suffering.

Let me end with a couple of verses by the Victorian poet Christina Rossetti which to my mind, and perhaps yours, could almost be Sonia speaking:

> When I am dead, my dearest,
> Sing no sad songs for me,
> Plant thou no roses at my head,
> Nor shady cypress tree.
> By the green grass above me
> With showers and dewdrops wet,
> And, if thou wilt, remember,
> And, if thou wilt, forget.
>
> I shall not see the shadows.
> I shall not feel the rain,
> I shall not hear the nightingale
> Sing on, as if in pain.
> And dreaming through the twilight
> That does not rise nor set,
> Haply I may remember
> And haply may forget.

Sir Malcolm Bradbury (1932–2000)
writer

by Professor David Lodge
(writer)

*Memorial Service at Norwich Cathedral
on 10 February 2000*

I want to speak about Malcolm as a writer and friend – the first, the closest and most enduring writer friend I have had – and I've written out my words because I want them to be the right ones. A memorial service is an occasion of thanksgiving for the life it commemorates, and I certainly have reason to be grateful that I knew Malcolm, and first met him when we were both young, setting out on our careers. In 1960, at the age of twenty-five, I was appointed Assistant Lecturer in English at the University of Birmingham. The Head of Department at that time was Terence Spencer, who was bent on expanding the department's rather traditional curriculum. He had appointed me specifically to teach Modern English Literature, and in the following year, 1961, he advertised a lectureship in American Literature. I remember being in his office one day when he showed me an application from one Malcolm Bradbury, saying casually, 'I don't think we need interview anyone else, do you?' In those days Heads of Department exercised their power of patronage like feudal barons. Sometimes, as in this case, it worked very well. I warmly endorsed Terence Spencer's judgement.

A few months later, Malcolm and Elizabeth arrived in Birmingham, in a smart VW Beetle – a distinctive and stylish vehicle in those days. He told me he enjoyed driving, because he had never been very good at operating machinery, and finding he could drive well had done a lot for his self-esteem. Very soon the Bradburys became firm friends of Mary and myself. Malcolm and I were the only members of the department under forty, and we both hoped to combine academic careers with creative writing. Each of us had published a first novel and was working on a second one. Malcolm was a couple of years older than me, and slightly ahead in the writing game: *Eating People Is Wrong* had made a bigger impression than *The Picturegoers*, and was indeed a more mature piece of work. And he was already well established as a journalist, humorist and literary critic. He contributed to periodicals as different as *Punch* and the *Critical Quarterly*, and was able to switch, effortlessly it seemed, from one stylistic register to the other. I was impressed by this versatility, and inspired to emulate it.

As everyone here knows, Malcolm was a great wit, and a master of comedy. That was one of the reasons why we loved his company, and his books. Right from the beginning of our friendship, he encouraged me to develop a vein of comedy that was rather deeply buried in my own early work. I remember that, in our very first conversation, he commented favourably on a parody of Hollywood film credits in *The Picturegoers* – a passage which I had regarded as an insignificant detail. Sometimes a remark like that from a source you respect can make you see your own work in an entirely new light. I began to experiment with overtly comic writing. I even placed a few pieces in *Punch*. In 1963 Malcolm initiated a collaboration between the two of us and a talented Birmingham undergraduate, Jim Duckett, to write a satirical revue for the Birmingham Rep. I have written on other occasions about this venture, what fun it was and how much I learned from it.

Malcolm was a great collaborator. He was one of the first English literary novelists to get involved in the essentially collaborative medium of television drama. He welcomed the stimulus of other people's ideas, and could often see in them possibilities of which their originators were unaware. That was one reason why he was an outstanding teacher of creative writing. Another was his exceptional generosity of spirit. He never felt threatened by other people's talent, or attempted to make his students into disciples. His generosity as a reviewer has often been remarked on; and to his writer friends in adversity he was always supportive and encouraging.

There was, inevitably, an element of rivalry in our relationship, as between all artists working in the same field, but by a kind of instinctive tact we never allowed it to surface in a way that would disturb our friendship. When Malcolm was lured away from Birmingham to East Anglia, in 1965, I was in America on a fellowship. Had I been at home I should certainly have tried to dissuade him, though in retrospect it was probably good for our development as writers that we should separate, and have different experiences to write about. Even after Malcolm left Birmingham I would sometimes be in his company, perhaps in the bar at an academic conference, listening to somebody tell an anecdote ripe with fictional possibilities, and a knowing glance would be exchanged between us as if to say, 'Toss you for it?'

Malcolm himself agonised about leaving Birmingham, where he was very happy. He told me that on the day when he finally, definitively, irrevocably had to make up his mind, he went out with two letters in his pocket addressed to the University of East Anglia, one saying yes, and the other saying no. Just in time to catch the last post, he mailed the one that said no. The next day UEA rang him up and said, 'You don't really mean it, do you?' And he agreed that he didn't, and so he went to Norwich. It's a very representative story, because Malcolm hated to say no to anybody, as many people discovered to their advantage – literary editors, British Council officers, conference convenors, and secretaries of literary societies. He enjoyed telling such stories about himself, in which he figured somewhat like one of his own comic heroes – diffident, eager to please, directed by personalities more assertive than himself. It was in part a useful fiction: by humorously exaggerating his own helplessness, he charmed others into performing many of the more humdrum chores of life for him, giving him more time for the things that really mattered, reading and writing.

Of the pair of us, I was supposed to be more practical and efficient, so when we were both invited to speak at the annual MLA Convention in New York in late December 1978 I offered to book the flights so that we could sit together. We met at Heathrow and lined up to check in for the one o'clock PanAm flight. It was some years since I had been to America, and I discovered to my dismay that I had omitted to renew my visa. So much for my efficiency. Malcolm went off to the departure lounge, alone and despondent, and I, in a desperate effort to salvage my trip, took a cab to the US Embassy in London. I'll spare you the details of how I managed to get a visa just in time to catch the last plane out of Heathrow to New York, at 6 p.m., but I felt I was living the longest day of my life. Because of the time change, it was only mid-evening when I reached the New York Hilton, where the thousands of delegates were assembled. And there in the lobby, to my astonishment, was Malcolm, chatting to a circle of people, with his overcoat still on, and his suitcase at his feet, looking as if he too had only just arrived – which indeed was almost true, for reasons that were partly chance and partly character. His plane's departure had been delayed, he'd inevitably met other people on it going to the convention, and got talking to them, he had lined up with them for a bus from the airport instead of taking a cab, and at the Hilton he had unassumingly lined up again, still chatting, to get his room key, instead of going to the VIP desk reserved for guest speakers. And, typically, having finally got his key, he still couldn't tear himself away from the lobby, where the conference action was. His stamina on these occasions was legendary. (I learned recently from a colleague that Erasmus translated the first sentence of St John's Gospel, 'In the beginning was the Word' as 'In the beginning was the Conversation', and got rapped over the knuckles for it, but I think Malcolm would have approved.) He greeted me with astonishment, but also sincere delight that I had managed to catch up with him. Being Englishmen who came of age in the fifties, it was not our custom to embrace, but when he had heard my story, he put a comradely hand on my shoulder and said, 'You did well.'

I used that MLA Convention as the setting for the last chapter of *Small World*, which I wrote at the same time as Malcolm was writing *Rates of Exchange*, and I gave us a Hitchcockian appearance at a cocktail party, where the hero of the tale observes 'a shortish, dark-haired man . . . talking to a tallish dark-haired man smoking a pipe. "If I can have Eastern Europe," the tallish man was saying in an English accent, "you can have the rest of the world." "All right," said the shortish man, "but I daresay people will still get us mixed up." ' And of course they did. I was once telephoned by someone asking me to settle a bet that I was the same person as Malcolm Bradbury. I am frequently complimented on writing *The History Man* − a type of compliment difficult to handle gracefully. Letters were often addressed to me at the University of East Anglia, including one from the Rupert Murdoch Professor of Communications at Oxford. We were once interviewed together by a German radio journalist and I vividly remember the panic on her face as she realised halfway through that she had mixed up our identities. This kind of confusion was amusing but also exasperating to us. In spite of some generic resemblances between our novels, especially the ones about academic life, it seemed to us that they were essentially quite different in technique and thematic preoccupations.

Another writer friend gave me a diary at the beginning of last year, with a handwritten passage or sketch by a writer or artist on every page. The text for the day of Malcolm's funeral, which I attended, Monday, 4th December, had in one sense an uncanny appropriateness. It was contributed by the Irish novelist Brian Moore, who must have submitted it not long before his own death, and it was a quotation from Roland Barthes's essay on Chateaubriand. As many of you will know, Malcolm was working on a novel about Chateaubriand when he died. The quotation is 'Memory is the beginning of writing, and writing is, in its turn, the beginning of death.' But if I understand that statement correctly − and Barthes is an elusive writer − I don't really agree with it. It has always seemed to me that writing is a kind of *defiance* of death, because books live on after their authors have gone. Certainly the greatest consolation we have for Malcolm's passing is that we can re-experience his company, his character and his life-enhancing sense of fun, through his books. But that is not the same, of course, as a living, breathing, laughing friend.

Sir Stanley Matthews (1915–2000)

legendary footballer

by Jimmy Armfield

(radio commentator and former international footballer)

*Funeral Service at St Peter's Church, Stoke-on-Trent,
Staffordshire, on 3 March 2000*

It is my honour and privilege to speak on behalf of the FA and the
game, but you will excuse me if there is a mention of a little seaside
town in there somewhere.

Well, every sport has its first real champion, a person who lifts
their chosen activity to a level that others will probably never attain,
a person who first takes their sport into what I would call modern
times. When I think of boxing I think of Joe Lewis, when I think
of cricket I think of Don Bradman, when I think of tennis, I think
of Fred Perry and, of course, we in football had Stan. A true great
who had the temperament, skill, artistry, speed, balance and above
all humility. A man who could reach for the stars and yet somehow
still manage to keep his feet on the ground. All the trappings of a
champion, that was Stan. In that period of seven years in our time
together in the Blackpool team, I thought him to be the role model
for everybody who wore a tangerine shirt. Now I realise he was
the role model of every footballer in the land. Always fit, giving of
his best, dedicated and still striving long after others have hung up
their boots. He was reared and he was a man of the Potteries. His
father was a barber, and, I remember him telling me, taught him
the importance of speed and agility. It was something that never

left him. Maintaining supreme fitness was essential to Stan. He regulated his diet at a time when other sportsmen never thought about it. He could actually starve himself for a day. He believed in exercise, deep-breathing and in his time at Blackpool he was a regular on the beach every morning around eight o'clock and it paid off because, incredibly, I never once saw him out of breath in a football match. He loved all sports. I think tennis was his second love but once he told me he could have made the grade as a cricketer, and who am I to doubt that.

In his latter years, he seemed to love bright colours. I remember on one of his last occasions I saw him in Blackpool, he was actually dressed in leather bomber jacket, a baseball cap and he had underneath a pink shirt and a light blue tie. It didn't seem right somehow but that was Stan. He never chased the limelight although his ability meant, of course, it always found him. In his playing days he quite often refused interviews, not to be rude, he wished to retain privacy, he treasured that. His family and football were the two loves of his life. He loved to travel. I remember him going off to Ghana where he was once crowned prince of football – I can see the picture now – South Africa, Canada, Malta, the USA, Australia. He actually once had a share in a hotel on Blackpool promenade, he actually owned a racehorse but really nothing could take the place of football. And, playing days over, he tried to pass on his skills to the youngsters in far-off lands but passing on genius is impossible. He soon learned that in his brief term as Port Vale's manager. That speed off the mark, the feint, the flick, the dribble, the balance, the tormented defenders around the globe: it seemed to come easy to Stan and so did that self-control that became a crucial part of his make-up, although at times I know, playing with him, it was absolutely tested to the limit. But that was Stan, he was never Sir Stan to us because it didn't seem to ring true. He was the first real football man. He was often kicked and fouled but never retaliated. I never saw him lose his temper and, of course, he was never booked. Much has been made of his awards over the past few days, European Footballer of the Year, English Footballer of the Year, Cup winner, international star, etc., etc. But despite his global fame, Stan was very much a man of the people. His own background, growing up in the twenties and the thirties, and the war years in the Royal Air Force helped him to maintain a humility that was very much a part of him, humble but important. He always believed in striving to get a fair reward for his talent, I remember that well.

People asked me this week how do I picture him. You will forgive me here in Stoke but I always remember him seeing the back of a tangerine shirt with a number 7 on it, thankfully running in that direction and that's right somehow. That's right because the back of Stan is how most defenders remember him anyway. I picture him now coming to me after I had lost my temper once in a match at Chelsea and he said to me, 'You know, lose your head on the field, son, and you will lose control of yourself and your opponent will see that he can rattle you. It's no good.' It was advice I never forgot. I picture him now on his forty-second birthday. He was exactly twice my age on that day and we played at Charlton. He was brilliant on a mud-bath of a pitch and after the match we won, I was still on a high and remarked to our then manager, Joe Smith, 'It wasn't easy playing on a surface like that.' Joe, who incidentally came from just up the road at Newcastle-under-Lyme, very experienced, just said to me simply, 'Matthews didn't look too bad on it.' But then he never looked too bad even on his off-days. Like the rest of us he had good and bad days but just having him around was the real key to success. Make no mistake though, he was no soft touch. He was a real pro, he could be absolutely ruthless. I have seen him demoralise defences. People have asked me this week what it was like having him in the dressing room. Strange that. Funny, I always wondered what it was like in the other dressing room knowing that Stan was in ours. He made the manager's job simple. Joe Smith, our manager's team talk, I can remember it because it was so easy: 'Pass the ball around, plenty of movement of the ball and then get it to Stan.' His appearance was that important, but wherever he went in football that was also true. The game and life has lost a treasure and the people in football today, and all those coming up behind, should remember the heritage that Stan has bestowed on them.

Anthony Powell (1905–2000)

writer

by Hugh Massingberd

(writer)

*Memorial Service at Grosvenor Chapel, London,
on 4 May 2000*

The late Frankie Howerd – who personified Anthony Powell's maxim that melancholy should be taken for granted in anyone with a true gift for comedy – used to preface his patter with 'Welcome, my brethren, to the Eisteddfod'.

It seems not unfitting this morning – as Tony Powell traced his descent to the Lord Rhys who held the first recorded Eisteddfod at Cardigan in 1176. Indeed the Powell pedigree includes several bards such as Llywarch Hen (nothing to do with the Mitfords, but a descendant of Old King Coel, who as Tony pointed out *didn't* pronounce his name '*Cowell*'), a knight of the Arthurian legend, which so beguiled the great twentieth-century bard, author of thirty immortal books, we are celebrating today.

It is unfortunate that anyone keen on genealogy risks being branded a snob, a crashing bore – and probably off his rocker (as Peter Templer in *A Dance to the Music of Time* would have put it). In his *Memoirs* Tony recalled that his own father, Colonel Powell, 'was not merely bored by genealogy, he was affronted'. The colonel 'possessed little or no sense of the past; still less curiosity about the circumstances of other people, alive or dead'.

Tony, of course, was quite the reverse. Genealogy meant a lot to him, as I discovered in the 1960s when I was working on *Burke's Landed Gentry* (perhaps his favourite work of reference) and he pointed out a Lincolnshire connection between us through his mother's family, the Dymokes of Scrivelsby, hereditary Champions and Standard Bearers of England. (I will spare you the details, otherwise we will be here until the evening.)

Tony believed that genealogical investigation 'when properly conducted' – and Tony always liked to get things right – 'teaches much about the vicissitudes of life; the vast extent of human oddness'.

As for snobbery, Tony argued that genealogy actually demonstrates the extreme fluidity of class in this country. His *Journals* confirm that he was equally interested in the local duke, who burped his way through the National Anthem, as in the giggling girls who delivered the Sunday papers to the Chantry, his home in Somerset, where he lived with his wife, Violet, for nearly half a century. The Chantry is bordered by Dead Woman's Bottom, but this historic name proved too fruity for 'the plansters' (as John Betjeman called them) who wanted it changed to the ever so dainty Chantry Vale. Tony countered by saying he would have his writing paper reprinted to incorporate Dead Woman's Bottom as part of the address.

Tony's inexhaustible curiosity about other people (and not only people, but animals, whether his cats Trelawney and Snook or the 'goat of unreliable aspect' in Sir Magnus Donners's tapestry) was the mainspring of his genius as a novelist. Indeed he regarded an interest in other people as the *sine qua non* of novel-writing – an attribute lacking in not a few novelists whose interest in people extends only to themselves.

Tony's fellow-novelist Iris Murdoch, herself an only child, thought that his solitary childhood was the key to his all-embracing imagination – though Tony said that in his experience it was children of *large* families who tended to exhibit the traditional foibles of the only child. Among the multitudinous family he married into, he noted 'the Pakenham habit of contradicting anything anyone else says'. But Tony stood no nonsense.

Although Tony did not have an easy relationship with his father, they had a bond through the colonel's rather unexpected admiration for nineties artists, particularly Aubrey Beardsley; incidentally, the wonky hour-glass on the front of what Dicky Umfraville might have called 'today's race-card' is taken from a Beardsley illustration for a poem by Ernest Dowson (another favourite of Tony's).

Tony had a highly developed visual sense and to the end of his life never tired of looking at art books or sifting through his eclectic range of postcards. Not least among 'the all he gave his country' (to adapt a pet catchphrase of his from one of his beloved von Stroheim films) was his stint as a trustee of the National Portrait Gallery.

As an antiquarian scholar and biographer, Tony effectively rediscovered John Aubrey and his *Brief Lives*. Like Aubrey, Tony delighted in recording quirky anecdotes of his own times.

There was, for instance, the story of the Norfolk parson who was officiating at a funeral in a church not his own – and arrived early to have a look round. Above one tomb he spotted a medieval iron helmet and, as there was time to kill, tried it on. Assuming this headdress was easy enough; removing it proved impossible. And so when the mourners and the coffin arrived at the church they were (as Tony, with typical understatement, put it) 'surprised to be received by a cleric wearing a knight's bascinet'. Thus accoutred, the priest duly pronounced the burial service – but Tony was characteristically exercised by the question of whether or not the helmeted parson had 'contrived to lift the vizor' in order to conduct the ceremony.

Like all fans coming face to face with their heroes for the first time, I was awestruck when I went to meet the legendary Anthony Powell at the Travellers' Club more than thirty years ago. Here was our greatest writer and the most eminent literary critic, whose witty novels had entranced me with their fastidious style, paradox, irony and throwaway dialogue that cried out for dramatisation. Indeed in the early 1960s, his first novel, *Afternoon Men* (1931), was dramatised successfully. This, in a sense, was the bohemian forerunner of *Dance*. Reading it as a schoolboy, I was struck by the author's description of an unprepossessing painter whose false nose at a party lends his face 'an unaccustomed dignity'. *Dance* itself was not only the finest achievement in fiction in the twentieth century, it *was* the twentieth century. Powell's universe seems more believable than the so-called 'real world'. His intriguingly connected characters live and breathe. One cannot walk through, say, Bayswater without expecting to bump into Uncle Giles sloping out of the Ufford (or some less respectable establishment in Shepherd Market); or Hyde Park without hearing Sillery's cry of 'Abolish the Means Test!'; or Pimlico without thinking of poor Maclintick, the embittered music critic, gassing himself.

That evening at the Travellers' – which Tony, incidentally, had joined back in 1930 – I stupidly expected a grand, aloof, formidable presence of chilling authority. Instead, there bustled into the Smoking Room a toothy, chatty, friendly man, full of dry jokes and spicy gossip. I was particularly struck by the master's charming voice. A measured, mellow, slightly sibilant drawl (redolent of Eton and Balliol), it held out the promise – unfailingly fulfilled – of constant amusement, stimulation, subtle, original, often oblique observation, so that every minute in his company bucked you up. Above all, Tony was extraordinarily funny, with a humorous curiosity and sympathy peculiarly his own.

It was a tonic to hear Tony's bracing views on the absurdity of power, politics and public affairs (so witheringly portrayed through the ambitions of Widmerpool, who yet always manages to back the wrong horse), as well as his strictures on the idiocy and incompetence of sub-editors, publishers, journalists and so forth. He took a robust approach to the arts. True aestheticism called for toughness, discipline. Tony was essentially a practical man prepared to get his hands dirty, whether hacking at the underground around the Chantry grotto; or preparing one of his farmhouse curries; bottling wine from imported hogsheads; or covering the gentlemen's lavatory with an elaborate collage. True to his military background, he was intolerant of sloppiness and had no time for sentimentality or self-pity ('the magic ingredient of every best-seller', as he put it). In his *Journals* he tells of how he suggested to the dotty fan prone to telephoning at strange hours that he should consult a psychiatrist: 'He said he had. Told him to do so again.' (Sound advice, which I took – hold on, it wasn't me . . .)

Yet there was usually a Bowra-esque element of leg-pulling and self-parody in such astringency – and, of course, in his famous last-paragraph wiggings in *Telegraph* reviews, correcting howlers. Above all, Tony believed that the only sort of writing worth reading was *sympathetic* writing.

In the last entry of his *Journals* Tony wrote: 'I realise more than ever how much I depend on V, and on the rest of my immediate family.' The devoted care given to Tony in his last years by Violet and the family is beyond praise. Special tribute should be paid to John Powell, Tony's younger son (a dear friend of my wife and myself, first encountered on a Dorset cricket field in 1987), whose selfless commitment and dedication were nothing short of heroic.

Anthony Powell died peacefully at the Chantry surrounded by his family. The only child had become the beloved patriarch of a flourishing dynasty: his elder son Tristram, the distinguished television director, and his wife Virginia Powell, the artist, have a son, Archie – also working in what Tony called 'the unruly world of television' – and a daughter, the glorious Georgia, married to Toby Coke. They have a son, Harry, and a daughter, Hope – Tony's great-grandchildren. And so the Powell pedigree goes on.

Tony felt his family motto – 'True to the End' – was on the feeble side, but, like horoscopes (in which he also took an interest), mottoes can have a facile fittingness. (Hence the old journalistic formula of trotting them out in police reports about disgraced peers.)

For Tony *was* 'True to the End'. He bore his long years of immobility with great fortitude, occasionally consoling himself with the thought that at least it was better than being back with his old regiment. His wartime service in the army produced what many of his fans would regard as the three finest novels in the *Dance* sequence (and indeed the best fiction of the Second World War), beginning with *The Valley of Bones*, evoked so strongly in Harold Pinter's reading from Ezekiel and in the closing hymn today. In that book, too, the narrator writes of the inexorable pull of ancestry towards *The Soldier's Art* (the title of the second novel in the war sequence).

Tony's penultimate words – typical of his courtesy and concern for others – were 'Help yourself to a drink.' And on his final appearance in the library at the Chantry, he noticed Violet seemingly reaching for *Burke's Landed Gentry*. He said, 'What are you looking up?'

On the day of the funeral, spring in Somerset suddenly turned to winter. Hilary Spurling had no doubt that the snow had been laid on by Tony himself. As Tony's ashes were scattered from a boat into the Chantry lake, it was like a vision of the Ancient World which so bewitched the author's imagination. Tristram read the dirge from *Cymbeline* ('Fear no more the heat o' the sun . . .'). John half expected a mailed arm to rise up from the water. And everyone thought of the last lines from *Dance*, which we are shortly to hear read by Simon Russell Beale, Widmerpool in Hugh Whitemore's television adaptation of *Dance*, which gave Tony (a hardened script-writer himself in his time) such pleasure at the end of his life. Indeed my abiding memory of one of my last visits to the Chantry is of Tony chuckling away at Captain Soper's reaction to Captain Bigg's suicide. 'In the cricket pav, of all places – and him so fond of the game.'

Violet said that Charles Addams's cartoon of a man in a cinema audience roaring with laughter, while everyone else in the house was weeping, represented Tony.

The conversation between Tony and Violet began in September 1934 when they first met in Co. Westmeath and happily carried on, whether over games of slosh, walks in Regent's Park or cultural cruises, for sixty-five and a half years. Anyone lucky enough to have overheard some of their hilarious and harmonious exchanges will know what a blissful fusion of souls this was – and how much Tony and his work owed to Violet's encyclopaedic knowledge, insight into human nature and zestful love of life.

Finally, many of us now echo the feelings of the narrator of *Dance* when he sees his enchanting composer friend, Hugh Moreland (one of the portraits that even Tony had to admit was drawn from life, in the person of Constant Lambert), for the last time. 'It was also the last time' (the narrator writes) 'I had, with anyone, the sort of talk we used to have together.'

Lord Charteris of Amisfield (1913–1999)

*Assistant Private Secretary and Private Secretary to
Her Majesty the Queen, 1950–77*

by Eric Anderson

(Provost of Eton)

*Memorial Service at St Margaret's Church,
Westminster, London, on 16 May 2000*

Martin Charteris was a lovely, lovely man. He was so successful in
everything he did that it was hard to believe that he was serious
when he said that neither he, nor any who knew him as a boy,
would in their wildest flights of fancy have expected him to be
Private Secretary to the Queen or Provost of Eton. His claim that
he was totally undistinguished at school, while erring a little on the
side of modesty, was however not far from the truth.

'Charteris' reports are bad and I am not at all satisfied with him,'
wrote his housemaster after his first term, enclosing a Maths report
which said: 'He has been more careless, untidy and forgetful than
any other in the division: 16th out of 16.'

Things were rather better in Science where he reported that 'Mr
Gardiner pronounced him the only hopeful specimen in a lag division about whose mentality he felt anxious,' but French seems to
have been a particular trial both to him and those who taught him.
In his first year he was second bottom. A year later his report began:
'French composition dreadful – total 4/60 – and I think some of
those must have been charity marks.' By the next year: 'Charteris
is not only bottom but easily bottom of this division. He must learn

309

that a pleasant manner and a disarming smile will not get him through his examinations.'

And Henry Marten, who by a nice symmetry later tutored the Queen whom Martin served with such devotion as Private Secretary, described him as 'the typical fourth former of fiction – untidy, unbrushed, unbusinesslike but brimming over with life and spirit'.

What is fascinating about his school reports is to see how early, as he became 'appreciably less inky and unkempt' (after the time, presumably, when the boys' maid who looked after his room had had to dust his soap each week), he began to reveal the qualities for which we all loved him.

He was commended in his first term for the way he memorised and recited poetry. He got good marks too for his English style, and even in Maths Hope-Jones wrote that 'Attempting to teach a cheerful and friendly boy like this is always a welcome and refreshing tonic. His half's work with me has certainly done me a lot of good: in my most optimistic moments I venture to hope it may have done him some as well.'

The Drawing master found Charteris 'a delicious character, it is very difficult to be angry with him'; his classical tutor confessed: 'Perhaps if I had liked him less, I should have got more work out of him,' and the head boy of his house wrote: 'He had great charm and irrepressible optimism. His friends were numerous and his enemies non-existent.' His housemaster complained that: 'Matters are not improved by the fact that an engaging personality disarms everyone with whom he comes into contact.'

Truly, the boy was father of the man.

But it was George Lyttleton, above all, who sensed his potential. When Martin was only fifteen he wrote of him: 'He should do well for he has some ability. Not in Latin, or in French, or perhaps anything in the academic scheme. But I feel it is there. I may be wrong.'

As we know, he wasn't wrong, but gloriously right. Martin's career was unplanned, and full of unexpected turns, but he was a success as a soldier, in the desert and in Jerusalem, as Assistant Private Secretary and then Principal Private Secretary to the Queen, as Provost of Eton and as chairman of the National Heritage Memorial

Fund. It is not difficult to see why, for he had integrity, judgement, a sense of duty and flair. His integrity was complete: it is inconceivable that he would ever for a minute consider doing what was not right. His judgement was excellent: those who served with him in North Africa admired the flair and courage with which he conducted skirmishes in the desert (throughout his life he was good when the going was tough), but also the imagination and judgement with which he worked out new tactics. Later, royal observers praised the originality and wise judgement with which he helped the royal family in its move towards a more open and approachable style of monarchy, always trying to ensure, as he put it, that the Queen should 'spread a carpet of happiness wherever she goes'.

He made no fuss about his sense of duty; it was simply second nature to him. In all his different careers he served and served unstintingly, doing his duty as a soldier, as a royal servant and then to Eton. As always with people in important jobs, inconvenient duty frequently interrupted family life ('If only I had served my family with half the zeal with which I have served my country,' he used to say, adapting Cardinal Wolsey), but none the less he was lucky in his family and they in him. At Eton and in Gloucestershire he loved the visits of his children and grandchildren. His marriage to Gay in wartime Jerusalem at a service attended by the best man, Martin's commanding officer, and a congregation of eighty nuns (Martin was billeted in a nunnery) was the prelude to the happiest of married lives. Gay says that throughout more than fifty years, whenever she heard his key in the front door, she always felt, with a lift of the heart, 'Ah, now life is going to get better,' and he in the last year of his life wrote to one old friend: 'Well one thing I am and that's happy – and with Gay as my wife I ought to be!'

Integrity, judgement, duty and flair may account for his successful career, but not for the love which he inspired in all who knew him – and which drew so many people to a memorial service at Eton in March and has brought so many others to this church today. What 'marked him extraordinary' was his talent, his gift, in fact his genius for fun and friendship. 'Only take the job if you think it will be fun,' was his advice to a friend and he applied the same test to all he did, with this difference – that if a thing was not inherently fun, he made it fun. As a result life with him was full of surprises. At the end of a long route march to keep his soldiers fit, his company was pounding along a beach to the finish. 'Right wheel,' shouted Martin, and the hot and sweaty troops, with Martin beside them, marched neck-deep into the sea. In Haifa, where he was a staff college instructor, he conceived the notion (probably correct) that battle-hardened troops could not be lectured at but required constant stimulus. So, on one occasion no lecturer turned up, but two minutes later soldiers shot out of their seats at the crack of a whip wielded by a richly mustachioed Mexican general in a ten-gallon hat announcing that he had come to inspect the unit. Of course it was Martin, introducing the topic of 'Dealing with the unexpected'. (Resourceful, unorthodox solutions were his speciality. When the Queen was presented with a young crocodile on a visit to the Gambia, it made the journey home on *Britannia* in Martin's bath.)

Eton gave fresh scope for his dramatic talents. A play early in his time as Provost is still remembered for his rendition of 'Tiptoe Through the Tulips' (both words and actions), and when Queen Elizabeth, the Queen Mother, made an evening visit it became the tradition that at the end of an entertainment of words and music from the boys, there would be an additional item, not advertised in the programme, in which he took the star role – for instance as the Russian novelist, Vladimir Brusiloff, in a brief adaptation of P.G. Wodehouse's *Clicking of Cuthbert*. 'No novelists any good except me. I spit me of zem all. P.G. Wodehouse and Tolstoy not bad. Not good but not bad. No novelists any good except me.' Nothing at Eton has ever been more fun.

He loved words. Those of us who heard him read in chapel, Sunday after Sunday, know that we shall never hear the Bible read better. Of course, he always read from the Authorised Version. He was a faithful president of the Prayer Book Society – drawn to it not for sentimental reasons but because, with his instinctive appreciation of words, he loved those standing models of our language whose phrases and whose rhythms are woven into the fabric of our literature and our lives.

Words gave him a lot of amusement too. When *Let's Talk Strine* came out, he and Bill Heseltine wrote a whole speech for the

Queen's Australian subjects in their own language – which however she did not actually make. He was luckier in the New Hebrides where it turned out that a monarch was considered too important to speak for herself and he therefore had the chance to address the great and the good on her behalf in Pidgin – practised daily with growing assurance to his shaving mirror each morning on *Britannia*, and indeed occasionally repeated in part for Eton audiences many years later.

He loved to laugh. He had a wonderful ability to deflate any situation which looked like becoming too pompous, to walk with kings but keep the common touch. Nervous visitors to Buckingham Palace found themselves put at ease by this royal servant who took the business seriously but was so natural and amusing both before and after. He had absolutely no side. He was unpompous, unorthodox but never undignified. He was the most unstuffy person to fill dignified public office.

Into his main public office as Private Secretary to Princess Elizabeth and later to Her Majesty the Queen, he fitted in his favourite words from P.G. Wodehouse, 'like a prawn into aspic'. He was for years at the very heart of the inner councils of the court and the country, and there were moments when he knew that history was being made. His charm was that with all those dealings among the great ones of the world, he was still the friend of everyone.

At school he had already charmed his beaks. An early dancing partner, equally charmed, tells me that dancing with young Charteris was like dancing with a tiger. 'I'm a jungle dancer with an iron rhythm.' Even the formidable Miss Gardiner, of whom the rest of the Private Office was in awe, was not proof against Martin's arm around her shoulder and his 'Good morning, Gubbins'.

When a young assistant private secretary confessed to nervousness about whom he might be beside at his first state banquet, Martin said, 'Oh, I never bother to look; I'm just relentlessly agreeable.' He was that to all of us and we all loved him for it. We loved him, though, for more than that, for we all sensed that it wasn't an act, that he really enjoyed being with us.

He really enjoyed the company of his brother soldiers in the desert as the moon came up and the wind dropped and the flies disappeared and they sat round on the sand with the whisky bottle circulating. He really enjoyed his colleagues in the Private Office. At Eton collecting his pension was almost a morning's work as he stopped for a word and a laugh with everyone who happened to be in the High Street on a Thursday morning. He loved the company of shooting-friends and gamekeepers, and the ghillies of his youthful summer holidays on the Uists.

He loved dashing round the country with his fellow-trustees of the National Heritage Memorial Fund of which he was the first – inspirational – chairman to look at a great house in danger, a great picture at risk of export or a tract of wild moorland that could be saved for the nation. He revelled in negotiating for the Mappa Mundi and loved the drama of hiring a helicopter to whirl his trustees to the Hebrides (where, characteristically, he fitted in a visit to Annie Macdonald who had helped in the house when he was a child). All the time serious business was combined with uproarious fun. Meetings started on time and finished on time; everyone felt they had had their say, but the memory afterwards was of how much everyone had laughed.

We all enjoyed being with him, because his zest was infectious. You couldn't but enjoy lunching with someone who said to the waiter: 'Only six oysters, thank you; my doctor's forbidden them so I can't have a dozen . . . Oh come on, make it nine. After all I may not still be here next year.' And I have to confess to having drunk larger whiskies in Martin's company than anywhere else – especially after the doctor rationed him to only one a day and he bought that enormous glass. There is no Nobel Prize for friendship, but had there been he would surely have been in line for it.

He was an artist as well as soldier, courtier and countryman. In the last few weeks of his life it gave him great pleasure to help the National Galleries of Scotland acquire the Botticelli which had been brought to Scotland by his great-grandfather. He was himself quite a good painter and a sculptor of real ability. He began when Oscar Nemon was sculpting the Queen. Martin amused himself by taking a lump of Nemon's clay and producing a bust of the artist while he worked, topping it off with a pair of devil's horns. Nemon was impressed, told him he should take it up and gave him some help.

Latterly he turned to fire-backs and claimed that if he lived long enough there would be one 'in all the best houses in England'.

You will find them in Stanway, Belvoir, Hatfield, Canon's Ashby, Waddesdon, Chastleton and the Castle of Mey, but sadly his last brief illness interrupted work on his fire-back for St George's Hall at Windsor. It was almost the only thing, though, which he left undone, and even that is to be finished by another hand. We mourn his going but at the same time we can celebrate a wonderful life of great achievements, a life lived with energy, zest and fun, a life which spread its own carpet of happiness before children, grandchildren, colleagues, companions, friends, acquaintances – for even people who met him only once tend to remember him affectionately. It was a life which was complete in a way which few lives are.

He had faced death before – when his hospital ship was torpedoed in the Bay of Biscay and again two years ago – and he was not afraid to die. One cannot help feeling that he organised his departure considerately. He said goodbye in the two last weeks to many of those who had meant most to him, and he slipped away a day or two before Christmas, with his family around him, knowing that they would be there with Gay for the next few days.

To a message of love from a friend in his last days, he replied: 'Tell her she can go on loving me. I shall be dead but I shan't be gone.' He was unforgettable and he lives on in the hearts of all of us who knew him. We shall remember him with admiration, affection and gratitude, and above all with delight. He was one of the best people any of us will ever meet, and we are all the better for having known him.

John Morgan (1959–2000)
etiquette expert and dandy

by Nicholas Coleridge
(managing director of Condé Nast)

Memorial Service at St George's Church, Hanover Square, London, on 19 September 2000

It is almost exactly two months to the day since John's funeral at the Queen's Chapel.

That was a very sad and bleak – but also beautiful – service; afterwards, a lot of people commented on how much John would have approved of the whole thing, and how it had met his strict criteria on music and protocol. This was a relief. I think that, even now, we are all still a little in awe of John and his famously high standards.

Today's memorial service is, of course, quite different from a funeral. As John himself wrote in his *Debrett's New Guide to Etiquette and Modern Manners*: 'Memorial Services celebrate the life of an individual rather than commemorating his death. At one time,' he went on to note, 'Memorial Services tended to be reserved for only the great and the good. Today, many far less illustrious people have them.'

I wonder what category John would have placed himself in? I would unhesitatingly place him into both the great *and* the good. John was definitely illustrious. As P.G. Wodehouse would have put it, he was a rare bird indeed: immensely knowledgeable over a wide range of subjects from art to classical music (obviously not rock music, of which he strongly disapproved) to fashion, luxury goods of all kinds, politics – yes, genuinely – and bespoke tailoring. We received more than a dozen letters of condolence from leading Savile Row tailors, each eulogising John as their most fastidious-ever customer, who knew more about the four-button cuff than any other gentleman. And, of course, John was an expert on all questions of etiquette: the correct places to go on holiday, the best restaurant tables, how to tie a tie (he felt very strongly on this subject: a correctly tied tie, he felt, should have a little dimple or dent in the middle of the knot. When he was unofficially advising William Hague on his wardrobe, he expended a lot of effort in getting his nuance across to the Leader). John actually knew about everything, about topics he had no reason to be knowledgeable about, such as how to bring up children and where to take a girlfriend on a first date.

In a world increasingly dominated by mass-market, dumbed-down thinking, John was a beacon of wit and civility. He was also immensely kind and thoughtful, never too busy to give time to other people, particularly if this involved a glass of champagne at Claridge's or a lunch in the Sotheby's Café: two of his favourite haunts.

I first met John properly when he joined Condé Nast eleven years ago as a style authority on GQ, and he was already fully formed as man of poise and taste. In the last five years of his life, we got to know each other very well and he became a friend; when neither of us had a lunch, we sometimes slipped out to his favourite sushi bar, the Ikeda. His opinions on many subjects were sound and intuitive, and I miss him immensely. There was a depth and a cleverness to John that was sometimes overlooked, lurking beneath the exquisite suits and hand-made shoes.

He had an amazing radar for knowing when any kind of party was taking place anywhere in Vogue House – he was like a heat-seeking or canapé-seeking missile. And then he would appear, always immaculate, hovering at the door, waiting to be invited in: which he always was, because he was such an asset, and because he knew everybody and could light up any room with his presence, and was greatly interested in – and was genuinely liked by – all the people in the glossy magazine world: which he recognised as the best kind of world.

He made an ally in Bridget Moloney, who oversees the Condé Nast kitchen. Bridget told me yesterday – and I never knew this before – that John had somehow persuaded her to provide him with a little plate of canapés every evening at six o'clock: honeyed sausages, quails' eggs, a smoked salmon sandwich, and a glass of champagne, which he ate at his desk in his big office. He was very keen on smart snacks, claiming to have low blood-sugar.

He was a person of immutable routines: every day at four o'clock precisely, his two assistants had to supply him with a pot of Earl Grey tea (in a warmed teapot, on a polished silver tray) and a chocolate bourbon biscuit.

He cashed his personal cheques with the cashier at Claridge's, a service offered to no other non-residents, so far as I'm aware. He also used the gents' cloakrooms at Claridge's, preferring them to the Condé Nast loos. He enjoyed being handed a white linen towel, which doesn't happen at Vogue House. He did all his grocery shopping in the Food Halls of Fortnum & Mason.

He was a person of severe opinions on certain subjects.

It horrified him when the new Chancellor of the Exchequer, Gordon Brown, refused to wear white tie at the Lord Mayor's Banquet at the Guildhall and rolled up in a suit.

He was horrified when Prince Edward and the Countess of Wessex decided to have a buffet at their wedding reception at Windsor Castle. John thought this was highly inappropriate. He could be a little stuffy at times, and sometimes needed teasing. He was horrified when I personally bought a pair of slip-on loafers with tassels, which he considered naff. He forced me to go with him to a very smart shop called G.J. Cleverley and buy mind-blowingly expensive brogues instead.

He was horrified when he discovered that the waitress in the Condé Nast boardroom served the food anti-clockwise. John felt it should be clockwise. He later checked this out with Claridge's and discovered that they too were serving food anti-clockwise. He quickly put them right too, and the whole world now does it clockwise.

He had the best taste. His clothes were genuine works of art, the products of months of collaboration and discussion with his tailors. He couldn't believe it when other men simply bought suits off the peg in ten minutes. Whatever event he happened to be going to – Ascot or Glyndebourne for instance – he loved to parade around the offices, from floor to floor, making sure that we all saw him in his top hat, tailcoat or black tie. I'm going to miss that.

His tiny flat – his set – in Albany was a study in micro-perfection. He adored living there. His stationery – the engraved letterheads, the writing paper as thick as card, the special John Morgan luggage labels from Smythsons – was really quite beautiful. The invitation for his last book party at the Royal Opera House was so thick, and the engraving so deep, that had you accidentally stepped on it in bare feet, your soles would have been cut to ribbons on the razor edges of the raised type.

Of course he could be a bit extravagant. There was sometimes something of Toad of Toad Hall in his reckless attitude to money. Occasionally I took it upon myself to lecture him gently on the subject, advising him to show some restraint. Then, he was always full of remorse: 'You're so right, Nicholas, you always know about these things.'

But, of course, within twenty-four hours he was back doing what he loved best. His midnight-blue silk opera cloak and matching shoes were one of the sights of Covent Garden; the amazing diamond evening studs he bought himself as a treat at Asprey & Garrard; the watches – he particularly adored Patek Philippe. 'They're not indulgences,' he would insist. 'They're essentials.'

At the time of his death, he was in the process of commissioning a giant portrait of himself, wearing the famous opera cloak, posing in the cloisters at Albany, in the manner of an eighteenth-century nobleman on the Grand Tour.

He had recently become a member of Mark Birley's Bath & Racquets Club gym, where I never actually witnessed him doing any press-ups, but often found him eating a large plate of smoked salmon in a white towelling robe. He loved to undergo deep massage from a Russian masseur from Chechnya.

Although I don't believe he always realised this, he had more friends than almost anybody else. He was a truly beloved figure, and an admired one too. I've never known more women insist that John was their best friend.

It was obvious that, like so many people, John had his bleak moments, some, as we now know, very bleak – but I like to think that in his life they were outweighed by his happy ones.

John was a true original. There should be more John Morgans in this world. It is ironic and awfully sad that his life and career have been cut short at exactly the time that he was reaching the pinnacle of his success.

And, of course, he quite rightly relished his success, which was based on real hard work and achievement.

He loved GQ, his colleagues and his editor, Dylan Jones. He loved Condé Nast, and I don't think it's presumptuous to say we provided a second family to him. He loved his columns on manners in *The Times*. He loved his work for the Conservative Party. He loved England, and Englishness, and the whole English social calendar, which he saw as something ancient and important. He loved the world of Bond Street, the shops and the craftsmanship. And he took growing satisfaction in his television – never TV – appearances, and his books.

John leaves a huge vacuum. At all those events so many of us go to – the Cartier Polo Day, the Royal Windsor Horse Show – I shall half expect to see him in his perfect suit and panama, with his Swaine Adeney Brigg walking-stick, swaggering about, adding culture and civility.

Since he died, I don't think a day has gone by without my thinking, I wonder what John would have recommended on that.

Only yesterday, thinking about today's memorial service, I suddenly thought: I know you wear a black tie at a funeral, but what's the correct tie for a memorial service? I must ask John. And then, of course, you remember he isn't here.

The answer to the tie quandary, incidentally, is contained in John's book. He wrote: 'A plain black silk grenadine tie should be worn by gentlemen at a Memorial Service.'

I do hope you all are. I do feel we owe it to dear John to get it right.

Derek Hill (1916–2000)

painter

by Lord Gowrie

(former Minister for the Arts)

*Memorial Service at St James's Church, Piccadilly,
London, on 28 October 2000*

When a friend dies it is often the small things that make us most sad. The big picture – the life and personality, the work, the kaleidoscope of recollection – is there for celebrating, not mourning, and at a memorial service we thank God for it, and for the part we have been allowed to play in someone else's life.

My own detail, small source of a great sadness, lies in a black Filofax book of names, addresses and telephone numbers. Under Hill – Dr Derek Hill CBE; he was proud of his honorary degree and his deserved recognition as one of the best painters of public figures of his time – under Hill, the entry reads: 'Best to avoid calling between 2 and 5 p.m. as he sleeps in the afternoons. Early morning only.'

Early morning, of course, works both ways. How often have I been dragged peremptorily from sleep – and I'm sure I'm not the only victim present by tones at once brisk and querulous. 'You *said* we were lunching today.' It was often true. But it was not always true. How often was the rest of the morning spent in frantic appeasement as arrangements made from dull necessity were discombobulated. It is hard to believe that the affectionate accusing tones I first heard in Co. Donegal almost fifty years ago will, for this slice of eternity, be stilled.

I last saw Derek a few weeks before he died. We were under the same roof, in hospital. Recovering from a hip operation, I would hobble on sticks down the corridors to visit him. Like many artists whose gifts allow them to impose a kind of order on a kind of chaos, Derek preferred to pitch his tent in the chaos. Polite and grateful to the hospital staff, he nevertheless employed that indomitable will to turn an orderly room into a replica of his Hampstead studio, a virtually impenetrable jungle of paintings and possessions. Derek never threw things, or people, away. In bed, he seemed covered more by envelopes than blankets: a whale beached under dunes of paper. Pill dispensers were everywhere, their tops suspiciously tight. I accused him of hidden caches of chocolate and cake. He denied it, but feebly. Visitors popped in and out. The atmosphere was festive. In Donegal, the best parties were often the funeral wakes. Derek knew he was dying and had the courage and inner strength to try to enjoy it.

We gossiped, as friends do. Derek, as this congregation bears witness, had a great gift for friendship. Of course he loved the great and good of his two countries, the droppable names – who among us, if we are truthful, does not? – and he painted so many of them. But his manner with obscure people was equal and in the 1960s he made some truly obscure people, natives of Tory, Europe's most westerly island, more famous, as painters, than himself. He took trouble over his friends in the way he took trouble over the composition, the skeletal structure, of his paintings – this being, I believe, his great strength as an artist. Be that as it may, both his artistic gift and his gift for friendship sustained a life which was solitary in emotional terms. The landscapes and seascapes of the west of Ireland, which I believe to be his best paintings, are unpeopled or inhabited only by lonely figures.

Derek thought of himself as a loner and in profound ways he was, yet he was also an intensely social being. 'All I want is peace,' he would say to his friends. Woe betide any who granted this wish by failing to include him in their invitations. This seldom happened. He was excellent company and had good tales to tell. His life as a traveller, a stage designer, an art collector, a painter of famous people, an expert in Islamic architecture, an infinitely *un*vain, *un*egoistic promoter of talents other than his own, an educator, a gardener and a chocoholic certainly equipped him as a raconteur. And everyone I have met who sat for Derek agrees that his ability to paint and converse at the same time was both relaxing and enchanting.

In that hospital room, Derek and I bade farewell without stating it. We talked of Berenson and Italy and the Tuscan landscape of his which he had brought from Holly Hill to hang on his wall. We talked about poetry and food and music (my favourite Hill portrait is a small back view of the pianist Rubenstein) and journeys and the possibilities and impossibilities of love. We talked of Ireland – my mother, as it were, and Derek's improbable mistress. I confessed that one of the mercifully few times in my life I'd suffered pangs of envy was when Derek was made a Freeman of the City of Letterkenny. We talked about Gracie, Derek's cook-housekeeper in Donegal whom he loved. Elizabeth David told him that Gracie was the best natural cook she had ever encountered. Gracie took the relayed compliment in her stride as she disapproved of Mrs David cooking Derek and me a paella with a cigarette in her mouth and a Damoclean half-inch of ash hovering over the rice. We talked of things great and small in the context of Derek's grand life – grand in the Irish as well as the English sense. And after the chat, and the enjoyment, I wanted to say, as we all want to say on such occasions, something true and kind or, as Philip Larkin wonderfully put it, something not untrue and not unkind. I told him that if in England he was still an underestimated painter – his own fault, as getting him to sell a good painting was like taking a mule to Ascot – in Ireland he was a national hero. That was and is true and I offered it as a bread-and-butter letter to someone I had the great good fortune to meet in my early teens and so become one of the many whose eyes were opened by Derek to what aesthetic understanding can do for sanity and happiness. God rest 'Muster Hull', as Gracie called him, and comfort all who miss him.

Major Desmond 'Kelpie' Buchanan
(1920–2000)
soldier

by Adrian House
(publisher and writer)

*Memorial Service at St John's Church, Northington,
Hampshire, on 9 December 2000*

I was hesitant when I was asked to talk about Kelpie today because some of you have known him for far longer and better than I. But I took courage from the strength of my admiration and affection for him, feelings shared by my wife Perella, who knew him for more than forty years, and our great friend Eric Newby who fought beside him nearly sixty years ago. So please will his older friends forgive me if I try to describe for his later ones Kelpie's outstanding achievements and qualities which we have all come here to honour today.

His life was full of surprises. Such was his vigour that I was amazed to discover the birthday he celebrated last month was his eightieth, and until then I never knew he was born in Jamaica, where his father was in the army. In fact his whole boyhood, the morning of his life, was coloured by the army. He went to an army school, the Imperial Service College, and when he failed to get into Sandhurst, by one tantalising place, he met the first of his great challenges with the first of his great gambles: he joined the Grenadier Guards in the ranks, then one of the toughest ordeals in the army.

The outbreak of war in 1939 coincided with the noon of Kelpie's life, packing it with glamour, drama and trauma. So impressive was his performance in the Grenadiers that he was soon the first man ever to be promoted from the ranks to a commission in the regiment. But he was a sore trial to his commanding officer: he spent too much time with sophisticated young ladies in The 400 nightclub; his beloved dachshund called Socks lifted its leg in the Mess; and his hair was so unruly that the colonel posted an order: 'In future Lieutenant Desmond Buchanan will be known as "Kelpie" '; Kelpie was the name of a seahorse whose luxuriant mane was then famous in a popular strip cartoon. Kelpie kept his nickname but soon left his battalion, to join a crack commando training unit in Scotland, with heroes like Lord Lovat and David Stirling.

A few months later he was sent to the Mediterranean and put on a submarine with eight other desperadoes, including Eric Newby, the future traveller and writer. They were to be dropped off the coast of Sicily to blow up an airfield there; being Kelpie he boarded the sub with Socks under his arm. Sadly the raiders ran into enemy fire, the submarine failed to rescue them, and they had to keep afloat in the sea for three or four hours. Eric and Kelpie saved the life of one colleague, determined to drown himself, before they were all taken prisoner by Italian fishermen in the morning. The submarine commander dolefully observed Kelpie's last wishes, sending Socks to Princess Aly Khan in Beirut

Typically, Kelpie met the second great challenge of his life by taking his second great gamble – escape. His efforts involved helping to dig a tunnel with a large chisel borrowed from the camp commandant; lying doggo for three days under an altar in a convent; and walking two hundred miles towards the Allied lines with a fellow-Grenadier, Anthony Kinsman. Outside Florence they were hidden by two French ladies for five weeks, in a windowless attic while four German soldiers worked in a room downstairs. The Allies reached Florence just in time to save their lives.

In the anticlimax which followed Kelpie moved into an uncertain afternoon. For short periods he was in the Foreign Legion, in the City, and married to Maureen Dufferin and Ava in Ireland. But, for all the fun, Kelpie wasn't happy and met his third great challenge with another gamble. He threw up everything and, with his last penny, bought an antique shop in London, and later Keepers, his house in Hampshire. His luck began to change.

In about 1970 he met and married Sue, and his life was transformed; Harry was born and his cup overflowed. But Kelpie always preferred a magnum to a bottle; he was already a special constable in Chelsea, now he became a prison visitor in Winchester and soon a churchwarden in the valley. As his evening approached first his heart, and later six strokes, nearly killed him, but mercifully Sue, his doctors and his fighting spirit saved him for the serene country life for which we remember him here.

If wit is the salt of life, laughter must be its sugar, often helping to sweeten the bitter moment; Kelpie loved laughing. When he was captured he pointed out to the Italian lieutenant that his spurs were upside down. The officer was furious but, much amused, his colonel told him to get properly dressed. On another occasion his sense of humour, combined with quick thinking, saved his life (I hope the rector will forgive me for mentioning it in church). During his escape he saw a German scout car driving towards him and since he was wearing jodhpurs sent to him by his mother from India he knew that if he walked on he would be recognised as a prisoner, recaptured and shot as a spy; if he ran off he would be chased and also shot. He therefore leaped on to the verge, turned his back on the road, dropped his trousers, squatted, and did his duty for England. The Germans sped by in disgust.

The French understand that the style is the man; Kelpie's style curiously evolved in the opposite direction to English architecture. It began as flamboyant; in the war it became decorated – in part literally, for he was awarded the Military Cross; afterwards he expertly practised the Early English pastimes of riding, shooting, stalking and fishing and towards the end his style had the perfection of classic simplicity.

But for many of us his overarching quality was his chivalry, embracing his courtesy, kindness and compassion – for his guests, for his friends, for the Italian peasants who helped him in the war (he got one a job at The 400), for the prisoners he visited, and for the dying. Integral with all this was his courage – his wartime bravery and the moral courage with which he repeatedly met his challenges.

Moral courage here in the valley, too, when he publicly defended a rector he felt was being unfairly criticised. When he left, nearly twenty years later, the rector said it was one of the most valued memories of his time in the parish.

On summer evenings Kelpie and Sue would sit out among their roses with their dogs, talking over the day and Harry's exploits in Africa or Oxford. Then, last thing at night, Kelpie would recollect what was closest to his heart, and pray for those he specially loved – his mother, Sue and Harry. Remembering this, on the night I heard of his death, I looked for a suitable prayer, and came across one which we will soon hear in the Commendation; I would like to end with a few words from it now: 'O God, those whom you give us you do not take away, because what is yours is ours also . . . for life is eternal, love immortal and death only a horizon.'

Auberon Waugh (1939–2001)
writer

by Patrick Marnham
(writer)

*Memorial Service at the Church of St Mary the Virgin,
Bishop's Lydeard, Somerset, on 24 January 2001*

After Bron's death last week there was an outburst of grief and praise. One of the many obituaries described him as 'the most controversial, the most abusive, perhaps the most brilliant journalist of his times . . . a hater of humbug in all its forms' and ended by saying that: 'If he was a reactionary it was in the best sense, of reacting against the folly and cruelty and oppression of his age.' And tribute after tribute emphasised the view of his peers that his work had been uniquely valuable and that he was irreplaceable. But together with this assessment of a lifetime's achievements there was a general sense of grief that would probably have surprised him. We can only hope that he knew what has now become clear, how greatly he was loved, not only by those closest to him but by all his friends. Bron was a steadfast friend, and never more so than when he was needed.

So much has been written in the last week in praise of Bron, that he must be wondering what there is left to say. The first time I saw him it was in the grounds of Cranmore Hall about thirty miles from here. Fifty or sixty small boys were standing around a bonfire on the night before Hallowe'en in 1955 singing from a school song sheet. He, aged fifteen, had come back to visit his old school and was also singing, very loud, very flat, and rather different words. He was already defying authority, heading for trouble and, of course, making a joke. And that defiance and those jokes continued for the following forty-five years. When news came that he was very ill, many refused to believe it. Instead we convinced ourselves that it must be another of his jokes. He must be lying doggo, ready to mount the next ambush.

One of the particular things about Bron was the way in which he seemed to burst fully formed into the world. He started as he meant to go on and his childhood was a succession of catastrophes. Many of us faced with an impatient and strong-willed father might have avoided too frequent clashes with authority. But for Bron the imposition of authority was like a red rag to a bull. There was the time at prep school when — finding a confiscated air-pistol in the room of the deputy headmaster — he removed it and shot a fellow-pupil, Gregory, in the leg. He had been intending, as he shortly afterwards explained, 'to kick up the gravel' around the boy's feet. Moving on to Downside he persecuted the headmaster. Faced with an enormous man who most boys found terrifying, Bron started to circulate a petition for his removal. And when news reached his father that the school gym had burned to the ground, Evelyn Waugh was immediately convinced that it must have been Bron. As the end of his school days loomed up things were going so badly that, although he had won a scholarship to Oxford, he seriously enquired about openings in the hotel trade.

Fortunately he was talked out of this and instead sent to Florence where thirty years later Harold Acton remembered his visit to La Pietra in 1957 when he rode up the drive on a beaten-up motor scooter wearing a straw hat and a black armband. Enquiring anxiously about the reasons for the black band — then the accepted sign of mourning — Harold Acton was told not to worry. Bron only wore it when he was on the motor scooter, to gain the sympathy of the traffic police.

The dreadful injuries he suffered in Cyprus, which nearly killed him at the age of eighteen, caused his entire prep school to be ordered to climb to the top of Glastonbury Tor to pray for his recovery, which gave him a certain satisfaction when he learned of it. Characteristically, when he recovered he turned the dramatic episode of his near-death into a joke for the amusement of the rest of the world.

Although such stories make us laugh they also illustrate some of Bron's qualities: total independence of mind, a contempt for majority opinions however shrilly expressed, and even his courage. Bron was not so much brave as fearless, which apart from being rare is potentially hazardous and must account for how he got into so many scrapes. The extent of another of his qualities, generosity, only became clear after he had died. We know now from what his friends have written of his private generosity to colleagues while he was editing the *Literary Review*.

Another distinguishing mark of Bron's life was the variety of his interests. If it is unsurprising to us to find him as a cornet of the Blues during national service, he himself was amazed that he had passed the board. His brother officers would have been more surprised to hear that after recovering from his wounds he had taken up an apprenticeship on the *Daily Mirror* as a caption writer for photographs of girls in swimsuits – which he always remembered as demanding work.

With this unpredictable progress went unpredictable opinions. It was always difficult to know which way Bron would jump on a new issue of the day. His commitment to the cause of Biafra during the Nigerian Civil War was straightforward and passionate. Having seen the effects of the government blockade and the famine it imposed he denounced British policy as wicked. But unlike others he never forgot what had happened and the failure of his Biafran campaign formed his settled view of politicians. This did not prevent him from once writing in 'Way of the World', in so many words, that the monarchy, the armed forces and the House of Lords were the only centres of excellence left in national life, and it is a measure of how unpredictable he could be that he stated that, even after the thousands and thousands of words he had devoted to mocking the absurdities of each. His writing was well described as 'a carnival of decay'. His diaries in *Private Eye* went way beyond journalism and will probably become his lasting monument. It was in his diary that he responded to the loyal publicity surrounding the news of Princess

Anne's first engagement with the information that the ring she was 'flaunting' bore 'a striking resemblance to one that had been stolen from one of his sisters in Blackheath three years earlier'. Bron could also be quixotic, as his sustained, one-man campaign to restore rhyme to English verse showed.

Perhaps it was this wild unpredictability that made one so impatient, when one left him, for the next meeting; the knowledge that only then would one be readmitted to the unmapped world of his personal comic genius. His humour was never intrusive, he did not impose his jokes or perform them, instead they grew out of his response to the company he was in.

There was occasionally a sense of melancholy and solitude about Bron that was unexpected in a man who was normally so convivial and who made so many of us laugh. He must have been frequently in considerable pain without showing it. That was a further sign of his courage, and of his great courtesy.

When his sister died, in 1986, Bron wrote a quite uncharacteristic piece in the *Spectator* about the grief and pain which lie beneath our daily experience. Only now, sharing that grief, and offering our love and support to Teresa, to their children, and to all his family, can we realise all that we lost when we lost him.

The Right Reverend Simon Phipps, Bishop of Lincoln (1921–2001)

by the Right Reverend David Wilcox
(formerly Bishop of Dorking)

Memorial Service at St Mary the Virgin Church, Shipley, Sussex, on 12 February 2001

Text from Iris Murdoch: 'I use the word *Attention* to express the idea of a just and loving gaze directed upon an individual reality.'

My friends, we have come to mourn the sudden loss of a dear friend but also to celebrate a remarkable life. The writer in *The Times* last week struck precisely the right note when he said that Simon combined gentleness, tranquillity and sweetness of character with deep psychological insight and considerable strength of purpose. And, I would add, a deep humility.

As I have reflected upon what I know of that life of nearly eighty years, it seems to me that the one word which comes nearest to capturing its meaning is the word 'attention': a just and loving gaze directed upon an individual reality. In the short time we have this afternoon, let's look together at a few episodes in Simon's life.

See him, first of all, just after the war, president of the Cambridge Footlights, which prepared the way for *That Was the Week That Was*. See him dressed (or partly dressed) as an artist's model and singing: 'I'm a Botticelli angel and I'm bored with looking sweet and faintly over-awed. I feel so bloody silly just holding up my lily, in that way that Botticelli so adored.'

He was, of course, a brilliant mimic. See him, for instance, mimicking Charles Raven, the Regius Professor, sweeping back his gown and telling of some 'profoundly moving occasion' (which happened to Raven rather often). Now, you can't mimic people unless, like Alan Bennett or Simon Phipps, you pay attention to people, to life, to detail.

Returning to Cambridge, after his curacy in Huddersfield, Simon became chaplain in his own college, Trinity, where this capacity for attention, attention to the individual, was very evident, as he concentrated entirely on the person he was speaking to.

The fine obituary to which I referred clearly saw Simon's next work as the happiest of his ministry. I mean his ten years in Coventry as industrial chaplain. He was a member of a very remarkable team of men under Bishop Cuthbert Bardsley, including Provost Williams, Stephen Verney and Edward Patey. It was during this time that Simon wrote his book *God on Monday*. It was here, among the working people of Coventry, that he developed a theology which, to a great extent, remained with him for the rest of his life. It was a theology which saw the priority not as attending to things to do with the Church but rather attending to the Kingdom of God; that is to say, attending to ordinary secular affairs and circumstances and trying to perceive what God is saying in and through them. This gave him an immediate link with ordinary working people, as he sought to address these matters in common-or-garden language. 'Love,' he would say, 'means taking *everybody's* interests seriously.'

In these ways, Simon was already giving attention to what lay outside himself, especially people in need. It was a form of love: a just and loving gaze directed upon an individual reality.

In 1968 he came to this part of the country, becoming Bishop of Horsham. It was during this time that Simon saw the vital importance of support groups for the clergy. It was this initiative, in particular, which led to his meeting and eventually falling in love with Mary Welch. At the same time, Simon came to see that there is a proper sense in which a priest, a bishop, needs to pay attention to himself, to himself in his relationships, and this became possible for him very largely through the insights of psychotherapy. Simon wrote:

Religion *can* become a matter of satisfying a critical God, by adopting a pattern of strict and punishing self-discipline. Then it becomes all rules and regulations which must be obeyed. But what are we playing at out there, when all the time there is God waiting for us in our rejected inner life, where he accepts all the very things that make us afraid?

To be responsible for myself is to face myself and then to go on from there. This can make us more free *from* the illusions of anxiety and thereby more free *for* faith.

In 1973 Simon and Mary entered upon a marriage which lasted for twenty-seven years, ended only by Mary's death last June. It brought to them both, and to many of us, very great happiness, but not without its struggles. Neither Simon nor Mary made any secret of the fact that the early years of their marriage were not without difficulties. They came through to a relationship (combining both a closeness and a separateness) which was able to embrace so many of us lovingly, a marriage in which others felt comfortable and loved.

The attention which Simon devoted to Mary in those first years undoubtedly affected the character of his next major ministry, as Bishop of Lincoln from 1974 onwards. He tended in later years to be self-deprecating about his effectiveness as a diocesan bishop, but others would regard such self-criticism as very unfair. During those years, he was responsible for some remarkable initiatives: he pioneered the development of Local Ordained Ministry for that large rural diocese (indeed, it is difficult to see now how it could otherwise be adequately ministered to), he actively campaigned for the ordination of women as long ago as 1978, he appointed a lay parish worker, to be in charge of a benefice. He developed the link between the diocese of Lincoln and the diocese of Bruges, finding a kindred spirit in Bishop de Smet.

In other respects, he did not, I think, give a strong lead to the diocese and there were those who found this a real problem, but it was partly because he felt that people must be treated as adults, and make their own decisions. He certainly felt deeply about the deprivation of many people in rural communities, and, above all, he ruled out whole days in order to travel around that vast area, visiting the clergy and their families in their homes. Paying attention to them: a just and loving gaze directed upon those clergy and those families.

When Simon retired to Shipley in 1986, there began another, extremely fruitful stage in his life and ministry. For one thing, he now had more time to paint and he was an accomplished artist in oils. It involved, once more, attention – both to his own painting and to the great painters. Michael Mayne wrote: 'If you are going to let a painting speak to you, you have to respect its silence and its stillness. It has demanded an intensely concentrated act of seeing on the part of the artist and it isn't going to give up its secret at a hurried glance.'

For another thing, he gave himself up to friendship, a vast range of friendships formed over the years with every kind of person: princesses and psychotherapists, priests and politicians, hospital chaplains and the villagers of Shipley. There was huge affection for him here. But people would come from a distance to 'Sarsens' for his guidance and find themselves (we found ourselves) loved and accepted.

He called us his *philadelphoi*, beloved brothers and sisters, and saw always the potential which was in us, what we might become. How typical of him to die at the very moment when he was speaking on the telephone to one friend and preparing supper for another! In many of us there is a tendency to be attention-seekers; Simon was an attention-*giver*.

My wife and I came back just the other day, and stood once more in that familiar study. There was his chair, with the back rest (his back gave him a lot of trouble) and all around were piles of books, many of them new, many of them carefully read and marked up with a highlighter, books of theology, literature, biography, art criticism, photographs of Mary, paintings and Michelin maps of his beloved France. And that is where he prayed for us, seventeen whole pages of names remembered day by day as he said the morning Office.

That, in the end, is the key to the whole matter: Simon used to say that prayer is a giving of attention to what is the case: namely that God *is* and that we *are*. Prayer is taking time to focus, to say Yes to God, to open the channels of grace on behalf of x and y and z.

And here too in this church, on many Sunday mornings at 8 a.m. and on the day before he died, he led the people in giving their corporate attention to God, which is the inward and essential element of worship.

The truth is of course that all this is only our *response*, for God himself gazes on us and with the creative eye of Holy Love. Simon used to say that he had an old American cousin who told him that when her husband proposed to her he said, 'I think you are about the most selfish person I have ever met! But you have possibilities.'

This is the great truth about us. None of us is just me as I am and that's that. There is always more to be discovered and explored and enjoyed and shared. That's how God sees us. It is the real self with all its weakness that He desires. He cannot transform us if we insist on only offering to Him our goodness, our successes, our strengths. His gaze is transforming: He does not leave us in our poverty but draws into being all we are meant to become.

Some of us saw Simon for the last time at the Eucharist in Worth Abbey a fortnight ago. His own last words to us in this life were: 'The peace of the Lord be with you.'

Peace be with you, dear Simon.

Ruby Ludlow (1921–2001)
countrywoman, housekeeper, family friend

by Nicholas Baring
(erstwhile merchant banker and foundation chairman)

Thanksgiving Service at St Nicholas Church, East Grafton, Wiltshire, on 26 February 2001

I am honoured to have been asked to offer this tribute to the life of Ruby Ludlow by her family and am grateful to Sarah and to Patience for the help they have given me in composing it.

She was born Ruby Noyes at Burbage in 1921, the youngest of five children. Her father was a woodman on the Savernake Estate, while her mother, whose family had links with the Forest of Dean, had been a cook by profession and at one time worked in London. All Ruby's childhood was spent at Burbage, where she went to the village school, leaving at what seems to us today the early age of fourteen to go into domestic service, at first locally and later somewhat further away. In the early years of the 1939–45 war she found herself working in a munitions factory near Reading – which wasn't much to her taste.

About the same time she met Reg Ludlow, whose roots were also deep in the Wiltshire countryside; he came from Marten. They courted and, once he had met her condition of providing a twenty-two-carat gold wedding ring, they were married in All Saints' Church, Burbage, in December 1942. Clothes rationing made it impossible to think of a wedding dress and she was married in a suit. They must, nevertheless, have made a very handsome couple.

Their early married life was geared to Reg's work on the land; they moved a number of times – never further than a few miles from Burbage – and then settled in a cottage on the village green here at East Grafton, which became the family home for some years for Ruby and Reg and, in due course, Adrian and Patience, both born in the early post-war period.

The time at East Grafton was a happy one for the family and led to some warm friendships, but in 1966 Reg's farming job came to an end, and with it their tenancy of the cottage. However, Ruby was not one to mope about misfortune and her indomitable spirit came to the fore in the search for a new home and employment. It so happened that at that time I was preparing to move into the Grange at Shalbourne. By an inspired piece of match-making Lew Wager, who lived next door, suggested that Reg and Ruby would be the ideal couple to move into the bungalow which went with the property and to look after the Grange. I remember very well at our first meeting thinking that here was a family with whose help life in a part of England to which I was new would be a pleasure.

And so it proved. Ruby and Reg moved into Per Ardua and became the linchpin of life at the Grange. I was unmarried at that time, but the relationship between us extended not only to my mother – with whom Ruby had a natural bond through their shared feeling for family and country upbringing – but also to my brother and sister and their families, who were frequent visitors and later, of course, to my wife and our three sons.

Ruby's and Reg's own life took an unexpected turn when their three-year-old granddaughter, Sarah, came to live with them at Per Ardua, adding a lively and at times distracting element to their existence. But otherwise the framework of life for Ruby and Reg remained unchanged for some twenty years, during which their partnership kept everything at the Grange in good order; this happy period and more than forty-five years of marriage sadly came to an end with Reg's death in 1988.

Shortly after that (and coinciding with our move from Shalbourne to Ham) a bungalow in the Barracks became free; it was to be Ruby's home for the twelve years of her widowhood. Though she always looked back with nostalgia to her days with Reg in the comparatively spacious surroundings of Per Ardua, she was glad to be able to stay in Shalbourne close to her friends, to the village shop, an important focus of social life and, most of all, to Sarah who within eighteen months moved back to Per Ardua with her husband Martin.

In her new home Ruby was able on a reduced scale to indulge her love of gardening and took great pleasure in the wild birds coming to feed at her bird table. In recent years, apart from constant contact with her family, she enjoyed the meetings of the Good Companions and, latterly, her weekly outings to the Day Centre at Burbage – her club as she called it – where she could share memories with some of her childhood friends.

A strong spirit of independence lay behind her insistence on continuing to live on her own, despite deterioriating health, which led to a number of spells in hospital and increasing concern on the part of her family. Her peaceful death in hospital following a fall at home in a sense averted what would have been a difficult decision for all concerned. For this we should be thankful.

Such then is the bare outline of Ruby's life – virtually all spent in this corner of eastern Wiltshire. You will each have a picture of what made her so special and her life so admirable. I will try to say in a few words how she seemed to me.

She was a very positive person, whose life was founded on a clear set of values. Material ambition did not feature in those; the importance of family life emphatically did. Adrian and Georgie and their son William; Patience and John; Sarah and Martin: she was deeply interested and involved in everything to do with them and never happier than when in their company – preferably, I suspect, all together.

That same human interest extended to others with whom she was close. Our sons became almost a second family for her; she followed their progress from their earliest days right up to the present and always was delighted to see or hear about them. They in their turn loved to visit her. The same applied to the Rogalys and in a lesser extent to our many friends who visited Shalbourne at one time or another. Her quick wit and immediate sympathy – neither of them in any way dimmed by age – enabled her to be in tune with a wide variety of people for all of whom she was an essential part of life at Shalbourne.

I'm sure the same traits were evident in her friendships in the village and elsewhere. She was an excellent listener, always ready to lend an ear to accounts of successes or failures, news of births, deaths and engagements, travels, anecdotes and anything else of interest. I shall especially remember the throaty chuckle with which she responded to anything which amused her – she had a great sense of humour.

While she was in no way a gossip, her acute observation and remarkable memory made her an excellent source of information, particularly about members of the older established Shalbourne families whose number sadly diminished during the more than thirty years she lived in the village. She was not, with very few exceptions, censorious about others; her own life, on the other hand, was governed by a strict code of conduct. She was totally straightforward and refreshingly direct; if there was something she needed to know, she would ask. To be able to live within one's means was important to her and bills were paid by return: 'out of debt, out of danger' was an oft-repeated saying. Unlike so many of us, she never felt there was a need for alcohol to lubricate the wheels of social life: tea was much more to her taste.

Her liking for bright colours in plants and flowers was matched by some of the vivid expressions which appeared in her conversation. Someone by whom she had not been impressed was described as 'not making much music for me'. Her family recall 'a face like a donkey's baby' as a favourite phrase, while one which sticks in my mind is 'straight griffin', equivalent, I think, to 'a piece of my mind' and used in her description of her reply to the distinguished judge in the High Court in London when she was called to give evidence regarding a contested will.

That was one of only a few visits to London, which held little interest for her. Nor did she ever wish to travel abroad. However, she loved her trips with Patience and John in England and Wales and had a particular fascination with the seaside. In spite of the pleasure of these excursions, she never liked being away for more than a few days, worrying how Reg, who was not a traveller, was getting on without her and missing her familiar surroundings.

Her life was a shining example of how much satisfaction can be gained from and dignity given to the daily tasks that go to making a home or helping others to enjoy theirs. Whether it was gardening – her ability to grow perfect Christmas roses showed what green fingers she had – or cooking – her treacle tarts are a legend with our sons – or looking after our flock of bantams, what might have been for others a chore was for her a continued source of pleasure and infused with a spirit of real generosity in that she never thought of doing for herself what she did for others.

I shall remember her best in her garden at Per Ardua, her small figure in a bright blue overall seen watering her flowers or going to collect the eggs from her chickens. It was a sight which, whatever the concerns of the moment, would remind one of the real point of rural life and of country people such as Ruby. We are much richer for having known her.

She will be much missed, most of all, of course, by her family for whom she remained such a central figure. Our sympathy goes out to them, but I hope that they will be comforted by the thought of how glad she was in the knowledge that they were happy in their lives and by the many glowing memories of her which they – and we – will retain

John Diamond (1953–2001)
journalist and broadcaster

by Dominic Lawson
(editor of the Sunday Telegraph)

*Funeral Service at the West London Crematorium,
Kensal Green, on 4 March 2001*

John was a brilliant writer long before he was a famous writer. I remember when I was at the *Spectator* commissioning him – I think I'd read him in the *Sunday Times* travel section – to write a piece on going to Geneva, one of the dullest of the great cities of the world. He wrote an incredibly funny article as only he could about such an unpromising subject. I knew that he was working on the *Sunday Times* where Nigella then was and I liked to ring Nigella up anyway when I came across bits of writing which I enjoyed and I read the Geneva article out to her, trying not to get giggles at it all the time. And a few weeks later, Nigella had what I think is called an unfortunate episode and I said to her, 'Why can't you for once go out with someone nice?' And she said, 'For example, who?' And I said, desperately trying to think of someone, 'Er, for example, John Diamond.' Anyway, a few months later, despite my advice, she did.

Now Nigella then was not the Nigella you know today. She was very shy and insecure and she found someone who loved her and this was more important – someone who made her feel loved. There is no better way to gain self-belief and self-confidence and I think that has made her what she is today. Of course, he adored Mimi and Bruno as much as he did their mother. And when in horrible instalments he lost his tongue, they always understood him when others couldn't. This was very, very important to him, to feel normal with the people with whom it mattered most. Except Mimi and Bruno pretended not to understand him when he was telling them off, which he did not like.

I suppose my fondest memory of John is just sitting with him in silence watching Mimi playing with Savannah and Bruno playing with Domenica, their cousins. John actually had a special bond with Domenica. Her tongue was too big and his tongue was too small and then non-existent and neither could express in words what they were thinking. But they sustained a wonderful relationship by making meaningful noises to each other. John's account of illness, of course, which is famous, is not the full picture. He said once, I think, that it was almost a musical act, 'Cheeky Charlie, the Carcinoma King'. There was, in fact, which did not always come out in his writing, a very, very deep anger. He would say, 'Well, wouldn't you be?' I think this was a huge burden for him and a huge burden for Nigella and it wasn't the real John who was, I think as you all know, the most generous-spirited of men.

We all want to know, I suppose, all of us here, was he reconciled at the end to death? Yesterday, I asked Nigella, really on behalf of us all, and she said yes, suddenly in the last two days he was and the old John, the John she fell in love with, free of all bitterness, very calm.

You probably all know that John kept notebooks, strange one-sided conversations. You'd be with John or John would come to your home and you'd find these notebooks littered everywhere with his side of a dialogue and try to remember what it was all about.

Yesterday, Nigella showed me this last book, John's last notebook, which I suppose he would wish you to know is matt black, Tolerton and Harvey. She asked me to read out the last pages, which may be difficult, I think, for you to bear but Nigella pointed out to me that John adored an audience. So I've transcribed it. It was quite difficult to read, obviously, because of the drugs he was on. The period also covers his final surgical procedure and a cast of characters.

There are some very close friends there, Nigella, of course, and Peter Rees-Evans, the surgeon who looked after him so well.

That's all I need, mates who insult the anaesthetist before I go under.

This must be afterwards:

Any chance of a little sedation, I feel a touch anxious. You are not allowed to do that outside Holland. Sort of okay I suppose, within the usual existential constraints. See if Bywater will finish the book. Don't worry, I've done the clever stuff. Stay with me is all. As long as the last is with you, that's okay. It's not finished but on the folder saying John there is a file saying to Mimi and Bruno.

And this, I think, is to Peter Rees-Evans, where he says:

Peter, thank you for everything you gave me a wonderful extra three years.

And then, I think also to Peter Rees-Evans:

I want no more resuscitation please Peter, I can't take any more of this, thank you.

And then I think this is to Nigella:

How proud I am of you and what you've become. The great thing about us is we have made us who we are. Kiss the children for me. I love you all, you are all.

Then I think this is the last note which just says:

Meanwhile can you take me under to relieve the pain and waiting, please.

And it's underlined twice . . .

Colin Cowdrey (The Lord Cowdrey of Tonbridge, 1932–2000)

cricketer: captain of England twenty-seven times

by the Right Honourable John Major
(Prime Minister, 1990–7)

Memorial Service at Westminster Abbey, London, on 30 March 2001

There is a moment when someone dies when raw emotion has a way of letting you know just how much they meant to you. When Michael Ancram phoned me with the news I had a prickling in the eye that came unbidden and would not go away. No more Colin. Millions — some of whom had never met him — felt the same. To those millions Colin was one of the world's greatest cricketers. To those of us who knew him, he was one of the world's loveliest of men. That is why this abbey could have been filled many times over.

Letters to the family poured in from all over the world:

From Australia:

When one thinks of Colin Cowdrey, one thinks of grace, elegance – and England.

From India:

Sad to see you go, Mr Colin. We loved you in India.

And from Sydney a prophecy, which I hope is true:

Bowlers, beware! That great firm of Cowdrey and May are about to renew their partnership!

There were many more such affectionate letters: from all those whose lives Colin had touched.

It's not just that Colin was a great cricketer – though he was: the prodigious talent of the boy ripened, to make the man the greatest pear-shaped batsman of our time. Although on a bad day he could have the cricketing equivalent of writer's block, most of his batting was pure poetry.

At Melbourne aged twenty-one, he scored a hundred for England that old men still babble about. I heard some of that innings over the static in the middle of the night, my ear pressed to the radio to avoid waking my parents, who thought that a ten-year-old should be asleep. Lovely people, my parents – but they never did understand cricket.

Colin the man was special too. In the early 1990s he came to see me at Number 10 with some South African cricket officials. As we sat in my study, beneath a portrait of W.G. Grace, he asked me to speak to some Commonwealth heads of government to help South Africa back into the world game. I did. They were admitted: but it was Colin's love of cricket that was the driving force.

He had a great affinity for the young. He helped me launch a sports initiative at a London stadium, following which we had an impromptu game of cricket with a veritable United Nations of children. An Indian boy bowled; I kept wicket; Colin batted and hit up a catch to a Jamaican girl. As she caught the ball, he cheered: 'Well played. Bravo! Well played,' an encouragement he used a thousand times a year. The girl skipped up and down, eyes shining and pigtails flying. Once again, Colin had used that extraordinary gift he had for making anyone in his company feel a hundred feet tall. If I ever saw the joy of life I saw it then. It was a very happy moment.

As Christopher has already said, Colin was a great writer of notes and a world-class user of the telephone. Whenever I faced political difficulty, Colin would be there. So we were in touch a lot.

The phone would ring and a voice would say, 'Morning, Skipper

– Cowdrey here.' Or there'd be a note – many notes. They were always upbeat. 'Bravo! Well played. 100 not out,' he'd write – even if I'd been politically bowled for nought.

Sometimes, if life was more than usually turbulent, he would phone those closest to me at Number 10 and ask if he could pop in for a drink.

For Colin, the answer was always yes. And when I walked into my flat above Number 10, late at night, he'd often be there – tumbler of whisky in hand – his gently smiling face and wise words bringing sanity and common sense to the frenetic world of politics. Colin never talked of this publicly – nor did I before now. But it illustrates the kind of man he was: a friend in bad times as well as good. Truly, a man for all seasons.

Colin's gift for letter-writing was no doubt hereditary. There is a letter written from Malabar, India, in October 1940 from Colin's mother, Molly, which paints a wonderful portrait of a happy cricket-mad boy 'enjoying himself' and loving cricket. 'And have you noticed his initials?' Molly wrote: 'MCC'. How proud she would have been of the extraordinary man her boy grew up to be.

But then family is a Cowdrey trait. Colin always spoke with such affection of Chris, Jeremy, Carol and Graham and his years with Penny. He was so proud of all their achievements – whether on or off the cricket field – with a hundred stories which he would recount with an air of wonder that he and Penny should have produced such a talented crew.

And his joy over Anne and her horses bubbled over like uncorked champagne. He would phone me when a horse won. 'She's done it!' 'Done what?' 'Won.' 'Won what?' 'That race . . . Anne's won.' And after a while even the horse got some credit, too.

Colin is a loss to us all, but the greatest loss is to his family.

A modest man, blessed with the gift of friendship. A gentle man with a God-given talent. Kipling had it right: 'If you can talk with crowds and keep your virtue, or walk with Kings – nor lose the common touch'. Colin *never* lost it.

In life, said a lesser poet than Kipling, it matters not who wins or loses, but how the game is played. And how well Colin played it.

Captain of Kent and England; President of Kent and the MCC; a Commander of the British Empire; a Knight of the British Empire; a Peer of the Realm. A man of Kent who left his mark on so many lives and had friends in every corner of the world.

And when Colin died, the England team wore black armbands for him and beat Pakistan in the gathering gloom at Karachi. As the unlikely victory neared, Colin's family and friends had returned from his funeral service and were gathered in his study at Angmering cheering them on. How he would have loved it. And how we missed him.

The day before he died, Colin was due to attend a meeting of the Master's Club followed by lunch at the Oval – to honour Sir Jack Hobbs – the man known universally in cricket as the Master. He couldn't make it and sent a note: 'It is with real regret that I cannot be at The Oval today to celebrate The Master's Birthday,' and he went on: 'what a magnificent season Surrey have had. Many, many congratulations.' This was a characteristically gracious ending to a note that may well have been the last he wrote before the Young Master went off to join the Old Master, at a far Higher Table than the Oval.

It's hard to believe we will no longer hear his voice at the end of the phone. Nor be cheered by the notes he would send. But yet – Colin isn't gone. How can he be when in our mind we hear his voice and see his face? No man is gone whilst those who knew him – and the family who loved him – remember him and talk of him. He left us too soon. For once, that immaculate timing was out – but it was a gem of an innings.

Colin played life as he played cricket: with a clear eye, a straight bat and a cover drive from heaven. On the field and off it he was a true Corinthian. And when the Umpire of Life gave him out he went, without complaint and without rancour, to join many of his old friends.

As for those he has left behind, we are blessed with an abundance of happy memories of the times we shared together. Well played, Colin. Bravo. Well played.

Anthony Storr (1920–2001)
psychiatrist and writer

by Kay Jamison
(Professor of Psychiatry at the Johns Hopkins University School of Medicine, USA)

Memorial Service at Holywell Music Room, Oxford, on 24 June 2001

No one I know thought more clearly about human nature than Anthony Storr. And no one I know wrote better about the pain and delights of being human in the modern world. Anthony understood in the deepest way the emotions and experiences that make us who we are. He was profoundly compassionate toward those who struggle with hopelessness, despair, uncertainty or paralysing anxieties. He believed that such psychological imperfections, however painful, are an essential part of our humanity and are a not inconsiderable part of what makes us invent, discover and create. He wrote once that 'Man, though successful biologically, is in many ways an unsatisfactory species; but, whatever he is, we have to live with him.' It was one of Anthony's great gifts that he was able to persuade so many of this essential truth.

Anthony was an unnervingly astute observer of people and an excellent doctor, capabilities which combined to give him a lasting respect for the power of irrational forces in the lives of individuals and their societies. He understood that aggression and hatred and perversion are a part of our species but that so too are love and music and the capacity to heal. He had a personal as well as a professional knowledge of psychological suffering, and he always believed, and taught, that life was well worth whatever effort it took to get through to the other side of the darkness.

This essential hopefulness, together with a tenacious belief in the power of good psychotherapists to heal their patients, was at the heart of Anthony's clinical work and writings. He understood his patients and he liked them, and he found utterly fascinating the personalities and varieties of temperaments that he encountered in his consulting room. The clarity of his clinical perceptions, and the sympathy with which he held them, found their way into most of his books, and his writing set the standard for a generation of psychologists and psychiatrists that followed. Indeed it still sets the standard.

His empathy for his patients is to be found everywhere in his work. In *The Art of Psychotherapy*, for example, he wrote:

> Human beings are endlessly fascinating; complex amalgams of all kinds of qualities, good and bad. If I had to choose one overriding impression which I have received from my practice as a psychotherapist, I would point to this ambivalent complexity. My life has been greatly enriched by my profession; and I am grateful for having had the opportunity of penetrating deeply into the lives of so many interesting, and often lovable, people.

Sympathy and a refreshing clarity of thought are central to Anthony's writings about psychopathology and human nature, but so too is an astringent scepticism toward any kind of therapeutic dogmatism, unwarranted adherence to flawed theoretical systems, and uncritical belief in governments or cult figures. In psychiatry, a field too often defined by its articles of faith, Anthony stood back, wrote wisely and sensibly, and was listened to. He sought and found that which was of value in a particular belief system, whether it was psychoanalysis or biological psychiatry, then he extracted the most thoughtful ideas or insights and left behind the rest. He was not an ideologue and he could not abide rigid intellectual beliefs. He thought that much of what was assumed to be true in modern psychiatry was absurd, and he said so often, clearly, and in a manner that caused our field to pay attention.

Anthony disliked the many arbitrary dichotomies in our field. He refused to join in the entirely unwarranted split between those who prescribe only medication and those who practise only psycho-therapy: he saw both as important in the healing of lives. He valued solitude, writing eloquently in praise of it, but he felt as strongly that life was made most meaningful by one's closeness to family and friends. He loved literature and music, but was also fascinated by the rapidly progressing fields of genetics and neuroscience. All, he thought, were essential to understanding the mind. He rejected the current psychiatric diagnostic systems as extremely unsatisfactory, as indeed they are, but he was equally scathing toward those who cling mindlessly to the tenets of doctrinaire psychoanalysis. His intellectual curiosity forced him to see mankind from diverse and original van-tage points, and his sense of delight – whether in a new bit of knowledge, a piece of music, his family, or in watching the pelicans in St James's Park – offset his scepticism in a distinctive and wonder-ful way.

Anthony's work, especially, I think, *The Art of Psychotherapy*, *Solitude* and *Music and the Mind*, have had and will continue to have a major influence on British and American ways of thinking about human psychology. Psychiatrists, psychologists, artists, writers and the general public have been influenced to a quite remarkable degree by Anthony's books, by his respect for the individual, and by his belief that a good doctor, great art, and a more compassionate society can make a difference.

Anthony expanded our notions of the origins and expressions of human imagination and, in the process, restored dignity to the discussion of psychological struggles of those artists whose creative works enrich our lives. He wrote compellingly of the social dangers of unchecked human aggression and paranoia, graphically elucidated the destructiveness of pathological narcissism, and passionately advo-cated the rights of those damaged by inhumane political systems. In all of these things he made original and important contributions to his profession and society.

Anthony's ability to reach across different groups was brought home to me a few years ago when I watched him address more than a thousand psychiatrists at an American Psychiatric Association meeting in San Francisco. Unlike most of us who give scientific talks, who gallop through our incomprehensible and boring slides of medication response rates or brain slices, Anthony spoke from a prepared text. The room was dead quiet. There was no rustling through papers or getting up for coffee, no whispering, no palpable restlessness. Anthony spoke about individual lives and how they had been affected, for better and worse, by suffering; and he spoke about the importance of respecting the uncomfortable reality that the border between what is normal and what is not is more permeable and shifting than many of us would like to believe.

At the end of his talk the audience rose and gave him a prolonged and heartfelt standing ovation, a tribute made all the more extraordinary by the rather jaded nature of many of the doctors and scientists in the room. Anthony's perspective on life was not just appreciated, it was needed. It will be missed.

I would like to end on a personal note. I first met Anthony Storr nearly twenty years ago, here in Oxford, when I was on a year's sabbatical from the University of California. He became my closest friend and, like many of you who knew him, I simply adored him. He was a remarkable listener and I talked with him about everything imaginable. He understood, effortlessly, the most disjointed thoughts and feelings, and he had an astonishing way of making sense out of chaos. He was kind beyond reckoning and was able to give excellent advice in such a gentle way that it was only later that you realised how very blunt he had been. I think Anthony's own experiences with depression, and with the lifetime repercussions from a deep childhood loneliness, made him able to understand the pain of others, and to encourage the channelling of that pain into something of more lasting value.

Several years ago, when I was struggling with a decision about whether or not to write a book about my manic-depressive illness, and was particularly concerned about the professional and personal consequences of doing so, Anthony strongly encouraged me to do it. He predicted, accurately, that I would find that most people would be more open-minded and compassionate than I could imagine, that some people would be cruel, and that whatever criticism came it would be endurable. He was right, as always. And, as was usual for him, he telephoned and wrote me often to see how I was holding up. He was a friend like no other.

My heart goes out to Catherine, whom he loved and admired; to Sophia, Cecilia and Emma, whom he thought were marvellous; to his step-sons, of whom he was so proud; to his grandchildren, of whom he spoke incessantly; and to all his friends and colleagues here, who will miss him. I am glad that so much of this celebration will be music, for that was Anthony's passion. Music, he wrote, in his great book on the subject, was 'a way of ordering human experi ence, of arousing our emotions, exalting life, enhancing life, and giving it meaning'. Music, he believed, is 'an irreplaceable, unde served, transcendental blessing'.

So, too, was Anthony. I learned from him, was befriended and encouraged by him, and I shall always miss him.

Lalage, Lady Wakefield (1906–2001)

Raj daughter, wife and mother

by Maximilian Wakefield

(soldier, racing driver, entrepreneur)

*Memorial Service at Bramdean Church, Hampshire,
on 6 August 2001*

Whenever someone close to Grandmother died she was fond of quoting the third-century BC poem 'Heraclitus', translated by William Johnson Cory. And so it is entirely right that I quote it to you now:

> They told me, Heraclitus, they told me you were dead,
> They brought me bitter news to hear and bitter tears to shed.
> I wept as I remembered how often you and I
> Had tired the sun with talking and sent him down the sky.
>
> And now that thou art lying, my dear old Carian guest,
> A handful of grey ashes, long, long ago at rest,
> Still are thy pleasant voices, thy nightingales, awake;
> For Death, he taketh all away, but them he cannot take.

Grandmother's nightingales will live for a long time.

Whatever Grandmother did she did brilliantly. She could sing, and was trained to do so as a child. She could speak several languages and French so well she was considered a local. She could paint and sew beautifully, she was phenomenally well read. She was in a league of her own when it came to horses and dogs. She was fearless and honest to an extraordinary degree. So, today we are all here to say farewell to someone we know differently from everyone else. So rather than try and conjure up your images I will take the next few minutes to talk about *my* grandmother.

I went to live with Grandmother at the age of four. She came from a line of six, or maybe more, Oxbridge Classics double firsts and indeed my grandfather, too, had a Cambridge Classics double first. Every ounce of that great intelligence was required when it was discovered that I was dyslexic. When I went to live at Mary Abbots with Grandmother she had recently lost her husband, and it seemed that I was yet to find my brain.

Together we soldiered through and Grandmother was keen that she prepared me for the challenges of life with some of her own qualities and these were: determination, fearlessness and honesty.

But what I remember most about Grandmother was her complete capacity for unconditional love and devotion. In fact in such stark contrast to my mother's regime that I was frightened it may end at any moment, as if it were a dream. To allay this fear, whenever I was out of sight of Grandmother, I would call out her name, just to hear her answer back. And of course she would be there, sitting in her chair, perhaps sewing or reading. Grandmother had a phenomenal mind and it seemed she could quote large tracts of any great literary work or poetry. These quotes were triggered by a key word. It would be quite normal for me to ask what we were doing tomorrow and the reply would come.

> Tomorrow and tomorrow and tomorrow,
> Creeps in this petty pace from day to day,
> To the last syllable of recorded time.
> And all our yesterdays have lighted fools
> The way to dusty death. Out, out, brief candle!

Not perhaps the answer a four-year-old was looking for. And nor was it the answer that a second-rate teacher of this four-year-old was after in response to the same question. Thus I learned the first painful lesson of a classical education.

Grandmother had every sympathy with the fact that I found spelling Catullus and Heraclitus difficult. But she had no sympathy for the illustrator of a very simple English book I was required to read for homework. Nipper, to me, was clearly a Red Setter, but for some biological reason Grandmother could not recognise the breed and the book was shut up and the homework left undone.

My spelling fell so far behind that the child of a neighbour, who attended the same school, asked Grandmother why my spelling was so bad. Grandmother delighted me with her response which was simply, 'Why is your bottom so fat?'

Grandmother had a very sharp wit and plenty of practice with her family kept it honed to a very fine point. I remember my father trying on my grandfather's overcoat he recently had altered, to his obvious delight. Grandmother looked up from her sewing and said, 'Yes, darling, you look very good in that overcoat.' Then, after the rightful pause, added, 'But not quite so good as you think you do.'

Grandmother had a mantra she based her life on which was 'Honesty is the best policy', and she twisted this phrase to make a trap for fools, though fools were not the only pickings.

Two fools I can think of were the two burglars who stole into Grandmother's bedroom in the dead of night. One was sent back out of the window, whence he came, under a barrage of flailing fists, and the other was shown the door and not allowed to leave until she had extracted the correct apology.

There were two times Grandmother was fond of claiming to be agnostic. The first was when she had queued for hours at a post office or Passport Office and was asked to fill in a box with the heading 'Religion'. And that was to prove some fault in their paperwork. The other time was in pursuit of a greater truth.

As I said, fools were not the only pickings and I suppose that most of her targets, in this pursuit of truth, fell under the heading of 'Cleric'. She would lull her opponent into a sense of security by professing to be agnostic. This, of course, was rubbish as she could quote this edition, the last edition and the next edition of any Bible forwards, backwards and sideways.

A former Archbishop of Canterbury used to spend a week a year on holiday with Grandmother as a guest of my Great-Uncle Lucius. I think he must have dreaded this week more than any other in his year's calendar, as debate would have raged from morning till dusk.

To all our embarrassment, Grandmother gave the Archbishop of the Indian Ocean an inquisition on his thesis on racism.

I know that Grandmother believed in God, and I know this because there was a story she would tell, but not often. Once while out riding Grandmother's horse bolted and was galloping down a slippery road; Grandmother felt that her end had come and found herself shouting out for Jesus's help. At that instant a man in flowing robes appeared in the middle of the road with his arm raised. The horse came to an instant stop and before Grandmother could look up and thank the man he had vanished.

But the truth was that Grandmother loved to help everyone no matter what creed, breed, colour or age. She was particularly interested in those that needed protection and encouragement. Grandmother may have loved to pursue but she loved to protect as well.

Perhaps the best illustration of this desire to pursue and protect is summed up in this simple story. Grandmother loved hunting and to make things more challenging she would do it side-saddle. There she would be crashing over fences, at the front of the field, pursuing a fox. Simultaneously, at home, she was raising a fox cub rescued from the same hunt. And thus one can see that Grandmother could enjoy both hunting and protecting at the same time.

Grandmother was brilliant with animals and my grandfather brought back from Tibet a lone, pregnant spaniel. From this single dog Grandmother was able to propagate the Tibetan Spaniel breed to the point that it had, and still has, its own class at Crufts. Grandmother would go on to judge at this show as well. But horses, dogs and foxes were not the only animals: there were pigs, owls, geese, parrots and goodness knows what else. Each was spoken to in the correct jungle howl or farmyard grunt. One of her animals, that lived and died long before I came along, went on to cause me great embarrassment. Duchess, the Tibetan spaniel, was lucky in that she could understand English fluently but spoke it with a rather odd accent. Grandmother, to my intense discomfort, regaled my friends with Duchess's adventures while I just wished she would tell them about her adventures point-to-pointing.

Grandmother would point-to-point side-saddle and one particular race she won was on a horse called Mistake, which meant that the papers reported that such and such a point-to-point was 'won by Mrs Wakefield's mistake'. That delighted her.

So it is obvious that Grandmother felt she knew what Whyte Melville meant when he wrote this:

> There are men both wise and great
> Who hold, in another state,
> All creatures that have loved us here below,
> Will give us Joyous Greeting,
> When we reach the Golden Gate,
> Is it Folly that I hope it may be so?

You could not throw Grandmother. She was simply bullet-proof. Whenever I made a mistake, regardless of scale, she would look at me and say, 'Ah, darling.' Once, when we were moving house, Father sat Grandmother in a chair, balanced high on top of a lot of furniture. That furniture was in a trailer and the trailer was towed slowly across Ireland for all to see. Grandmother sat high up, perched in the chair, quite unconcerned, reading a good book.

If Grandmother were to take a fall it would be by her own choice, and never off a horse, but on to a glass of Guinness, at lunch, and whisky and water in the evening. When she drank the Guinness she would quote the advertising slogan, 'See what toucan do.' Now, I am pleased to remember the things the two of us did do.

So what was Grandmother, a curious mix of emotions and devotions, devotions to her family, her husband, children and grand-children? She had pride in their achievements, one of which, Uncle Hardy, we can see about us here in the perfect execution of this service and its preparation. Indeed, I was so proud when Grand-mother came and watched me in a school play or when I passed out of Sandhurst and, of course, when she saw my children William and Edward had both inherited her famously red hair. But beyond us as family is her devotion to you, her extended family. I once went up to London to see Grandmother at the Lister Hospital on Christmas Day and found her chatting to Bernard Neville on the telephone, and this was long after I thought she had lost the power of speech. I thank you, Bernard, for taking such an effort and to Sue Rogers, Richard Storey, Robert Guinness and the Jackson family, to name but a few. Thank you all for making the journey here today.

There is no way to say adieu, but on the subject of death Grand-mother was fond of quoting Hamlet's last words in the play of the same name and so I will finish with them today:

The rest is silence.

The Earl of Longford (1906–2001)

politician, penal reformer and author

by His Eminence Cardinal Cormac Murphy O'Connor

(Cardinal Archbishop of Westminster)

Memorial Service at Westminster Cathedral, London, on 10 August 2001

It is good to remind ourselves of what shapes our celebration today. For this liturgy of the Requiem Mass tells us that we are to comfort one another with words of faith; that we are to praise God for His majesty and glory; that we are to invoke in the Holy Eucharist the death and resurrection of Jesus Christ, which for we Christians is our ultimate hope – and we express our faith in God's love for Frank Longford as we pray for the repose of his soul.

I suppose the obvious Gospel reading for today might have been Matthew 25, with Jesus telling his disciples of the last judgement and how the King would say to those admitted to eternal life, 'For I was hungry and you gave me food, I was thirsty and you gave me to drink, naked and you clothed me, sick and in prison and you visited me.' And the virtuous will ask when did we do this to you, Lord? And Jesus says, 'In as much as you did it to the least of my brothers and sisters, you did it to me.' In many ways that was Frank. But I chose the Gospel of the Beatitudes because it seems to me that if we are to connect a reading with a man's life, then for Frank Longford the Beatitudes sum it up.

For all his life long, Frank was taken up with the quest for holiness and the Kingdom of God. How happy are the poor in spirit, theirs is the Kingdom of Heaven, happy the gentle, happy the merciful, happy the peacemakers, happy those who hunger for what is right, they shall be satisfied. He witnessed in his own life all of these things.

He also wrote about it. As you know, many of his books were about what it meant to be holy – books on humility, on saints, on the virtue of hope, and indeed there was one entitled *Bishops*, because I suppose Frank rightly thought that bishops were called to be holy. I am inclined to think that he did not make much money from his books because he gave away so many. I picked one up from my library the other day, one he had kindly given to me eleven years ago and inside was the letter he wrote. 'My dear Cormac, I venture to send you a little book I have just written on forgiveness. I hope you will like it – and even if you don't I know you will be kind about it!'

But I noted that in all the books of his that I possess, each one is dedicated to his wife Elizabeth. In her he was especially blessed. She was everything to Frank and he to her. Elizabeth, you have our profound sympathy on your great loss. But you know you will be sustained and supported by the love and affection of your family and of your many friends.

There are some who think that religion is a refuge from risk, but it never should be and it certainly wasn't for Frank. In many ways he was a controversial figure and at times was mocked and scorned. But it never unduly worried him, for he was concerned with another kingdom. Did not Jesus his master say that the Kingdom belonged to those who were poor in spirit and merciful and peacemakers? Perhaps above all, he said, happy are those who are persecuted in the cause of right – theirs is the Kingdom of Heaven. So when Frank spoke out against abortion or against pornography, or spoke up for penal reform and visited the forgotten ones in prison, he was only living out simply and bravely the injunctions of the Kingdom of God. Those actions were not bees in his bonnet. Frank believed them to be true, so he was a free man. As Jesus said, 'The truth will make you free.'

The values of the Kingdom of God will always turn the values of this world upside down. And that to me is the inner meaning of the long and varied life of a great man. So if the tributes that have been paid to him have emphasised the seemingly more colourful and eccentric side of his life, rather than his career in politics and publishing and banking, who is to say they are wrong. For the world needs to hear and see a witness to the values that are different from those espoused by our society. For Frank, another Francis was his hero. A man of Assisi who stripped himself naked, gave back his possessions to his father, was at first mocked by his townspeople and then was recognised as someone who sang and rejoiced in God's world and everything in it – sang of his poverty and of his love for the poor and dispossessed – and so inherited the Kingdom of God.

So today we pray for the repose of the soul of Frank Longford and ask God to forgive him any faults he will have committed in this life, for like all of us he was human and vulnerable and has need of God's mercy. But we can also be sure that Frank Longford will inherit the fullness of the Kingdom of God, still incomplete in this life. But the glimpses of that kingdom we see in the lives of good people such as Frank. He, too, will have heard the voice of the Master and the promise he gives in the Gospel today to those who live out the Beatitudes. 'Rejoice and be glad for your reward will be great in heaven.'

Keith Beaumont (1930–2001)
Shropshire farmer

by David Palmer
(farmer and Master of Foxhounds)

Funeral Service at Nash Church, Tenbury Wells,
Worcestershire, on 14 October 2001

I have an immense responsibility to portray to you the life of a very exceptional character.

Keith was born in 1930 at Byton near Presteigne, into a farming family, and from a very early age was no stranger to hardship and tough physical work. Horses immediately played a large part in his life as he learned to work with heavy horse teams, both farming and hauling timber from the forestry.

At eighteen he came to live with his uncle and aunt at Aston Bank Farm, where his regime of hard physical graft continued. He met and married Maureen Corfield from Dean Lodge who he always called Maun, or, as you will hear, with good reason, Mother, when they were both twenty-one years old. For the first few years of married life they lived with his in-laws at Dean Lodge, where Jean and Nicholas were born. He always found the hard work ethic difficult to shake off, and endeared himself to his young bride by going baling while Nicholas was born!

No one could deny that Keith had a fairly fiery temperament, and when he eventually fell out with his uncle he set up his own contracting business. Keith and Maureen moved to the Old School at Nash in 1960, and it was their home for sixteen years. The old classroom became his workshop, as well as the auditorium for some pretty high-class swearing!

The family continued to grow pretty rapidly, and in due course Robert, Sarah, John and Mark were added to the family. Throughout this time Keith had kept his love of horses, and having converted the old school lavatories to stables hunted with the Ludlow Foxhounds together with his great friend and soulmate Cliff Bevan. Incidentally, at one early stage of developing his own business he had scraped all his money left to buy a baler, and having bought it had no money left to buy a tractor to pull it, and Cliff came to the rescue and loaned him his. Not to be left behind, Keith's three eldest kids also went hunting with their dad after their ponies had been herded into the schoolroom overnight. I am informed rather ruefully by those three that the quality of the ponies varied somewhat, and that the only advice they were ever given was to 'kick on'.

Apart from his hunting and his family, Keith's life at this time consisted of work, work and work, which made him tremendously fit, and he gloried in tug-of-war matches.

In 1975 Maureen's father Mr Corfield died and Keith bought Dean Lodge where the family have been centred ever since, together with Flavia, Maureen's sister, who has been a rock of strength especially in these later years of Keith's failing health.

Fox-hunting had by now become an absolute passion, and Keith and his friends Ray Godwin and Roger Beaumont learned to cut quite a dash across the Ludlow country.

I think there are probably quite a lot of Keith's friends here who got to know him through other branches of his life, and I wonder if you realise what an outstanding horseman he was. He possessed a combination of immense courage, fitness and from somewhere the God-given gift of judgement of pace and distance. He could ride across country on fairly ordinary (certainly inexpensive) horses like no one else, and his reputation spread throughout the hunting scene in these parts.

I got to know him in the early eighties and when in 1982 I came to be Master of the Ludlow Hounds Keith, Ray and Roger were in their heyday, and very apt to go off jumping mad things regardless of what the hounds were about. In 1985 we cured that by making him Field Master, a job for which he was perfectly suited, possessing a detailed knowledge of the country, great riding ability, and a proper understanding of the farmland we crossed and the technicalities of fox-hunting. He wore the red coat that went with his position with great pride.

I think the Ludlow Hunt became in many respects the centre of his life, and my memory is crowded with incidents from those years:

- The opening meet when we both jumped a hedge into a dried-up pond and Keith broke his wrist.
- The time soon after his recovery from bypass heart surgery when we tried to swim the Teme, and he, a non-swimmer, got washed off his horse (incidentally called River) and only survived by holding on to his stirrup leather while the horse swam to the opposite bank.
- Those generous whisky-befogged lawn meets from Dean Lodge when there always seemed to be a fox nearby.
- The time he thought I had given him the slip from Gaudy Wood, and he jumped five hung steel gates in a row to catch me up at Ray Godwin's Foxley Farm.
- When we bet him he couldn't put a visiting Master of Foxhounds on the floor, and he jumped over a huge iron gate only to find that his would-be victim had gone off to change horses, and he finally got his man at four thirty that evening.
- When Miss Mary rang to say how on earth had a new steel gate at Downton Hall become bent. Who on earth would want to jump it, and then answering her own question: 'Keith, I suppose.' Incidentally, Miss Mary had a soft spot for Keith who had always worked so hard for her in helping with the work on the point-to-point course.
- The fact that Robert married a feisty horsewoman, and the glee with which we on the sidelines watched as they squabbled away. How could a man whose idea of tack cleaning was to rub it over with a twist of hay from a bucket of cold water work in harmony with Steph? When Keith's horse was plaited we knew all was well, and when there were stable stains and straw in its tail we knew just how things were.

The list goes on: years of work and advice as vice-chairman of the Supporters' Club. Pride in puppies walked at Dean Lodge, and whoever will forget his appearance in Christine Lockyear's plays? Can anyone who was there not remember him appearing from under the bedclothes with Margaret Kimnel, and after declaiming, 'It is I, Leclerk from the Clee Hill,' completely forgetting the rest of his hard-learned lines, and just basking in the huge ovation he was receiving from the audience.

He came to this area with very little in the way of family, and together with Maun he made his own, of which he was justifiably proud – so many proud boasts began with the words 'our boys'. He leaves behind now eleven much loved grandchildren.

You know that I have left a lot unsaid about this larger-than-life character. A father, grandfather, a man's man, farmer, contractor, a man who loved and laughed, and who has left this world a richer place of his having occupied it.

Thank God we knew and loved him.

Peter Townend (1921–2001)

social editor of Tatler

by Nicholas Coleridge

(managing director of Condé Nast)

Memorial Service at St George's Church, Hanover Square, London, on 6 November 2001

We are here, of course, to celebrate the life of Peter, for a quarter of a century the social editor of *Tatler* and the person who, single-handedly, perpetuated the idea of the Social Season. He was a remarkable and unusual man, certainly slightly eccentric and a much loved figure – as today's enormous congregation attests. Wouldn't Peter have enjoyed captioning us all and correcting the spelling of our names, when the photographs of today's service came in to *Tatler*? I can see him now, bent over his desk on the third floor of Vogue House just up the street, peering at the transparencies, giving a little running commentary on who everyone is, and delighting in pointing out errors of identity: 'That isn't the Marchioness of Arbroath,' he would exclaim. 'That's her sister-in-law, the Countess of Strathduggan, whose mother ran off with a gypsy, but we won't talk about that.'

I hope he's looking down on us all today, from some Members' Enclosure in the heavens, and seeing who's here in the church – I think he'd be very touched. And I think he might be surprised, too, to realise quite how fond of him so many people were, and how greatly we all appreciated his role in our lives.

He had many, many friends – of all ages. When he had his

heart attack, literally hundreds of people rang up, swamping the *Tatler* switchboard, to find out how he was. Men in their eighties and nineties, who had known Peter for fifty or more years; debutantes' mothers; debs themselves of all vintages; spare men, whom Peter had shoehorned into scores of dances over the years; a couple of dukes, waiters from Claridge's, his barber from Trumpers, stewards of the Jockey Club: all rang, eager for news and sending best wishes for a speedy recovery. His network of friends cannot be overestimated. As they rushed him into intensive care at St Mary's, Paddington, the pretty duty nurse exclaimed, 'I know exactly who this is. I was a deb a few seasons ago, and Peter helped organise my dance.'

In a way, he spent much of his life helping other people, generally unpaid for his troubles. He ran the whole deb business as a *pro bono* service, because he thought it was important, and gave a lot of pleasure too, but nobody paid Peter for doing it. He was an institution. Over the years he organised, or scheduled, or was somehow involved with, I estimate, more than seven thousand balls, dances, cocktail parties, teas, charity galas, tombolas and fairs, dress shows and the rest of it. Think how much business he brought to marquee companies, caterers, florists and discotheques: all thanks to Peter who made it his life's work to ensure the parties ran on time, and didn't clash. Had he chosen to, with his skills he could have run Railtrack, a good deal more efficiently and elegantly than the prevailing management there.

He was an extraordinary man. His life followed an immutable timetable. Over Christmas, he began writing to several hundred feasible debs' mothers, always in that trademark turquoise ink on turquoise writing paper, casting his net, bringing in his haul, consulting his reference books: 'Ah,' I hear him say, 'old Lady Arbroath's granddaughter the Honourable Fenella Sporran will be eighteen in July.' Sometimes he interviewed more marginal, less landed candidates to see if they'd do for his list, and then set it all in motion: the Berkeley Dress Show, the annual drinks party he gave at Raffles for suitable young men – his debs' delights – and then all the events of the summer he so enjoyed: Ascot, the Royal Academy Summer Show and Goodwood. During the season, he would appear at the

Tatler offices in morning coat and sometimes even a top hat, to check the Bystander pages before they went to press.

He was extremely adaptable, in his obstinate way. He survived six changes of ownership at *Tatler* and at least nine different editors. Over the years, I think several incoming *Tatler* editors initially thought they could manage perfectly well without Peter Townend, until they quickly discovered they could not. He simply knew things that nobody else knows; like whether such and such a person's Christian name is spelled Clair or Claire or Clare. Peter always knew. In fact he knew how to spell all names, not just smart ones. Shortly before he died he was the only person in the *Tatler* offices who could correctly spell Lionel Ritchie, the pop star – not one of the Northumberland Richies.

His long tenure at *Tatler* coincided with a rapidly changing Britain. He seldom welcomed change, but he went along with it. His social pages, which once championed the Winter Ball, the White Knights Ball and the Rose Ball, were soon contaminated, as he saw it, by funkier, more egalitarian parties, at which the Honourable Fenella Sporran cavorted with rock stars, and many of the young men at the raves found no place on Peter's respectable list. The social stars were no longer the Lord Lieutenant of Derbyshire, but supermodels and self-publicists and entrepreneurs.

But, in his typically Peterish way, he recognised the inevitability of change, and got on with it, and was frequently very amusing about it too. I think we all know that Peter had a mischievous eye and a waspish tongue on occasions.

I first met Peter myself twenty-five years ago, when he period-ically deployed me to make up the numbers during chronic man shortages at dances. And very grateful I was too, aged eighteen, because it was generally immense fun. Later I worked with him on *Tatler*, when Tina Brown was the editor, and he came back to my life again when Condé Nast acquired *Tatler* in the mid-eighties. He never really changed. Editors came, saw, conquered, retired; Peter was always there. He had a particular rapport with the present editor, Geordie Greig, who used to take him to lunch at White's.

He had his feuds, of course. It is no secret that he was delighted to outlive another venerable social editor, on a rival magazine, with whom he'd never got on. And he could be dismissive of European titles, complaining that ninety per cent of them are absolutely bogus, invented by impostors.

But I think of Peter as a life-enhancer, not a feuder. Which of us can justifiably say that they have brought more happiness to the world than Peter did? Through his parties, he set up more happy marriages than Cilla Black through her game shows. And he was the funniest of lunch companions, which was why he ate lunch in a different restaurant with a different friend every day of the year. People loved to take Peter out. His favourite restaurants were the Ritz and Claridge's, though he was equally happy at that tiny bistro 19 Mossop Street, next to the Admiral Cod pub. At night, he frequently skipped dinner altogether and subsisted on canapés.

He adored *Tatler*. *Tatler* was really his family. He loved the sub-editors and the art department and the fun of it all. When the registrar at St Mary's asked Peter, 'Who's your next of kin?' he sat up on pillows in his hospital bed, and pointed to Geordie Greig and said, 'He is!' which was the first Geordie had heard of it. But it was appropriate and understandable, because Geordie, as head of the *Tatler* family, was *de facto* next of kin. And Geordie was hugely touched.

The serious point to be made about Peter was that he was a genuine scholar – a scholar of genealogy. People tend to mock this particular discipline, confusing it with snobbery, but Peter's interest was overwhelmingly academic. He was a historian of people and families, and had incredible knowledge. Having begun life as an archivist for the local council in Wolverhampton and later for the Royal Navy, he was a meticulous editor of *Burke's Peerage* who knew his subject inside out. If a regular historian knew as much about, say, Henry III or Edward the Confessor as Peter knew about his own area of expertise, they would make him a Fellow of All Souls and give him a Nobel Prize, and we'd all be saying, 'What a brilliant and learned man he is.'

I don't think that another Peter Townend will come along again for a very long time, if ever. His passing really does mark the end of a particular era. It's hard to imagine dances in the future without him there, leaning up against a pillar at the Café Royal in his dinner jacket and trademark comb-over hairstyle and slightly wonky bow-tie, surrounded by young men and pretty girls, soaking it all up.

I imagine that somewhere up in heaven he is already hard at work on a new reference book, tracing the lineage of the angels and archangels, and all their various connections, and writing letters to the saints who have daughters who will shortly become eighteen.

Professor Edward (Teddy) Hall (1924–2001)
Professor of Archaeological Science

by Sir John Smith
(preservationist)

Memorial Service at Logan Hall, London University,
on 15 November 2001

Teddy had very many friends, as you can see. Each of us has a different picture of him, even if only a little different; and many of you knew him, or at least some aspect of him, a good deal better than I did. Therefore you must forgive me if I leave out what you think is important, or put in what you think is unsuitable.

We first met sixty-five years ago, when he turned up at school. What attracted me to him was that he liked a project. The main interest of most boys seemed – at least in those days – to be games and popularity, but Teddy, though good at games, and popular, was never much bothered about fashion; if he had been he would not have specialised in Science, then deeply unfashionable at Eton. Throughout life he was unconventional in the best way – that is to say he was not militant, exhibitionist, or self-conscious about it, as some people are. He had nothing against convention; he understood it, but just was not interested in it. For example he could dress extremely smartly when he chose, such as when marrying Jeffie – look at the photographs – but most of the time he did not bother much about it.

As I said, he liked to have a project on the go. There was a long succession of these while we were at school. The first was a device that revealed what day of the week any particular date in the past had been. We tried it out on the dates given in the old Authorised Version of the Bible – one of the few occasions on which Teddy referred to that work. Next there was a scheme to get round sugar rationing by extracting dextrose from potatoes. Then there was a gun that worked off blasting powder, which in those days one could buy across the counter at any good ironmonger. It became quite sophisticated and fired a shell that went off in mid-air, but eventually it broke Teddy's wrist, and had to be abandoned.

When the war came we were encouraged to Dig for Victory, and an allotment was pegged out for us on the unkind earth of Dorney Common. Teddy soon tired of digging, and reflected that all the soil did was supply the vegetables with chemicals, and that it would be much less work if they grew in sand, or even on wire netting, and were periodically flooded with a nutrient solution. We managed to get an American book on the subject, and Teddy fitted up one of his mother's greenhouses with the necessary tanks. However the scheme demanded constant attention, which it did not get; the plants died, the liquid in the tanks turned black and began to smell, and in the end Teddy's mother wanted the greenhouse back.

As you would expect, she had quite an influence on Teddy's character. She was resolute – tough would be too strong a word – intelligent and full of go, but not at all tiresomely so. To say that she had a sense of purpose would be about right. She was a keen spender. Her chief interests, at least by the time I knew her, were in dairy cows and dogs. One could not open a door in their house without finding a poodle or two, waiting to come through it from the other side. I liked her, and she used to give both of us sound advice, which we seldom took. However she did somewhat neglect Teddy when he was at school. He arrived there with the usual complete outfit but, so far as I could see, none of it was ever renewed. His cuffs frayed, and rose slowly up his lengthening arms, his underclothes fell to bits, and quite soon he could no longer get into his overcoat – not that he had ever worn it very much, even in the coldest weather. Teddy's father was a gallant and much decorated regular soldier, but surprisingly mild. I think it was a combination of all these influences – heredity and upbringing – that made Teddy easy-going, but energetic and determined with it, tough in mind and body.

Another modest project of ours was to revive the Sussex iron industry. We got a long way with that, and had ordered the blowing machinery for our blast furnace; but we got fed up with mining the iron ore. It was the digging again. I wish I could tell you more about these projects, but I have to get you to the drinks on time.

I left Eton before Teddy. He was never much of a letter-writer – at least to me – but I have a few from that period, including one of fourteen pages, written, so he says in it, during a Divinity lesson. Then he joined the RNVR and served in landing craft. At the end of the war we were both released from the navy, with unflattering speed, and got ourselves into New College at Oxford, where we shared a set of rooms. They had been occupied by a don and our sitting room had four bookcases. We sawed two of these up and turned them into window seats, which we thought would make for a more balanced existence. Teddy, all his life, liked music, in those days overtures mostly – Rossini, Glinka, that sort of thing. We had a gramophone, and he would stand there conducting it vigorously with his soldering iron, a serious expression on his face. Part of Teddy's success and charm all through life was due to his ability to look serious. I have often seen him gazing, with the utmost and very flattering concentration, into the eyes of someone who is talking absolute rubbish.

It was the custom to invite people round for coffee after Hall, and Teddy made us a percolator five feet high out of laboratory equipment. He was always, perhaps surprisingly bearing in mind the rest of his no-nonsense character, keenly interested in food and drink. I would not describe him as greedy; he was more of a perfectionist, critical and analytical about cooking, and about wine – for which many of us here are grateful. He was not an aesthete. He came to art through science – at some points they are not far apart: clocks and porcelain for example, which were two of his enthusiasms. Nor was he really, in spite of all, a romantic. He was too much of a debunker. That was the aspect he liked about the Piltdown Skull and the Turin Shroud. Before we left New College, I remember walking with him, on a warm spring evening with a big yellow moon, into the dim, deserted cloisters behind the chapel. I was rather moved by it. 'Extraordinary waste of space,' said Teddy.

So we were happy in those rooms; but outside the walls of our college there were girls, adorable creatures in New Look skirts, thirsting for knowledge as they pedalled about the university with books in the baskets on the handlebars of their bicycles. Teddy was susceptible to feminine charm. He had always been perfectly nice-looking, but somewhere along the way his nose had got broken and this I think improved his chances. He now bought a French four-seater open Delage car, made in the late thirties, with a blue art deco body that had plenty of chrome about it: a most beautiful object anywhere, but in post-war Oxford a sensation. Cars were few in the streets, and hardly another undergraduate had a car at all – none had been manufactured for seven years, and new ones had not yet appeared. There was one man at New College, who had lost both his lower legs in the war, and he had an old banger of sorts, but that was about all.

Before being allowed to keep a car at Oxford in those days one had to be interviewed by the Proctors. When Teddy appeared before them with details of his Delage they asked him doubtfully whether he could not bring up to the university something smaller and less exotic. 'I'm afraid it's the only car I've got,' said Teddy, which flummoxed them; and so he got permission. As he was, throughout life, good-natured and extremely generous anyway, he was now, with his natural advantages, irresistible. I remember a friend – whom I see in front of me as I speak – saying, 'There'd be something wrong with a girl that didn't fall in love with Teddy.' He stole all the young ladies to whom I paid court, and very annoying it was when they called me 'Teddy' by mistake. Moreover, if circumstances obliged him to introduce me to one of his discoveries, he would take care to pronounce her name indistinctly.

However, enough of that. When we had to leave our rooms in New College Teddy went to live over a dairy in Walton Street that belonged to his parents. He used to keep his Science tutor at New College, Dr Staveley, in a good mood by turning up at his tutorials with a couple of bottles of rich rationed Jersey milk for Mrs Staveley. Years afterwards I happened to meet Dr Staveley and I asked what he had thought of Teddy as a pupil. 'Ingenious,' he said, which I do believe is a fair summary of Teddy's professional career. He liked exploring byways, which is one way to make new discoveries. His flat over the dairy also had the advantage that at night he could steal down to the churns of milk waiting to be sold in the morning, and skim them for cream with which to make crème brûlée, an unheard-of luxury in those days, and much appreciated by his friends.

So Teddy was a bit of a scamp, a word one uses – or at any rate I use – for people of whom one might sometimes disapprove if one were not so fond of them. I have more stories of Teddy in this role or vein, but the drinks at the BM beckon. He was a scamp, with a bit of buccaneer thrown in as well. Perhaps that came from his grandfather in Australia.

After a time he moved from the dairy to a flat in the Banbury Road, where he gave generous parties for his friends and the friends of his friends. I stayed there with him once for a couple of months, on and off. Sometimes he did not come back to sleep, and then it was always even money whether he had been out on the tiles or working all night in the Clarendon Laboratory. What he did there I know not, except that he did a great deal of it. He had an extraordinary capacity for work, whether with his head or his hands.

When I got a job in London he used to come and stay with me. He had been in the habit of staying at Claridge's, but he fell out with them soon after the war, when they charged him for boiling an egg he had brought with him for breakfast. He showed me the bill: 'To cooking own egg – 10/6', at that time a large sum. He was never a snob about luggage – or indeed about anything else – and used to arrive at my flat carrying whatever he needed for the evening and the night in a stout cardboard box with 'Goldsmiths and Silversmiths Company Ltd' printed on the lid in heavy black letters. On one occasion he arrived unexpectedly, and said that he might be out late, so I gave him a latchkey and, as he was short, lent him some money. To air my spare bed for him I filled and put into it two of those old stoneware hot-water bottles. I heard him come in at 5 a.m. After breakfast next morning, when he had gone, I found that he had drunk the contents of both of them. Some time later a package arrived for me from him with a note saying, 'I seem to remember that I owe you 35/-, so I have bought you this cylindrical slide rule with it.'

On another occasion he said, 'I mustn't drink too much; I'm appearing in court tomorrow.' I said that I supposed he was giving expert evidence. 'No; speeding for the third time.' 'My dear fellow, you'll lose your licence.' 'I know,' he said, 'I'm rather looking forward to it. I'm arranging to have a glamorous blonde chauffeur.' Needless to say he got off – just a little to his disappointment.

By the time he was over thirty we all began to wonder who he could possibly marry, and who could possibly come to the wedding. He solved this problem 'at a stroke' – as it used to say in the *Boy's Own Paper*: you know, 'with one bound Jack Strangeways was free' – by discovering the beautiful timeless Jeffie, and marrying her six thousand miles away in South Africa. Of course I then saw rather less of him, but he was there, and the hospitality at Beenhams with such a hostess thrown in was if anything more generous than ever. I remember once there was so much caviare that the toast ran out. He liked fireworks, and the aerial maroons at his earlier displays were so big that they caused disturbances at Littlemore asylum. He even provided entertainment, and indeed employment, for the grown-up children of his friends. Teddy enjoyed himself, and did his best to see that others did as well.

He mellowed a bit with the years. About five years ago he and I were discussing a new disease that is afflicting the world. I suggested that perhaps it was nature's reply to better medicine. 'It makes one wonder whether there might not be a God after all; it's a bit worrying,' he said.

Shortly before he died, and when he was very ill, I went to see him in the John Radcliffe Hospital, that enormous gleaming white affair, a city in itself, that so damages the skyline of Oxford. I was on the top floor, trying to find out where he was, when I was accosted by a handsome but stern-looking nurse who asked if she could help me, which usually means, What are you doing here? I explained that I was looking for Professor Hall. 'Ow, you mean Teddy,' she said, so I realised that the old magic was still working.

Well, I have had to leave out a lot; but that is the Teddy I saw

– able, energetic, skilful, friendly and generous, an enjoyer, loved by many, well liked by one and all. I still feel that he is just around the corner. We will remember him all our lives. There was no one like him. But wait a minute. I have forgotten science. He has two sons with many of his qualities, and also grandchildren. I am sure that one day, soon perhaps, God, or whatever Teddy thinks it is, will dip His glittering ladle into the pool of Hall family genes, now enriched by those of Jeffie, and up will come Teddy himself again, once more to charm and benefit his generation.

Sir Nigel Hawthorne (1929–2001)

actor

by Nicholas Hytner

(director of the National Theatre)

Memorial Service at the Olivier Theatre at the National Theatre, London, on 9 January 2002

The last half-hour of *The Madness of George III* was like a party. The audience had suffered with Nigel so much, so painfully, that after he got better, the play could have gone on all night. They were overjoyed. They didn't want to let him go. The Lyttleton rocked. In a word, they loved him.

I think it was because they saw beyond his matchless technique to his heart. I would often watch *George III* and be surprised that Nigel had stopped doing something that always worked. 'It was getting stale,' he'd say, when I talked to him about it. 'I wasn't believing it any more. Give me a couple of weeks and I'll find it again.'

He always did, but never before he could do it truthfully. They loved him for that. They loved him because, secure as he was in his wonderful relationship with Trevor, he exposed himself – the thing itself, a poor bare forked animal and he didn't care who knew it.

They loved him too because they knew his amazing timing was nothing to do with calculation, and all to do with an irresistible sense of humour.

You had to have your wits about you in a big way. His first big scene with Mr Pitt, the Prime Minister, would start, 'Married yet,

Mr Pitt, what, what?' To which Julian Wadham, as Pitt, would reply wearily and superciliously, 'No, Your Majesty.' And the King would launch into a hymn of praise to married life, twinkling with malicious merriment at the distaste on Pitt's face. One night, Nigel asked as usual, 'Married yet, Mr Pitt?' and Wadham, his mind God knows where, answered, 'Yes, Your Majesty.' A barely perceptible flash in the King's eye. 'Who to, Mr Pitt, what, what?' Blind panic from Wadham. 'The sister of the Duchess of Bedfordshire, Your Majesty,' thus altering history at a single terrified stroke. Then a viciously timed pause, and: 'What's she like, Mr Pitt?'

At which Wadham threw in the towel and changed the subject.

They loved him because even as the King they could see he was the outsider. He used that: always subversive, never cosy. Always, bubbling beneath the surface, his fury that it took everyone so long to realise how good he was. So always generous, always thrilled by the talents of others, particularly young talent.

Always bursting with energy too. They loved him for his guts and they loved his gusto. They saw how much he loved what he was doing.

You couldn't hold him back. Early, far too early, in the shoot of the film of *George III*, he had to gallop through Windsor Great Park with Anthony Calf, who played the equerry Fitzroy. Anthony is a notably proud horseman, and first take he dug in his heels and as the pair of them careered towards the camera he overtook the King and beat him to us. I was happy enough, and not that keen to go for another take. I didn't want Nigel falling off, to be honest. But Nigel was furious, as he sometimes was. 'We're doing another!' he cried from the saddle. 'I'm not having him ride faster than me. I'm the fucking King!'

It was, honestly, the best time we'd ever had. I can see him now, take two, spurring on his horse, flying towards us, miles in front of Anthony Calf, his face flushed with triumph, the King of England, the fastest rider, the great actor, the happiest man in the land.

Lady Longford (1906–2002)
biographer

by Sir Nicholas Henderson
(diplomat and author)

Memorial Service at Westminster Cathedral, London,
on 12 February 2002

'Now that tree over there,' said Thomas Pakenham, pointing to a Wellingtonia in the garden at Bernhurst. He was starting a speech at Elizabeth's ninety-third birthday party in the garden there and he was immediately interrupted by barracking from brothers and sisters. The next member of the family to speak was met with the same cross-fire from the others, and so it went on.

When it came to Elizabeth's turn to reply to these heckled greetings she said, 'Now go on, interrupt me. I like it. The more give and take the better.' I do not recall any of the children taking the risk and doing so, but I do remember thinking how Elizabeth's example helped to explain the readiness and ability of all of them to express themselves distinctly and fearlessly.

Having heard Elizabeth on the hustings when young, I have always thought that, if she had stayed in politics, she would have reached the top. She had all the qualities: clarity of mind and expression, conviction, courage, presence and warmth; and no inhibitions about being in the limelight.

But to return to family life at Bernhurst: Thomas has said that he had to battle for an hour to get a word in edgeways at the dinner table. This, he thought, explained the literary output of the

Pakenhams. Ten talkers in one family and no listeners. It was inevitable that half at least would be driven to take refuge in authorship.

I know Elizabeth's reaction to this. It was that she never remembered Thomas being checked from talking; and he never seemed to mind whether or not anyone was listening.

Talk was always plentiful at Bernhurst. I can't say that this could have been said of the fare. Elizabeth was not interested in food. She kept it all locked up. To stave off hunger the children had frequent resort to the vegetable garden. In retrospect it struck them that she was the only person who had positively liked food rationing.

While practical, she did not relish housework, least of all meal-management. I recall a lunch when there was not quite enough of some dish to go round. Only one sausage was left.

'Go on, Frank,' Elizabeth said from the other end of the table, 'you have it.' To which Frank protested that he could not take food out of his children's mouths. 'Go on.' Again from Elizabeth. So Frank went on and ate the sausage, to cries of 'Oh Dada' from the young.

All eight children were born at home. There was no fuss. Elizabeth was strict, particularly with the elder children, but direct rather than fussy. She wanted them to be able to stand on their own feet, to compete and be ready if necessary to take risks. No molly-coddling.

During the Blitz on London Antonia, then only nine, was sent off by herself from Oxford by train to visit a doctor in Harley Street – not once, but for several consultations.

Michael was packed off by himself on foot and by bus to a day school in London during the height of some IRA campaign. After the war, Elizabeth and Frank left London for Bernhurst on Friday evenings. Kevin, the youngest of the family, had to be at school in London on Saturday mornings. He was made, by himself, to find some friend with whom to spend Friday night.

If all this sounds a bit ruthless it was matched by no less constant devotion by Elizabeth – in her own way. Before Antonia and Thomas went to the Dragon in Oxford Elizabeth taught them Latin so that when they started school they were way ahead of the class. She helped Antonia to prepare for her interview to get into LMH by insisting that she read Arnold Toynbee, then in vogue – not a summary of his history but the whole of at least one volume. Then in the interview she would be able to say, 'As Toynbee wrote, in volume eight, chapter seven we learn that . . . etc.' Antonia did just this with the desired result. Lucy Sutherland, the principal, may have been baffled but she was no doubt also impressed.

After Thomas had failed to get a scholarship at Christ Church, Elizabeth made enquiries and found out that he had had no practice at school in writing essays. During the holidays she therefore made him write essays which she corrected. He thereupon won an Exhibition at Magdalen.

Elizabeth habitually read aloud to the children. She wrote to them at school and afterwards. At LMH Antonia received a letter from her urging her to work hard – and reminding her that she owed twelve and six for tennis racquet repairs.

Elizabeth kept Progress Books for each of her children in which she recorded their physical and mental development and how she thought they would turn out. These were kept until they were twenty-one, at which time they were shown to the child – not always with the happiest outcome. One of the daughters was pre-dicted in the Progress Book as likely to do best as a home-maker. She was not flattered.

Elizabeth had a passion for writing. She never had a study and did a lot of her work in the drawing room at Bernhurst, in the early days surrounded by children playing, quarrelling and screaming, 'Catherine's stolen my pillow', or 'Judith's taken my book'. Eliza-beth continued writing imperturbably. She could isolate herself.

Frank told me that often if he went to London for the day he would leave her in the morning in the drawing room writing and when he returned in the evening she was still there and had been writing uninterruptedly since he left.

Not a hedonist, she was nevertheless a great enjoyer. She adored her garden which she had made entirely, planting every shrub and tree. She loved swimming. She started painting again. She took pleasure in the company of her friends and rejoiced in their success.

She took trouble with her appearance and in the mind's eye I see her now in her wedding dress that she wore on the sixtieth anniversary of the wedding. She was not vain. 'No one so successful was ever so unself-important,' Diana Cooper said. I would add, nor so unselfish.

She liked to see a purpose in pleasure. Swimming was healthy. She took the children to Tintern Abbey. It poured with rain. Judith read Wordsworth to them as they all huddled together under a dripping umbrella and stared at the ruins of the abbey below.

'All happy families are alike,' Tolstoy wrote. The Pakenham family were happy but they were not like any other I have met, and their mother was likewise different from any other mother I have known – in the way she combined an all-embracing love for her children with an equal determination to make them independent.

To remember Elizabeth is not to be sad, but to feel fortunate and heartened in having known her.

Christopher Bowerbank (1940–2002)
architect

by Alan Jenkins
(literary editor and poet)

*Memorial Service at St John's Church, Notting Hill,
London, on 9 May 2002*

'Death is not an event in life,' the philosopher said, but Christopher's exit was nothing if not an event in the lives of all who loved him.

It was, like so much he did, uncompromising. Not for him the lingering dissolution, the humiliating subjection to doctors' orders, the embarrassment of protracted farewells. We did not see him 'shrunken' his word, when he described to me the shock of seeing his mother on her death bed, among the paraphernalia of the geriatric ward. And all who loved him will count that a blessing, even while we register no less profound a shock.

For it is almost impossible to think of Christopher gone from our lives; of Christopher not hurtling determinedly along the road of his own life, foot to floor, towards some new excitement or difficulty. Both excitement and difficulty he relished equally, with a deeply resourceful relish, a justified confidence in his readiness for anything.

How much he gave to his work, the price his dedication and perfectionism exacted, only those who worked with him truly know. I believe it would surprise many who saw him mostly in more convivial circumstances. For thirty-five years, Bowerbank, Brett and Lacey was the cornerstone of his life. He cared passionately about it, and about the livelihoods and the professional well-being of his partners and workmates, through good times and harder times. He was often troubled by the responsibilities it carried. Just as often, he enjoyed the rewards — though not usually the financial ones — it brought.

It also brought challenges, frustrations, and these he faced with defiant gusto. Sometimes he sought release or escape with an intensity that could be alarming. But who would have had Christopher tone himself down? His way in adversity was to laugh, dare it to do its worst, and get on with the next thing.

Christopher was driven, not by ambition but by curiosity — as anyone who heard him talk about architecture, or literature, or the history, the landscape and the buildings of this country, or those of Serbia or Byzantium, will know. And how he could talk! With the eloquent precision (and sometimes the hyperbole) of an age when speech was valued; with passionate enthusiasm or mocking denunciation. His rigour in argument was exhilarating — and could be disconcerting. He made you sit up and listen; he made you laugh; he made you raise your own game. Because he always spoke his mind, he encouraged you to do so too.

Many here will recall his delight in nature, in the English countryside, in the seals with which he exchanged meaningful looks as their heads bobbed above the waters off Rousay, in the birds of that island, and of Wiltshire; will recall his excited 'I say, look at that!' as an owl swooped at nightfall across the convent garden at Stourhead. The same passion leaped out when he took you round a building he loved, whether it was a burial chamber in Orkney or the Blue Mosque in Istanbul.

Perhaps even more of us will remember — or remember up to a point — the lunches that turned into dinners, the conversations that went on, vodka-fuelled, until dawn, the phone calls out of the blue, just as we were leaving the office, that meant Christopher was looking for trouble. To bump into him somewhere, sometimes just to hear his voice — 'Steady on, actually' — meant a quickening in the pulse, a sense of accelerated possibility. Something would happen, and it would be fun. Then it would become funnier, and more and more outrageous, every time Christopher told the tale.

I loved this disdain for unadorned fact; it showed not just exuberance but a kind of generosity towards his listener, one among the many forms of generosity that came naturally to Christopher, as it came naturally to love him for them.

For Christopher's greatest pleasure was the pleasure he took in his friends, his London friends, his country friends, his Orkney friends – all of us, once, of that privileged company, now so bereft. If we did something worth while, he was proud of us. If we made fools of ourselves, he was there to commiserate – and roar with laughter. He revelled in our enjoyment of his hospitality, of the houses he threw himself into with such verve, and that always spoke so profoundly of him. You almost certainly know something of the sheer disbelief I still feel, that we should have come together, not at Christopher's bidding, for some marvellous party, perhaps to celebrate his marriage to Emma – not for that, but to say our final farewells to him; disbelief that I shall not be going, tonight or any night, to meet Christopher in one of his haunts, something I never did without a lifting and a lightening of the heart.

No one could say that Christopher was a particularly open or straightforward man. Nevertheless it so happened that I first came to feel I really knew him at a time of great turbulence in his life, and he was an indispensable friend to me through a few such times of my own. He had his dark days, certainly, in the nearly twenty years I knew him, and his difficult moods; a person of his complex temperament and intelligence will always be prey to those. What I carry with me, though, will be his huge gift for loyalty and affection, innumerable kindnesses, 'tough love' or at any rate gruff love, of a very English kind, that was returned, deeply and patiently, by the woman with whom he wished to spend the rest of his life; and by many of us, to an extent that would have astonished him.

Because he died much, much too young and because, whatever he did, his capacity for joy and for the adventure of life was that of the boy he had once been, I want to end with this poem by the Orcadian poet George Mackay Brown:

> That one should leave the green wood suddenly
> In the good comrade-time of youth

And clothed in the first coat of truth
Set out alone on an uncharted sea;

Who'll ever know what star
Summoned him, what mysterious shell
Locked in his ear that music or that spell,
And what grave ship was waiting for him there?

The greenwood empties soon of leaf and song.
Truth turns to pain. Our coats grow sere.
Barren the comings and goings on this shore.
He anchors off the Island of the Young.

Dorothy Tutin (1931–2001)
actress

by Patrick Garland
(writer and theatre director)

*Memorial Service at St Paul's Church, Covent Garden,
London, on 21 June 2002*

'I left no ring with her, what means this lady?' Don't worry. This
is not an attempt to imitate that haunting and beautiful tremulous
voice, described by a critic – it must have been Kenneth Tynan –
'cooing like a turtle dove with laryngitis'. But I can hear her in my
mind's ear, and I can see, that moment on stage in *Twelfth Night* in
that wonderful production by the young Peter Hall, with the even
younger Dorothy Tutin as Viola/Cesario, and Geraldine McEwan
as Olivia, and Patrick Wymark as Sir Toby Belch, and Richard
Johnson – rather unlikely, as he was later to be Romeo – as Sir
Andrew Aguecheek, and Max Adrian, of blessed memory, as Feste,
and that wonderful autumnal interpretation of that most beautiful
of plays.

When I heard of Dorothy's death I was struck by a very, for
me, strange, a very unexpected, thought. I suddenly recognised
something that I hadn't done, because we had always kept in touch
and when I was at Chichester I saw a lot of her, so it had never
occurred to me before that all my early experience of Shakespeare
– of those great romantic comedies in particular – *all* took place
with Dorothy Tutin playing the leading lady, playing the heroine:
her Viola, Rosalind, Portia (to Peter O'Toole's wonderful Shylock),

Desdemona, and I suddenly felt how one's experience of our greatest poetic dramatist is peopled, is populated, by the actors of our time and of our youth, because we are as young as they are. And it is this perpetual memory that I feel can never be taken away. She was unique, as all actresses are unique, all special in their own way, special in their own voice, special in their own look. These wonderful creations of Shakespeare came to life under her lips, under her breathing.

What was it she brought on to the stage? I remember it well, unforgettably if you like. It is the quality of lyric grace, a special kind of poetry that came out of her and not from the printed page, not even Shakespeare. I think it was as if she came from *off*-stage – wherever that particular universe was – on stage, in an imaginary world and had somehow improvised or written the words that she was saying. It wasn't that they came out of her mouth having been learned, it was as if she was writing them as she went along. And this is a very special quality that only the finest artist gives. You could say the same perhaps about Casals playing the cello or Oistrakh playing the violin or Richter playing the piano, as if it has been made up as you go along so that the experience is so immensely vivid and so fresh and so spontaneous, that you remember it, you remember it in your ear. Philip Larkin said that writing a poem was like trying to recall a tune that you had long forgotten and I feel that acting is like that, it brings back a tune, a melody, of something that you feel you once knew and it revives it in your mind.

Dorothy, of course, went on to play so many other great roles. I've been astonished in a way to see how disparaging she was of her own career. It reads like a mighty line of roles to me, and yet she somehow in her own creative process was always disappointed, always searching for something else. But I was not surprised to discover, although I did not know it before, that her first wish, her first inspiration was to be a musician, and, of course, it is this *music* of her, her great musicality, that I think is always memorable. And so the great line of classical roles went on and, still playing Shakespeare, there was a most memorable Catherine of Aragon only just a few years ago, at Chichester, always played with gravity, with great sincerity, and with instinct. But I shall always recall that wonderful magic of her first years where she brought on to the stage the living world of Shakespeare's comedy, often shot through with poignant, sometimes heartbreaking moments, but yet nevertheless always joyful, always firmly in the realm of comedy, the business of *life* and tragedy, the business of death, and she could harmonise these two wonderful spirits. The only role that she didn't play – and I think these days she would have done because fashions have changed – which I would so much have wished to see her in, is the role which I think she resembled in her own life, namely Ariel, the wonderful spirit-creature who came on and was incapable of speaking in prose, couldn't express herself other than in poetry. How this all happened is to me a mystery, and I just leave it in her own words through the interpretation of Shakespeare's Viola.

> Time thou must entangle this, not I
> It is too hard a knot for me to untie.

Sir Peter Parker (1924–2002)
industrialist and student of William Blake

by Sir Richard Eyre
(theatre and film director)

Memorial Service at St Martin-in-the-Fields Church, London, on 9 July 2002

Nobody could know Peter without thinking that, in spite of a life that was richly achieved and fulfilled and in spite of being loved and admired by his family and friends, in some way he had missed his vocation.

Peter's vocation was to be an actor. He was a theatrical man – by which I don't mean self-advertising or flashy or superficial, or any of those patronising adjectives which get attached to our profession. He was theatrical in demonstrating a love of metaphor, a love of poetry, a love of heightened speech and behaviour, a love of living in the present tense – a love of performance in all areas of life. For him, acting wasn't a carapace, a cover to conceal feelings, but a way of revealing them, a way of expanding life rather than reducing it. If there's a reason that he didn't become an actor perhaps it was because in many ways he was already larger than life – or life, perhaps, was smaller than Peter.

If he was disappointed by failing to follow his love of theatre professionally, he concealed it perfectly, and he channelled his passionate enthusiasm into giving his time, his wisdom and his expertise to many theatres, most conspicuously the National Theatre, the Young Vic, and the Globe Theatre. Without him the theatres would be much less than they are.

There may be many amateur actors who have the nerve – or foolishness – to play King Lear at the age of twenty-five, but there are few that have the skill. Peter not only played it – in two different productions – but played it to great acclaim in a production which toured the US.

A few years ago I told Peter that I was planning a production of *King Lear*. We discussed the pitfalls of the play, and the paradox of Lear being an old man and yet requiring the energy of a young one. And we talked about the endless fascination of a play that is about fathers and their children – and children and their fathers. We swapped favourite passages. This was one of Peter's. Lear is consoling Cordelia with a description of their future, father and daughter alone together probably for the first time – and certainly for the last time – in their lives:

> We two alone will sing like birds i'th'cage.
> When thou dost ask me blessing, I'll kneel down
> And ask of thee forgiveness; so we'll live,
> And pray, and sing, and tell old tales, and laugh
> At gilded butterflies, and hear poor rogues
> Talk of court news, and we'll talk with them too,
> Who loses and who wins, who's in, who's out,
> And take upon's the mystery of things
> As if we were God's spies; and we'll wear out
> In a walled prison packs and sets of great ones
> That ebb and flow by th'moon. Have I caught thee?
> He that parts us shall bring a brand from heaven
> And fire us hence like foxes. Wipe thine eyes.
> The good years shall devour them, flesh and fell,
> Ere they shall make us weep.

Sir Peter Parker (1924–2002)

industrialist and student of William Blake

by a railwayman★

Memorial Service at St Martin-in-the-Fields Church, London, on 9 July 2002

1976–1983 = eight years of inspirational leadership.

We speak on behalf of all railway folk from heart.

Within months he was deeply involved in the warm and wide railway community – he made us feel like a family again.

So his passing has come as a sudden and tremendous shock. A blow to us all. We expected him to go on for ever.

We have mourned the loss of a great chairman but today for Gill, Lucy, Alan, Oliver and Nathaniel, the grandchildren, and all of us, this is a time of comfort and celebration and of real treasured memories.

Not only was he a born leader but so natural and willing.

Not surprising we all give thanks for Sir Peter and his:
> Friendship – his favourite expression: keep our friendship in good repair.
> Fellowship – could talk to you on a personal, family, political, business topic.

★ Anonymous by request.

Leadership – unrivalled: what can we say burns head and shoulders 'above them all'.

Who can forget his encouragement to share his philosophy of a 'fistful of priorities'!

And after the sad Serpell Report assured us 'there *was* life after Serpell'.

Reminded of two short passages in the Bible: Genesis: 'Jacob died old and full of days' (old here means experienced) and we all know the experience and conviction he brought when handling various:
Government and MOT.
Senior cabinet ministers.
Union chiefs.
Industrial leaders.
Staff.
Media, customers and public.

Full of days and never missed opportunity of promoting transport.

Then Ecclesiastes: 'the charm of a man is his kindness'.
His charm was his kindness and always reflected in his positive outlook: for him the glass was never half empty but always three-quarters full.

What kindness, what charm, what memories, what talents.

Threaded through all this was the unique family quality.
Was a wonderful husband: constantly concerned for Gill and his desire to involve her in all things railways. Thankfully Gill always ready to join in despite being a busy London GP.
And during that, Sir Peter fully supporting, she was the author of a book about her very special garden.

There is a saying in business that behind every successful businessman stands an astonished wife! But Gill was a loving, devoted, supportive wife. Fully endorsing all he did.

Sir Peter and Lady Parker had a partnership of love over fifty years. Culminating in a fortnight's relaxing cruise with friends off the Turkish coast.

What a family man he was: mention their names, his eyes sparkled with joy and enthusiasm! Is it any surprise, one way or another, they all follow his wonderful example in life. They share his optimism, quick wit, his charm as well as his looks.

Loved to get out of the Kremlin out of the bunker.

While touring north of Scotland was asked by BBC radio reporter, 'Why have you come up here, Sir Peter?' 'Oh, we are doing a thistle-stop tour.' One young hack on Isle of Skye asked, 'Shall we see trains on Skye?' 'Well, if you keep looking you might just see Skye trains.'

But he was a good dynamic chairman – deserved and got loyal support from its board and all at the rail HQ. He was loved and respected in the five regions.

> We thank them all and they are unanimous in their appreciation and of his memories.

Among very many I mention two people in his daily life on BR: Gwen Cowan, his loyal and hardworking secretary; Peter Barlow, his constant journey companion.

> Gwen: a tower of strength as well as keeping us appropriately informed, also kept us well in line.
>
> Peter Barlow and Sir Peter journeying west from Paddington and as the young Peter went for two coffees, the guard announced, 'Sorry for the delay – due to technical difficulties.' When Peter returned the chairman was bothered about the jargon and was told there had been a fatality on the line ahead.
>
> 'Go tell the guard to be a bit more explicit and truthful.' The next announcement came up: 'Ladies and gentlemen, we have the chairman on board and I must tell you there has been a fertility on the line.' How he loved that!

Everything came to him so effortlessly with so much humility – which hid so much talent.

There was just no limit to his talents.

> He was a man's man – Burns said, 'A man's a man for a' that and a' that.'

He was fond, too, of quoting Blake – how well read he was.
A man for all seasons.
An outstanding leader of industry.
An ideal chairman for British Rail.
His life was full of days.
His grasp of transport issues was unrivalled.

And we all miss him.

But above all 'the charm of that man was his kindness'.

We will all of us always treasure these vivid and wonderful memories of Sir Peter.

But there are very special memories for Lady Parker, Alan, Oliver and Nathaniel. So take great comfort and celebrate the experience of a loving husband, wonderful father and a very proud grandfather.

John Miller (1931–2002)

painter

by John le Carré

(author)

*Memorial Service at St Mary's Church, Penzance,
on 2 August 2002*

'Very old, very dear friend' – as you wrote to me not long ago –
I'm not speaking to you alone this afternoon, but for each one of
the hundreds of people gathered here to mourn you, to honour and
remember you, and to *thank* you, and your Maker for your good
life.

Each one of us here believes that he or she was a special person
in your life. Perhaps the most special. And each one of us is right.

It was because of you that I came to Cornwall at the lowest point
in my life, just as so many others of us here came to you in their
distress. We laid our lives at your feet, knowing we could trust you,
believing absolutely in your good heart and good head, and not
pausing, in our self-obsession, to wonder whether you might have
a few problems of your own.

It was you, inevitably, who led me over the cliff to the ruined
cottages that eventually became my home. It was you who for
forty-five years have been present at every turning point, good or
bad, in my life, now gently holding me back, now urging me on,
now dabbing away my tears: never manipulative, never anything
but the true voice of love, decency, common sense and acceptance
of our human foibles.

Today this church is full of people for whom you did the same.

No wonder so many of us came to you. No wonder even priests and monks confessed themselves to you, and children flocked to you, my own included. All of us knew that your love was humble and unfeigned. We knew you were the rarest and best of men, a clear-eyed visionary who could see the bit of God in each of us.

But you were earthy too, with enough larceny in you to cut a path to the lost boy or girl from the housing estate, or the gypsy at the roadside, or the Russian lady who one day presented herself at your door and announced that she proposed to live the rest of her life with you. And she did.

How you could laugh! The laughter bubbled out of you at the most unlikely times – irreverent belly laughs. I can hear them now. They scattered our self-pity to the winds, gave us back our sparkle, and got us up and running again.

So thanks for that too. Oh, and by the way, in case anyone should ever suppose you were some kind of arty non-combatant, let it also be known that you were a good man on a dark night too. As an army officer and a special soldier, you had a few nights that were about as dark as they come, and you served your country in the same selfless spirit that you served your friends.

So thanks for that too.

Thanks for the adventures, and the romps. And thanks for your numberless acts of charity, public and private, at home and away, visible and hidden. The loans that never come back, the paintings you gave to hospitals, hospices, cathedrals, schools and to your friends. And to friends who couldn't afford them, and, too often, to the friends who could.

Thanks for never giving us up, even those of us who exploited you rotten, because we too, in our sad way, needed you.

Thanks for the *time* you gave us – as if you had nothing better to do with your life than give, and listen to our woes! How often, I wonder, did you quietly lay down your paintbrush for a friend?

For many of us you were quite simply our virtue, the walking standard that we came to live by; the emotional anchor, the moral compass. From you, John, we learned to be less greedy, less selfish, less envious, kinder, more tolerant. From you, we learned to let

Creation speak to us – and through us. From you we learned what all schoolchildren should learn: that in every human relationship we have first to love, and then to understand. And, having understood, forgive.

Because from time to time you and Mike had a great deal to forgive. Generosity on the scale that you practised it could never go unpunished. The sanctuary you provided to so many of life's refugees – Jane and I were two of them – placed you firmly on the Wanted List of the intolerant.

The unfree envied your freedom. Your happiness threatened them and so did your independent spirit. So the weak conspired to destroy the strong. And failed miserably. Instead, you and Mike became one of the triumphant partnerships of our lives. Neither of you was imaginable without the other. Your loyalty to each other was indestructible. But anyone who thought Michael was second fiddle was in for the shock of his life. Without Michael, John could never have been John.

As an occasional anarchist, you liked to poke fun at the pomp and ceremony of tradition. But your other heart thrilled to it. Did I hear you complain when you were appointed a lay canon of Truro Cathedral?

But as ever with John Miller, the paradox bespoke the man. Your real heart was not with cathedrals and bishops, but with the lowly; with the brown brothers, the disciples of St Francis, the practitioners of self-denial and humility and unqualified love – ideals which lay at the very heart of your mysticism and your painting.

How on earth did John Miller come to be such a brilliant communicator? Well, you were a visionary who felt compelled to share his glimpses of the infinite with his friends. We know that. And by friends I mean, of course, the whole mess of suffering, sinning, striving, rumbustious, dreaming humanity.

The breadth of knowledge that you brought to your calling – literary, technical and historical – never ceased to amaze us. You were a closet polymath, and a closet workaholic. Your fights with the demons of your art were as real as any other painter's fights. More real, perhaps, because they were also dialogues with God.

Perhaps the gift of empathy is the clue to your magic. When

you sat with your dying friends, you died with them, as we shall with you. When your father died, you died one death. When your mother died, you died another prolonged and rather beautiful death. When Marika died, you nursed her to rest. In death as in life you took our pains on your own back. For all your dreaming, you could grab reality by the scruff of the neck and haul it uphill for us.

And the same night you'd be singing Noël Coward better than Noël ever could; and Flanagan and Allan; and Jack Buchanan; and reciting 'Gunga Din' until we wept.

Like all the best saints, you were a shrewd old trooper, dipped in all the oceans, and when need arose you could fight your corner with the best of us. Only your limitless consideration for the other fellow, never cowardice, held you back. And when you were winning round after round, your ludicrous concern for the loser far outweighed your will to win: which made you, as you very well knew, an impossible opponent.

A string of books won't cover the lives you've led on your way from there to here, but there isn't a single dishonourable page in any of them. Special soldier, restaurateur, actor, architect, antique dealer, but always, eternally, artist. For as long as we survive you, none of your lives will be forgotten. For as long as our children survive us – and all the many children who have been lucky enough to know and love you and nourish themselves with your creative humanity – you will be revered and honoured as the miracle you have been to them.

What waits to be written about you in the last book of all is the same riddle that was always out there for you: the single flickering light that you painted, far out to sea. The helpless, plucky little boat halfway to the horizon. The featureless man or woman rising or descending in shafts of brilliance. The strip of light between heaven and earth, sky and sea, death and immortality.

It seems to me now that all your life you have been quietly waiting for this moment. Nobody I have ever known was better prepared for death than you were. Who else would lie smiling up at me while I read these words to him? But you did. And you worried for me, that I would be too upset to read them. I had come to comfort you. But you got there ahead of me, and comforted me instead.

We shall never know a better man than John Miller – or a happier one.

Here's what William Hazlitt wrote: 'Happy are they who lie in the dream of their own existence, and see all things in the light of their own minds; who walk by faith and hope; to whom the guiding star of their youth still shines from afar, and into whom the spirit of the world has not entered! They have not been "hurt by the archers", nor has the iron entered into their souls. The world has no hand on them.'

John is this happy man.

John Thaw (1942–2002)
actor

by Sir Tom Courtenay
(actor)

*Memorial Service at St Martin-in-the-Fields Church,
London, on 4 September 2002*

John and I were students together at the Royal Academy of Dramatic
Art. I remember him standing in the queue in the RADA canteen
wearing a dark grey jersey and a manner that didn't invite conversation. I was the only one of us in the first term at RADA who
dared speak to him. The first time I tried all I got for my pains was
a grunt, but something about him made me persist and we soon
became pals. He was only sixteen when he started at RADA – I was
twenty-one, having already been to university – and his forbidding
manner was just a cover-up for his shyness.

Ignorant though I was, I soon realised just how full of feeling he
was in his acting, feeling which, like me, he wasn't then always able
to control. His arms were a terrible nuisance to him. I remember
him doing a piece from *Richard II* with astonishing passion and
conviction, trying desperately to keep them down by his side. In
fact we both had arm difficulty at RADA: mine went like this . . .
John's went like that . . .

Within a term or two, John came to join me in a huge maisonette
in Highbury Crescent – a place that got gradually fuller of aspiring
actors – and we became very close. We had various little routines
we used to act out. One was impersonating Arthur Mullard who

403

lived just round the corner. When there were several young actors present, Arthur always got the name of the one he was addressing wrong, and he would have to go all round the room, correcting himself. To John he might say, 'You see, Tom er Michael, Nick, John.' John liked it best when he got it right the first time, but was so used to getting it wrong he'd start his journey round the room all over again. 'You see, Jo——, To——, Nick, Michael, John . . .'

We spent a lot of time talking as though we didn't have any teeth. Don't ask me why. John was very partial to this and very good at it. 'The thing is, Tchommy . . .' We carried on doing this in our maturity, even into last year's BAFTA awards – privately, be it said, not publicly.

Looking more of a juve than John, I was discovered while still at RADA and thrown into the profession at the deep end. We were best pals by this time and it would not have been surprising if he'd been resentful of the extraordinary things that were happening to me. Not a bit of it. Though he did christen me Golden Bollocks.

When he first moved into Highbury Crescent he brought with him his collection of gramophone records, including a new Cannonball Adderley LP of which he was very proud. I couldn't conceal my indifference to it and by way of a riposte put on one of my records. It would have been music by Schubert or Beethoven probably. Anyway whoever wrote it, it did the trick, and he never looked back. One of my most vivid memories is of him lying on a sofa listening to my record of Casals playing the opening of Bach's sixth solo cello suite and unable to move or speak in his rapture. So I introduced him to something that gave him joy for the rest of his life, which pleases me. Though small recompense for the affectionate, humorous and sweet friendship I got from him.

Dudley Moore (1935–2002)

musician and actor

by Eric Sykes

(writer and actor)

Memorial Service at Magdalen College Chapel, Oxford,
on 16 November 2002

Well, what is there to say now? Everything I was going to say has already been said. Even Steven has played that wonderful cello. I'm glad I left mine in the car now.

But one night, moons, moons ago, a producer friend of mine said, 'Would you like to come to the theatre tonight, opening night?' I said, 'No.' He said, 'I thought you liked theatre.' I said, 'I do. Sometimes when I'm working I go six nights a week for a month or a week if it's not so good.' But anyway I went and it was *Beyond the Fringe* I saw, and it was a revelation to me – I'm born of the old vaudevillian tradition – to see those four lads on the stage, and also I must say that Peter Cook and Alan Bennett and Jonathan Miller were quite brilliant, but the one who stood out was Dudley Moore. And he stood out because he had this quality that he could walk on to the stage as if he didn't belong there, as if he was just going across to the other side to get a glass of water and he came across the footlights. I think we will all agree that there was some quality about Dudley that made you want to protect him, made you want to put your arms around him and see him through.

I didn't know until this week that he was an organ scholar. I had no idea, I mean the school that I went to we didn't even have a piano – and he was an organ scholar. I must admit, I mean the organ is not my favourite instrument. I think that it is very good for J.S. Bach, I think that's marvellous and the wedding march but other than that. And er . . . I've lost the thread now. It all happens when you get on a bit; I don't know what I'm doing in this bus shelter. I said to the producer who wanted to take me there this morning, I forgot. He said, 'Come to the theatre, you know.' And I said, 'No, a bus driver doesn't get himself dressed up and go down to the depot on his day off.' (That felt like a lead balloon anyway. I've worked to a smaller audience than this.)

Now the thing about Dudley is there is not a lot you can say about him unless you knew him intimately and I didn't. After *Beyond the Fringe*, he went his way, I went mine and we didn't meet until *Not Only . . . But Also* came on the television and I think that was the most brilliant and the funniest thing I've ever seen on television. Black and white, but to see those two sitting in the pub with their macs on, mufflers on, flat caps and the wonderful things they did, honestly, about:

> 'I had a dream last night. I dreamt I was in bed and there was a tapping on the window and I looked at the window and do you know who it was?'
> 'No.'
> 'It was Sophie Loren.'

Now this kind of humour, it had never been heard of, neither had Sophie Loren at that time. But this was it. One day they rang me up, a very great compliment and I always felt very honoured, and said, 'Would you like to be our guest next week on the show?' And I said, 'No, I don't want to be. Honestly, I love it, I think it's the best thing that has ever been on television, I think it is the funniest and I can't improve on it. I would hate to come into it because I couldn't give it anything it hasn't already got.' 'Oh no.' So that was Thursday. On the Friday they turned up at my office, Pete and Dud. 'Come on, Eric,' they said. 'No, no, I've told you I'm not going to do it.' So we had one of those afternoons, like, wouldn't it be funny if. 'I'll tell you what, why don't we do . . .' 'I'll tell you what, let's dress up as gladiators . . .' 'And then what?'

'Hang on a minute, I haven't finished.' It was one of those afternoons and they had it in their mind that Dudley would be a monster, with all the scaly thing on him, like that, and his head under his arm. And I'm sitting next to him on a settee and Peter is the director of the film and that's how it started. And then that's Friday finished and I thought, All right, I'll do it yeah. 'I'll see you Monday,' because I thought, Well, over the weekend I'll write it. I'll write all this down and I can learn, you know. They said, 'Monday? No, we'll see you tomorrow morning.' I said, 'Tomorrow's Saturday.' He said, 'That's when we do the show.' Can you imagine? 'That's when we do the show.' So we sat down.

I didn't see them until seven o'clock that evening and the show was on at eight o'clock and I didn't see them, then they said, 'Ah that last sketch, now,' and they did the sketch and 'Right, we're on,' and we went. Now there was that settee and I was sitting next to Dudley with his scales on and his head under his arm and they started off on a routine that we hadn't even talked about. And it was such a funny routine, this is where the brilliance comes in. They talked about ooh the monster and Pete was saying, 'Now it's a good idea, you are the hero,' to me, 'and you're lying on the bank, composing a poem and there is a lake there, old placid lake reflecting the azure blue of the sky and then the monster pops his head up.' And of course I looked at the two of them, they were waiting for me to say something. Well, all I could do, I could do what I'm doing now, I started to laugh and so they carried on. But there was always a twinkle in Dud's eyes and Dud said, 'Pete, Pete.' He said, 'Yes.' He said, 'When I'm under the water like that, you want me to pop up. How long is this poem going to be?' He said, 'Oh, I'll shoot you separately, let you come up out of the thing.' He said, 'How deep is the lake?' 'Oh,' he said, 'it's bottomless.' So he said, 'I'll tell you what we'll do, I'll shoot you separately.' 'Before you start shooting, can I ask another question?' He said, 'Yes.' 'While I'm under the water, how will I hear the cue?' Well, I can't tell you what, I was laughing. I didn't say a word actually after that. I was sitting down there laughing like that. Then Peter started to laugh, then Dud, then the audience until we were doing nothing but laugh. When you've got that hysteria you know that you'll never work again. But it's that hysteria – and of course in those days you see there was no cutting and no doing it again – and it stopped, the programme stopped in the middle of all this roaring about with laughter. Then the man who has to read the nine o'clock news said [laughing] 'Here is the news.' That was Dudley.

And when Jimmy Edwards and I were doing *Big Bad Mouse*, we came from Chicago and we came to Washington and on the stage at the National Theatre Washington was Pete and Dud. So that was absolutely wonderful, I mean it was really, I can't tell you again. I was watching my peers, the people I respected. Jim and I, that same night, took Peter out to dinner and I said, 'Where's Dud?' 'Oh,' he said, 'he won't come tonight.' And I said, 'Why?' Pete said, 'It's my fault,' and I said, 'Why's that?' 'I told him I was having dinner with the Archbishop of Canterbury.' And the show that we did, we followed them in that week in Washington, and the shows were similar, lots of laughs, lots of everything. There was only one slight difference between our show and theirs: they were packed.

I don't know what else to say against, thing. You see, like I said, the organ has never been my favourite. I think Reginald Dixon put me off the organ at the Tower Ballroom, Blackpool. Never in my wildest dreams can I ever see Dudley sitting up at the organ, swaying backwards and forwards, playing 'O I do like to be beside the seaside'. All I can say is that there are millions of organists around the world, there are millions of organs but there was only one Dudley Moore.

Dudley Moore (1935–2002)
musician and actor

by Michael Parkinson
(writer and broadcaster)

*Memorial Service at Magdalen College Chapel, Oxford,
on 16 November 2002*

I came here today in the car with Laurie Holloway, piano player, knows a thing or two about music, and just to check my opinion, I said to him, 'You know, how good a jazz pianist do you reckon that Dudley was?' And he said, 'Well, people assume that had he stuck at it, he would have been a great jazz musician.' He said, 'In fact he was already a great jazz player, probably the best that we've ever produced.' He said, 'But the point about Dudley' (and I've known him for forty years) 'is not so much that he was a great gifted musician but that he was a nice man.' And 'nice' is a word that we shun nowadays but we didn't ought to; it means pleasant and kind and gentle and he was all of those things.

I thought before I came here that I would have a look at the obituaries about Dudley. It proves my point, my opinion, my theory, that the only blessing of death is that you don't have to read your obituaries. I mean there is one glorious example in one of the broadsheets, who ought to know better, at the very end of a long obit about Dudley, which says and I quote: 'For a long time he lived with Susan Anton who was 11 inches taller', as if that explained everything. I mean maybe it did, who knows. Generally speaking, reading the obituaries, what came across was somebody I didn't quite know. I mean I didn't know Dudley that well, really well, he wasn't a close personal friend. He was somebody I had had an agreeable relationship with over thirty or forty years. Whenever we met, we enjoyed each other's company, we laughed a lot. I admired him inordinately as a musician. He threatened one day to accompany me as a singer and he did that, but I'll tell you about that in just a moment. But they said, this was the tenor of the obituaries, they portrayed him as someone who had a desperate sense of failure: the working-class lad from Dagenham who felt he didn't quite belong in exalted company. And there is also the suggestion that he was the serious musician who sold his soul to showbiz. One writer put it, quoting again from one of these obituaries: 'success took the place of achievement' – the assumption being of course that the two are incompatible. Dudley, they suggested, died a man unfulfilled.

Well, who knows about that except Dudley, but if it be so I can't think of anyone who had a better time being unfulfilled than Dudley did. Unfulfilled, well I mean he was, as we have already said, a great jazz player. His musical satires of Benjamin Britten and Beethoven were brilliant. He was one-quarter of a group that redefined British humour in the sixties. He was one-half of a comedy partnership on television which still informs and inspires comedians and audiences forty years on. And then he became a film star; maybe that was his problem, a box-office success, a sex symbol or sex thimble as he called himself. Unfulfilled? I don't think he had the time to be unfulfilled. He couldn't be bothered with any of that.

In the sixties there was a club in London, called Burke's; it was a restaurant, and Dudley would go there sometimes and play the piano and everyone went to see him, all the visiting Americans, everybody. And I arrived there to watch him one night, to hear him late and drunk, I have to say, and I sat down at my table and wasn't quite aware of my surroundings and who my company was, except that I knew my friend was on the stage playing. And we'd had this running gag about him playing for me for many, many years. He then made the announcement that I was in the audience and that I had agreed to sing 'Moon River' with him. Now this was news to me but I was already at that point of drunkenness where it didn't matter. I was Frank Sinatra, there was no two ways about that. I went up on stage and I barely know the lyrics to 'Moon River', but I didn't care and my friend smiled, that wonderful daft smile he used to have, you know, when he was up to mischief. He gave me a key which sort of informed me, but when I started singing he did that wonderful Les Dawson thing, he started playing off-key. Of course, I was about five lines into this song and I knew that things were going terribly wrong and that it wasn't as it should be. Even in my drunken haze, I understood that and I turned to my accompanist and he looked at me like this and gave me a big smile and he went . . . and I turned and followed his gaze and there was Andy Williams in the front row like this. I had been spectacularly set up by him.

You see that's how I remember him. Someone once said that when comedians die, when funny men die, all they leave behind is the echo of remembered laughter. Well, that will do for me and I am sure it would do for Dudley Moore.

Karel Reisz (1926–2002)
film and theatre director

by Harold Pinter
(playwright)

*Memorial Service at Golders Green Crematorium,
London, on 1 December 2002*

One of the things Karel loved most in the world was playing bridge. He would call and say, 'How would you fellows like to play some cards on Friday?' 'We'll be there,' I'd say. As we sat down at the table he'd clap his hands together and say, 'This is the life!' He was of course a very accomplished and eminently rational player but every now and then he allowed himself a wild gamble. 'Six spades!' he would declare. On seeing his partner's cards he would say – with a twinkle in his eye – 'One of two things will have to be right.' But more often than not he would actually make six spades and he received our congratulations with modesty and grace.

He was a man of true grace. But he was also tough.

He directed four of my plays with great skill and dedication but the longest working period we spent together was on the script of *The French Lieutenant's Woman*. On one occasion I showed him a scene I'd written which was to follow the Victorian love scene in Exeter. Jeremy Irons and Meryl Streep playing the actors playing the Victorian characters are at Exeter station where she is catching a train to London. Jeremy says, 'I want you,' and Meryl says, 'But you've just had me – in Exeter.' Karel looked at me across his desk with a gleam in his eye. 'Audacious,' he said and winked. I can never forget that wink.

Noel Davis (1927–2002)
casting director

by Gyles Brandreth
(writer, broadcaster, former MP)

*Memorial Service at the Brompton Oratory, London,
on 3 December 2002*

Good afternoon. I'm not Alan, I'm Gyles. It's just that in the service sheet the billing is alphabetical.

It's good to laugh amid the tears. Noel gave us so much laughter. More than anybody I have ever known.

Michèle, my wife, and I last saw him twenty-four hours before he died, at the Chelsea and Westminster Hospital. He was in the Adèle Dixon Ward, named after Adèle Dixon, the musical comedy star. Noel, weak, frail, so near death, took off his oxygen mask and whispered, 'I knew her.' He then told two funny stories about her, and *then* – wait for it – one of our favourites about Coral Browne. What a man. Hilaire Belloc was right:

> From quiet homes and first beginning,
> Out to the undiscovered ends,
> There's nothing worth the wear of winning,
> But laughter and the love of friends.

Laughter and friendship: the life of Noel Davis.

He was born in Liverpool on 1 March 1927. He was christened Edgar. He later changed his name to Noel after Noël Coward. They had much in common: lower-middle-class parents, only children, theatrically minded mothers, and a devastating wit used only to amuse, never to wound. Kind, good, gifted, funny – it's an irresistible combination.

Our Noel left school, left home, left the Merchant Navy as soon as he was able and came to London to work in the theatre. It was here in London in the early 1950s that he made so many key friendships – with Robert Shaw, Mary Ure, Margaret Rawlings, Gerald Cross, so many – and, most significantly, of course, with John Schlesinger.

Those who didn't know them well I think sometimes misunderstood the balance within their friendship. John might have been richer and more famous, but as friends they were always equal – their friendship was a two-way street, loving, giving, generous in equal measure on both sides.

Noel, John would admit, was the better actor. Noel was a fine actor. I only saw him on stage once. In *My Fat Friend* at Windsor, playing the role created by Kenneth Williams. Noel got as many laughs as Kenneth, but got closer to the truth. Noel's great success on stage, of course, was in *The Creeper* at the St Martin's in the mid-sixties. He was billed above the title and his co-star was his lifelong hero, Eric Portman.

On the night Noël Coward came to see the play, Eric Portman brought the Master to our Noel's dressing room. Portman introduced the Noels to one another, 'Noël Coward, Noel Davis,' and then left the room. Coward said, 'That's typical of Eric. Larry [Olivier] would have stayed and stolen your thunder.'

It wasn't long after *The Creeper* that Noel decided he wanted to give up acting. He said the decision was triggered by a fit of hysterics during a rehearsal. When the director asked him why he was laughing, Noel, through the tears, squealed, 'I can't go on. It's just so ridiculous, us all standing around like this, pretending to be other people.'

I think he found the key to his second career when he and I teamed up in 1973 to run the Oxford Theatre Festival – eight plays, three West End transfers, seventeen fringe shows, all cast by Noel, who had never cast anything before but who knew everybody and had an unerring instinct for who would be right for a part.

We were going to do a play called *The Missionary* in which Sir Ralph Richardson was to play the title role – the only human in the piece. The rest were to be animals. Noel cast Anna Massey as the Giraffe. 'It's an instinct,' he said. She took the part.

Noel also knew, and this is what made him so special, who would be fun to work with and who would be a nightmare. He would mark up his copy of the *Spotlight* casting directory with comments scrawled by each actor's photograph: 'V good', 'Should be useful ten years from now', 'She's death, dear, death!' and, his favourite and mine: 'NEVER, NEVER, NEVER TO BE USED – until we need them.'

It was in the aftermath of Oxford that John gave Noel his big break, inviting him to cast the film *Yanks*. From then on, there was no turning back. Noel cast more than forty films for the cinema and television with so many fine directors: John, of course, time and again, Clive Donner, Peter Yates, Peter Medak, Franco Zeffirelli, Ridley Scott, Ron Howard, Kevan Reynolds, among others. And James Dearden and Stephen Whittaker, two brilliant talents whose parents Noel had known and loved and whom he regarded in a way as the sons he never had.

Of Noel's films – and often he was asked to make a cameo appearance in them as well as casting them – we'll all have our favourites. The star of what is my favourite – and perhaps Noel's too – is going to speak next. (Alan Bates appeared as Guy Burgess in *An Englishman Abroad*, written by Alan Bennett, directed by John Schlesinger.)

Noel relished his work as a casting director. He particularly enjoyed casting Sir John Gielgud in his final screen appearance in *Merlin*, for which Noel was nominated for an Emmy – something I don't think he ever talked about. Of course, he did work to earn money as well as work of quality, but if ever an experience on a film was less than happy, he managed to turn it to good account with a subsequent anecdote. He had a vast repertoire of stories about his experiences with Warren Beatty, for whom he cast *Reds* – all of them unrepeatable here and most ending with the words, 'God is not mocked'.

Noel kept his faith with God and God was good to Noel. In the last thirteen years of his life he gave him a perfect guardian angel in the handsome shape of Harry Audley.

And now we say goodbye to a fine actor, a great casting director, a wonderful host and a matchless friend, who could tell stories as no one else could tell stories. At the weekend Gerald Gouriet reminded me of the night Noel, the piano salesman's son from Liverpool, reduced the Lord Chief Justice of England to helpless paroxysms of laughter. That was at the Garrick Club.

I remember the first time Noel dined there as a member. I was his guest. We kicked off with two bottles of champagne, we braced ourselves with Bloody Marys, we took in a fine Chablis and then slummed it a bit with the club claret. At this point Noel and Sir Laurence Olivier – who was sitting at the head of the central table – blew kisses at one another. After the port, Noel escorted me towards the door where, suddenly, we found Sir Richard Attenborough and Lord Mountbatten of Burma advancing towards us. 'Ah,' said Noel happily, 'the two Dickies together at last.'

They both seemed to know Noel, but Noel wasn't in the mood for small talk. 'We're going dancing,' he said. And together we tripped down the stairs of the Garrick Club, where, as we reached the street, a huge limousine appeared. The doors opened and out of the car stepped Yul Brynner. Noel fell to his knees, yanking me with him, effected a deep salaam and cried, 'Welcome to England, O King of Siam.'

As I recall, we ended the evening in a nightclub called Heaven.

And, now, Noel is on his way to the real thing. Noel Davis is going to heaven. Aren't they lucky? And aren't we blessed to have known him?

Laughter and friendship: the life of Noel Davis.

Anne Bernstein (née Faber) (1944–2002)
journalist, wife and mother, magistrate

by Lord Cavendish of Furness
(landowner from the north of England)

Memorial Service at Chelsea Old Church, London,
on 9 December 2002

Brooding on how I might get even remotely close to doing justice this morning to Anne's memory, her voice came suddenly and vividly to mind saying: 'Don't be pathetic, Hugh. Get up and comfort my family and my friends. As for me, no whitewash; tell it to them as it was.'

I will try to take her at her imaginary word . . . or nearly so. Aside from kinship and more than forty years of friendship, I have no claim to having greater insights into Anne's warm and wonderful personality than many others here today.

But I rather doubt if *anyone* knew her as a passing acquaintance; knowing her was to experience an overwhelming feeling that you mattered to her.

And this morning, reciprocating Anne's feelings for each of us, we commemorate her life, her achievements, her disasters, her triumphs over disaster, her zest for living, her laughter and her prodigious gifts of love, warmth and friendship. More sombrely, we remember her indomitable bravery.

For me remembering gratefully these things and many, many others does bring a sense of peace and consolation; I hope it is so for others.

Anne's lovely qualities were not just a feature of later years; she always had them. Someone quite recently described her as being at 'full blast'; I cannot remember her being anything but 'full blast'. No whitewash, I promised her; her early years were wild; sometimes almost disconcertingly so. She was reckless, beautiful, irresponsible and, when now and then I was able to catch up with her, huge fun.

Even then, a serious thread ran through this frenzied existence; she was a respected researcher with the BBC where she was, as ever, well loved and admired; and where she met Michael, the father of two wonderful children, Sophie and Will.

With her talent for getting people to open up, she was tremendously well suited to this work that included light-hearted programmes, satire, politics (in the blood) and current affairs.

While still in her early twenties, and this is central to the story, a shadow began to fall over Anne's life in the shape of chronic addiction. At much the same time, the same shadow, I am permitted to say, was cast over David's life and mine and the lives of many of our friends and relations.

We are talking here not of youthful excess, but a way of life, hugely damaging to ourselves and to all around us.

A then rather new approach to the problem came on line and thus Anne became an alumna of that institution situated in Totterdown Lane, Weston-super-Mare, known to some of you as the Cavendish Arms.

Anne's programme of recovery represented as complete a watershed in her life as it is possible to imagine. She once told me that her personality was such that there was perhaps no avoiding the misery and despair of addiction in order to enjoy the freedom and peace that she worked first to win; and then to keep for the rest of her life.

Unsurprisingly, even this she undertook with larger-than-life style. Emerging like a bright new star, she was an inspiration to so many who needed help or who, but for her, might have faltered.

Meanwhile she rebuilt her life and her friendships, finding a new career first working for some years in the House of Commons and then, until ill health prevented her, as a greatly respected magistrate for ten years serving in a part of London brought low by deprivation and crime. It was entirely natural to her to use her energies and her talents in the cause of public service; not making a fuss about it; just doing it.

A senior colleague on the Bench in paying tribute to Anne spoke admiringly of her habit of getting rather quickly to the point – there's no denying she had a low boredom threshold – and more warmly said of her that she was wise, intelligent, reliable, knowing, funny: 'the sort we dream of . . .'.

Anne's qualities went beyond the boundaries of work and friendship; she touched a chord wherever she touched life. Most tellingly I think is how young people reacted to her, including a goddaughter who is one of our own children, one of a number, I suspect, who for the rest of their lives will hold dear her memory. I might have thought Anne's forthright views and robust opinions might have been a tiny bit daunting; not so; as I have seen again and again, young people simply adored her.

If Anne was a delightful and appreciative guest who liked the good things of life, which she did, then she and David were also stunningly generous and stylish hosts. The comfort and warmth of their hospitality were legendary.

Two final reflections: in the same way that Anne so obviously minded about all of us, her friends, it seems to me that the one thing she would hope for *from* us is that we should lend loving support to those who remain and were closest to her.

Carol: after losing her husband, Julian, and her son, Mark, now is without her only daughter and probably closest companion and friend.

Sophie and Will of course.

Her brothers, Michael, David and James.

An almost endless list of relations, godchildren, nephews and nieces.

Those very great friends who stood by Anne in the shadow years of addiction. The self-same people and new friends who were with her in these last years of illness.

And finally, I want to say something about David. I need hardly say that David's devoted and tender care of Anne these last two years has been remarkable and humbling to see.

It was touching to see how Anne found even greater reserves of affection with which to repay him. There could never be a hint of false sentiment between David and Anne; but in those last weeks and months, transcending all the pain and the disappointment, it was impossible not to feel a truly moving and romantic exchange of love between them.

The beautiful reading that Will chose was a call to faith. It seems to me that faith can be strengthened by giving thanks for a life that was precious to us.

Anne's huge and generous heart is finally still; this morning, we cherish that dear memory so as to keep alive in our minds what it really meant to have received her love and her friendship.

Lord Dacre of Glanton (Hugh Trevor-Roper) (1914–2003)

Regius Professor of Modern History at Oxford, 1957–80

by James Howard-Johnston

(step-son; Fellow of Corpus Christi College, Oxford)

*Funeral Service at St Thomas the Martyr, Oxford,
on 4 February 2003*

I do not have a memory like Hugh's. Its cubic capacity is much smaller. The materials stocked there are much less variegated. The retrieval system is poor. All I can offer are shards of memory, small, jagged pieces.

My first encounter with a Trevor-Roper (I must have been twelve, Xenia ten) was with Hugh's brother Pat, who drove us on a hair-raising journey in a small, fast, flimsy car across London to my mother and Hugh's wedding reception. Of the reception itself I remember nothing.

The first episode involving Hugh to come to mind was the subject of a favourite anecdote. The grey Bentley which embodied most of the proceeds of *The Last Days of Hitler* – a car being an essential part of a don's equipment and therefore qualifying for tax relief – that massive vehicle had an encounter with a bus on a Northumbrian country road. The bus, packed with passengers, ended up on the far side of a hedge. Hugh was charged with dangerous driving and advised to plead guilty by his solicitor, Evill (the name Evill, long forgotten, suddenly popped up from the deep recesses of memory as I was thinking about Hugh one night last week). Hugh jibbed at this, went to court and applied all his skills honed in Germany in the late months of 1945 to cross-examining the bus's passengers. Naturally they began contradicting each other and Hugh got off. The Bentley was reconstructed and was still going strong in the mid-1960s.

Another memory (long submerged) surfaced last week as I was thinking about Hugh, about the time when I nearly shot him. I was about fourteen and learning to shoot. We (I suspect my Uncle Dawyck was there and witnessed the scene) were on the small bog immediately below Bemersyde Hill. In those days aerial prey did not pullulate at Bemersyde. So excitement seized me as a snipe rose and flew zigzagging to my right. I swung, fired and then saw Hugh in the line of fire. He simply remarked that the shot had whistled past his ear, and never mentioned the subject again.

Hugh was a formidable figure in the 1950s and 1960s – not only by virtue of intellect and learning and powers of expression. He could be, often was, severe, forbidding. And he had a temper. That temper was a weak spot, which my younger brother Peter exploited (between the ages of eight and fourteen or so). Whereas other antagonists – Evelyn Waugh, Arnold Toynbee, R.H. Tawney, Lawrence Stone – were routed in engagements with Hugh, Peter almost always came off the better. Strong-willed, irrepressible, ready to fill conversational voids with chatter, absolutely safe under the protection of an indulgent mother, Peter would on occasion drive the conversation in directions Hugh did not like, or would needle Hugh in an exasperating way – until there would be an angry expostulation or an abrupt, wordless departure from the room.

I suffered from depression in late adolescence. Hugh did not understand the condition, but patiently, week after week, month after month, did what he could to spark interest in external phenomena. He chipped away at a dark cell from the outside until eventually a chink of light showed. There followed a phase of guided reading, of being taught to look and observe properly, for which I remain for ever grateful to him.

Chiefswood, a rather gloomy house which had been created out of a cottage by Scott's son-in-law Lockhart, was where we lived then. Hugh's study, with Aubusson carpet, Aubusson chairs and book-lined walls, was the most cheerful room in the house. He liked reading aloud. Regularly we would gather after supper for long sessions. Jane Austen, Turgenev, Cervantes and Scott were favourite authors. Hugh had his own idiosyncratic Scotch accent for the many passages of direct speech in the Waverley novels. One session – he was reading *Emma* by that mistress of suspense – went on right through the night. One other specific memory has lingered: at the point towards the end of *Fathers and Sons*, when Bazarov bids a final farewell to his parents, tears came into Hugh's eyes and he could not continue for a while. The inner Hugh within that tough outer carapace had shown itself momentarily.

We must leap forward from the mid-1960s – past the phase when he would go pale and flutter his right hand at his side whenever the subject of his great work on the Civil War came up (eight hundred and fifty pages had been composed in his neat hand), past the most expensive monosyllable in televisual history (his No when asked whether the first moon landing would have the same effect as the discovery of America; he said he was like a tube of toothpaste, he needed to be squeezed hard by interviewers, but on that occasion the follow-up questions never came), past the translation from Oxford to Cambridge when somehow he forgot a favourite maxim about winning rather than scoring, past elevation to the House of Lords and the arguments in favour of the old prayer book which he deployed on a deputation to the Archbishop of Canterbury – to the fifteen years of retirement which he spent in the Old Rectory, Didcot.

Hugh mellowed in a quite remarkable way. The steel shutter, which used to come down when conversation deteriorated or someone of whom he disapproved materialised, stayed up more and more often. Jealous as he had been of time spent away from historical reading and writing, ready as he had been to slip silently off to his study at every opportunity, he had always made exceptions for his pupils and friends. It was hard to know what the criteria for his affection were, but once it was gained, he was unstinting in the time he gave, the trouble he took, the ideas he shared. In old age the criteria multiplied and his generosity to others increased in scale and frequency. More than ever he enhanced the lives of those about him.

History remained at the centre of his life, but it was sometimes squeezed by other concerns – above all, concern for my mother in her decline, as Alzheimer's gradually sliced away memory and

thought. For some two years, Hugh looked after her virtually un-
aided, cooking four meals a day, leaving the house only once a
week. On one occasion as I was talking to her, trying to exercise
her failing memory, I asked her about Hugh, when had he come
into her life? She could not remember. I tried again: had he been
in her life when she was at Cambridge? She thought for a while,
then hesitantly replied, 'Yes,' adding, 'But that was another Hugh.'

She was right. In some ways Hugh had changed out of all recognition. That was even plainer a few months later when it became
clear that she must go into a nursing home. Hugh found himself
bounced into the decision by Xenia, me and three professionals. At
this he burst into tears and turned to the wall. It brings tears to my
eyes when I remember it.

Hugh in old age was an example to all of us. He showed fortitude,
cheerfulness and resilience in the face of accumulating ailments and
frailties. He always made light of them. If they featured in his
conversation, it was only to provide the stuff for eloquent disqui-
sitions. There was nothing dutiful about the visits he received
because of the pleasure he gave his visitors.

Then, in the first half of December, his cancer bolted, its pace
quickening rather than slackening. An extraordinary intellect, full
of learning, bubbling with ideas, amused at the vagaries of human
nature, was still evident in the last fortnight which he spent in Sobell
House. But the time came, late on Friday twelve days ago, when
the pain grew yet worse and morphine, harbinger of death, was
needed and began dulling his mind to bare consciousness. Within
thirty-six hours he was dead. A great man was snatched from us.
The only real consolation – and it is a considerable consolation –
is the prospect of several posthumous works, above all the publication of the letters, which, from the first, capture both the intellectual
power of his mind and the warmth of his character.

Hugh's children are his step-children and his pupils. We were
privileged to know him. We will not forget him.

Sir Hardy Amies (1909–2003)

couturier

by Sir Roy Strong

(historian, writer, diarist, gardener)

*Funeral Service at St Matthew's Church, Langford,
Oxfordshire, on 14 March 2003*

Edwin Hardy Amies, Knight Commander of the Royal Victorian Order, Royal Designer for Industry, dressmaker by appointment to Her Majesty the Queen. This is the man whose passing we mark today and of whom we have read so much during the last week or so. That was the public man, but what of the private one? It seems appropriate in the atmosphere of this ancient church in his beloved, adopted village of Langford to recall the person he referred to as 'Moi' – 'me'.

He has a whole chapter devoted to 'Moi' in his endearing autobiography *Still Here*. It opens as follows:

> I am no longer six foot tall. As the years increase the spine shrinks. This is one of the many things you have to suffer without complaint. I weigh less than 170 lbs: so I am not fat. Pino, the men's tailor at my shop, makes the waistband of my trousers 33 inches. This is tight but bearable: there is a small but ugly roll of fat above it . . . I should like to have a waist of 32. I must not be more than 34 inches. With a 40 inch chest, these are the standard measurements of a size 40 suit. If I keep to these measurements I can try on a Hardy Amies man's suit anywhere in the world and judge its fit, finish and quality.

This simple paragraph tells one quite a lot about Moi. It tells us that he was vain of his appearance, but, a redeeming feature, that he was funny with it. It captures his honesty and directness about himself. Although he revelled in being a knight of the realm and was never happier than when a duchess loomed, that went hand in hand with never passing himself off as other than what he said he was, trade, nor concealing that his origins were, in fact, quite humble. In his autobiography he's hugely amusing about his induction into English upper-class mores. 'You must not, dear Hardy, call the lady who prepared your meal Cook. She must be Mrs Whatever her name is.'

The fact that he wished to retain his elegant figure also had a business side to it. In that way he could check up on suits sold under his name and, as we know, he was an astute businessman. And note one final phrase: 'This is one of the many things you have to suffer without complaint.' In this Hardy was typical of his generation. Any suffering should be borne with stoicism.

I first met Hardy at a costume ball in 1970 to which he went attired as King Richard II, fully aware of the incongruity of wearing a sweeping late fourteenth-century costume while retaining his huge owl-like spectacles. I therefore only knew him thirty years, but we shared a great friend in Bridget Bernstorff, who was one of what he called the 'clan' which went back to the 1930s and included other people we knew like John Fowler, the decorator. Looking back over those three decades of friendship, what sticks in my mind most about Hardy?

High on my list would come self-education. Although he had a natural eye and a quick intelligence, he was happy to listen and learn from others. He was incredibly well-read, self-taught about history, art, music, gardening, to name only four obsessive areas. That ability was fuelled by another magic gift, the one above every other which keeps people young, curiosity. Every day to Hardy was an adventure. That curiosity went hand in hand with another quality, self-containment. Hardy was a person complete within himself. And that is rare.

He was, as we've all experienced, a past master of the put-down. The last I had from him was at a dinner given for Rosemary Verey, the garden writer's eightieth birthday, where I was explaining to him the placement at table to which came the withering response: 'Roy, never use the word placement. It's the word the French use for what they do with their money.' But beneath the bristle and one-upmanship there was the kindness. When Rosemary's husband David Verey died Hardy rang her up every day for a year regardless of where he was in the world. When poor Bridget Bernstorff was suddenly seized with Alzheimer's while in London it was Hardy who had to deal with somehow getting her back to Germany.

I could cite other instances, for he was a complex and contradictory man, waspish yet incredibly thoughtful. Wildly indiscreet at one moment but, at the next, maintaining a dignified silence when it came to things which really mattered. He was at heart a romantic, for why otherwise his fascination for the Stuarts whose portraits festooned his bedroom, especially those of his heroine, the star-crossed Elizabeth of Bohemia, the Winter Queen.

Above all Hardy was patriotic. How brave he was in the war we shall never know, for his service in the Special Operations Executive of the Intelligence Corps bound him to a silence which he never betrayed. He saw himself as an English gentleman and for three decades he was able to live out that role amidst old oak and flagstones, blue and white china along with needlepoint cushions and carpets of his own making and a garden paved with Cotswold stone and filled with old English flowers and roses. He had made a long journey from Delaware Mansions, Elgin Avenue, Maida Vale, where he first saw the light of day on 17th July 1909. Let us give thanks today for all the creativity, wit, delight and service which he gave not only to his sovereign but to so many others as he made that journey, and also as he embarks on this his own last.

Lynn Chadwick (1914–2003)
sculptor

by Rungwe Kingdon
(bronze founder)

Funeral Service at the private chapel at Lypiatt Park,
Gloucestershire on 2 May 2003

If Lynn walked into the room now I bet he would say, 'Nobody but people!'

He often quoted that line from his favourite film *Harvey*. He might even suggest we could see 'a pooka or two'.

To quote another of his phrases, 'it's a terrible problem'. How do I manage to say something about his awesome achievement and what he has meant to us in just a few words?

They say you should never meet your heroes. I'm happy to say that this hero contradicted the theory. Mind you, most things about him were contradictory: he could be fierce or gentle, intimate or distant, warm or cold, encouraging or dismissive, but his wit, humour and generosity are the features for which we will most remember him.

Of course, the majority of people who never had the benefit of meeting him will know Lynn Chadwick, the artist: a visionary and radical sculptor whose unique objects will continue to amaze, move and affect people for ever.

Those early, energetic, wonderfully crazy, vital images turned the art world on its head. It is no wonder that the prizes and honours, exhibitions and awards were showered on him from all over the world. Somehow Lynn had tapped into the human unconscious and liberated images we can't help but respond to.

The only thing Lynn might readily say about his work was the admission that he saw himself as some sort of a channel for an energy that re-formed itself through his mind, eyes and hands into the images we are now so familiar with. They are the natural successors to great icons of artistic achievement across time and culture: Palaeolithic beasts, African ancestor figures, huge Easter Island heads, Assyrian lions and Egyptian anthropomorphic gods. It is not a self-conscious relationship, just an instinctive one from a truly original mind. It will, I fear, be a very long time before the world can enjoy again an iconography of such intensity and originality.

All of us here have the good fortune to also know Lynn the man. That wasn't always necessarily easy: I for one have been frightened of him at times and his betrayed look of hurt if he disagreed with an opinion could truly feel a rejection. However, who here hasn't also been charmed by the open, generous man whose wit and humour could have us all in stitches? His deep, outrageously dirty belly laugh amusing us all the more.

Lynn's appetite for life is well known. In the sixties Lypiatt was a byword for wild bohemian life, even within the liberated artistic community, and his magnetic personality combined with his good looks attracted all the beautiful people of the day. Always one with an eye for a beautiful girl, Lynn once stated that during the war the only way he stayed awake while flying his plane over endless grey sea and in endless grey sky was by having what he termed 'impure thoughts'.

I think those same impure thoughts were with him only a few days before he died when he was trying to persuade Emma, one of several pretty young women who cared for him in his later years, to go swimming.

'You don't need to bother with a bathing suit here,' he encouraged.

How many lunches or suppers have we shared where Lynn's unique perspective on life and humanity, nature or art, have made us realise what a complete individual he was? Who of us haven't wandered around the house and garden and marvelled at the restrained, organised beauty of the place, all so perfectly fitting with his aesthetic?

Many among us here have enjoyed personal and precious times with Lynn, but the constants in his life were his family, their latest activities often provoking memories of their childhood trips to France or here at Lypiatt, the familial nostalgia tempered by a genuine interest in what they were currently involved with.

Lynn was fully aware that his achievements and hopes were largely realised through the enormous support he enjoyed from Eva. Words would fail him in trying to understand how she managed to run the business, house, estate, family and achieve in her own chosen field.

He said, 'I can only do one thing at a time but Eva can do it all at once and all the time.' Love and pride literally glowed out of him at her recent graduation.

Eva's lavish and delicious meals, always centred on the salad and vegetables of the garden, are legendary, and Lynn, who always stopped work for lunch, enjoyed them with gusto. We will always remember meals like that with Lynn recounting some funny story or other with the red wine flowing.

Lynn was a disciplined worker; without fail, from eight till lunch and from two to five. It's how he achieved such an enormous body of work. Those of us who worked with him would know if we were even half a minute late: just that look – and then down to work. He could stand for hours at a time welding knot after knot of knitted steel, building up the nodes of his intersected frames, beating and forging rods into legs and feet, looking, trying, cutting, grinding, removing, trying again, feeling for the attitude that would make it work as a sculpture, totally absorbed by the search and the activity.

Then with the frame all welded up he would start to model the surface. Here he might accept help and Claude would often make the mixes and help apply the layers of stolit. However, when it came to shaping the breasts of the female figures, Lynn would take the tools and mix and say: 'Leave those to me' – those impure thoughts again?

Lynn really loved Lypiatt. He spent years shaping it exactly how he wanted it, growing forests for the future, planting flowers for the season. As with the sculptures, he was creating an atmosphere, and what an atmosphere!

Cold frosty mornings, frozen cobwebs across the sculptures; blazing summers, drinks and strawberries on the lawn; autumn mornings, mists with trees and sculptures looming into view on a mushroom-hunting trip; or like now, wonderful spring, that optimistic ambiance of bluebell time. Lynn was always impatient for the bluebells: 'Are they out yet? Shall we go to the woods?' How strange that he should die at the height of bluebell time – I think his favourite time of year.

Lynn was always himself. He didn't have to pretend to be anything to anyone. He was fond of a story told to him by some clients who were stopped and searched going through Customs. 'They didn't even know who we were!' said the indignant clients and Lynn's reply was, 'And who *were* you?'

I think we all know who Lynn was – both the sculptor and the man. His influence will last a long time in his sons, daughters, grandchildren, friends and all of us who worked and cared for him, let alone his awesome body of work.

For Claude and me his influence and encouragement have been enormous. He once told me don't worry what '*they*' think – just do what you feel is right; some of the best advice I've had. I'm going to miss him terribly – I think we all will.

Lord Jenkins of Hillhead (1920–2003)
historian, politician and Chancellor of Oxford University,
1987–2003

by Giles Radice
(former Labour MP)

Memorial Service at the British Embassy, Paris,
on 12 May 2003

It is highly appropriate that we should be holding this thanksgiving service for the life of Roy Jenkins in the British Embassy in Paris. Among foreign cities, Paris was undoubtedly Roy's first love. Roy's father, Arthur, miners' MP and parliamentary private secretary to Clement Attlee, Labour's first Prime Minister, had a passion for all things French and took Roy to Paris, first on a family holiday when he was ten and then, in 1938, before Roy went to Oxford, to learn French in a *pension* off the boulevard de Port-Royal in the *treizième arrondissement*. Roy liked the wide boulevard, with its *pavés*, plane trees and what he called, with the customary Jenkins precision about time, 'its very early Third Republican feel'. During that summer and the next, when he worked as a guide for the Workers' Travel Association conducting British visitors to and from his much beloved Parisian railway stations, Roy developed a deep affection for and a surprisingly good knowledge of the city. In his charming work *Twelve Cities* published last November, in which the opening essay is about Paris, Roy wrote that, though he met very few Parisians, he got to know the Métro system inside out, finding its characteristic smell 'evocative rather than offensive'. He also learned to ride and

432

smoke Gauloises on the rear platform of the Paris buses and took pride in acquiring an 'almost taxi drivers' grasp of the City's street plan'.

It was a mark of his growing love for France and his foreboding about the future that, as war drew near in late August 1939 and he made his way back to his home in Pontypool, Roy took with him a large *tarte aux pommes* as a gift for his mother and a memory of France. As he served his country, first in the Royal Artillery and then decoding German ciphers at Bletchley Park, one of the most prominent of his personal war aims was being able to return to Paris.

After the war and by now an MP, Roy often came back to France both on official trips and on holiday and it continued to be important in his life. It was his experience as a delegate to the Consultative Assembly of the Council of Europe at Strasbourg during the crucial period leading to the Treaty of Rome which converted him to the Europeanism which was to be such a big influence in his life.

When he became one of Wilson's ministers in the 1960s, he usually stayed at the British Embassy. Although he enjoyed his stays here, he recounts in *Twelve Cities* what happened on an extremely tricky visit to explain to French ministers why the British government had announced, without consultation, that they had wanted to cancel the Concorde project. Emerging fresh from his morning bath, ready to face a round of ministerial appointments, he found that every stitch of clothing had already been packed by the *valet de chambre* and put in the boot of the Embassy car departing for the airport. Catastrophe was only just averted. In a characteristic aside, Jenkins wrote: 'from that morning I learned two lessons: that excessive service can be more of a menace than a convenience, and that one should always keep as close as possible to one's luggage.'

It would be wrong to say that, during his ministerial and Brussels career, Roy never clashed with his French counterparts. As President of the Commission, he had one or two notable passages of arms with President Valéry Giscard d'Estaing, despite Giscard having been one of the initial backers of his appointment. But, all the same, Roy remained a committed Francophile throughout his life, with a number of extremely close French friends, including, of course, the de Beaumarchais. He was most certainly a firm supporter of a strong Franco-British entente. Today we greatly miss his wise counsel on this and other matters, including the UK and the euro.

Roy Jenkins' death is indeed an enormous loss for both British and European public life. Not since the death of Churchill have there been such unanimous and glowing tributes about a British politician, not only in the UK but across the Continent. Why this almost universal feeling of loss? Certainly, Roy Jenkins had a distinguished ministerial career; he was a brilliant reforming Home Secretary and a skilful and courageous Chancellor of the Exchequer. Yet he failed in his ambition to be Prime Minister.

Part of the answer was given by his old rival, James Callaghan, who did become Prime Minister, when he said that Roy was 'one of the outstanding statesmen of his era'. The word 'statesmen' is key. Roy Jenkins was prepared to give up his chance of the top job in British politics for what he saw as a greater cause – British membership of the European Union. He left British politics to become the first and so far the only British President of the European Union because he believed the time was right for a British President. And, instead of retiring, he came back in British politics to help set up a new party, the Social Democratic Party. Although I did not follow Roy Jenkins out of the Labour Party, I always understood that the motives for his action were public-spirited. He wanted a more effective party system than that then offered by the Conservatives and Labour. I also acknowledge that New Labour owes much to Roy's courageous initiative. The point about Roy Jenkins, one well understood by the voters, was that he was a principled politician who, at crucial moments, was prepared to put the causes in which he believed above personal ambition or party.

Another reason why Roy's public life had such an impact was that, unlike many politicians, he continued to live it until the day he died. He remained an influential elder statesman, acting as adviser to the Liberal Democrat leaders Paddy Ashdown and Charles Kennedy and, intriguingly, striking up a close friendship with Tony Blair. 'I think Tony treats me as a sort of father figure in politics,' said Roy and he was right. Blair admired him especially for his unrivalled historical perspective and his disinterested advice. As the Vice-Chancellor of Oxford University, Colin Lucas, said so eloquently in his address at the Oxford memorial service, Roy Jenkins was a first-class Chancellor of Oxford. Self-mockingly, Roy described the post as 'impotence assuaged by grandeur', but he took it seriously and in doing so helped enhance Oxford's reputation. As if this was not enough, the quality of his literary output remained extremely high. His life of Gladstone published in 1995 and his *Churchill* published in 2001 were the late flowerings of a writer at the height of his powers. Neither claimed to be based on original research but they were distinguished by shrewd judgement and political insight. To Roy's delight, *Churchill* proved to be a triumphant bestseller, deservedly selling half a million copies on both sides of the Atlantic.

To illustrate what I mean about living life to the full, here is an extract from my diary entry for Sunday, 4th June 2000 when Roy and Jennifer came to stay with us in Lincolnshire after a European Movement dinner:

> Roy's energy is phenomenal for a man in his eightieth year. He is up early and, by breakfast, has already written 700 words for his *Independent* article. After breakfast, we go to see Lincoln Cathedral before driving back for lunch at which Roy drinks his usual liberal quota. He then retires to my study where he finishes his *Independent* article . . . At about 4.30 pm, we go to Belton, the splendid seventeenth-century manor house . . . back to tea, more writing by Roy (finishing off his latest Churchill chapter) and dinner at which he drinks more claret. At 10.30 pm, after much talk about Europe, Blair, Brown, Crosland and Healey, the Jenkins retire to bed, as Roy is to do a BBC *Today* programme interview down the line early in the morning.

This brings me to my concluding point. Roy was above all an extremely generous, warm-hearted man, with a priceless gift for friendship. His friend, the journalist and well known thriller writer, Robert Harris, who lunched with Roy about once a fortnight in or near the Jenkins' most hospitable country home at East Hendred, has paid tribute to Roy's 'lack of rancour, the broad toleration of all points of view, the unhurried pleasures in food and drink and conversation'. There are some here today, like Nicko Henderson, who knew Roy for over sixty years. All of us who got to know him found him a wonderfully stimulating companion who lit up an occasion by his presence. Under the guise of writing a book, *Friends and Rivals*, about the complex relationship between my political heroes, Crosland, Jenkins and Healey, I became one of Roy's lunching companions, if not in the Robert Harris class, then at least a dozen times in the last two years. It was always such fun because Roy was so alive and engaged. I never thought of him as old – indeed sometimes he seemed younger than me. His curiosity and zest for life continued to the end.

Being deprived of Roy's company is a great loss for all of us. For Jennifer, his wife, counsellor and support for fifty-eight years, and for his family it is a devastating blow. Roy Jenkins was an exceptional man. We shall not look upon his like again.

Dame Diana Collins (1917–2003)
freedom activist

by Ronald Blythe
(writer)

*Memorial Service at Mount Bures Church, Essex,
on 5 June 2003*

Diana sometimes spoke of this moment, this day when I would stand up in this little church to say the funeral words, and she would be 'elsewhere', as Thomas Hardy called the destination of the soul. She spoke of it with happiness, having made her plans and her requests. And, as she approved the great change-makers of the Church, it might have pleased her to know that we are saying our goodbyes on 5th June, the feast day of an English saint of whom it was reported, 'He made an immediate impression as one who moved with power, and the results of whose mission were lasting.' This was St Boniface of Crediton, the man who enlisted women mission-aries as well as men for his great task of Christianising Germany.

Diana would have hesitated to describe herself as a woman with a mission. What activated her was that the unparalleled evils of the twentieth century, and many of its laws, lacked all common sense, let alone love and understanding, and that they could only be destroyed by the kind loving rationalism which ruled her thinking. But – like Boniface – she certainly moved with power, to the alarm of those who had little knowledge of the strength of her will, and the tirelessness of her dedication to a task once begun. We now see her as belonging to an historic tradition of Englishwomen who demolished the unjust barriers of their time, in Diana's case with that open, smiling face, with that flow of energy, with that right kind of conviction. Unconventional, unorthodox, and strangely unworldly in many ways, she would write after the birth of her son Richard: 'I was lifted to a real peak-experience: once again I felt that joyous affirmation of life. Traherne was right. Blake was right – Blake was *always* right. Everything that lives is holy: I felt like singing my own Magnificat.' William Hazlitt wrote: 'We are sure to judge wrong if we do not feel right.' Both John and Diana Collins made right judgements, as time has proved. Their judgements were not confined to a crisis here, a decision there, but, as we can now see, were part of an interlinked chain of right feeling and right action which altered politics and attitudes, laws and society over the past half-century.

Unlike most reformers, Diana made sure that her public work never threatened her private idyll. As a child at Sutton she was 'Running through a meadow . . . The meadow is all wild flowers and grasses . . . There are moon daisies, buttercups, dandelions, young red sorrel, and masses of tiny flowers . . . The wind is blowing in my face, and rippling the grass. It must be early summer, before the hay harvest. Skylarks and blackbirds are in full song . . . It must be a Sunday evening, for the sound of church bells is carried clearly over the waters of the river.' It could be today in fact. That sensational running through the June countryside would happen wherever she happened to be, in Oxford as a student, in Oxford as a young mother, in the unlikely 'countryside' of Amen Court, in the straggling gardens of rural vicarages where John took his working holidays, and most of all, here at Mount Bures, where there is never a shortage of wind and bloom. Diana never lost her Suffolk freshness, her waking up to the new day.

Her marriage to John in 1939 was what made their often quite terrible tasks bearable. The sheer labour of going down into 'the pit', as it were, alone could have destroyed either of them. But supported by each other's love, by the lively boys, by the loyal and believing friends, and in Diana's case by poetry, landscape and her special vision of the world, they spent much of their energy descending to the degradation into which governments had thrust their people, to lift them from it. 'Action!' being the get-going word of Fascism, Christian Action would be the slogan of the Collinses. The latter have never been very popular words in the Church of England and Diana's funny but unmalicious description of it in her book *Partners in Protest* as it was when she and John arrived at St Paul's reminds us what a world of difference there is between the Church then and the Church now. Governments became troubled when Christian Action flowed from religion into politics.

It began to happen when John was an RAF chaplain at Yatesbury, Wiltshire, during the Second World War, where he created his Fellowship of the Transfiguration. And it came into its now celebrated power with the formation of the Campaign for Nuclear Disarmament – CND – after the United States of America dropped the atomic bomb on Hiroshima – on the Feast of the Transfiguration, August 6th 1945, as it happened. His and Diana's work, for now they must be seen as one, reached its influential peak with the International Defence and Aid Fund for Southern Africa. Each of these institutions in their quite different ways altered world thinking. In all three the historian will find the heart, hand and mind of Diana Collins. As well as this she helped to abolish capital punishment, support homosexual law reform and the women's movement in the Church of England. She was robust, good-hearted, wonderfully intelligent without being intellectual, and someone who put Christ's teachings to work. These she interpreted in their original state.

Diana and John knew William Temple, Bishop Bell, Trevor Huddleston, Nelson Mandela, Walter Sisulu, Martin Luther King, Oliver Tambo and all those extraordinary brilliant brave men and women who were to revolutionise late twentieth-century attitudes and laws. I once accompanied her to hear Archbishop Tutu lecture at Essex University. When he saw her I watched him run to her with open arms and an amazed smile, like a child running to a mother. It had not occurred to him that she lived nearby.

Through Defence and Aid Diana helped to save many lives, and through her warm personality and with her warm speaking, she helped *us* to escape many hurtful myths. She became a good writer and one of her often repeated regrets to me was that she had not become an author in the full sense, to which I always responded that what she achieved in other ways was so great that we all had to be thankful that she did not sit at a desk. She loved her writer friends, especially J.B. Priestley and his wife Jacquetta Hawkes, Iris Murdoch and Victor Gollancz, and she remained a great reader until the day she died.

Something of the making of Diana can be traced in the letters which her brother David wrote to her from the Western Desert and Italy when she was at Oxford and which she generously allowed me to put in my book *Private Words*. I quote from one of them because it reflects the fierce desire which the young at that time possessed to change the post-war world. Alas, David would be killed at Monte Cassino, aged twenty-four. This is what he wrote to his sister:

> Churchill's speech is attaining good circulation among the officers and men. It does not really say very much, but it *does* commit any government to fairly substantial measures of reform. We had a Brains Trust this morning in which inevitably the Beveridge Report was discussed and I was able, I think, to allay some of the uneasiness. If it is not accepted in toto I feel there will be a revolution.

There *was* a revolution in 1945 – a very English kind of revolution – and all through the following decades much of its thinking spread through the Empire and to the United States, altering everything. But racism, as we still know to our cost, proved hard to eradicate. An English clergyman and his wife, and their friends, an American Baptist pastor and a group of heroic South African patriots, have destroyed the worst of it. It is the convention at a time like this to say that the departed has left the world a better place. This is the least we can say about Diana. She changed the world we all once knew – that prejudiced place. Her most delightful asset was her simplicity, her innocence even. She lived here among us at Mill House for over thirty years, adoring her big flat garden, searching for the spire of this little church through her trees, coming here to read without fail the lessons in her fine voice – cutting out the barbarous bits when possible. I was with her here when Richard was killed in the car accident. So I will end with her confession –

her credo, her apology, her self-explanation. It is from *Partners in Protest*.

With experience of life, beliefs develop and change. For John the dynamism of his faith sprang from the question-mark at its heart. 'I have become more and more doubtful about an increasing number of formularies of the Christian Gospel,' he wrote, 'but more convinced of the basic truth of the Gospel these formularies are intended to preserve.'

Like John [writes Diana] I have less and less belief in dogmatic formulations, unless they are seen as symbols of a deeper truth . . . I no longer find theology helpful. I return to poetry and to a search for that inner light cultivated by the Quakers. I am no longer 'hot for certainties', but I know that the person who or whatever he was, or is, that I want to follow is the man of Galilee, Jesus of Nazareth. It is his teaching, the drama of his life and death, the paradox of worldly retreat and spiritual triumph, of death and resurrection that speak to me most powerfully.

Sir Hardy Amies (1909–2003)
couturier

by Selina Hastings
(biographer and writer)

Memorial Service at St James's Church, Piccadilly, London, on 17 July 2003

I first met Hardy nearly twenty years ago, one Sunday lunchtime while staying with Jim and Alvilde Lees-Milne in Gloucestershire. But although this was our first *actual* encounter, in fact I had fallen for him several years earlier, while reading a piece in the *Evening Standard* in which half a dozen celebrities were asked to describe their favourite meal. Hardy told the reporter that when he entertained a guest to lunch at his apartment in New York, he always served lamb cutlets lightly grilled on a bed of rock salt, followed by Cheddar cheese and Cox's orange pippins. How delicious, I thought, and what a perfect person this man must be! And so indeed he turned out.

That day at lunch with the Lees-Milnes, Hardy enchanted me with his high spirits and his wickedly funny stories, and he I suppose recognised an appreciative audience and invited me, I think the very next week, to go to a concert, and then drive down afterwards to spend the night at Langford.

And so our friendship began, characterised by glamorous invitations from Hardy, to hear Mozart at Covent Garden and Glyndebourne, to dine at Mark's Club or Launceston Place, or to weekends in the country. My attempts to reciprocate were not always terribly successful. The first time he came to dinner at my house, he looked round my kitchen/dining room and said with a kindly smile, 'It's so *amusing* how people live nowadays, I find!'

Going out on the town with Hardy was an education in itself. He taught me how to make the best dry martini, not with an olive or lemon-peel but with a curl of orange. We would sit upstairs at Mark's Club drinking a couple of these, Hardy's stories growing more outrageous by the minute, or if we were dining at Launceston Place, he would telephone ahead from the car to make sure the drinks would be ready waiting on the table. 'And if they're not,' he'd say, putting down the telephone, his spectacles glinting dangerously, 'there's going to be a *screaming* row!' Once I remember we drove up together from London to Chatsworth, for the wonderful annual garden party given for the Heywood Hill literary prize. At about eleven o'clock we reached the outskirts of Chesterfield and Hardy asked his driver to stop outside a particularly dreary-looking pub. In we went, and Hardy then devoted the next half-hour to patiently instructing the bemused girl behind the bar how to make a martini to his precise specifications, getting her to do it again and again until she got it *exactly* right.

Of course over the years I was the recipient of a very great deal of Amies lore on the subject of dress. My clothes were always hopeless, but the hyper-critical Hardy was on the whole forbearing about my appearance – though on our very first date, as he let me in to the flat in Cornwall Gardens he said, '*Very* nice dress, darling. Pity about the hemline.' With staggering generosity he several times gave me dresses, which he had made for me at Savile Row, every one of which I still have and will always treasure. Not moving in that world myself, I had no real understanding of the glorious effects to be achieved by couture, and was amazed when I wore my first Hardy Amies outfit to experience at first hand the transformation of even such deeply unpromising material.

The occasion for this particular dress was a gala evening at the Opera House, followed by a black and white ball at the Savoy. Hardy had very kindly asked me to go with him, and about five days before the event it had obviously struck him that it was all too likely I would utterly disgrace him by turning up in something totally 'naff' – a favourite word – from Marks & Spencer or Monsoon. 'You'd better come into the shop, darling,' he said, 'and we'll see if we can fit you out.' Round I went to Number 14, slightly quaking, and Hardy accompanied me upstairs where Diana, beautiful and kind, was waiting with a rack of gorgeous creations in satin, velvet and tulle. Settling comfortably in an armchair Hardy then proceeded to issue instructions, prodding me from time to time with his walking-stick, as though I were a heifer in a cattle-market, in order to illustrate his points. It was rather a nerve-racking ordeal but the results, I have to say, were sensational.

Over the course of time I learned that it was 'naff' for women to show their knees, to wear scarlet, or tight skirts, or to let the hair cover the nape of the neck. The rules for men were equally strict: it was, for instance, naff to wear black in the evening: an evening coat (the term 'jacket' was *not* to be used) must be dark blue, but a blue so dark it was impossible for the human eye to detect it *wasn't* black. Another taboo concerned cufflinks. One evening at a party I ran into that exquisite dandy, Bunny Roger, who was an old friend and one-time business partner of Hardy's. Bunny in white tie was wearing the most beautiful ruby cufflinks which I enthusiastically admired. 'Oh, please don't tell Hardy you saw me in cufflinks,' he said. 'He told me *never* to wear them. He says they're *ageing*.' Then, lowering his voice, Bunny added gloomily, 'Aren't Hardy's diktats *terrifying!*'

(The diktats, by the way, are still being issued as it were from the grave, as you will have seen if you read in the paper the notice of this memorial service, at which we were specifically told, 'no black cloth' was to be worn. Very dark blue, presumably, being perfectly acceptable.)

In his heart of hearts Hardy was more interested in men's clothes than in women's and his personal wardrobe was always a major preoccupation, the ghillie collars, the five-button coats, the specially woven tweed from Harris. One evening when he and I were getting pleasantly tipsy over our martinis I started to ask him about his war. We know *now* what an outstandingly gallant and adventurous war he had, but he himself was reticent in the extreme and would never, to me, talk about his experiences. On this occasion he did, however, tell me about his last day in the army, when he was summoned to 'sign off'. 'Amies, I want to congratulate you,' said the colonel. 'You've done an excellent job and you'll be much missed.' 'Thank you, sir,' said Hardy, shaking the man by the hand. '*Just* a minute, Amies,' said the colonel as Hardy turned to go. 'There's something odd about your uniform. What *exactly* are you wearing?' 'Oh, do you like it, sir? I designed it myself. Khaki's such an unbecoming colour, so this is Loden which I had sent over specially from Austria.' 'And good God, man, the buttons! Those don't look like regimental buttons!' 'No, sir. But pretty, don't you think?' Holding one out. 'Do you see? A pansy resting on its laurels.'

Part of Hardy's war was spent in Intelligence in SOE, training resistance fighters to be dropped in Belgium. Again I tried, but failed, to draw him out about this, although he did tell me that one of the men in his Mess was Kim Philby. Kim Philby! I was riveted. 'What was he like?' 'Oh, always trying to get information out of *me*, darling.' 'What sort of information?' 'What do you mean, what sort of information? Why, the name of my tailor, of course.'

This wit and frivolity, accompanied, as one knew very well, with a kind and loving heart, made Hardy irresistible as a friend. He had such love of life, was always so ready to enjoy himself, to rock with laughter at the silliest joke; he revelled in gossip, and adored his excursions into the beau monde. A self-confessed snob, he used to say that in his youth his social climbing had been so energetic he would take an alpenstock to parties, and indeed he began his ascent at an early age, with introductions to the Astors at Cliveden and to the notorious Lord Beauchamp at Madresfield. (I remember Hardy, with his beady eye for detail, saying he would never forget, while staying at Madresfield, the chink of the footmen's bracelets as they changed the plates at dinner.) Of course he could be tough and tenacious, as he had to be in the highly competitive world in which he was so successful, but he was wonderfully resilient and rarely let anything get him down for long.

For this reason it was particularly heart-rending to see how he suffered, and how stoically he bore that suffering, first over the death of his beloved friend, Ken Fleetwood, then of his adored sister, Rosemary. Rosemary provided Hardy's family life, and it was immensely engaging to see them together at the Old School, one on each side of the fireplace, bickering cosily away like the most devoted of old married couples. Rosemary, who hated London, was the first to settle in Langford. Previously she and Hardy had shared a handsome house in Eldon Road. Years after this had been let go the owner lent it to Hardy for a party, and it was here that I first met Miss A, as she was generally known. It was a warm summer evening and most of the guests were sitting in the garden. 'This is a wonderful house,' I said to Rosemary. 'Why did you and Hardy ever give it up?' 'I'll tell you exactly,' she replied. 'For me, it was nothing but work. I spent all day going round with my Black & Decker while Hardy lay on his bed eating chocolates and reading *Vogue*.'

During the last year or so, when Hardy was living entirely in the country, it was a joy to visit him and find he still retained his old love of life and intense interest in what was going on around him. Accompanying that dapper little figure on his daily walk round the village one would be entertained to all the local gossip, some of it enjoyably waspish, and then after a turn round the churchyard, we'd often end up having a jolly lunch in the pub – except for a brief period when he was banned for being too dictatorial over the exact size, number and shape of the pieces of chicken in his chicken curry.

Hardy's gallant spirit reminded me of something I once read about one of his favourite composers, Mozart. Rebecca West it was who wrote that for her the most wonderful thing about Mozart was that however hard or terrible had been the experience at the end of the day Mozart always went home whistling, with his hands in his pockets. And that's how I think of Hardy.

Sir Paul Getty (1932–2003)
philanthropist

by Christopher Gibbs
(art dealer)

*Memorial Service at Westminster Cathedral, London,
on 9 September 2003*

To see this cathedral thronged with so many people he loved would
have delighted him, but to realise that all were gathered together
to give thanks for his life would have astonished him, for Paul was,
above all else, both humble and modest. He was also very conscious
of his particular frailties, striving with increasing fervour – and success – to live a happy and fulfilled life within their confines. It is
this secret battle which was at the heart of his being – his suffering
and the way he opened himself to the transforming stream of grace,
to the healing love of Victoria and those close to him, his family,
his friends, all of you here today and the many unable to be with
us, or gone before, that makes his life so deserving of celebration.
So while we mustn't ignore the woes that at times in his life crowded
thick upon him, it is how he turned them around and put them to
work that calls for fanfares and, whether we were privy to his
troubles, or as many oblivious of them, brings us here together to
give thanks and praise to God for Paul, his unusual, courageous and
lovable servant.

Paul was born seventy-one years ago aboard ship off Genoa. His
mother Anne, almost a child bride and the daughter of a Hollywood
producer, was on her way to meet her husband, a then unknown

oil man more than twenty-five years her senior. The ceiling of the Wormsley library shows the conjunction of the planets on that September day when the sun was in Virgo. The marriage was brief, producing Paul and Gordon, and the boys spent much time in Los Angeles with their grandmother Getty, to whom discipline was the surest expression of love. She died in 1941 and Anne, now in San Francisco, took over, a wilful and indulgent charmer whose mordant wit her son inherited; she spoiled her Pabs, encouraging him to stay up late and drink with her. He was sent to school with the Jesuits at St Ignatius, learned to love poetry, forged enduring friendships and remembered the arrival in California of the saint's withered arm in its jewelled reliquary. He moved on to the University of San Francisco, studying the liberal arts, sowing wild oats and wooing Gail, the lively daughter of Judge Harris. He loved the Harrises, a close-knit family who talked ideas and politics, and it was here that he first heard the voice of Caruso. They married and a third Paul was born, followed in time by Aileen, Mark and Ariadne. Leaving university, he was called to soldier in Korea, arriving there the day the war ended, ingeniously landing a job in the PX, thereby becoming a man of influence and discovering a taste for the oriental and its R & R pleasures and somehow – there are pieces of paper to prove it – being honourably discharged from both the army and the navy.

So far he'd seen little of his father, although there had been visits to Europe, and one that moved him deeply to bomb-torn London and a weekend stay at moated Hurstmonceaux Castle. Now he was to learn the ropes of the family business, living with his growing family over the Golden Gate Bridge and working as a petrol pump attendant by day. This traditional initiation swiftly progressed to a job in the Italian arm of the company in Milan, then in Rome, living in a villa on Via Appia Antica, and later in beautiful rooms overlooking the Michaelangelo piazza of Ara Coeli. But the wonders of Rome proved so beguiling, so seductive that the marriage foundered, and Paul found himself alone. Always of a bookish disposition, a movie buff from his teens and a lover of music with a special knowledge and delight in the human voice, he was good at being alone, would almost rather listen to music, look at his books, see again some loved movie of the golden age. He liked companionship, but was then shy and uneasy in a crowd.

Then Paul met Talitha, a beautiful troubled Dutch siren, raised in a Japanese camp and in high London Bohemia, wounded, vulnerable. Out East they tried the local panacea. In *Dolce Vita* Rome, in swinging London and in the beautiful getaway palace in Marrakech they'd bought on their honeymoon, they sought a paradise they couldn't find. Tara was born and flourished, but Paul and Talitha, try as they might, could not heal one another's pain. Talitha died in Rome and Paul came to the old house in Cheyne Walk, and like Rossetti, a predecessor there, mourned and suffered alone, among the wonderful books he had begun to collect, his music, his movies, and too often the deadening television. He ate little, saw few, rarely left the house or even went upstairs, dulled his pain. This bleak picture had other sides to it. Victoria was often there, loyal and loving. Colin Franklin and later Bryan Maggs brought him books and he spent many happy nights identifying tools on bindings, measuring the margins of his incunables, in the deep waters of bibliomania, tabulating, cataloguing, annotating, with all the Virgo's zeal. There were many nights too listening to opera, always alert for those high Cs or relishing the antics of Eric Blore and Edward Everitt Horton. Here Mick Jagger taught him the rules of cricket and for a while Gail and the children lived upstairs. Here too Father Gordon Albion came to stir up his Catholic soul. Faith and mirth, the best pair of spurs, were to keep him going all his life.

His father's genius for business left little room for family life. Paul was in his twenties before, by chance, he met his brother Ronald at the company headquarters. It was about this time too that his father earned the difficult-to-live-with label of the richest man in the world a brief kind of glory, but given a splendid after-glow at the museum that bears his name. Paul knew the difference between liking and loving and loved his father. While his father lived he had a sufficiency but was not a rich man, despite the name he bore. Though his father had delighted in, even envied, Paul's successes in the beau monde, he deplored his descent into addiction, unaware of the darkly falling curtain of depression. Then there was the terrible episode of young Paul's kidnapping and how to respond to it, and this had not brought them closer. His father's death therefore in 1976 brought changes and fresh challenges for which he was unprepared.

Thirty years ago little was known about depression, anxiety and the psychology of addiction. Now, thanks in part to the chair endowed by Paul's Charitable Trust at the Maudsley Hospital, we know much more. Despair and guilt, a sedentary life, eccentric timetable and diet took their toll and Paul was forced to spend years recovering in the tender care of the London Clinic. A few loyal friends helped vary the rhythm of institutional living. Monsignor Miles came from Spanish Place to brighten his flame of faith. Victoria was often there, and between episodes of *Mash* and the cricket began visits from new friends like Gubby Allen who led him into the heart of the cricketing establishment and the rebuilding of the Mound Stand. As was his wont, he endeared himself to everyone who looked after him, from the chairman of the trustees, to the doctors and nurses, and Nora who emptied the wastepaper basket.

He began to plan for the future. He knew he wasn't cut out for business and it was now too late to embark on a career in one of the fields for which his incisive intelligence and well-stocked mind equipped him. He had wanted to be a marine biologist, might have been a film or an opera critic or scholar of book binding. Now, encouraged by his early efforts at philanthropy, when from the sofa he'd slept on he had called a surprised television company to say he'd pay for some stranded seals to be flown to freedom, there he founded the J.P. Getty Junior General Charitable Trust with its brave credo of helping unpopular causes – occasionally causes unpopular with him – and gave the National Gallery its fifty-million-pound endowment. In his giving Paul followed his nose, strongly supporting causes that lifted the spirit, gave him joy, like the National Gallery, the British Film Institute and English cricket, and the boost in morale for those who shaped the future in those endeavours, transforming the possibilities into realities, spilled over into the lives of millions. He wanted others to go out and do likewise, was proud of Mark's generosity to the National Gallery. He didn't care to trumpet his giving, have his gilded name cut in stone, or even be sculpted as an out-of-sight gargoyle, loved the text about the right hand not knowing what the left hand doeth. He became a connoisseur of the begging letter. His all-time favourite was from an African who had found his name on a piece of newspaper floating in the desert and wrote to say that he always had the greatest difficulty in keeping awake and therefore found work a bind and could kind Mr Getty send him immediately a million pounds.

Mrs Thatcher came and sat on the end of his bed and said, 'We really must get you out of here,' and in due course out he got to a new flat overlooking St James's Park and to Wormsley, which he'd bought and not seen for three years. Discovering the joy of giving, feeling at home in two new nests, tasting freedom, took time, huge courage, fresh discipline and strong support. The motor of his life had become his faith, the framework his observances. From these flowed a new rejoicing in life's possibilities, a healing of old wounds and a growing openness to humanity. The lonely obsessive activities diminished or were shared with like-minded souls, and with brave and beautiful Victoria ever at his side, he began to reunite his family and to entertain in a wonderfully generous and all-embracing fashion. He forged at Wormsley a paradise peculiar to himself and loved to share it. The estate which had slumbered awhile was reordered and revived, woods replanted, footpaths opened up, an organic farming policy inaugurated, lakes created. A Gothic library was conjured to house his treasures, guarded by Bryan Maggs and opened whenever there was a cricket match on the newly made pitch with its grassy amphitheatre and thatched pavilion. Here, as in his box in the Mound Stand at Lords, he discovered a gentle English rapture beyond dreaming – delicious food, champagne and Pimms, sometimes music, tides of friends old and new, hoary heroes of the game, young blades and their belles, off-duty monsignori and scallywags for whom he had a special tenderness, all gathered together to relish the game of games. Remembering those summer afternoons, Paul beaming in his wheelchair, I think of Cardinal Newman's definition of an English gentleman: 'His great concern being to make everyone at ease and at home. He has his eyes on all his company; he is tender towards the bashful, gentle towards the distant and merciful towards the absurd – he is seldom prominent in conversation and never wearisome – he submits to pain because it is inevitable, to bereavement because it is irreparable and to death because it is his destiny.'

In winter there were shooting parties, when after a banquet of oysters for the guns he'd watch pheasants plummet from the frosty Chiltern skies and note with pride that he could now tell the bare form of an ash from that of a beech. There were balls too in the summer, glamorous, wild and elegant, scooping up friends from all corners of his life, fireworks lighting up the woods, dancing till dawn. And there were family gatherings, with Mark at his farm-house with Domitilla, Alexander, Joseph and Julius, Paul at Reed's Farm with Anna and Balthazar. Sometimes his dear Aileen from California with Caleb and Andrew and lately the joy of Ariadne and Justin with August and Natalia down the road and Tara, his Jessica and their little Orlando at the home farm and always Victoria with her boys Tarik and Zain to whom he was a father too.

In 1993 he took delivery of a splendid yacht and began exploring the Mediterranean and the West Indies for weeks at a time. *Talitha G* gave him further chance to spoil his friends, with her well-loved captain and crew, to take them to remote places, to attend Mass on tiny unfrequented islands, gather grandees from the local cricketing world, bird-watch and whale-watch. It was on board ship in 1994, before a company that included a former Captain of Hampshire, that he married Victoria, crowning their long happiness. He had become a British citizen in 1994 and the honorary KBE he had been granted eight years before was now Englished and he given the dubbing he so royally deserved – for valour in battle as much as for open-handedness.

His love of England was a romantic's, rooted in the movies and in literature. It was about history, freedom, courtesy and honour and a feeling for the divine harmony and balance in the way things are ordered. It encompassed the Holy Catholic Church; the crown; democracy, in the guise of the Tory Party; the army (in particular the SAS and the special forces); cricket; fox-hunting; landscape and architecture; the MCC; Pratt's and the Roxburghe Club. There were heroes: Churchill, Wodehouse, Matthew Arnold, Gerard Manley Hopkins, Rossetti and Swinburne, Wilde and Beerbohm, Brunel and Denis Compton. But if he looked back he looked forward too, was swift to explore, and master the new technology, relished *New Scientist*, never missed *Tomorrow's World*, but remained delighted to trade rare clarets for wooden gramophone needles with an Eton beak and to hear the voice of Count McCormack pour from a giant horn.

He was a man loving and forgiving, loved and forgiven. By a long and arduous climb he came from the pit of despair to the sunny heights of his last decade, was granted and gave out again riches in full measure. He seemed to demand the entire gamut of mortal experience to merit the happiness of his last years, when every Sunday he would drive to the ancient church at Stonor where the sanctuary lamp has glowed since the Middle Ages, with Victoria beside him, stopping, as they returned to gaze upon his earthly kingdom. He looked forward always to the great feasts of the Church and to die as he did in Holy Week had deep meaning for him. We followed his coffin through the familiar lanes. At each crossing stood a young SAS man with bowed head, waist-high in the cow parsley, honouring their patron. Family, friends, neighbours, doctors and nurses came together to a place where he felt close to his Maker, and thence to the sylvan glade above the house, the Campo Santo whose creation he had watched from the windows, while high above wheeled the red kites which, bred first at Wormsley, now circle ever wider over Middle England. Dear, gentle, clever Paul, we will miss your friendship, your kindness, your courage, your generosity and your laughter. May the Lord who loves us and knows us so much better than we know ourselves bless you and keep you always. Amen.

Hugo Young (1938–2003)
journalist

by Alan Rusbridger
(*editor of the* Guardian)

*Service of Celebration at Westminster Cathedral,
London, on 20 November 2003*

In the *Guardian* archives there is a famous photograph of the funeral of C.P. Scott in 1932. The cortège stretches into the distance down a grey, drizzly Manchester street. But what strikes you are the pavements – crowded seven or eight deep as far as the eye can see – hundreds upon hundreds of Mancunians come to pay their last respects.

To a *journalist*. To the man who, remarkably enough, edited the *Guardian* for fifty-seven years.

People look at the picture these days and smile. They smile at the sheer impossibility of the image. Could it ever happen again? Could a journalist ever again, by the simple power of his or her writing, provoke such a welling of trust, of love and – in death – of loss?

The answer to that question is in this cathedral today.

Hugo envisaged something much more modest than this. The day before he died he sent me a heart-stopping final e-mail acknowledging that he had little time left. He suggested we hold a service in the small church – barely more than a chapel – in which he and Lucy were married thirteen years ago. It did not occur to him that hundreds of readers who had never met him would ask if *they* could come and celebrate his life in this fashion – never mind hundreds more colleagues and friends, as well as those you might call his professional subject matter and, of course, his family.

We all wanted to be here today – whatever difficulties – because all of us had been powerfully touched by Hugo. By what he wrote, by what he stood for, by what he was.

The tributes that flowed in during the hours and days after the announcement of Hugo's wretchedly early death came in numbers that surprised us all. Many from friends. But many from people who knew him only through his writing.

There were common themes.

People spoke of Hugo's integrity, his decency, his fairness. His kindness, his modesty.

His faith. His values. His conviction. His courage.

His unsentimental humanity.

His prose. His learning. His clarity.

His serenity. His passion.

You didn't have to know Hugo personally to appreciate all those qualities: they shone through his work, over forty years on the *Yorkshire Post*, the *Tablet*, the *Sunday Times*, the *Observer* and, for two rich decades, in the *Guardian*.

Several of the letters came from other journalists who barely knew him or not at all. For some, he had been their political education. For one or two, Hugo was the reason they had become journalists. He was a beacon of enlightenment to all of us working in what can sometimes seem a tarnished world. He was a beacon to readers and – usually, though not inevitably – a beacon to those about whom he wrote.

One Cabinet minister wrote this week: 'We shall all miss him, even those of us who sometimes really copped it at his hands.'

There was something even worse than copping it from Hugo. Harry Evans, who worked so closely with him at the *Sunday Times*, said the thing they all feared was being at the receiving end of Hugo's disappointment.

Hugo was often at his best writing away from politics. He could write about baseball stars as well as he could about Prime Ministers. Looking back on one year – 1996 – he could find no heroes in politics. But he sang of Ian McKellen's *Richard III*, of Harrison Birtwistle's music, of Pinter's poetic drama, of Jasper Johns, of Andras Schiff . . . And, best of all, of Ganguly's century at Lords.

Also away from politics and writing was the chairmanship of the Scott Trust, established seventy years ago, after the death of the *Guardian*'s greatest editor. There could have been no better choice. No journalist of our times better embodied the values and standards which Scott himself both described and represented.

Hugo didn't believe in using the role to grandstand or to lecture. The job was simply to protect the tradition, the independence and the values of the *Guardian*. What each new editor learns to call 'the heretofore'.

He had had enough first-hand experience of other models of newspaper ownership to cherish the unique role of the Trust. It was a period of great, sometimes difficult, change. Throughout it all – and through all the assorted commercial missiles and legal boulders which were periodically flung our way – Hugo was a rock: to editors, to directors and to journalists alike.

You'd ring him up worried about something, or unable to think your way through a problem. He'd get you round his kitchen table – it could be for breakfast, or a drink.

He'd listen – he was a world-class listener.

He'd think – he was a world-class thinker.

And then he'd give you straight, tough advice in sentences that could have been written by Macaulay himself.

The last nine months of Hugo Young's life seemed, almost literally, like borrowed time. Last Christmas – already suffering from the illness which was eventually to kill him – he contracted pneumonia and was rushed into hospital. On Christmas Eve his heart stopped beating and, but for the immediate attentions of the medical staff, he would have died then.

He stayed in hospital for seventy-seven days. For nearly four crucial months Hugo's voice was missing from the *Guardian*. His last column before being taken ill had been written with UN weapons inspectors active on the ground in Iraq. By the time he returned into print – in late March – American troops were pushing towards Baghdad.

George Orwell wrote of the frustrations of trying to write while terminally ill and in constant pain. 'Your brain frankly strikes at work . . . whatever you write, once it is set down on paper, turns out to be stupid and obvious.'

Hugo was the opposite. His brain was absolutely not on strike, but working overtime. Nor was there anything obvious about this writing: on the contrary, it seemed sharper and more intense than ever – and ever more urgent. He read and researched as widely and keenly as ever before. Each column was of the minute. Each column was timeless.

I have a last memory of him, lying on a silver four-poster bed, surrounded by jottings and articles torn from newspapers ten days before he died. He knew he had little time left. But he'd received a passionate four-page letter from the Prime Minister protesting at something he'd recently written. Nothing on earth – or, you might tentatively add in this building, in heaven – was going to stop him writing one final column.

The two dozen or so pieces he wrote this summer and autumn drew together all the themes that had threaded through his writing over thirty years or more: social justice, liberalism, Europe, America, judges, war, peace, the constitution, government, governance.

He wrote with a passion that seemed to surprise even himself. He wrote with a fire that made everyone sit up and take notice. He wrote with a conviction that – when his death followed on just six days from his final column – left countless thousands of readers feeling quite lost.

The editorial conference the morning of Hugo's death was full of people too stunned to speak.

What was it that made his words matter?

The answer lies partly in Hugo's own history and methods: thirty years of meticulous research, reading, lunching, filing and phoning. You had only to peek inside the study at his Hampstead home to see the care with which he worked: his library of books and cuttings; the careful notes of conversations and interviews, so lightly alluded to in his writing. He believed in the primacy of reporting – of getting it right. What he said mattered in the body politic because it was so well informed. People trusted him. So they told him things, knowing he'd get it right. He was fair. He had an artist's sense of perspective.

But it was also about Hugo's character. Nothing he wrote was for effect, or advantage or calculation or influence. He didn't write to please editors, or proprietors or politicians or mandarins – or even readers. He simply wrote what he believed. That this should have had such an effect may suggest how rare and precious this gift was.

We meet on a day Hugo would have loved to have been alive for.

It's a question we will have to get used to asking: What would Hugo have thought?

He would, I think, have disapproved of another American President, Woodrow Wilson, making a detour to Manchester in 1918 to visit C.P. Scott. He was astonished at Lyndon Johnson seeking advice on the Vietnam War from Walter Lippman. He was not so disingenuous as to imagine that his columns had no effect on the subjects he wrote about. But that – in contrast to so many modern columnists – was not why he wrote.

Hugo occupied a very distinctive position in British life. Several people have remarked how you could have imagined him at the top of the law, the civil service or even the Church. He understood those worlds, and mixed easily in them. But in the end he preferred to stand outside them. He wanted the freedom to observe, to explain, to dissent. He was proud of his life in newspapers and frowned on colleagues who also dabbled in politics.

'Isn't journalism enough?' he asked.

The greatest emptiness will be felt by Lucy with whom he shared so much love, richness and happiness.

By his parents, Gerard and Diana.

And by his children, Cecily, Dominic, Emily and Victoria.

His friends and colleagues miss him – acutely – every day.

Hugo's death has left a yawning hole:

in the *Guardian* and the Scott Trust;

in British journalism;

and, most of all, in the wider public and political debate in this country – and beyond.

Those of us here today remember his full life.

Above all, perhaps, we remember his last year.

A year in which the world, as never before, needed his serene, but passionate voice.

He was allowed the privilege – the gift – of that small sliver of extra time.

For all of us, it was far too short.

But what a blazing, glorious use he made of it.